W9-ADM-191

INSIGHT GUIDE
ISTANBUL

125×47 tablecloth
add 6-8" each side

DISCOVERY CHANNEL

APA PUBLICATIONS
Part of the Langenscheidt Publishing Group

ABOUT THIS BOOK

Editorial
Project Editor
Melissa Shales
Managing Editor
Emily Hatchwell
Editorial Director
Brian Bell

Distribution
UK & Ireland
GeoCenter International Ltd
The Viables Centre , Harrow Way
Basingstoke, Hants RG22 4BJ
Fax: (44) 1256-817988

United States
Langenscheidt Publishers, Inc.
46–35 54th Road, Maspeth, NY 11378
Fax: (718) 784-0640

Canada
Prologue Inc.
1650 Lionel Bertrand Blvd., Boisbriand
Québec, Canada J7H 1N7
Tel: (450) 434-0306. Fax: (450) 434-2627

Worldwide
Apa Publications GmbH & Co.
Verlag KG (Singapore branch)
38 Joo Koon Road, Singapore 628990
Tel: (65) 865-1600. Fax: (65) 861-6438

Printing
Insight Print Services (Pte) Ltd
38 Joo Koon Road, Singapore 628990
Tel: (65) 865-1600. Fax: (65) 861-6438

©2000 Apa Publications GmbH & Co.
Verlag KG (Singapore branch)
All Rights Reserved

First Edition 1988
Fourth Edition 2000

CONTACTING THE EDITORS
Although every effort is made to
provide accurate information, we
live in a fast-changing world and
would appreciate it if readers
would call our attention to any
errors or outdated information
that may occur by writing to us:
**Insight Guides, P.O. Box 7910,
London SE1 1WE, England.
Fax: (44 20) 7403-0290.
insight@apaguide.demon.co.uk**

his guidebook combines the
interests and enthusiasms of
two of the world's best known information providers: Insight Guides,
whose titles have set the standard
for visual travel guides since 1970,
and Discovery Channel, the world's
premier source of nonfiction television programming.

Insight Guides provide both
practical advice and a broad
understanding of a desti-
nation's history, culture,
institutions and people,
while Discovery Channel ,
through television and the
Web (www.discovery.com),
helps millions of viewers
explore their world from
the comfort of their own
home while encouraging them to
explore it first hand.

How to use this book

Fully revised and updated, this new
edition of *Insight Guide Istanbul* is
carefully structured both to convey
an understanding of the city and its
culture and guide readers through
its sights and activities:

◆ The first section, marked
by a yellow bar at the top
of each page, takes a
whistlestop tour through
the city's long and influential **History**. The following
Features section looks at
Istanbul's people, food, art
architecture, carpets, culture
and nightlife.

◆ The main **Places** section, indicated by a blue bar, is a complete guide to all the sights and areas worth visiting, both in Istanbul and the immediately surrounding area. Each region has a detailed, full-colour map whose numbered dots, coordinated with the text, show the principal places of interest.
◆ **Travel Tips**, marked by an orange bar, is a handy reference section filled with detailed information on travel, hotels, restaurants, shops, sport, festivals and other practical issues of benefit to travellers.
◆ **Photographs** are chosen not only to illustrate the historic attractions of this ancient city, but as a vivid portrayal of the many faces and moods of modern Istanbul.

The contributors

An experienced team of writers and editors in both Istanbul and London worked hard to update and expand the previous edition of *Insight Guide Istanbul*. The project editor was **Melissa Shales**, an English freelance travel writer and editor, based in London, who also edited the award-winning *Insight Guide: Turkey*. She was also responsible for the history section in this guide.

The bulk of the new writing and updating, including the features and places sections, was the work of **Molly McAnailly Burke**, an American freelance journalist and former editor of the Cultural Supplement of the *Turkish Daily News*, who has worked in Istanbul for several years.

Three chapters were produced by American journalist **Michael Kuser**, who runs a business magazine in Istanbul. The Away from the City chapter was based on original material by **Bernard McDonagh**.

The Travel Tips were written by English travel writer, **Emma Levine**, who also contributed the feature on Sporting Istanbul, and Turkish tour guide, **Henol Güçlü**, with additional material by **Elizabeth Meath Baker**.

Contributors to previous editions of *Insight Guide: Istanbul* whose work survives in this edition include **Thomas Goltz, Sevan Nihanyan, Raoul Perez, Yorgo Pasadeos, Lyle Lawson, Marian Ellingworth, B. Semantha Stenzel, Alev Alatlı, Murat Belge, Engin Ardiç, Sevin Okyay, Metin Demirsar, Gabrielle Ohl, Jak Deleon, Biltkin Toker, Andrew Eames, Canan Silay** and **Lale Apa**.

The book was proofread by **Nicholas Inman** and indexed by **Peter Gunn**.

Map Legend

—··	International Boundary
⊖	Border Crossing
—•—	National Park/Reserve
----	Ferry Route
Ⓜ	Metro
✈ ✈	Airport: International/Regional
🚌	Bus Station
❶	Tourist Information
✉	Post Office
🏠 † ⸸	Church/Ruins
†	Monastery
☾	Mosque
✡	Synagogue
🏰 🏛	Castle/Ruins
∴	Archaeological Site
∩	Cave
🗿	Statue/Monument
★	Place of Interest

The main places of interest in the Places section are coordinated by number with a full-colour map (e.g. ❶), and a symbol at the top of every right-hand page tells you where to find the map.

CONTENTS

Maps

Snap shots
on the street

Travel Tips

Places

PORT OF FELICITY

Istanbul has had its fair share of disasters, from conquests to earthquakes, yet it has emerged as a enticingly vibrant city

When Sultan Mehmet II conquered the Byzantine capital of Constantinople in 1453, his awe as he dedicated the Basilica of Haghia Sophia to Allah is well recorded. No city in the world has such a continuous imperial history, or is so splendidly set as a fortress, port and commercial crossroads.

The remains of palaces and religious edifices, both Byzantine and Ottoman, still command views over three bodies of water: the Bosphorus, the Golden Horn and the Sea of Marmara, which were without parallel for military manoeuvres as well as international trade, turning Istanbul into one of the most strategically placed and coveted locations in the world. Yet such desirability has its price, and the modern city, weighted under its illustrious past, suffers at times from an identity crisis as it tries to balance the past with the demands of the present. Even in the Ottoman era, a large section of the population of Istanbul was not Muslim – this "Levantine" culture accounts for much of the cosmopolitan flavour of the city today, as well as the tension between "natives" and migrants from elsewhere in Turkey who number up to 500,000 a year. With a population topping 12 million and a growth rate nearly treble the national average, it is nonetheless easy to understand why migration to the city continues, for Istanbul also provides nearly half the country's wealth.

Lay aside images of odalisques, hookahs, turbans and torpor that epitomised the decadence of late Ottoman times, for these are now confined to museums as Istanbul leap-frogs into the future and its stockmarkets thrive as a major artery of international exchange. You may find yourself searching for remnants of old Byzantium in the most unlikely of neighbourhoods where scant regard is paid to their maintenance, and worry that the demands of the present threaten the glories of the past. Concern is rightly due, for there is little incentive for restoration outside the tourist neighbourhoods of old Stamboul as wealthy Istanbullites move to satellite cities in the outskirts.

Today the lure and fascination of this "Queen of Cities" goes far beyond the splendours of history. Its vibrant culture of youth and intellectual vitality may surprise the first-time visitor, with its café society, designer shops and intense technophilia. To see only one aspect of Istanbul – the imperial – is to miss an exciting moment of change as this megacity comes to grip with its disparate elements, and goes some way in explaining the country's continued reverence for Atatürk, whose commitment to secularism and attempts to forge a unified national identity are among the most important issues at stake in Turkey today. ❏

PRECEDING PAGES: cushion merchant in the bazaar; the Pierre Loti Café, Eyüp; passionate about football; all dressed up, at the Topkapı Palace.
LEFT: the Bosphorus Bridge, a link between Europe and Asia.

Sexta etas mūdi

Onstātinopolis imperialis ac famosissima ciuitas: olim bizantiū (vt supza scriptū est) appellata. e cū admodū parua esset: eā postmodū constātinopolim noiarūt. Constātin⁹ eīm impatoz cognomē ne magn⁹: dum statuisset imperij sedē ex vzbe roma in ozientē trāsferre: quo facili⁹ parthoz excur tiones cōpesceret. Tradūt aliqui autozes in troade pfectū: ibi regie vzbis fundamēta iecisse: vbi quon am agamenon: ceteriq; grecoz principes aduersus pziamū fixere tentozia. Sed admonitū in somnis a ho saluatoze locū aliū designāte: ceptū opus (cui⁹ diu mansere vestigia) infectū reliquisse. atq; in traciā na gāte bizantiū petiisse. Cūq; sibi locū diuinitus ostensum dixisse: mox vzbem ampliasse: noua menia exisse: sublimes excitasse turres magnificētissimis tuz priuatis: tuz publicis operib⁹ exoznasse. Tātiq; decozis adiecisse: vt altera roma nō imerito dici posset. Scriptozes vetusti qui florentē videre: deozum oti in terris habitaculū q̃ impatozis putauere. Nomē vzbi noua roma impatoz indidit: sed vicit obsti tatio vulgi: vt a cōditoze poti⁹ Constātinopolis vocicaret. Quā ei⁹ successozes impatozes passim tuz pu licis edib⁹: tuz priuatis ciuiū pallacijs τ quidē supbissimis exoznare curarūt. Et adeo vt exteri eo veniē s vzbis splēdoze admirati: nō tam moztaliū q̃ celestiū eā domiciliū dixerint. Erant muri vzbis τ altitu ne τ crassitudine toto ozbe celebzes. antemuralia vero oppoztune comūta. Triangulare pene vzbis ēmā fuisse tradūt. Duas partes alluit mare. nec muri desunt: ad ppulsandos nautales impetus idonei s reliquū est ad terras vergens: post alta menia τ antemuralia. ingēti claudit fossa. Habetq; hec ciuitas ndecim poztas: dignitatē ipsi⁹ pre se ferētes. quarū noia hec sunt: aurea: pagea: sancti romani: carthasea gia: caligaria: xilina: bacmagona: phara: theodosia: τ sylaca. Extāt in ea preter cetera magnificētissima lificia templū Sophie iustiniani cesaris opus: toto ozbe memozabile nongētis quondā sacerdotib⁹ ce bzati: mirabili ope: pciosa materia cōstructū. Ea deniq; vzbs tanto splēdoze insignita fuit vt toti⁹ ozien s columen: τ vnici uocte grecie domiciliū habita fuerit. vbi tria magna cōcilia celebzata fuerūt: videlicet b theodosio seniore: sub agathone papa: τ sub iustiniano principe. Eam cū thurci ppter ei⁹ dignitatem u exosam habuissent. Anno salutis nr̄e. 1093. a belzete quodā eoz principe: cū ingenti thurcoz manu ossessam: deinde capta fuit. Inde galli cū venetis p quinq; τ quiquaginta annos possidere. postea palea goz clarissima familia genuēsiū ope a gallis ademit vsq; in anni. 1453. glozisissime possedit. quo an

Constantinopolis

no Machometes Ottomānus thurcoȝ impatoȝ eā cepit diripuit̄ȝ. Sic nobilissima vrbs in man² infide/
liū venit. Ab e² cōditione: Mcxxx. vl² circa. Tātoȝ tpe paulo pluri² senioȝ roma steterat. qñ pmo a gothis
capta est Athalaric² eñ anno ab vrbe ōdita. Mclxiiij. romā irrupit. at hic ne basilice sctoȝ effringerēt edi
xit. Rabies aūt thurcoȝ nil sanctū: nil mūdū: i² vrbe regia reliqt. sacratissia ei² tēpla machometee spurcicie
vedicarūt. Legimº thebanoȝ res gestas: lacedemonioȝ ȝ atheniesiū illustria facta: fuit corinthioȝ nō cōte
nēda respublica. clare oli micene: larissa potēs: pluresȝ mēoȝabiles vrbes quoȝ si nūc reqȝas muros: nec
ruinas inuenias. Nemo solū in ȝ tacuerint queat ostēdere: sola ex tāta ruina vetustatis cōstatinopolis supa
bat: ȝ tñ mirabiliū opeȝ: tñ armoȝ: tñ lfarū: tñ glozie habuit: vt oīm ciuitatū damna: hec vrbs sola re
cōpesare videret̄. Et licet post diuisuȝ imperiū siue trāslatū ad frācos sepe cōstatinopolis i man²bostū ve
nerit: nūȝ tñ basilice sanctoȝ vstructe: neȝ bibliothece cōbuste: neȝ despoliata penit² monasteria. Itaȝ
māsit vsȝ i hūc annū vetuste sapie apud cōstātinopolis monumeñts. Nemo latinoȝ satis videri doct² pote
rat: nisi p tempȝ cōstatinopoli studuisset. Inde nobis plato reddit². inde aristoteles: demostenis: xenopho
tis: thucididis: basilij: dionysij: origenis ȝ alioȝ multa latinis opa (diebºnris) manifestata sunt. Nūc sub
thurcoȝ impio sec² eueniet: seuissimoȝ hoim: bonoȝ moȝ atȝ litteraȝ hostiū. Nūc ȝ ȝ homero ȝ pindaro
menādro ȝ oibº illustriozibº poetis secūda mors erit. Nūc grecoȝ phoȝ vltimº patebit interit². Innume
rabiles eñ ex hac celeberrima vrbe in oi scia atȝ virtute pclarissimi extere viri: inter quos cognoēto io
hānes crisostomº ipsiº vrbis eps̄. Atticus eps̄ cuiº de virginitate liber extat. gennadiº: cassianº ȝc. Et no
uissime emanuel crisoloras ȝ grecas lfas tpe cōstātiesis ȝcilij in italia cū ingenti vtilitate retulit. Precisus
est aūt nunc fluuiº oīm doctrinaȝ. musaȝ desiccatus fons. Fateoȝ multis locis apud latinos studia lfarū
esse illustria. vt rome: parisius: bononie: padue: senis: perusij: colonie: vienne: salamatice: oxonie: papie:
liptzk: ertfordie. Sed riuuli sunt oēs isti ex grecoȝ fontibº deriuati. Ȝ fonte precide riuū: pcisus arescit̄.
Nihil aūt sub luna ppetuū. Quomodo aūt impatoȝ thurcoȝ machometº aio voluerat vrbe in medio thur
coȝ esse sitam: que suo imperio nō pareret: suoȝ nomini decus maiº accedere posset: si eā vrbem expugna
ret: machinas bellicas admouit. ȝ insultū magna vi in eā fecit atȝ tandē expugnauit: vt hec ciuitas in po
testatē venerat infideliū spurcissimoȝ thurcoȝ hoc infelici anno ȝ vtriusȝ sexus pe rsone cum imperatoze
paleogolo neci vediti fuerant. sub Friderico tercio impatoze oīa clarescent.

Ecclia sancte sophie

Decisive Dates

c. 1 million years BC Earliest human remains outside Africa discovered at Yarımburgaz, near Istanbul.

c. 6500–5400 BC Çatalhöyük (central Anatolia) is the world's second oldest known city (after Jericho); a community of around 5,000, domesticating animals, irrigating crops, weaving and trading obsidian.

c. 3000 BC Interconnected city states trade with Greece and Syria. Sophisticated metal-working is proved by the hordes of treasure found at Troy II.

c. 1250–650 BC The legendary Trojan Wars, later described by Homer in *The Iliad* and *the Odyssey*.

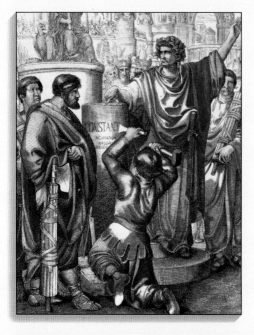

c. 675 BC Megarian Greek colonists found the city of Chalcedon on the Bosphorus (modern Kadıköy).

c. 660 BC Byzas founds the first city of Byzantion.

546 BC The Persian conquest of Anatolia is begun by Cyrus and completed by Darius the Great and his son, Xerxes. Byzantion is occupied in 512 BC.

479 BC City reverts to Greek rule under Pausanius of Sparta, later the Athenian League.

334–323 BC The campaigns of Alexander the Great.

278 BC Celts settle in Bythinia (Marmara). Byzantion repulses their attack but agrees to pay tribute.

179 BC Rhodes, Pergamon and Bithynia join forces to capture the city.

129 BC Byzantion becomes a Roman protectorate but retains its free city status.

193 AD City sacked by Emperor Septimus Severus as punishment for taking the wrong side in a Roman civil war, then fully absorbed into the Roman Empire.

258 Chalcedon destroyed by invading Goths.

313 Roman persecution of Christians ended by Emperor Constantine.

325 The Council of Nicaea proclaims Christianity the official religion of the Roman Empire and lays down the tenets of faith still followed today.

BYZANTIUM

330 Constantine moves his capital to Byzantium, building the world's most glamorous city and naming it Constantinople.

337 Constantine converts to Christianity on his deathbed.

395 Emperor Theodosius divides the Roman Empire between his sons; Constantinople becomes the capital of the eastern Empire.

476 The western empire falls to barbarian invaders. Its revived form, after centuries of darkness, becomes the Holy Roman empire.

532 Nika Revolt results in the deaths of 30,000.

537 Aya Sofya dedicated by Emperor Justinian.

668–718 First Arab invaders bring Islam to the empire, making several unsuccessful attempts to besiege Constantinople.

726–787 Iconoclasts borrow from Islam and ban religious images of the human form. Many Byzantine churches are literally defaced.

1054 The final split between the Catholic and Orthodox churches; the Catholics are based in Rome, the Orthodox in Constantinople.

1071–1461 Persian Selçuk Turks rout the Byzantine army at the Battle of Malazgirt. By 1078, the Selçuks have built a new empire covering most of Anatolia, imposing their language, culture and name on the people. The Byzantine Empire shrinks to the area immediately round Constantinople, the Aegean and parts of the Black Sea.

1096–1204 Crusaders head east to halt the spread of Islam. In 1096, the First Crusade restores the western empire; eastern cities such as Edessa and Antioch become Norman, Christian principalities.

1204 The infamous Fourth Crusade sacks Christian Constantinople, ruling it as a Latin kingdom; emperor flees to Nicaea.

1261 Constantinople is recaptured by the Byzantine Emperors.

1243 The Selçuks are defeated by the Mongols.

1288 Minor Muslim warlord, Osman Ghazi, with lands around Eskihehir in central Anatolia, begins to build a powerbase which grows steadily into an empire over the following 150 years. Bursa is captured in 1326, Nicaea in 1331, and Edirne in 1362. Constantinople is surrounded.

THE OTTOMANS

1422 First Ottoman siege of Constantinople.

1453 The Ottomans, under Mehmet II, eventually conquer Constantinople; the last Byzantine Emperor, Constantine IX, dies in battle defending the city walls; the city is renamed Istanbul (Islamboul; City of Islam).

1455 The Grand Bazaar and Yedikule are built.

1470 Fatih Cami is built.

1478 Topkapı Palace is completed.

1512–20 Selim I consolidates Ottoman rule over all Anatolia, conquers Persia and Egypt, and assumes the title of Caliph, head of all Islam.

1520–66 Süleyman the Magnificent reigns over the golden age of the Ottomans.

1556 Suleymaniye Cami is built.

1616 Sultanahmet (Blue) Cami is built.

1622 Janissaries revolt and murder Sultan Osman II.

1683–99 The failure of the Siege of Vienna, defeat at the Battle of Zenta and the Treaty of Karlowitz mark the end of Ottoman expansion in Europe.

1774 The Ottomans lose Crimea to Russia. Empress Catherine the Great dreams of liberating Greece and reviving an Orthodox Byzantine Empire.

1807 Istanbul is devastated following another Janissary revolt.

1826 Janissary corps destroyed by Mahmut II.

1845 First Galata Bridge crosses the Golden Horn.

1853–56 The Crimean War. Britain and France side with the Ottomans against Russia.

1856 Sultan Abdülmecid I moves the court to Dolmabahçe Palace.

1875 Tünel opens – the third oldest underground in the world.

1888 Orient Express opens for business on the new through rail link from Istanbul to Paris.

1908 Young Turks Revolution in support of Western-style liberalism leaves Sultan as figurehead to a more democratic government.

1914–18 Turkey enters World War I as a German ally; Mustafa Kemal leads victorious resistance at Gallipoli in the Dardanelles.

1919 The Ottoman Empire is carved up by the Allies in the post-war Treaty of Sèvres. Mustafa Kemal leads the Turkish War of Independence.

PRECEDING PAGES: medieval vision of Constantinople.
LEFT: Constantine names his new city.
RIGHT: a Turkish encampment during the last siege of Constantinople.

THE REPUBLIC

1923 Mustafa Kemal, now called Atatürk (Father of the Turks), abolishes the monarchy and becomes president of the new Republic of Turkey, with its capital in Ankara. All foreigners are thrown out; almost 1½ million people are moved as Greece and Turkey exchange minority populations.

1923–38 Atatürk reforms the constitution, giving votes to women, establishing equal rights, disestablishing religion and adopting the Latin alphabet. He rules as a benevolent dictator and dies in 1938 at the Dolmabahçe Palace.

1939–45 Turkey remains neutral during World War II, declaring war on Germany in the last few weeks.

1946 Turkey is named as a charter member of the United Nations.

1952 Turkey joins NATO.

1960, 1971 and 1980 Kemalist military factions lead military coups after political and economic crises. Each time, they restore democracy after stablising the situation.

1973 First Bosphorus Bridge opened.

1988 Kurdish separatists (the PKK) begin an armed insurrection in the southeast; Istanbul suffers intermittent bomb attacks.

1995 Customs Union agreement signed with EU.

1999 Massive earthquake rocks the area surrounding Istanbul. An estimated 40,000 people die, and up to US$3 billion worth of damage is done. ❑

THE GREAT DAYS OF BYZANTIUM

Intrigue and murder, great art and high culture, battling bishops and barbarian hordes – these were the potent ingredients of the Byzantine Empire

There is a wealth of evidence, including 6th millennium BC pottery unearthed in the courtyards of the Topkapı, to suggest that Istanbul is far older than the known physical evidence suggests. However, the first known settlement on the site of the modern city was Chalcedon, a colony of the Greek city state of Megara, founded in 675 BC on the Asian shore (modern Kadıköy). Only 17 years later, a man named Byzas, also from Megara, pinpointed a far better site across the Bosphorus and the first city of Byzantion was born. Said by legend to be the son of Poseidon, Byzas was told by the oracle at Delphi to look for a site "opposite the land of the blind". He chose this one because only a blind man could have ignored its potential and settled on the opposite shore.

Ancient Byzantion

For nearly 1,000 years, Byzantion remained a semi-independent city-state which ran its own affairs while paying lip-service and tribute to its varying political masters.

Yet, even then, the cycle of conquest, collapse and rebirth that has characterised the city through the ages was already apparent. It was first sacked by Persian King Darius in 490 BC. In 409 BC, the Athenians attacked by sea, building the fortified settlement of Chrysopolis (now Üsküdar) nearby. Philip of Macedonia (father of Alexander the Great) laid siege but failed to capture it in 339 BC. In 279 BC, the somewhat shortsighted King Nicomedes of Bithynia (modern Marmara) invited the Celtic mercenaries to settle on the west bank of the Kızılırmak river. A robust, warrior people, they called their new land Galatia (Galata) and from here, they preyed upon the wealthy Hellenistic city-states, appearing before the gates of Byzantion in 278 BC and extorting a payment which ruined city finances for decades to come. In 133 BC, the whole region was shocked

when Attalus III, the last king of Pergamon, bequeathed his kingdom to Rome, opening the door to Roman expansion into Asia Minor. Byzantion allied itself to the empire in 129 BC, remaining an autonomous protectorate for the next 200 years. It was only fully absorbed into the empire in AD 73.

The Roman years

The *Pax Romana* brought both security and prosperity to the city but, in AD 196, Roman Byzantium backed the wrong claimant to the imperial throne, with disastrous effect. The winner, Septimius Severus, besieged the city, slaughtered many of its inhabitants, including fleeing refugees, and razed it to the ground. He then rebuilt it, named it Colonia Antonina after his son Antonius Caracalla, added the Hippodrome, a grand colonnaded forum; mosaic-paved promenades; the Baths of Zeuxippus, with 60 bronze statues reputed to be the finest in the Empire; and a vast necropolis whose surviving statues and sarcophagi indicate a level of

LEFT: the magnificent dome of 6th-century Haghia Sophia (Aya Sofya). **RIGHT:** the Barberini Ivory, depicting 5th-century Emperor Anastasios I Dikoros.

civic refinement hardly equalled by the later splendours of the Byzantine and Ottoman eras. No trace now remains of this imposing classical city, buried by the grandiose building projects of Constantine.

By the 3rd century AD, tremors began to shake the foundations of the Empire. Internally, it was challenged by a religion consciously opposed to classical civilisation and its values – Christianity. Externally, its borders were being menaced by barbarian invaders. In 268, a Visigothic attack failed to breach the city walls, repulsed by Claudius II Gothicus, in whose honour a column still stands on Seraglio Point.

new phase which was to last for the next 1,000 years. The most pressing issue facing the Empire was the grim struggle for supremacy between paganism and Christianity. The major breakthrough was made when Constantine adopted the cross as his symbol at the battle of Milvisan Bridge in 312. In 313, he declared Christianity the official religion of the Empire. Yet even the converted Constantine was not immune to lingering lapses into paganism and was only baptised shortly before he died.

In 324, Constantine instituted a thorough reorganisation of the Empire's administrative structure, ending 150 years of intermittent civil

Later emperors were to become energetic, often harsh reformers. Diocletian (284–305) reorganised the army and government and tried to combat a more modern problem – inflation, ordering a price-freeze throughout the empire. However, his two most radical initiatives failed: he tried to create a new capital for the Roman empire at Nicomedia (İzmit), and, in 303, in an attempt to wipe out the religion, he unleashed a ferocious persecution of Christians.

Constantine

Constantine the Great (306–337) tackled the same problems from a different angle and, in doing so, catapulted the Roman Empire into a

war, during which provincial warlords ruled from their strongholds while the Senate pretended to function in Rome. At the same time, he decided to leave the traditional seat of power at Rome and establish a new, Christian city in Asia. The building of New Rome was thus part of an ambitious plan to reshape an empire and the unprecedented, planned creation of a city designed to serve as the centre of the world.

Constantine originally chose the site of Troy, replete with Homeric associations, for his new capital. The walls were nearly complete when he changed his mind and selected provincial Byzantium instead. Astonished courtiers watched as Constantine marked the bounds of the new city, way beyond the edge of the old one. Asked why he did so, he replied that he was following an angelic guide. The scale of the construction lived up to the grandeur of the occasion. A city that equalled Rome in size and architecture was created within six short years.

The shortage of architects and artisans was solved by setting up schools in the most distant provinces of the empire to train the most talented youths. And, when the artistic talents of the age proved inferior to that of earlier generations, the ancient cities of Greece and Asia were ransacked for their most valuable monuments, their trophies and relics, to add to the glory of the new capital. In AD 330, the capital moved officially to Byzantium.

The advance of the holy men

By 325, splits within the new religion again threatened state security as the church thrashed out agreed explanations of its central truths. Constantine took a robust approach to the problem, calling the various factions to the Council of Nicaea (İznik). He seems to have prepared the way carefully, holding propaganda sessions in advance of the main meeting, and banishing as criminals any who refused to sign up to the agreed doctrine, which formalised the system of belief still stated in the Nicene Creed and appointed the Emperor head of the church.

Four of the six subsequent Councils, held to amend the original compromise, took place in Constantinople itself or its suburbs; two moved elsewhere because factional balances within the city made it seem wiser. They were rowdy affairs, with cheering crowds, street fights, and even the occasional lynching.

The church became the physical, social and political focus of the city, occupying the turbulent energies of its uprooted crowds and the political talents of its faction bosses. Constantine's great-nephew, Emperor Julian (361–363), attempted to turn the clock back, but he was too late. He was killed while doing battle with the Persians in 363; all subsequent emperors were Christians.

LEFT: Emperor Justinian the Great, surrounded by his entourage.
RIGHT: sad remnants of the great Bucoleon Palace.

SAINTS ON STICKS

Early Christian holy men sought bizarre ways to demonstrate their faith. Daniel the Stylite (AD 409–493) passed the last 33 years of his life on a pillar at Rumelihisarı (Anaplous), attracting visitors like Emperor Leo I and his family.

Glittering city

Within a century, Constantinople had became the world's most populous city. Its walls, which had scandalised pundits in 325 by their "preposterous" extent, had to be rebuilt during the reign of Theodosius II (408–450) about a mile beyond the original perimeter. It was the greatest city of the western and near-eastern worlds, with a population hovering around one million, when the next biggest town in Europe barely approached

100,000. In fact, for almost 1,000 years, it was the only city around: Rome and Athens barely survived as smallish towns festering in the ruins of the barbarian invasions; Paris and London were rustic villages; only Ctesiphon and Baghdad were brief rivals to its glory.

For a long time, the volume of trade in the market probably exceeded all of Europe put together. It was a veritable supermarket of luxury, only dreamed of by the most hedonistic Roman. Middlemen, especially, had it good, as Constantinople delivered silks, spices, drugs, gold and grains to a hungry world. The specialisation of labour required an orderly pattern of production, resulting in institutionalised guilds through which the state could easily control supply, price, and profit.

Constantinople had a university, when the West could boast only a few monasteries where monks copied manuscripts and tended the goats. There were splendid palaces and administrative halls, an overgrown bureaucratic apparatus, and meticulous rules for court ceremonial and official procedure, at a time when the petty kings of Europe lived in dank forts and got drunk with their boon companions. Many of the most accomplished artists of the time flocked in, master weavers, goldsmiths, carpenters, musicians, and architects.

Their work included The Church – Haghia Sophia (Aya Sofya) – which remained the world's largest man-made enclosed space for a thousand years, and The Work of Art, a fantastic golden tree with mechanical birds which sang separately and in harmony, of which medieval travellers have left awed descriptions. Nothing but bits of worn masonry now remain of the labyrinthine Great Palace leaving only the Kremlin – a copy by a marginal civilisation in an inferior age – to convey a picture of what it was once like.

Much later, when European courts decided to civilise, they would turn to the Byzantine model for their lessons in royal decorum and palatial glitter, the compilation of Byzantine court manners by Emperor Constantine VII Porphyrogenitus (913–959) serving as the classic primer on palace etiquette.

Bread and circuses

As it swelled, the city suffered many of the natural consequences of mass immigration: overpopulation, urban violence, political turmoil. The ancient economy could never find a satisfactory answer to the problem of employing such concentrated masses. Grand public works temporarily allayed the problem, but inevitably ran against a depleted imperial treasury and overtaxed provinces. A system of benefits was developed on an unprecedented scale. Along with free Hippodrome tickets, public baths and gymnasia, all residents of Constantinople were entitled to free rations of bread, meat, oil and wine, upon presenting a coupon at one of over 80 stations, the entire wheat crop of the Nile Valley commandeered to feed the city.

Innumerable monasteries and churches maintained hostels for the homeless and kitchens for the poor. They provided security, solidarity, shelter, and perhaps employment for the bewildered immigrant; taught him city ways and the Greek language; saved his son from youthful crisis and crime. In return, they demanded unconditional loyalty, using it to consolidate their power and expand their resources.

At first frequently, later on twice a year until 1200, huge crowds gathered with the imperial family for public games and spectacles in the Hippodrome, cheering and shouting slogans at the charioteers, enjoying the music, animal shows and parades paid for by the city budget. The *vox populi*, often clamorous and explosive, was heard on these occasions. Many magistrates and several emperors lost their offices, and sometimes their lives, on the Hippodrome steps; others built their careers through careful cultivation of organised Hippodrome crowds.

The Blues and Greens, and other lesser groups, were originally formed to provide charioteers and acrobats for the games. However their fanatical support base turned them into formidable political forces. Their cheerleaders could organise the frenzy of the crowds; their support network could whip up riots or empty the streets at will; their protection was sometimes essential for finding employment or safely operating a shop. The Blue street-gangs which terrorised the city in the 520s provided a convenient vehicle for the political ambitions of Justinian. But even the support of the Emperor and his wife Theodora did not prevent the Blues from joining their rivals, in 532, in the great Nika revolt (*see page 151*). Justinian was saved from panic and an inglorious escape by the contemptuous determination of Theodora. He eventually regained the upper hand and restored order after the massacre of some 30,000 people.

Imperial ambitions

Throughout the 5th and 6th centuries, the eastern Empire thrived, largely unaffected by the

Justinian I has gone down in history as the builder of Aya Sofya and the codifier of Roman law, but these were only parts of a vast imperial programme which also aimed to reconquer the western territories lost 60 years earlier to the Germanic chieftains. His armies conquered north Africa and part of Spain relatively easily, but the reconquest of Italy required a long and enervating war. To finance it and his vision of a strong, centralised empire, Justinian's rapacious minister, John of Cappadocia, squeezed the cities of Anatolia and Greece, weakening what remained of the classical urban institutions. The contradiction was felt acutely by

chaos caused by Goths, Vandals, Franks and other sundry barbarians to the west. It was a period of great splendour under emperors such as Theodosius I (378–395), Theodosius II (408–450) and Justinian I (527–565). Greek began to replace Latin as the language of the court and the administration. The educational system became explicitly Christian. Imperial power grew and municipal traditions waned as senators cast off their pagan culture and sought careers as monks or bishops.

LEFT: Byzantine women often ran the state.
ABOVE: mosaic of Christ between Empress Zoë and Constantine IX Monomachus in Aya Sofya.

contemporaries, such as the official historian Procopius, who publicly eulogised Justinian, while privately lambasting him as a devil in human form. Nor did Justinian's legacy endure. Within his lifetime, the empire was struck by plague and soon after he rescued Italy from the Goths, it was overrun by the Lombards.

At the end of the 6th century, the Danube frontier was attacked by the Avars, a Central Asian people similar to the Huns. The empire battled bravely but, as the frontier collapsed, the Slavs flooded the south. Emperor Maurice (582–602) struggled to contain the challenge but, in 602, his armies revolted and he was assassinated by a usurper, Phocas. Meanwhile, in the east, the Sassanid Persians marched across Anatolia to reach the Sea of Marmara at Kadıköy, seizing Byzantine provinces as far away as Egypt. It was Persia's greatest triumph since Alexander's defeat of Darius in 333 BC.

A quiet life was impossible for the next 100 years. Anatolia suffered an economic and cultural collapse, although Constantinople itself survived. In 628, Emperor Heraclius was finally able to muster his army and expel the Persians. But the effort left both Persians and Byzantines unable to resist the arrival of a new enemy on their frontiers: the Arab armies sweeping out of the desert under the banner of Islam.

Islam

To the Byzantines, the Arabs at first appeared to be wild, primitive tribesmen, a notion quickly overturned when the Byzantine host was routed by Muslim horsemen under Khalid Ibn Walid, the "Sword of Islam" at the battle of Yormuk (in present-day Jordan). In 674, the Arabs began their first great siege of Constantinople, which lasted 4 years. It was repulsed, as was a second in 717–718, but the Byzantines lost most of their eastern provinces.

In 726, Emperor Leo III copied the Arab Caliph in banning pictures and representations of human beings, fomenting a new religious crisis as the Iconoclasts battled supporters of

images. By 843, icons triumphed and images were gradually restored to the churches.

Byzantine revival

On 3 September 863, a Byzantine general, Petronas, finally defeated the Arab armies of Omer Ibn Abdullah, the Emir of Malatya, at the battle of Poson, and turned the tide. Just at this point, his brother, Chief Minister Bardas, was murdered by the homosexual lover of Emperor Michael III, a Thracian peasant, who was crowned joint emperor in 866, before murdering Michael to become sole ruler (*see page 29*).

From this sordid beginning emerged Byzantium's most glorious dynasty. Over the next 200 years, the frontiers were expanded in all directions, with wars fought and won against the Fatamids in Egypt, the Abbasids in Baghdad, and the Bulgars and Russians to the north.

Under the ferocious Basil II ("The Bulgar Slayer"), the late Byzantine state reached the apogee of its glory. With the aid of Varangian soldiers sent by Vladimir of Kiev (in return for a royal princess, given to Vladimir as a christening present), Basil first crushed the revolt of two generals who meant to usurp and divide the empire between them before turning to the Balkans to deal with the Bulgarian Czar, Samuel. In 1014, the Byzantine army captured 14,000 Bulgarian soldiers who were all blinded and sent back to Samuel, in groups of 100, each led by one man who only had one eye put out. When Samuel beheld the gruesome spectacle, he fell into delirium tremens and died within two days. His kingdom was annexed to the Byzantine state.

Basil II also extended the eastern frontier of the empire to the Armenian kingdom of the Bagratids in the north, and in the south to Amida (Diyarbakır), Edessa (Urfa) and Aleppo. In the west, he restored much of Italy to the Byzantine sphere, and was preparing for a decisive campaign against the Muslims in Egypt and Syria when he died in 1025, an unmarried warrior with no heir.

In many ways, his death signalled the end of Byzantium, with the ruling house riddled by intrigue. Basil's ageing, younger brother, Constantine VIII, next took the helm and was succeeded by his daughter Zoë (*see page 29*).

The final break with the Catholic church in Rome isolated Byzantium from its natural allies in the west, while civil bureaucracy castrated the Byzantine war machine, leaving the frontier defences in the hands of local aristocrats and their personal armies of mercenaries.

The arrival of the Turks

This could not have occurred at a worse time: to the north, Turkish tribesmen ransacked the Danube provinces; far more ominous were the Selçuk Turks who had replaced the Arab threat. Their small but powerful army swept across the southern and eastern areas of the empire, then, in order to buy time as they consolidated their victories, their leader, Togrul entered into lengthy negotiations with the emperor.

Meanwhile, the day-to-day situation on the borderlands between the Byzantine and Selçuk lands was anything but peaceful, with various Armenian and Byzantine landowners enrolling private troops from amongst the ranks of the Turcoman *ghazis* (warriors for the faith) and Byzantine *akritoi* (mercenaries), all of whom promptly started looting, leaving both sides to accuse the other of bad faith. By the late 11th century, with the situation desperate, the widowed Empress Eudocia married Romanus IV Diogenes, who decided to preempt the Selçuks and reconquer Armenia.

In 1071, he crossed the Euphrates (the classic demarcation of east and west) to confront the Selçuk army at Manzikert, north of Lake Van. His army of 150,000 mercenaries vastly outnumbered Alp Arslan's 14,000 irregular Turkish horsemen, but the Byzantine troops could scarcely have selected a worse venue. The light-riding Turks feigned a retreat, lured the main Byzantine force into a loop, and showered the heat-exhausted Christian host with arrows before closing on three sides with the scimitar. Large numbers of Armenian mercenaries deserted to the Turks. The booty for the victors included Diogenes himself.

He managed to ransom himself and signed a treaty with the Turks, but his defeat turned into a total disaster on his return to Constantinople, when he learned that he had been deposed during his captivity. He was subsequently blinded by the new emperor and died of his injuries in 1072. The freshly signed treaty was no longer valid and Anatolia lay open to the Turks.

LEFT: mosaic portrait of Emperor Alexander VII (912-3) in Aya Sofya.

RIGHT: crusaders sack Constantinople in 1204.

The Crusades

The Byzantine defeat at Manzikert was a final alarm call to Christian Europe, already facing a steady tide of Muslim expansion from Iberia. Pope Urban II, determined to save the Holy Land, called a Crusade against the Infidel Turk.

Byzantium, far less troubled by Islam than by the loss of its lands, joined the First Crusade of 1097–98, but there was a heavy price to pay. The crusaders' progress across Byzantine land was marked by wholesale pillaging. A reluctant empire was persuaded to allow free passage during the Second Crusade of 1146, again suffering widespread destruction. Meanwhile,

THE SELÇUKS

In the mid-11th century, an obscure Turcoman people, the Selçuks, set up a state in Iran, with Isfahan as their capital. The Abbasid Caliph in Baghdad was so taken in by their military prowess, that he gave their leader, Togrul Bey, the impressive title "King of the East and West", designating the Selçuk warlord as his temporal deputy. However, the Selçuks under Togrul and his successor, Alp Arslan, were not content with only a small piece of the disintegrating Arab Empire. Recent and enthusiastic converts to Islam, they persuaded themselves that they were the rightful heirs to all lands conquered during and immediately after the time of the prophet Mohammed.

the western crusaders regarded the "heretical" Eastern Orthodox state as little better than the Selçuks. They did take Antioch, Edessa and eventually Jerusalem, but they set them up as Norman principalities, paying only the most tenuous lipservice to the empire.

When, in 1175, Byzantium complained of the Westerners' cavalier treatment, Holy Roman Emperor, Frederick Barbarossa, persuaded the Selçuks to attack Constantinople. Byzantium suffered another horrific defeat and the Balkan states seized the moment to break away. In 1185, the Normans sacked Thessalonika. Two years later, the Third Crusade took Edirne. In

1204, the notorious Fourth Crusade gave up all pretence of fighting the Turks and laid siege to Constantinople. The motley crew of French and Italian crusaders massacred a good portion of the population, looted almost all the art and valuables, demolished the palace, and put the rest of the city to the torch. The Byzantines reatreated hastily to Nicaea, and Count Baldwin of Flanders was crowned head of a new Latin Empire of Byzantium.

An inglorious finale

The eventual Byzantine recovery of the city in 1261 by Michael VIII Palaeologus was little more than an interesting historical footnote.

The last centuries of Byzantine rule offer the painful picture of a race of survivors crawling around the ruins of a destroyed civilisation. The reconstituted "Empire" of 1261 barely reached beyond the suburbs of Constantinople, a rump state that became ever more dependent on the surrounding Ottoman Turks. Devoid of funds, and with a population reduced to less than a tenth of its former numbers, little could be built, much less rebuilt. Instead, the principal method of raising money seems to have been the sale of whatever could still be unearthed in the city in terms of treasure and artwork. Still, the city struggled to survive for another 200 years until the sultans, their harems filled with Byzantine princesses taken in exchange for peace, finally grew tired of the presence of the ancient city of Constantine in their midst and the Ottomans surged forward to sweep Anatolia clean.

In May 1453, Constantine XI, last Caesar of the Roman Empire, set out for a final, hopeless stand. He was last seen charging on foot against Turkish soldiers that poured over the battlements near the Edirne Gate.

His army consisted of the Genoese, who dominated the city from their colony across the Golden Horn, building the mighty Tower of Galata at a time when the emperor lacked the funds to repair the leaking roof of his palace, and the Catalans, who pillaged the city and sold its citizens into slavery when not fighting for it. Emperors had flirted with Roman Catholicism since their return to the city after 1204, and finally adopted it in 1438 in a last-ditch attempt to rally European support.

Their disgusted vassals went over to the Turks in droves. Haghia Sophia, reconsecrated as a Catholic cathedral, was shunned by the Greek population of the city. Public opinion, murmured by the monks of the Studion and Phenar, had preferred "the turban of the Turk to the mitre of a cardinal."

Once the days of pillage were over, the abbot of the Studion was consecrated Orthodox Patriarch of Rome by the turbaned Conqueror. The people of Constantinople, whether converted to Islam or content to stay within the sphere delimited for them as Christian minorities, carried much of the culture of old Byzantium into the newly resplendent Empire. ❏

LEFT: Emperor Theophilus with his bodyguard, from the Scylitzes Chronicle.

Byzantine Intrigue

It was an era of palace murders, blindings, outrageous torture chambers, and a bureaucracy so self-serving as to deserve a new adjective: *Byzantine*, a word that has entered the languages of the world as a synonym for intrigue, dirty dealings and general corrupt civic behaviour, conducted by an exclusive palace élite in a manner which cannot possibly be comprehended by normal mortals.

Clearly, not the whole of Byzantine society was corrupt, but endless examples are documented by contemporary historians themselves. Procopius, the official court historian of Emperor Justinian (483–565), lauded the emperor in public, but also maintained a diary annotating the sleazier aspects of the time. Here is what the (uncensored) Procopius has to say about a certain stage starlet: "For the time being Theodora was too undeveloped to be capable of sharing a man's bed or having intercourse like a woman; but she acted as a sort of male prostitute to satisfy customers, and slaves at that, who when accompanying their owners to the theatre seized their opportunity to divert themselves in this revolting fashion... But as soon as she was old enough, she joined the women on the stage... Often she would go to a party with 10 young men or more, all at the peak of their physical powers and with fornication as their chief object in life, and would lie with all her fellows."

Procopius's fulminations might have just disappeared as a rather imaginative example of late-Roman pornography but for the fact that Theodora went on to become the mistress, then empress of Justinian the Great. And one fact does give credence to his litany of accusations: Theodora had a convent constructed on the Asiatic shore of the Bosphorus for the benefit of her former colleagues in the world's oldest profession.

Certainly the ruling families showed a remarkable propensity for a "bit of rough". After numerous small scandals, the next big one hit when Basil, a penniless youth of Armenian descent, drifted into the city from Thrace as a teenager. At first, he slept out in churches, then he got a job as a groom, first in a wealthy household, and later, in the palace itself, where he doubled as a champion wrestler.

Basil quickly became the emperor's favourite, but neither he nor his master was taken seriously

RIGHT: Byzantine palace dungeons, an elegant setting for unspeakable torture.

by first minister, Caesar Bardas. Basil solved the problem by murdering Bardas. He was first appointed in his place, then crowned joint emperor with Michael on 26 May 866. The sequel was predictable: on 23 September 867, Basil murdered Michael III to become the empire's sole ruler.

Another 150 years later, Empress Zoë's tempestuous marital life seems to have begun at the age of 50, when her father, Emperor Constantine VIII, died, leaving three middle-aged daughters as heirs. The eldest was a nun and, on his deathbed, he saw his second daughter, Zoë, married to an elderly distant relative, Romanus III Argyrus, who took the purple with his wife.

Six years later, Romanus was drowned, probably by Zoë's new young lover, a peasant from Paphlagonia. The couple married in remarkable haste next morning, while the body still lay beside the pool, and Michael IV took the throne. When he also died a year later, an adopted nephew greedy for the throne, Michael V Calaphates, tried to banish the empress to a convent. She had him blinded and deposed and, at the age of 64, decided to marry again. Her new husband, Constantine IX Monomachus, arrived with a mistress who seems to have been a welcome member of an increasingly bizarre household. Zoë died aged 72; her husband reigned another five years before her sister Theodora took over, the last of the Macedonian dynasty. ❏

HUB OF THE OTTOMAN EMPIRE

Within a century of the conquest, Istanbul was once again capital
of one of the most powerful empires that the world has known

s the Mongol forces swept over Anatolia in the early 13th century, an exhausted band of retreating Selçuks, led by Alâeddin of Konya, were cornered by a detachment of the Mongol barbarians from the east. Just as all hope seemed lost for the Turks, a wall of horsemen appeared on the crest of a nearby hill, seemingly pausing just long enough to choose the winning side and claim a division of the spoils. Their chieftain signalled his men forward, drawing his scimitar as he charged.

But, instead of joining the apparent victors, the horsemen spurred their steeds towards the Mongol flank, and carved their way through to the surprised relief of Alâeddin. Grateful for his life, the Selçuk commander asked the leader of the gallant horsemen his name: Ertugrul, came the answer, father of Osman.

So legend tells of the emergence of Ertugrul Ghazi and his 444 horsemen, and the birth of the Ottoman Empire. Even if the historical accuracy of the episode is somewhat doubtful, the fact remains that his intervention helped stem the tide of the Mongol invasion, Ertugrul emerged as the possessor of a small fiefdom near the town of Eskişehir in western Anatolia. This was to serve as the base from which the Ottoman Empire spread first across Anatolia into Europe, Middle East and parts of Asia.

The beginning

At the time, the Ottomans, who numbered fewer than 4,000 souls, had not yet converted to Islam. However, as the Mongols destroyed the Selçuk state, and the rump Byzantine empire fed its own confusions, the power vacuum and the need for order grew. The Ottomans waited for their opportunity.

In 1301, the Ottoman state came into direct conflict with Constantinople for the first time, near Baphaeon. Although inferior in numbers,

the Muslims easily bested Christian morale and routed the forces of Andronicus II Palaeologus. The defeat of an imperial army by a still obscure Muslim clan sent shockwaves through the empire. The reverberations (and promise of further booty) brought Turkish adventurers, disgruntled Greek noblemen and holy warriors

PRECEDING PAGES: the magnificent Blue Mosque and Topkapı Palace, from the air.
LEFT: interior detail of the Blue Mosque.
RIGHT: Beyazıt the Thunderbolt (1389–1402).

DREAMS OF WORLD DOMINATION

Upon his succession as clan chieftain, Osman Ghazi spent the night in the house of a pious Muslim who introduced the young warlord to the Qur'an. Osman read deep into the night, finally falling asleep on his feet to dream of a giant tree springing from his loins. Its branches grew to such heights as to cover the great mountain ranges of the known world while its roots were watered by the great rivers – the Tigris, Euphrates, Danube and Nile. A wind blew through the vision, turning the leaves of the branches into swords, all pointed towards the direction of Constantinople, which appeared as a fabulous, bejewelled ring ripe for the plucking.

from across Anatolia flocking to join Osman, eager for battle. Each confederate led his own troops into battle, and received provinces and fortresses in return. The sultans lived simply, as the first among companions, often without a fixed residence, and ruled by consensus. At Nicomedia in 1308, Byzantium was routed a second time and the Ottomans gained effective control of the entire Anatolian hinterland, moving their capital to Bursa.

Empire building

Osman's son, Orhan Ghazi (1324–59) reorganised the nascent empire, conquered the Selçuk

the last crusade was routed by his son, Beyazıt the Thunderbolt. Some 10,000 knights were slaughtered within hours, with a cowering knot of survivors fording the Danube to safety. Middle Europe was left undefended.

But, just as Beyazıt prepared to turn on Constantinople, his attention was grabbed by the arrival of the iron-willed Mongol, Timur. One overwhelming battle left the Ottoman army in tatters, Beyazıt himself in chains, forced to serve as Timur's footstool and dragged through the streets of Anatolia in a cage, insulted and ridiculed by his former subjects until, in utter despair, he took his own life.

lands to the south and east and set his sights on Christian Thrace, crossing the Dardanelles and Sea of Marmara. His first actual step into Europe came at the invitation of the Byzantine pretender, John Cantacuzene, in exchange for his aid in a civil war. When peace was finally agreed, Orhan's role as a king-maker in Constantinople was firmly established, along with his first tenuous claim to the crown.

The second half of the 14th century saw the steady expansion of Ottoman territory, at the expense of both Constantinople. Within a year of his succession, Murad I (1362–89) controlled all of Thrace, including Edirne, which was to become the Ottoman's second capital. In 1396,

The conquest of Constantinople

There was precious little left of the Ottoman domains: Bursa had been sacked and Timur's hordes ranged as far as Smyrna (modern Izmir) to uproot the last colony of crusaders on the Mediterranean coast, with the skulls of his victims heaped in a pyramid to mark the occasion.

It was 50 years before the Ottomans gathered strength to continue and sorted out their endless wars of succession. In 1421, Murad II retook Anatolia, overran Greece and first turned the cannons on the walls of Constantinople.

By 1453, it was a foregone conclusion that Constantinople, by now a shadow of its former self, with a population of scarcely 40,000, would eventually fall to the Turks. The Byzantine hinterland had been reduced to a few farms near the city walls and for centuries the city had been little more than a Turkish dependency. Within months of his succession in 1451, Mehmet II announced the final siege of the imperial city, building the castle of Bogaz Kesen ("Throat Cutter"; now known as Rumelihisarı) on the upper Bosphorus, equipping it with heavy ordnance never seen before in eastern warfare, and marching his troops up to the Byzantine walls. When the last Byzantine emperor Constantine XI Palaeologus protested, Mehmet beheaded his envoys and sent a Turkish fleet into the Sea of Marmara.

In April 1453, the siege opened formally, with Mehmet petitioning Constantine for a complete and unconditional surrender. The Byzantine emperor replied, in equally formal manner, that it was Mehmet alone who had made the decision to break the peace, and that God would favour the righteous. There was to be neither surrender nor mercy.

Mehmet's cannons and siege machinery battered the city's walls for nearly two desperate months but, on 29 May 1453, Mehmet ordered the final assault, promising his men a 3-day respite from the fighting to boost their flagging morale. Wave after wave of Ottoman soldiers stormed the walls and, finally, resistance collapsed. The Byzantine Empire was no more.

Mehmet the Conqueror, entered the city in true imperial style, wearing his majestic turban and riding on a white stallion. Constantine's Christian city had become "Islamboul" – the City of Islam.

Superpower

With the conquest of Byzantium, Mehmet II inherited all the millennial prestige and traditions of a great empire. It gave him and his successors – Beyazıt II (1481–1512), Selim the Grim (1515–20), and Süleyman the Magnificent (1520–66) the opportunity to establish a lasting order over vast territories following centuries of feudal chaos. During their age of glory, the four great sultans undertook to create one of the most centralised ruling machines in history.

At the fall of Byzantium, the sultan invited

what he called "governors of Rome and Frankistan" to submit to his will as his vassals. The ultimatum was driven home as country after country fell like dominoes: Greece, Serbia and Albania were taken by 1468; the Rumanian principalities by the turn of the century; Croatia and most of Hungary by 1526. The elimination of the remaining Turkish and Greek states of Anatolia was followed by the conquest of Syria, Palestine and Egypt in 1516–17.

Nothing came out of the first siege of Vienna in 1528, but Turkish cavalry put the fear of god in the heart of German princes by their raids into Bavaria and Bohemia in following years.

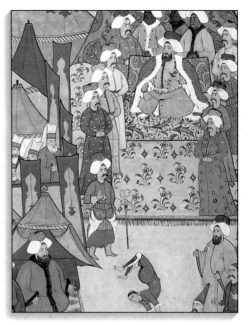

Ottoman privateers controlled the north coast of Africa, and almost squeezed the Spanish and the Venetians out of the Mediterranean.

The sultans put their military muscle to diplomatic use as well. For a while they pursued an alliance with France against the Hispano-Austrian Empire of Charles V. Due to the cultural barriers and mutual ignorance, however, they failed to convert fear into loyalty and menace into real power and influence.

What else "might have been" is best expressed by a remarkable document that Pope Pius II addressed to Mehmet II shortly after the conquest: "Be converted to Christianity," wrote the pontiff, "and accept the faith of the gospel.

LEFT: a 17th-century artist's impression of the entrance to Aya Sofya.
RIGHT: acrobats entertain the sultan.

Once you have done this there will be no prince on the whole earth to outdo you in fame or equal you in power. We shall appoint you emperor of the Greeks and the Orient, and what you have now obtained by violence, and hold unjustly, will be yours by right. Many will submit to you voluntarily, appear before your judgement seat, and pay taxes to you… The Roman Church will embrace you in the same love as other kings, and all the more so accordingly as your position is higher."

The proposal was never a terribly realistic one, but it is tantalising to imagine the possible consequences of a restored East-West Roman

Empire. Even without Western alliances, within a century, the Ottoman state had grown into the most formidable superpower of the old world, its territories extending further than the Eastern Roman Empire at the peak of its power. It reached its zenith during the reign of Süleyman the Magnificent (*see pages 168–69*).

Day-to-day dictatorship

At home, the Ottoman conquest ushered what is arguably its most splendid age as the capital city – and market – of a vigorous, young power which commanded a hinterland spreading from the Yemen in the south to Vienna in the north, and from Algiers in the west to the Persian Gulf

in the east. More to the point, it was an Islamic empire, grounded in a religion which actually encouraged trade.

The city had become the primary metropolis of the Muslim world, a city of administrators and bureaucrats, but also now the chief market in the Middle East, and the final destination of a thousand caravans. Muslim Turks, Arabs, Albanians, Bosnians and Tatars were joined by Christian Greeks and Armenians who accounted for almost a third of the population, and Jewish refugees from Spain who made up 10 percent. By the end of the 16th century, Istanbul was once again the largest city in the world, with 700,000 souls.

In keeping with both Turkish and Byzantine traditions, the sultan was regarded as ultimately responsible for "the poorest widow and the weakest orphan" in his vast empire. This – in marked contrast to Europe – checked the emergence of a hereditary nobility. It also gave the empire an extraordinarily egalitarian aspect. The sultan appeared, above all, as the protector of his subjects, to a remarkable extent regardless of status, wealth, or creed. His annals record an incredible preoccupation with the day-to-day administration of minute aspects of the everyday life of his people.

The palace regulated the economy in a meticulous and authoritarian manner, with priority given to consumer protection. Prices, manufacturing methods, shipping procedures were set down by law to the infinitesimal detail. The monarch took a direct interest in the quality of yoghurt and sherbet sold in the market, the ingredients that went into candles, the standard temperature of hamams, and the hazard posed by chickens in flourmills. The grand vizier, and even the sultan, personally inspected the markets in disguise, searching for irregularities of production, distribution, quality and price.

This centralised control required a huge civil service. And when that grew unwieldy, further layers were added to control and inspect the bureaucracy. Everything was recorded. The Ottoman archives are one of the greatest achievements of this civilisation: all property, all actual and potential sources of income in every part of the empire were inventoried.

LEFT: miniature of Süleyman the Magnificent.
RIGHT: the "Gilded Cage" in the Topkapı Harem, a prison for pretenders to the throne.

Taxes to feed the system were laid down on this basis from the capital. The sultan's treasury strived to gather all, and redistribute all, according to single-voiced imperial policy.

Imperial slaves

At the centre of the imperial system were the *kapıkulu* ("servants of the Porte"), imperial slaves trained for the highest military and administrative posts. Reflecting Ottoman distrust of any privilege or power independent of the sultan, they were recruited neither from a hereditary class, nor from the ranks of the Islamic institutions or the companions of the early sultans. They owed their sole allegiance to the sultan. Technically, they could neither hold property, nor enjoy the protection of ordinary courts. Some amassed fabulous fortunes; others held sway over continents: but it took only the displeasure of the sultan for them to lose it all – including their life.

The most important military component of the *kapıkulu* was the élite corps of janissaries, or "new troops" (*see page 163*), who were known for their fanatical *esprit de corps*, and equally fierce loyalty to the sultan. Most ministers, governors, and army commanders rose from their ranks through rigorous criteria of

POMP AND CIRCUMSTANCE

There were musicians, puppets shows and theatre, but the supreme form of Ottoman entertainment should perhaps be sought in the ceremonial display of imperial pomp that sultans regularly put up to the delight of commoner and dignitary alike. The procession of the sultan to the mosque on Fridays, the public festivities held at the Hippodrome for weeks at an end at the circumcision of princes, the majestic ceremonies performed on imperial births and accessions and the reception of ambassadors have been recorded among the most memorable features of Ottoman culture by both locals and visitors, and reflected in the boldly colourful miniatures by local painters.

A brilliant account is left by de Busbecq, envoy of Francis I at the court of Süleyman the Magnificent: "Around the sultan stood officers of high rank, troops of the imperial guard, the janissaries… an immense crowd of turbans with innumerable layers of the whitest silk, the brilliant costumes of every form and colour, and the shine of gold, silver, silk, and satin all around. Words cannot convey a true idea of this strange spectacle. I have never seen anything so beautiful… The janissaries, lined up apart from the other troops, were so motionless and silent that at first I thought them to be statues, until they at once inclined their heads in response to my salutation."

merit, much remarked by European visitors of the time. Few were even ethnic Turks. Ibrahim Paşa, the greatest of Süleyman's grand viziers, was of Greek origin; Sokollu Mehmet, who in effect ruled the empire under three successive sultans, was a Bosnian peasant.

Brotherly love

Chastened by the squabbles of his ancestors, Mehmet II instituted a drastic rule whereby all surviving brothers of a sultan were executed at his accession. Mehmet III had to dispose of 19 brothers in this fashion.

When this produced desperate fratricidal

wars, it was decided instead to keep all heirs to the throne under lock and key in a "gilded cage" (*see page 167*). Osman III (1754–57) passed 50 years here, all but losing the power of speech. Süleyman II (1687–91) spent 39 years copying and illuminating the Qur'an, and most of his brief subsequent reign begging to be restored to his peaceful prison. Selim III (1789–1807) came out after 15 years, seething with hostility toward the institutions of state, only to be overthrown.

In-laws were potentially equally worrisome and few sultans married any woman whose status might require formal treatment. Süleyman the Magnificent's beloved Hürrem (Roxelana)

was a Russian slave bought at the market; Selim acquired his beloved Nurbanu, a Jewish girl, by the same means. Kösem Mahpeyker, wife of Ahmet I (1603–17), was the orphan of a Greek village priest. Naksidil, mother of Mahmud II (1808–39), was probably Aimée de Rivery, a French creole of Martinique who was carried away by Algerian pirates.

The New World disaster

As early as the end of the 16th century, the Ottoman Empire began a slow and steady decline. It started with events outside its borders and way beyond its control.

For centuries, the Turks had grown wealthy by controlling the vital trade routes to the East – the Silk Road overland from China, and the sea lanes from India through the Red Sea to the Mediterranean. One of Christopher Columbus' motivations in sailing west was to find a way to China and India which avoided the fleets of such Turkish admirals as Piri Reis. His success in discovering the New World and Vasco da Gama's later voyage around the Cape of Good Hope to India were unmitigated disasters for the Turks. Not only did they lose their control of the trade routes to "distant Cathay," but the groaning shiploads of silver and gold flooding into Europe from the New World effectively debased the Ottoman currency.

Additionally, the Europeans' daring voyages gave new importance to naval, geographical and military science – and better ships, captains and guns meant better battles. Inexorably, the Europeans took control first of the Atlantic, then the Indian Ocean and finally even the Mediterranean. In 1571, within months of the Turkish victory at Famagusta, Cyprus, a grand coalition of Spain, the Vatican and Venice, surprised the Turkish fleet at Lepanto in the Gulf of Corinth, effectively destroying Ottoman sea power forever.

On an intellectual level, too, the profound astronomical discoveries with their algebraic and geometrical spin-offs were a thing of the past, with a strict and rigorous interpretation of Islam preventing further intellectual growth. This attitude was in sharp contrast to Renaissance Europe, where intellectuals, freed from religious dogma, were making huge advances in science, rational thought, technology and industry. Even the printing press, which had been used for 250 years in Europe, was only sanctioned by the Islamic clergy in 1727.

As the once glorious empire crumbled from within, formerly cowed rivals were only too eager to nibble away at the edges. The Treaty of Zsitva-Torok delivered Hungary into the hands of the Hapsburgs, who also stopped paying tribute to the Ottomans in 1606. The second Ottoman siege of Vienna resulted in failure (1683). Russia gained the Crimea and parts of the north shore of the Black Sea in the Treaty of Küçük Kaynarca (1774); while Napoleon invaded Ottoman Egypt in 1789, although nominal Ottoman control of the region was reestablished by 1801.

regicide to taint Ottoman history. Osman II (1618–22), unhappy with the less than enthusiastic performance of his troops during his unsuccessful Polish campaign, decided to form an army of Asiatic conscripts. On learning of the scheme, the Janissaries revolted, beheaded the grand vizier and forced the young sultan to ride on a broken-down nag amid insults, before raping and then strangling him in the dreaded prison of Seven Towers.

The bias towards rampant consumerism stifled innovation and investment. The systematic levelling of society extinguished provincial magnates and civic notables, and with them all

Janissary revolt

Internally too, the very strengths of the golden age turned into the empire's greatest weaknesses. The Janissary system became corrupted as soldiers were allowed to marry and become involved in commerce, while their sons and other outsiders were admitted to the ranks. Numbers swelled, and there were frequent mutinies to exact more money from the sultan. The "slave soldiers" had become power brokers with the distinction of committing the first

LEFT: young recruit to the Janissary corps.
ABOVE: the main gate of Istanbul University, on Beyazıt Square.

vestiges of economic and cultural vitality in the provinces. Istanbul itself continued to flourish through the early 17th century, but could not maintain its splendour as the provinces decayed. The lifeblood of the empire receded from the provinces to the city, to the palace, and finally to the inner sanctuary of the harem.

The only reason that the empire struggled on for another 100 years was strictly due to the rivalries and exigencies of European power politics. England and Russia took turns (to be replaced eventually by Germany) to prop up and force-feed the terminal "sick man on the Bosphorus" so as to prevent each other from grabbing his legacy. ❏

STAMBOUL

RECOLLECTIONS OF EASTERN LIFE

BY

PREZIOSI

1858

LA BELLE EPOQUE

As the state faced bankruptcy and talk of revolution got louder, Istanbul found that its political agenda was being increasingly dictated by western Europe

Throughout the 19th century, the empire's balance of trade went haywire as the industrial revolution in Europe turned the fading Ottoman Empire into a source of cheap raw materials and a vast market for manufactured products. Economic concessions given to the Western countries worsened the situation with favours ending as "capitulations". In 1839, a series of imperial reforms made it possible for non-Muslims to serve in government posts and every stage of the administrative hierarchy. Not only were the postal service, street cars, tobacco, electricity and railway now managed by foreigners, but they also had legal privileges. Any legal matter involving a foreigner or a non-Muslim Ottoman who asked for the protection of a foreign consulate could not be tried in an Ottoman court.

Long-distance trade, which had suffered badly during the decline of the empire, revived impressively, but those benefiting from it were almost exclusively European firms, through their Levantine associates and the Christian and Jewish communities. As they expanded their enterprises across the extent of the empire, the commercial centre of the capital shifted from the old Bazaar district across the Golden Horn. By the middle of the 19th century, Pera (modern Beyoğlu) had become the real social and economic centre of the city.

The alternative capital

Pera had been the place where foreigners lived, a foothold of the West in Istanbul, since first colonised by Gauls in pre-Roman times; in the 13th century, the Genoese rebuilt it as a fortified trading colony and it was never penetrated far by the conservative orthodoxy of either Byzantium or Islam. Until late into the 20th century, in fact, few Muslims ever lived there. Native minorities – Greeks, Armenians, and Jews – moved in mainly after the 1830s, as

shopkeepers, clerks and professionals. Apart from them and foreign diplomats and political exiles, the true inhabitants of the district were the Levantines, descendants of Westerners settled in Istanbul, who formed a distinct social layer and rapidly acquired the character of a Constantinopolitan "nobility".

From the 1840s onwards, the district underwent a rapid, monumental change. In 1854 an informal municipality was set up, boulevards and streets were named. The great foreign and multinational banks – Credit Lyonnais, Ottoman Imperial, Bank of Salonica – built their offices along the Grande Rue (İstiklal Caddesi). The illustrious bankers Corpi, Lebet, Camondo and Zarifi (Greeks and Levantines) held court there: between them, they mortgaged the imperial treasury several times over. The stock exchange was set up in Galata: daily rates were reported in journals published in Pera in several European languages. Government bonds were issued through the Galata market to

---

LEFT: a 19th-century book cover depicting life in the Old City.

RIGHT: westernising Sultan Abdülmecid.

European buyers. The English and Americans, Jesuits and Lazarists, Jews and Armenians all opened their own schools, joined in 1868 by the Imperial Lycée of Galatasaray, modelled on French public schools, which still continues to provide many of the Republic's prime ministers, diplomats, writers, and journalists. The streets were lined with luxurious private mansions, but the district's finest buildings were were undoubtedly the embassies of the Great Powers, whose palatial architecture still fascinates tourists today (*see page 205*).

The area became the commercial centre of the city where hundreds of stores and elegant hotels catered to all possible needs. In 1855, the arrival of gas lighting on the main avenues facilitated nightlife. Entertainment, which was limited in traditional Istanbul to activities at the imperial palace (and to the folk arts of the humbler classes), acquired a new life as foreigners began to organise soirées, dances, theatre, and opera. Many Europeans, including writers and poets as well as merchants and diplomats, came to see for themselves the mystical capital of the Orient. A veneer of modernity only added to the already irresistible attractions of a city halfway between the East and the West, where *savoir vivre*, adventure and love were overlaid by the exoticism of a distant culture.

Westernising Turkey

Over the summer, most inhabitants abandoned Pera for the cooler shores of Bosphorus or Princes' Islands, soon followed by the Turkish court who deserted the Topkapı for the sophisticated attractions of the Dolmabahçe, Yıldız and Beylerbeyi Palaces. They were at the vanguard of a profound conversion to European ways among the educated classes of 19th-century Istanbul society. More and more young Turks were sent abroad for study, especially that relating to the military arts. Inevitably, a taste of the social and technological progress in the lands of the traditional enemy made a great impression on these travellers. In the words of the poet Ziya Paşa:

"I passed through the lands of the infidels, and saw cities and mansions,

I wandered through the realm of Islam, and saw nothing but ruins."

On the whole, however, Muslim Turks kept aloof from Pera itself until the early 20th century. It was only during the final brief period between the Young Turk revolution of 1908 and the post-war Allied occupation of 1918–22 that Pera became a centre of gravity for the "westernised" Turkish élite of the empire.

Reform

Territorial losses continued throughout the 19th century. Russia annexed Bessarabia (1812); Greece became an independent principality (1827); Moldavia and Wallachia became autonomous principalities (1829); and British occupied Egypt (1882).

Attempts to reform the ailing empire began in earnest with Sultan Mahmud II (1808–29). In

CRIMEA

Trade with the empire became so valuable to the West that the Muslim Ottomans were saved by Christian England, France and Italy when attacked by Russia in 1854. The small but bloody Crimean War inspired an English woman, Florence Nightingale, to establish a war hospital in Istanbul. Here, she invented modern nursing practice, with its life-saving emphasis on cleanliness and hygiene. In recognition, she became the first woman in the world to receive a medal of honour from a sultan. Literature inspired by the war included English Lord Tennyson's epic, *The Charge of the Light Brigade*, while Russian novelist, Leo Tolstoy, wrote *The Sevastopol Tales*.

1826, he abolished the decadent Janissary corps. It was a bloody affair. After obtaining the support of the clerics and the people, the sultan asked each Janissary battalion to spare 150 men for the new corps he was forming. The Janissaries refused and overturned their camp kettles in the traditional signal of revolt. But Mahmud unfurled the sacred banner of the prophet and opened fire on his own élite corps from the Seraglio. Four thousand Janissaries were killed in their barracks, with thousands of others slaughtered in the streets of Istanbul and in the provinces as a general purge began.

Next the sultan produced a generation of French-speaking bureaucrats who were trained in the newly formed translation bureaux. Certain elements within the new bureaucracy desired reform from within, and edicts of 1839 and 1856 attempted orderly tax collection, fair and regular conscription, and the establishment of banks, public works and commerce.

Strangely enough, "equality" held little attraction for many Ottomans, and was resisted fiercely by non-Muslims, who, until then, had been exempted from military service. As prosperous tradesmen and farmers – often under the protection of foreign governments – they had no intention of interrupting business for the sake of a 5- to 7-year period of national service. Although paved with good intentions, the road to reform proved very rocky.

First constitution

Large-scale borrowing with high interest rates led to state bankruptcy in 1875. In 1881, the Ottoman debt was placed under receivership by the international commissions. The Regie Ottomane and the Public Debts Committee acted as the empire's *de facto* financial administration until World War I.

In 1876, the increasingly autocratic Sultan Abdülaziz was deposed and one of the most controversial of the sultans, Abdülhamid II (1876–1909) came to the throne. He established the first written constitution and the first elected parliamentary government in the history of the Ottoman Empire, or indeed, the Islamic world. However, the parliament only met twice before being dissolved in 1878. Meanwhile, a growing

Pan-Slavic movement in the Balkans culminated in war with Russia, which resulted in independence for Serbia, Montenegro and Bulgaria. Masses of refugees flooded across the frontiers, cutting some of the Ottomans' wealthiest provinces off from the state forever.

The crisis prompted Abdülhamid to suspend the new constitution and dissolve parliament. For the next 30 years, the empire lived under oppression and censure. However, the sultan's autocracy fomented opposition, and a secret society, the Committee of Union and Progress, began working to restore the constitution and, eventually, to depose the sultan.

The Young Turks

In 1908, in an uprising which became known as the Young Turks Revolution, army officers in Macedonia revolted, forcing the sultan to call for elections and reopen the parliament. The following year, Abdülhamid II was forced to abdicate in favour of Sultan Mehmed Reshad V (1909–18) who ascended the throne as a mere figurehead. The Ottoman sultanate was a thing of the past, in all but name.

Nevertheless, the days of democratic rapture were short-lived. Responding to threats – both perceived and real — the CUP triumvirate of Enver, Cemal and Talat soon took over the government at the expense of the other alliance

LEFT: a new architectural style for a new town – Art Nouveau was a favourite in Pera.
RIGHT: a Pera bar girl before World War I.

partners and ruled alone as crisis after crisis rolled over the tottering empire.

Dissent from within was matched by intrigue from without, as the European powers vied with each other to establish influence over the "Sick Man of Europe," cajoling and threatening by turns. The most successful of the suitors was the Kaiser's Germany, which, itself a newly formed nation-state, was attempting to play catch-up pool with its rivals in the Grand Game of Asia. Military delegations, trade and projects such as the Berlin-to-Baghdad railway were amongst the means used to woo the Ottomans to the imperial German side.

Things got steadily worse. Turkey found it hard to recover from the loss of Libya to the Italians in 1911, and its humiliating defeat at the hands of the Bulgarians, Greeks and Serbs during the Balkan War of 1912, when the Bulgarian army advanced to the fields of today's Yeşilköy Airport and Istanbul was only saved by bickering and internecine war between the Balkan allies.

The Balkan Wars – and the deteriorated state of the city – were amply covered by such cub-reporters as the young Ernest Hemingway (who loathed Istanbul) and the doyen of war correspondents, G. Ward Price, who was not terribly fond of the city either. He warned potential visitors: "Never set foot on shore, for the sordidness and squalor of that city's ancient streets and the incongruous modernity which is gaining ground in its more prosperous districts destroy the romance and seduction of what was once the capital of the Eastern Roman Empire."

World War I

When war finally broke out in August 1914, the Ottomans equivocated; but the English acted prematurely and seized two warships being built in dry dock for the Ottoman fleet. Collections had been taken throughout the Muslim world to pay for them and Ottoman fury finally turned the tide. Two German warships being pursued by the English and French navies in the Mediterranean were suddenly "donated" to the Ottomans as they steamed towards the Dardanelles. And, with a change of uniform but not of crew, the new Turkish warships sailed through the Bosphorus and into the Black Sea to lob shells at Russian ports in the Crimea. To the chagrin of many in Istanbul, Ottoman Turkey discovered that it was a Central Power.

Egypt's nominal loyalty was severed when the British ousted the last Ottoman Khedive in 1914, and the former province became a major base for English activities in the Middle East, including the Arab Uprising against Ottoman rule, led in part by the romantic Lawrence of Arabia. Meanwhile, to the northeast, the forces of Czarist Russia, with the aid of local Armenians, pressed inexorably west as far as Erzurum, successfully annexing large areas within the motherland – Anatolia.

Gallipoli

Within this sea of disaster, the only successful Ottoman military action during the war was the defence of the Dardanelles in 1915, when the combined French, British and Australian-New Zealand (ANZAC) forces landed at Gallipoli. One of the leaders of the "Young Turks" rebellion, a certain Colonel Mustafa Kemal (later to become known as Atatürk), commanded a brilliant but brutal defence for the Ottomans, winning a reputation for invincibility and heroism that stood him well several years later when he started building the Republic of Turkey.

The Gallipoli campaign was instrumental in the fate of other individuals and nations too: Sea Lord Winston Churchill, the architect of the ill-fated invasion, was obliged to resign and join the dough-boys in the trenches in France; Australia and New Zealand acquired a new sense of nationhood as a result of their horrendous casualties; and Czarist Russia, unable to export wheat or import weapons – in interesting contrast to the flow of trade today – collapsed in 1917, to resurface as the Soviet Union.

The end of the empire

When the Ottomans finally capitulated to the Allies in November 1918, the empire was but a pale reflection of its former self. The peace treaty eventually signed in Sèvres in 1920

made expediently and secretly by the Allies. Italy was to be given several of the southern provinces, while Russia had been promised Istanbul itself, the "key to the Crimea."

The 500-year reign of the Ottomans was over, but everywhere her "children" sprang up in her wake. Today, 31 nations owe a significant part of their heritage to the Turks, be it as banal as military terminology, as basic as food or as sublime as architecture: Albania, Bulgaria, the two nations on Cyprus, Greece, Hungary, Bosnia, Croatia, Slovenia, and the former Yugoslavia in Europe; the Ukraine, Armenia, Georgia and Azerbaijan in the former Soviet

stripped the rump state of many of her former provinces: Iraq and Palestine were ceded to the British, while Syria (including Lebanon) was given to France under the new League of Nations' mandate system. Separate Armenian, Assyrian and Kurdish states were also envisioned, all of them, strangely, to be established in the same eastern provinces – an insubstantial promise that has caused bloodshed ever since. Not even the Turkish homeland of central Anatolia was sacred, thanks to various agreements

LEFT: Dolmabahçe Palace, an extravagance of Western design by a reforming emperor.
ABOVE: weary Turkish troops in World War I.

Union; the Middle-Eastern states of Bahrain, Egypt, Iraq, Israel, Jordan, Kuwait, Lebanon, Oman, Saudi Arabia, Sudan, Syria, the United Arab Emirates and North and South Yemen; and Algeria, Libya and Tunisia in North Africa.

Strangely, the Turks were the last to emerge from the ashes of the empire and raise a beacon of nationalism. It took the ignominy of military defeat, the disgrace of Sèvres, invasion by the Greeks and, finally, one man at the right place and time, to ignite the spark that established a national identity and a modern nation state. The place was a harbour on the Black Sea Coast; the time May 1919, and the man Mustafa Kemal, the hero of Gallipoli. ❏

ATATURK'S REPUBLIC

With the end of World War I and the collapse of the Ottoman Empire,
the stage was set for the meteoric rise of Kemal Atatürk

On 30 October 1918, the Ottoman empire collapsed. Backing the wrong side in World War I cost millions of lives, huge chunks of territory and, finally, their empire. The Treaty of Sèvres that the Ottomans were forced to sign in 1920 was literally the death warrant for the pathetic "Sick Man of Europe," a mere redrafting of earlier secret protocols for the dismemberment of the empire between the French, British, Italians, Armenians, Kurds and Greeks, On 15 May 1919, as the first Greeks landed at Smyrna, the latent patriotism of the Turks was fanned into flame.

The War of Independence

Within days, Mustafa Kemal, the brilliant saviour of Gallipoli, slipped out of Istanbul, ostensibly to supervise the disbanding of the eastern armies. Once safely away from the court and Istanbul, he renounced his rank and titles and devoted all his energy to building a nationalist army. On 23 April 1920, he convened the first Grand National Assembly in Ankara.

Local committees in the southeast fired the opening salvos of the War of Independence. The battle-weary French soon withdrew from Turkish soil, while Kemal swiftly pushed the Armenians and Georgians back to their modern boundaries. The Italians then decamped, leaving only the British to aid the Greeks.

Kemal and Ismet Inönü, a close friend and accomplished tactician, next checked the Greek advance during the 22-day-long Battle of Sakarya. The following year, at the Battle of Dumlupınar, the bulk of the Greek army was annihilated; its commander-in-chief was taken prisoner; and the ragged remnants chased into the sea. The liberation of Izmir, on 9 September, 1922, paved the way for the withdrawal of British troops from the Dardanelles.

Kemal and his circle now turned their attention to the task of rebuilding their effectively

LEFT: the Turkish Memorial at Gallipoli, Turkey's only military victory in World War I.
RIGHT: Kemal Atatürk (1881–1938).

leaderless nation, ravaged and impoverished by conflict. As the Allies sent invitations to peace talks, the Istanbul government, now totally out of touch with modern reality, called for "a joint stand." On 1 November 1922, the Grand National Assembly declared that, while the Ottomans retained the right to the caliphate, or

religious leadership, of the nation, the temporal power of the sultanate was abolished.

On 17 November 1922, Sultan Mehmed VI slipped out a side door of the palace to board a British warship, *HMS Malaya*, which spirited him away to Malta and eternal exile. Next day, his cousin, Abdülmecid, was elected Caliph, an office he was to hold only so long as Kemal found the outward symbols of religion useful.

Kemal and his reformers wanted to model their new nation on the West, but all existing institutions were unmistakably Eastern. What was more, the Turks were conditioned to see themselves as an *Umma* (Muslim community), not a nation, and had long been discouraged from involvement in politics, industry, commerce or any other potential source of power that could challenge the absolute authority of the Ottomans. The government faced the almost impossible tasks of creating a national consciousness, absorbing Western civilisation and reinterpreting Islam. On 3 March 1923, with the new Caliph attempting to gather support in Istanbul, the Grand National Assembly abolished the caliphate and banished all male members of the royal family from the country.

On 24 July 1923, a new peace treaty signed in Lausanne lessened the harshness of Sèvres, and secured the sovereignty and territory of the

Turks. On 29 October the Grand National Assembly unanimously endorsed the proclamation of the Republic of Turkey. Its first president was Mustafa Kemal, head of the newly founded Republican People's Party (RPP).

Wrenching changes

Within days of the Caliph's removal, the remaining kiosks, pavilions and palaces along the shores of the Bosphorus were sacked by mobs acting in the spirit of Russia's October Revolution and with Ankara's tacit approval. In autumn of 1924, the imperial banner above the Sublime Porte was removed, while the Grand Vizierate was converted into the office of

the provincial governor. The Ottoman Debt Administration building in Cağaloğlu was transformed into the Boys' Lycée of Istanbul (now co-educational). Topkapı Palace and Aya Sofya, the very symbol of Ottoman Islam, were opened to the public as museums.

In 1925, all convents run by a host of religious sects were banned, primary school education was made compulsory and religious law was abolished. In 1928, Arabic script was discarded and replaced by the Latin alphabet. Even wardrobes were touched by the winds of reform. The fez, the headgear of officialdom, and turbans were banned. Hats and caps, personally modelled by Mustafa Kemal, found a surprising acceptance.

The westernisation of women was not merely cosmetic; new political rights led towards greater emancipation. Women were encouraged to compete with men professionally while the civil code adopted from Switzerland ensured their equality before the law, although the reality has still not caught up with the ideal.

Nationalist antipathy towards Istanbul did not stop at the symbols of the former royal family. Although nearly 40 percent of the city's population of 600,000 in 1927 was non-Muslim, a language campaign, replete with the equivalent of "Red Guards" to enforce it, was initiated under the banner of "Citizen, Speak Turkish!" Over 30 French and Italian language schools were closed, in keeping with efforts to impose a monolithic identity on a multi-ethnic fabric. The city was far too cosmopolitan for the new "Turkish" nation, which meant to find its "authentic" traditions not in the salons of Pera, but in the coffee houses of the hinterland.

Building the economy

In spite of the economic benefits of Lausanne, the new order masked deep economic setbacks. Debt relief was refused and Ankara's powers to set tariffs were restricted. However the leaders of the new state refused to be discouraged and reached eagerly towards what they perceived as the key to the Western supremacy – capitalism. Banks were set up with state funds to back private enterprise and a vast array of incentives were offered to businessmen. Then, in 1929, came the Wall Street Crash. The Great Depression had a disastrous effect on Turkey's crop exports, and discredited capitalism in the eyes of Turkey's military-bureaucratic élite, who saw the apparent immunity of the planned Soviet economy from the global catastrophe.

In an economic U-turn, the state put a series of State Economic Enterprises (SEEs) at the forefront of the drive towards industrialisation. Self-sufficiency became the order of the day. The first Soviet-influenced Five-Year Development Plan (1934-1939) helped a rapid build-up of the country's industries.

Changing of the guard

The leaders of the Republic were also casting increasingly worried glances at the regathering clouds of war in Europe. Against such a background, the death of Atatürk on 10 November, 1938 came as a major blow. Next day, his life-long friend and comrade-in-arms, Ismet Inönü, was sworn in as president.

Inönü devoted his energies to keeping Turkey essentially neutral during World War II. This required an iron hand, a skilled tightrope act between the warring sides – and a certain departure from treaty obligations. If anything, sympathies tilted toward the Nazi side after the German invasion of Russia – the traditional enemy of the Turks. German submarines and supply ships allegedly used the Bosphorus as a route into the Black Sea. The same channel served as an exit for German dead from the Crimea, as witnessed by the German War Memorial Cemetery in Tarabya.

It was a gloomy era for Istanbul, a virtual ghost-town with only a few spies and con-men stalking victims in the better bars. The centres of spy action were the Pera Palace and the Park Hotel, venue for singing duels between the British and the German delegations when they were not occupied making "preventive purchasing deals" – buying up every scrap of cloth which could possibly be used for bandages or tons of hail-damaged wheat.

The depopulation of the city was aided by the gouging new tax law, which allowed local officials to set exorbitant capital levies on the minorities amounting to over ten times that paid by Muslims or resident foreigners. Corruption abounded, with vindictive officials arbitrarily deciding who should pay what amount, and defaulters shipped out to hard-labour camps in the east. The policy, abandoned in 1944, effectively brought legal business to a standstill, as honest brokers were thrown into jail while bribers and blackmarketeers went free. Many established Istanbul families were either forced to leave or chose to abandon the city, their old houses given over to tenements and decay.

Post-war boom

A few weeks before the end of the war, Turkey finally threw its cards in with the Allies, just in time to qualify for UN membership, ensure American protection from Soviet threats and American assistance in rebuilding the economy.

Istanbul rapidly became a growth city as banks, business and industry moved in.

The honeymoon of the 1920s and early '30s between Turkey and Russia had long since returned to mutual hostility, thanks to Ankara's repeated crackdowns on domestic communists. Now the situation nearly exploded into fresh violence when Moscow demanded control of the Turkish straits and asserted territorial claims over previously Armenian districts on the eastern borders. The Soviets eventually withdrew their demands only after the United States and Britain firmly backed Turkey, and an American battleship, the USS *Missouri*, was sent to Istanbul as a symbol of solidarity.

LEFT: Greeks escorting Turkish prisoners following the Greek landing at Smyrna, 15 May 1919.
RIGHT: one of Atatürk's new young Turks.

Democracy

After years of autocratic rule by the RPP, Turkey's courtship of the United States had no little effect on the eventual development of a multi-party democracy in Turkey, a prerequisite for receiving aid under the Truman Doctrine. (It also led to Turkey's later involvement in the Korean War (1950), admission to NATO (1952), and controversial recognition of Israel.)

In 1945, a group of former RPP members, headed by Adnan Menderes and Celâl Bayar, formed the opposition Democrat Party. Their platform included the relaxation of state controls over business and agriculture and more

freedom of religion, a potent combination which proved enormously popular with an odd cross-section of voters, including feudal landowners, the traditionally conservative rural masses and the emerging urban middle class. By 1950 the DP was in power, with Bayar as president and Menderes as prime minister.

Erratic progress

The DP's markedly pro-American tone encouraged a continuous flow of US economic and military aid. In return, Turkey granted the USA facilities for an air base, electronic surveillance stations and bases for Jupiter missiles (later dismantled as part of the deal ending the Cuban

crisis). Despite the strain this placed on relations with the country's Islamic neighbours, Turkey proudly stood by her Western friends during the Cold War years and beyond.

The DP's populist policies and new incentives to free enterprise also led to massive, chaotic expansion. The newly established industries in Istanbul soon attracted hundreds of thousands of unskilled and semi-skilled workers from the vast Anatolian hinterland. From less than a million in 1950, the city's population rose to over three million by 1970. Festering rings of squatters shacks (*gecekondu,* meaning literally "put up at night") began to spread like mushrooms over any unclaimed land. Initial efforts to provide a modern urban infrastructure were abandoned, and the city sprawled out along the Marmara shore. Meantime, massive imports of foreign goods and overly generous public spending left the country with a massive trade deficit and national debt leading to repeated currency devaluations.

As his popularity declined, Menderes also became increasingly repressive, censoring the press, jailing political opponents and manipulating elections. He was finally deposed on 27 May 1960, in a popularly supported military coup. A year later he was sentenced to death by military tribunal. Perhaps strangely, this and later coups are regarded as progressive by many Turks, who consider the military guard on Atatürk's ideals a safety valve on extremism.

Descent into chaos

Under coup leader, General Cemal Gürsel, the constituent assembly drafted a new, more liberal constitution and free, if unstable, elections were held. The right to strike was confirmed in 1963 and Turkey's first socialist party was formed. Meantime, followers of the now-banned DP flocked to the new Justice Party led by conservative politician, Süleyman Demirel, whose career spanned more than 30 years. In 1965 and again in 1969, the Justice Party was swept into power, promising commitment to a free market and foreign investment.

In Istanbul, several areas of Greek settlement such as Arnavutköy or Tarlabaşı near Taksim were hard-hit following the expulsion of more than 30,000 Greek nationals in the wake of the Cyprus crisis of 1964. Now, poorer neighbourhoods were often composed of homogeneous migrants from one area, so that Zeytinburnu in

Europe had collected a nearly exclusive population of industrial workers from the east who supported social democratic parties, while Gaziosmanpaşa – the sprawling slum along the airport road – became the abode of the ultra-conservative migrants from Yugoslavia and Bulgaria who backed centrist parties.

Street politics

Urban polarisation had political ramifications as well. Whole slum areas became "liberated" zones controlled by extreme leftists or rightist militants, where you were identified as a friend or foe by the newspaper you carried or the cut

helped several pro-Islamic factions reestablish themselves on the political stage. Assuming victory, and hoping to shake off the Islamist coalition, Ecevit sought early re-election, but right-wing opposition forces closed ranks, and gained control of the government.

Throughout the late '70s Turkey's government was a chaos of extremes, the economy was in a dire condition, with a morass of foreign debts and uncontrolled public spending. Left-right feuding, sectarian violence and separatist activities erupted, leaving 5,000 dead by 1980, many more tortured or wounded, and the country on the verge of civil war.

of your beard or moustache. This explosion of political activism continued throughout the late 1960s and '70s. Strikes, political polarisation and street violence brought repeated military intervention and the ultimate alignment of Demirel with the far right. Even the socialist leader Bülent Ecevit had to compromise. In the elections of 1973, his reshaped RPP was forced to form a coalition with Necmettin Erbakan's Islamic fundamentalist National Salvation Party – a so-called "historic compromise" which

LEFT: funeral of a leftist political leader.
ABOVE: political demonstrations in the streets of Istanbul frequently turned into ugly, full-scale riots.

On 12 September, the generals once again stepped in. This time, they were determined to make a thorough job of reestablishing order. General Kenan Evren and the commanders of the armed forces formed the notorious National Security Council, and assumed totalitarian powers, caring little for domestic or foreign reaction. The cities were placed under total curfew, all political parties were banned and their leaders detained, including the former leftist mayor of Istanbul. Tens of thousands of suspected terrorists were rounded up and tried in military courts, with 25 executed for major crimes, though the radical right and Islamists suffered a great deal less than Marxists, trade unionists, university professors and other left-leaning intellectuals. It was late 1982 before the curfew was lifted, and nightlife slowly returned to the sobered streets of Istanbul. Martial law was finally lifted in 1986, two years after municipal elections were held.

The Ozal era

General elections held in 1983 were a landslide victory for the populist appeal of Turgut Özal and the ANAP (Motherland Party). Combining a sweeping liberalisation of the economy with Islamist sympathies and a blind eye to profit by any means, Özal reached the hearts of the

pro-Islamic Refah Welfare Party formed a short-lived coalition government, their brief victory now generally viewed as a protest vote against government corruption rather than a desire to overturn 75 years of Republicanism.

And now...

Recently, the Turkish parliament has been characterised by colourless non-majority centrist coalitions. Current projects include long overdue tax and family law reforms, and heavier penalties for fraud. Turkey undoubtedly has the capital and expertise to become a major player in world markets. Unfortunately the battle

common people. A sudden relaxation of trade restrictions created an influx of foreign goods and Turkish business people were encouraged to enter the world arena for the first time. Vast amounts of money were spent on developing tourism and foreign investment was welcomed. Inflation soared, but opportunities existed as never before.

If Özal is regarded as a hero of free-market capitalism, he is also remembered for shady business practices and blatant nepotism which helped set the stage for the corruption that still undermines credibility in Turkish politics today.

He died in 1993, succeeded in the presidency by Süleyman Demirel. Shortly afterwards, the

against the Kurds and ongoing human rights abuses continue to drain the economy and damage the country's reputation abroad. Economic growth is an impressive 7 percent a year but inflation is an inexcusably high 100 percent, while in 1999, the economy was devastated by the earthquake (*see page 57*).

In Istanbul, massive immigration has forever changed the complexion of the city. Old Istanbullites still yearn for a pristine past; rural newcomers dream of streets paved with gold. Are their dreams so different?   ❏

ABOVE: the army marches on, self-appointed guardians of Atatürk's ideals.

Atatürk: Father of the Nation

Gigantic bronze statues – the bigger the better for aspiring governors – occupy the choicest spot of every town. His towering figure and cold blue eyes bore little physical resemblance to the Central Asian ancestors he identified for his people, but Mustafa Kemal is the idol at the heart of one of the most enduring personality cults in modern history, the literal "Father" of the modern Turkish nation.

With their adopted religion of Islam and many centuries of autocratic rulers demanding filial obedience, the Turks have always been accustomed to following a succession of father figures. What sets Atatürk aside for true reverence is his success in reversing the fate of a doomed nation.

Born the son of a customs official in the now-Greek northern Aegean port of Salonica in 1881, Mustafa had his first violent row with the chief "Mullah" of the district religious school at an early age; an experience which seemingly left him with a lasting hatred for religious fundamentalism. Conversely, he had always been favourably impressed by the tight-fitting uniforms worn by the men of the local military academy, and he secretly enrolled by taking the entrance exams.

At the academy, his mathematical prowess soon won him the name Kemal, or "the complete one". While there he also developed a keen interest in the works of Rousseau and Voltaire, dreaming of future glory as the Napoleon of the East.

His clandestine activities soon resulted in a transfer to Damascus as staff captain – far away from the locus of power. Even so, he set up a revolutionary society which later merged with the pan-Ottoman Union and Progress Party (UPP) headed by the ill-fated triumvirate of Enver, Cemal and Talat. Unlike them, Mustafa Kemal remained a strict legalist, calling for the separation of the military from politics, and evoking the lasting suspicion of the better known leaders of the time.

In 1911, Kemal volunteered for service in Libya, which was then under attack by Italian troops. However, the breakout of the catastrophic Balkan Wars the following year brought him home to help Enver recapture Edirne, although the latter was given all the credit. Enver went on to drag Turkey into the

mess of World War I, then died in Central Asia at the head of a cavalry charge. When Talat and Cemal also died, assassinated by Armenian separatists, Mustafa Kemal, the only undefeated general of the savaged Ottoman armies, took up leadership of the struggle to save the heartland of the lost empire. He saw himself as the generator of a new and different nation known as "*Türkiye*," or the Land of the Turks. He led the country to victory in the War of Independence, abolished the monarchy and became its first president, secularising the state, liberating women and westernising the nation. He died from cirrhosis of the liver, on 10 November 1938, at the age of only 57. His life-

long friend and companion, Ismet İnönü, was sworn in as president to continue his work.

Today, half a century on, Mustafa Kemal, now Atatürk, is still idolised by his people, a source of often contradictory wisdom for all. Man or woman, rich or poor, right, left or centrist, all look to his quotations, whether those painstakingly translated from the old Ottoman script, or the ones he made up on the spot to suit the occasion.

Above all, the official memory of cadet number 1238 is jealously guarded by the officer corps committed to preserving his heritage. Every year, when his number is called out at the roll call of the graduating class of new cadets, there is but one solemn and uniform response: "He is among us." ❏

RIGHT: gold bust of Mustafa Kemal Atatürk.

A CITY UNDER STRAIN

With overpopulation, traffic gridlock, sub-standard housing and rampant corruption, Istanbul's quality of life is being eroded

Istanbul is a city under continual pressure, and, some say, ready to explode. For visitors unaccustomed to megacities, the sheer volume of crowds in the bazaars of Eminönü or Beyazıt, the Saturday night crush in İstiklal, the honking and banner-waving after a match, the riot squads, Panzer tanks and truncheons

adding to tension at political demonstrations and, above all, the relentless traffic jams, especially on the Bosphorus Bridge at rush hour, may induce severe claustrophobia in the unprepared. Istanbullites also have an astonishing tolerance for noise pollution, and from early in the morning until late at night expect to be assailed with the cries of street hawkers, sweatshop machinery, hundreds of electronically amplified calls to prayer, send-off parties for the army's new recruits, fireworks, and Arabesque music wailing from buses and taxis.

Why is it so crowded? The chief problem is unchecked expansion. When the Republic was founded in 1923, the population of Istanbul was only 600,000, similar in size to the original Byzantine city. Today it tops 12 million, with an annual influx of up to 500,000 a year, most of them migrants from poorer regions to the east. Istanbul provides nearly half Turkey's wealth, and, with a growth rate nearly treble the national average, public resources are stretched to their limits trying to solve enormous inbuilt problems of waste disposal and water supply, of education and welfare, and of pollution, transportation and traffic congestion.

Gridlock

As the latter affects all levels of society equally, it tends to top the complaint bill in city surveys. Not even a chauffeur-driven Mercedes can fly. There are well over a million cars on the road today, and, according to statistics, up to 100 more a day join them. A long-awaited underground system from Taksim Square to Levent 4 is meant to open in 2000, though it has been delayed time and time again. The existing tram, which begins at the ferry docks in Eminönü and runs out of the central bus garage at Esenler, is unnervingly packed at all times. Taxis are a bargain, but even the most honest driver can do nothing against a traffic bottleneck, infuriating one-way systems or narrow streets blocked by pedestrians and handcarts.

Tenements and shanties

With its population continuing to swell, housing is at a premium in Istanbul. Rents are radically higher than in the rest of the country, leading to the growth of shanty towns and perilously shoddy buildings, a fact which stood out glaringly in the shockingly high death toll of the 1999 earthquake (*see page 57*). Of course visitors don't see the worst. The areas flattened in the quake disaster cluster around the industrial hellholes of İzmit and Adapazarı far outside the city centre, while the most wretched of the urban poor live five to a room in Dickensian tenements in areas such as Tarlabaşı, once a part of Beyoğlu before a motorway cut through its heart. Others build illegal apartments on the rooftops of existing buildings, in historic neighbourhoods such as Tünel, around the Galata Tower, without concern for the added strain on the original structure.

In areas like Ümraniye, famed for a garbage dump explosion in the mid-1990s which claimed many lives, Gaziosmanpaşa, Sultanbeyli and Küçükarmutlu (adjacent to the desres neighbourhood of Etiler), these sub-standard buildings are called *gecekondu* ("overnight" houses). Usually built on government land, the term refers to the method of rapid construction and instant occupation intended to make tearing them down impossi-

ments, which were initially were considered expedient as they provided a work force for factories at no cost to the bosses.

Votes for sale

Gecekondu builders know that eventually, come election time, a pledge of votes for particular groups and individuals will be rewarded with an "amnesty" on illegal properties, granting rightful titles of ownership. Since 1949 there has been at least one amnesty per decade, and more often two. It is now calculated that 45 percent of Istanbul's buildings have no planning permission, and that 73 percent of these are on

ble, no matter how unsafe, illegal, badly planned, or lacking in basic amenities they are.

Once they were single or at most double-storey dwellings, but little by little families added floors or built newer structures of 4-5 storeys, easily finding tenants or buyers amongst the more recently arrived rural poor. Thus the chain of slum landlordship begins, and the socially poisonous shanty towns expand.

Today, there are more than 300,000 such buildings, generally near industrial develop-

state-owned lands. Until the last decade, it was the fashion of the liberal-minded to defend *gecekondu* building as the right of the poor. But research has increasingly shown that *laissez-faire* rural migration and shanty town building sets up a cycle of exploitation with enormous social consequences.

A fundamental shift

As the city becomes ever more divided politically and socially, old Istanbul families cling to the cosmopolitanism of the past, and despair of the influx of Anatolians who have severely altered the demographic balance and voting patterns of the city. Three generations on, many

LEFT: over 60 percent of Turkey's population is under the age of 25.

ABOVE: historic houses are usually left to rot or burn.

shanty dwellers still have not integrated into city life, contributing to a mafia mentality and a younger generation who have never acquired the skills to move beyond the margins of society. They, in turn, often feel dispossessed and looked down upon, and rally around politicians most sympathetic to their needs, responding eagerly to the utopian promises of Islamic fundamentalist parties or far-right nationalists.

Black market tax

Property problems in the city, however, are not specifically the preserve of the poor – a decade of 100 percent inflation has also taken its toll,

in a kind of tax amnesty designed to meet IMF conditions. It led to the sudden disappearance of something like US$20 billion out of the country. The government immediately backed down. The new coalition of 1999 has shown willingness to carry on with IMF-led reforms, including tax reform and privatisation, but no one is holding their breath. Meanwhile many apartments and buildings sit empty for years, have 20 owners or none at all (such as when original Greek owners have fled) or, as in the case of derelict historical buildings, mysteriously burn down. A vacant lot is a gold mine; the standard procedure is for the contractors to

along with messy inheritance rights and the value of land versus housing. A large section of society (especially those with capital) has become increasingly invested in the tax loopholes afforded by the rampant inflation and is resisting all government efforts towards reform. A change in Turkish tax law has long been cited as an absolute necessity for economic stabilisation, and ultimately the reduction of inflation, but "*rentiers*" have a great deal to lose if they cannot bury the true value of their property under Turkish lira prices of the past.

Politicians know this, and tread warily, further entrenching the "ghost economy". In 1998 an attempt was made to register "black money"

give land owners several apartments in a new highrise in exchange for the property.

These are tensions the visitor to the city should try to understand as they pass from slums of Karaköy or Tarlabaşı to the portals of plenty in Nişantaşı, Bebek and Suadiye. From the wailing Arabesque music in your taxi to the Pavarotti in an Ortaköy café, or the cost of a night out in a Beyoğlu *meyhane* versus a dinner at *Club 29*, it is clear that the vast gap between Istanbul's privileged and poor is a source of struggle to come. ❑

ABOVE: mass demonstration in support of the now banned Islamic Refah (Welfare) Party.

Seismic City

It started just a little after 3am in the wee hours of Tuesday, 17 August 1999. If you lived at the northern end of the Bosphorus, near the Black Sea, you knew you were experiencing a mighty earthquake, but not necessarily a deadly one. All electric supply had been cut, and it wasn't possible to know what exactly was happening elsewhere.

Sleepy neighbours in nightclothes huddled in doorways. Some had had the foresight to invest in battery-powered torches with radios inside, because they knew a "big one" was coming – they just didn't know when. There was approximately one a century, according to the statistics, and Istanbul's next one was overdue. History records that a quake brought down the original dome of Aya Sofya in 550, while in 1766 most of the 15th-century Fatih Cami was destroyed.

"There has been a major earthquake in Istanbul…" said the disembodied voice. The Richter scale reading, people were told, was 6.7, the epicentre in İzmit, an industrial hellhole specialising in the manufacture of cars and tyres, some 50 miles from Istanbul's heart on the Marmara Sea.

It took several days for the truth of the disaster to sink in, and for accurate information to filter through. A 640-km (400-mile) region had been affected, and the initial Richter reading had been far too low. Then came the worst televised images – huge highrise buildings which had simply toppled over like toys, revealing foundations sometimes less than a metre deep; burning oil and gas depots reminiscent of the Gulf War; human limbs sticking out of collapsed flats which had come down like layer cakes; buildings in which the entire structure dropped one floor due to a glassed-in shop at ground level so structurally weak it could not support the 5 or 6 floors above it; concrete with so much sand mixed in you could crumble it in your fist; contractors who had gone into hiding, and surveys whose results were never heeded; the laxity of building inspection, the rumours of bribery, and aftershocks which kept coming, and coming – 200 in one day alone – and people so fearful that panicked survivors in stricken zones died jumping out of windows. The official death count of around 14,500 never told the truth; it is estimated that around 40,000 people eventually died, their bodies

never found under the bulldozed rubble. Sales of sedatives in the city skyrocketed.

It isn't that Istanbul's building regulations are inadequate, it is that they are not followed. Even if building contractors themselves know what they are doing, the untrained, underpaid day labourers, usually poor Kurds from east Anatolia, do not. Now imagine these concrete hives built on an enormous fault line where land masses grind together as they move in opposite directions, sometimes reaching speeds of 8,000 kmph (5,000 mph) or more and shifting the ground both vertically and horizontally.

Who is to blame? Religious radicals had a field day claiming it was God punishing the secularist

government for banning headscarves in universities, as did foreign journalists hostile to the Turkish government and the military over Kurdish and human rights issues. Bereaved families wailing on television blamed anyone at all, even if they themselves would have been perfectly happy to bribe an inspector, or get something built on the cheap.

What good can come of this? In June 1999, President Demirel was still voicing his commitment to building Turkey's first nuclear power plant at Akkuyu, on the Mediterranean coast, despite research indicating a fault line off shore. With 96 percent of the country at risk from quakes, half of it under severe risk, one can only hope that the very worst will never happen. ❑

RIGHT: poorly constructed buildings simply crumpled under the strain.

QUEST FOR IDENTITY

*As Turkey modernises at a breathtaking rate, its self-identity is in crisis,
caught between Atatürk's liberalism, Islamic values and Internet culture*

Ne mutlu Türküm diyene! ("Happy is he who calls himself a Turk!"). Atatürk's famous quotation of 1927 is inscribed on walls and monuments throughout Turkey, but for all its patriotic sentiment, its exact meaning is increasingly difficult to define. What is "Turkishness" in a country which has been populated for 9,000 years by many races and religions, a country which regards its heritage as Asian, but hankers to belong to Europe?

The Republican rewrite

After the carve-up of the Ottoman Empire in 1919, the founders of the Republic preferred to deny the recent past and look further back in history for their national heroes while launching the new nation into the future via sweeping "Western" – style reforms. The Ottomans were reviled as sordid, and voluptuary, and so soon after the War of Independence, any identification with the Greeks was incomprehensible.

Greek-born Atatürk looked to the few thousand glamorous, nomadic Selçuk Turks who swept into Anatolia a scant 800 years ago, imposing their civilisation and language on a much larger indigenous population. At the same time, he saw the urgent need to create a forward-thinking Western-style society if the country were to survive. Seventy-five years on, the principals he laid down are still officially the guidelines of the Turkish Republic.

Unfortunately, the cult of personality which developed after the great leader's death and the force-feeding of his ideals through sloganeering led to an intellectual sloth that found it easier to repeat clichés than explore changing realities and ask difficult but essential questions.

Winds of change

Today, Turkey is in the midst of vast demographic change, due to population explosion

and rural migration. Some 3 million Turks now work and live in western Europe. Foreign tourists continue to swarm into Turkey. Films, television, music and the Internet have all played their part in breaking down barriers and, far from the "imposition of foreign culture" feared by conservatives, there has been an

explosion in creativity which has inspired a reassessment and appreciation of Anatolian culture among the young. Even ten years ago, few would admit to Kurdish, Laz, Circassian, Tatar or Greek roots; still fewer admitted membership of the various minority sects of Islam. Today, the single identification with Central Asia is losing credibility as the Turks redefine themselves in line with the diverse cultural mosaic that is their true heritage.

The pitfalls

This new confidence still masks a country of deep divisions, with a serious backlash against the rapid internationalisation which led, in the

PRECEDING PAGES: at Mihrimah Mosque; the "crying boy", ubiquitous symbol of Islam, with older believer.
LEFT: Islamic woman wearing a headscarf.
ABOVE: Atatürk teaching the new alphabet.

mid-1990s, to an urban upsurge in radical Islam. As the secular fight back gets underway, political parties calling for a return to Islamic law are banned under the constitution. Major reforms in the education system have raised the age limit for entry into religious schools, and there have been periodic purges of radical Islamisists within the Turkish military, whose commitment to the secular republic is unwavering. But the threat of a return to *Shari'a* remains a source of genuine concern to most Turks.

Where the religious parties are gaining most support is through the fundamental political and economic problems that still divide the country.

The class gap is frighteningly vast, especially in big cities, where rural migrants are visibly disdained by their middle-class, urban brethren. Financial and political corruption still goes largely unpunished; inflation has been running at nearly 100 percent; and the tax system, though under reform, remains punitive to the poor and easily avoided by the wealthy. State education is notoriously poor and, though universities are largely free, most young Turks need to study at a private lycée in order to pass competitive entrance exams.

Unfortunately, even the most well-meant attempts to lodge justifiable political criticism are met with a hurt defensiveness, a situation grossly inflated when the comment is made by a foreigner. Turkey's image abroad – and the country's own sense of how it is perceived by foreigners – remain central to the nation's self-esteem. Propaganda about the 19th-century "sick man of Europe" gave the Turks a palpable national inferiority complex and an appallingly poor, and poorly-informed image elsewhere. Debate around the country's promotional efforts in the west continues to dominate both mass media and public opinion, stemming from perpetual exasperation at being prejudicially represented in Western media.

The role of women

There is hardly any other topic where the psychological distance between "Islamic" and "Western" nations is more pronounced than in the status of women. Since the 19th century, European art, literature and popular culture have depicted Eastern women as docile, submissive creatures, clad in an all-enveloping black sheet when they are not dancing before their master in exotic, transparent silks. Thus modern visitors are often shocked when they find Turkish women sitting in a bar enjoying a cocktail after a hard day's work at a bank or an ad agency. Equally, many modern Turkish women are appalled when they visit their rural sisters, slaving in the kitchen after a day's labour in the family field while their husbands return to yet another game of cards or backgammon at the local teahouse.

Over a thousand years ago, the Turks adopted many of Islam's more conservative traditions, including the seclusion of women. The public area of the house was called the *selamlık*; the part reserved for women was the *harem* ("forbidden sanctuary"). It was the province of all women, including daughters and aunts, not a prison for sex slaves. The Muslim husband required the permission of the first wife before taking another woman, whom he would have to support in the same style as the first. Most men could simply not afford to practise polygamy, either financially or psychologically.

Social revolution

It took the major social upheavals of World War I and the subsequent War of Independence to change radically the status of Turkish women. Suddenly, many women found themselves working in munitions factories, while the wives and daughters of the élite classes became vocal supporters of Atatürk's fight for independence.

On 17 February 1926, the country adopted a new code of civil law which drastically altered the traditional family structure. Polygamy was abolished along with religious marriages, and divorce and child custody became the prerogative of both women and men. A minimum age for marriage was fixed and the legal status of women was greatly improved. Women gained rights of inheritance and equality of testimony (which previously regarded the testimony of one man as equal to that of two women).

Female suffrage was granted at local level in

male authority continues to pervade much of modern Turkish society. Realistically, the man is usually still legally regarded as the "head of the family" and his opinions hold more sway in the courts. New legislation is currently being framed to abolish these inequities, grant women an equal say in family matters and 50 percent of the family home in divorce settlements.

Meanwhile, alimony can be very difficult to claim, and inheritance rights are also a big issue due to the vast amount of unregistered income in the country. Better-educated and better-off women ensure their name is included on family property deeds, but uneducated rural women

1930, and nationwide in 1934. More recent changes to Turkish Civil Code have officially allowed married women to keep their maiden name, work without the permission of their husbands, and to be the legal head of the household – especially where the woman has her own property and a good lawyer.

Theory and practice

However, theory is one thing, and practice another. Even among the upper classes, the traditional Islamic ethic of female submission to

LEFT: the older generations have witnessed changes in their lifetime. **ABOVE:** women at prayer.

have little understanding of their legal rights and many remain trapped in abusive marriages. Divorce is still a scandal in religious communities and all too often their own families will not take back those who leave their husbands.

Meanwhile, although it is amongst the educated and urban working classes that the feminists have found most converts, paradoxically it is in the same community that many "new fundamentalist" women have emerged, from those severe enough to wear the "body bag" black *chador* to the more moderate (frequently middle-aged) "rain-coat brigade" in patterned scarves and loose overcoats, or fashion-conscious younger "new Islamic" women. ❏

WHERE GOD HAS 99 NAMES

Not only was Istanbul the birthplace of state-sponsored Christianity,
it was also for a time the headquarters of Islam

Constantine is credited with forming the first Christian capital of New Rome at Constantinople in AD 324. Yet he had inherited an already ancient city with many competing gods and religions of its own, set in a land which had been a crossroads of cultures and beliefs for more than 5,000 years. From the bull shrines and fertility figurines of neolithic Çatalhöyük, to the planet worshipping Sabians of Harran, Anatolia was fertile with faith, and Constantinople itself thought to have been colonised on the advice of a Greek Oracle.

Seraglio Point, where Topkapı Palace is today, was the site of an acropolis with temples to the entire Greek pantheon, and the church of Aya Irini, the oldest Christian site in the city, was probably built over a temple of Aphrodite. Certainly the ancient Persian religion of Mithraism, or Zoroastrianism, which worshipped a god of light, fire and air, was dominant in the 2nd century AD, is considered to have paved the way for Christianity and is still practised by certain Kurdish tribes. It was an early form of monotheism, sharing many Old Testament stories of adoring shepherds, the flood, and the ark. Mithras, the sun god, was born on 25 December, and its holy day is on Sunday. Wisely, Constantine did not try to ban the old beliefs, but instead absorbed their symbolism and practises into the new religion – he himself did not officially convert to Christianity until his deathbed, and it only became the state religion some 60 years later.

Jewish Istanbul

Judaism has also had a long history in Turkey. The Fertile Crescent between the Tigris and the Euphrates, known as Mesopotamia, may have been the "Garden of Eden", and in Genesis, Noah's Ark landed on Mount Ararat in eastern Turkey, his sons forming many of the tribes of Anatolia. Abraham, the earliest of the Hebrew

patriarchs, is believed by Muslims to have been born in a cave in today's Urfa and almost certainly lived in Harran in the 18th century BC. King Sargon is said to have resettled 27,000 Israelites in northern Mesopotamia in 720 BC, and Alexander the Great encouraged many Jewish merchants and traders from Palestine to

settle in newly conquered Greek lands. By the 2nd century AD there are thought to have been a million Jews in the cities of Asia Minor as a result of the destruction of Jerusalem and the temple, and, by the 6th century, they formed an important opposition group to disputational Christian factions in Constantinople and had a large settlement at Balat.

Even before the Conquest of Constantinople, the Ottomans were so hospitable to Jewish refugees that in the early 15th century a rabbi of Edirne entreated the Jewish communities in Europe to leave behind the torments they had endured under Christians "and seek safety and prosperity in Turkey" as part of their path back

---

LEFT: young Sufi boys at the Galata Mevlihanesi.
RIGHT: Byzantion was a pagan city for over nearly 1,000 years before the arrival of Constantine.

to the Holy Land. In the summer of 1492, 150,000 Sephardim escaped death or conversion under the Edict of Queen Isabella and King Ferdinand of Spain. They were officially welcomed into the Ottoman Empire and settled in Istanbul as well as other parts of the empire, receiving land, tax exemptions, encouragement and other assistance from the government.

These new citizens established the first printing press in Istanbul in 1493, and, as years went by, a number of

JEWISH REFUGE

"The Catholic monarch Ferdinand was wrongly considered wise," said Sultan Beyazıt, "since he impoverished his country with the expulsion of the Jews, and enriched ours."

The foundation of Islam

Islam as a religion suffered few of the internal contradictions that plagued early Christianity, and one of the main reasons for its powerful success was the *Declaration of Icma*, the agreement of Islam, based on the Prophet's statement, "My community will never disagree in an error," which meant that local practices were allowed to be considered Muslim even if not practised by others. This remains one of Islam's disconcerting strengths today. In the

famous Ottoman court physicians and diplomats were members of the Jewish community, which numbered 30,000 at the beginning of the 16th century, making it the largest and most important in Europe.

In the 1930s Atatürk invited many eminent Jewish professors to escape persecution in Germany and settle in Turkey, and during the war provided a safe passage for many to Palestine. Since the late 1940s, the Jewish community has dwindled considerably due to emigration to Israel, but Istanbul still has a large Jewish high school, 16 functioning synagogues, and a newspaper with about 4,000 subscribers in Turkish and Ladino.

words of H. G. Wells: "Islam prevailed because it was the best social and political order the times could offer. It prevailed because everywhere it found politically apathetic peoples, robbed, oppressed, bullied, uneducated and unorganised and it found selfish and unsound governments out of touch with any people at all. It was the broadest, freshest and cleanest political idea that had yet come into actual activity in the world and it offered better terms than any other to the mass of mankind."

ABOVE: Balat Synagogue, home to part of the city's small but still thriving Jewish community.
RIGHT: Byzantine icon of the Virgin.

In the 7th century, Arabia was occupied by disparate independent and aggressive tribes with varying pagan beliefs, all looking for new territories. Mohammed's revelations offered a simplified form of absolute monotheism which could unite them in a common purpose. Within ten years he was able to build a nation of Islam ready to take on the world. Although the verses which later comprised the *Qur'an* were not written down until after the prophet's death, they contained readily accessible maxims and stories as well as rules for government, law and domestic affairs. Where there was confusion or contradiction, the *Sunna*, a collection of anecdotes, traditions and sayings (*hadiths*) attributed to Mohammed or based on his deeds were added. The *Icma* took care of the rest.

Mohammed believed himself to be the messenger of God, sent to confirm revelations brought by previous prophets. According to the *Qur'an*, Jews had corrupted the scriptures and Christians worshipped Jesus instead of God alone. Islam had come to bring them to the correct path preached by the prophet Abraham. Islam means absolute submission to the will of God, as well as a direct route to the divine. In the words of Mohammed: "between Him and His creatures there are no intermediaries."

Conflict in Constantinople

During the 7th and 8th centuries, Christianity in Constantinople provided no better example of "bullied, uneducated and unorganised" in the iconoclastic controversy, which arose out of a period of economic recession. Leo III concluded God must be angry and, searching for an answer, blamed idolatry. In 726 he whipped up

sentiment for the immediate destruction of icons, which was fervently carried on by the next emperor, Constantine V, whose cruelty in the persecution of iconodules so divided Byzantine society that icon worship was restored in 787.

It was the Crusades that eventually put an end to hopes of a unified church as Rome found a convenient way to flex its muscles over the east and find a safety valve for restless European peasants and lordlings made insecure by continuous wars, raids, feudal destruction and overpopulation. By the 4th Crusade in 1204, the booty-grabbing rabble originally sent to

WAR OF WORDS: ECUMENICAL INTRIGUE IN BYZANTIUM

Byzantine Constantinople is famed for the schisms and intrigues which erupted into riots, street fighting and political factions as the new religion tried to standardise its beliefs. The First Ecumenical Council in 325 established that Christ was "truly God, one in essence with the Father" but, at the second meeting 60 years later, debate over the doctrine of the Trinity ran at such a high pitch Gregory of Nyssa complained every ragpicker and servant in the city was discussing it and the Patriarch of Constantinople denounced the lot as akin to the noise of wasps or magpies. The Fourth Ecumenical Council in 451 proclaimed the single nature of Christ as "truly god, truly man," which divided the Latin Catholic and Eastern Orthodox churches from the Oriental Orthodox of the Syrian and Armenian churches – the latter held to the Monophysite position of Christ's composite nature. This split, formed along class lines, was to lead to the famous Nika riot in 532 that destroyed half the city and left 30,000 dead. But the 6th council, in 680, held in Aya Sofya, had more worrisome things to discuss than matters of abstract theology. Islam was on the move, a power so rapid and forceful that only 50 years after Mohammed led the Hegira (Hijra, flight or migration of the prophet and followers to Medina) the Muslims were battering at the doors of the city.

help rout the Muslims ended with the Latin takeover of Constantinople and the death knell for eastern Christian power.

Living with Islam

After the Conquest in 1453, the remaining Christians of Constantinople were considerably better treated by the Muslims than they had been by Rome. Mohammed's dictats offered pagans the choice of conversion or death, but "People of the Book," who included Christians, Jews and Zoroastrians, should be allowed to

CENSORSHIP

While the press was revolutionising Europe by spreading the doctrine of Protestantism, Selim I organised a *fatwah* against anyone involved in printing – although foreign books could be imported.

maintain their place of worship as long as they did not add to their numbers, bear arms or go on horseback. They were also subject to a special tax called the *jizya* which exempted them from military service as they could not be expected to take part in wars on behalf of Islam.

The protected sects (*dhimmis*) were treated as semi-autonomous communities within the state, whose own religious leaders were responsible to the Caliph's government. In practice, however, most old churches were turned into mosques and new churches and synagogues were built, as long as they were no higher than Muslim buildings and their bells or services were inaudible to the Muslim public.

Islam played a crucial role in the Ottoman Empire, maintaining solidarity among its diverse Muslim elements and providing the ethical and legal structure for its subjects.

Following the 16th-century Turkish conquest of Egypt, the Ottoman sultans took the title of "Caliph" (leader of the entire Islamic world). Under them, Muslim scholars (the *ulema*) decreed on religious matters, taught religious sciences, operated mosques and schools and controlled the courts. Early Ottoman theologians were influenced by the teachings of Al-Ghazali, an 11th-century Persian scholar who rejected the idea that scientific knowledge violated Islamic doctrine. As a result, many Muslims achieved fame in the fields of science – notably astronomy, mathematics and medicine, and used mathematics and astronomy to fix the *Qibla*, the prayer niche of mosques, toward Mecca. However, as the empire declined, the Turkish *ulema* became open to widespread corruption and closed to change and progress. One reason was the resistance to printing.

Islam and calligraphy were intertwined, so machine printing was considered blasphemous – along with public clocks, as time-keeping was the preserve of the *muezzin* during the call to prayer. These bans isolated the empire from all intellectual and cultural development, including science and technology. In 1580, the Mufti incited a riot that destroyed an observatory in Galata built in 1577 for Murad III; it was nearly 300 years before another was built.

Christian communities today

Today, the many small and continually diminishing Christian communities of Istanbul attest to events of a thousand years ago. Though the official seat of the Eastern Orthodox Church has been in Istanbul since the 4th century AD, and His All Holiness Ecumenical Patriarch Bartholomew, spiritual leader of world Orthodoxy, continues to reside at Fener in Istanbul, it is in an all but symbolic capacity. Until the fall of the Ottoman Empire, between a quarter and a third of the population of Istanbul spoke Greek and professed Orthodox Christianity, and the Greek community ("*Rum*" – as in Roman – in Turkish) maintained freedom to run its own affairs. There had been political conflicts over the centuries, however, with attempts to stir up Greek risings leading to bloodshed on all sides. Seeking a solution, an exchange of populations following the Greek War of Independence compelled over a million Greeks to leave Turkey. About 500,000 Turks returned from Greece.

The Armenian and Syrian Orthodox Churches are also present in the city, though in diminishing numbers. The Armenians are perhaps the oldest Christian community in Turkey, converts since the 3rd century and allowed a great deal of autonomy by the Ottomans. In the 15th century, the Armenian Patriarchate was in the Church of Surp Kevork in Samatya, near

The Surianis, another group of early Christians whose main community is in eastern Tur Abdin, still speak a dialect of Aramaic, considered the language of Jesus. Some have settled in Istanbul and a new Syrian Orthodox church, St Mary's, was dedicated in Tarlabaşı in 1963, built of stones from Tur Abdin.

The Roman Catholics arrived with the Crusaders, Genoese, and other European expatriate communities – their Cathedral is St Esprit in Elmadağ, though there is a much older church, St Benedict, in Karaköy. Protestant communities, largely centred on the Anglican Christ Church and the Dutch Chapel in Beyoğlu, owe

Yedikule. Sadly, in the latter half of the 19th century, Armenian nationalist sentiment was inflamed by the Russians, who promised them an independent state if they joined the Russian side in World War I. Well over a million people were killed on all sides of the conflict, vast numbers of Armenians were exiled and today Turkey's Armenian population numbers only around 70,000. The Patriarchate is now in Kumkapı in the Surp Astvadzadzin (Holy Mother of God), built originally in 1645.

LEFT: all Qur'anic script is considered sacred; a man carefully repairs an ancient manuscript.
ABOVE: students at an Armenian school.

their history in Istanbul to missionary activity since the early 19th century. Sultan Abdülmecid recognised them as a legal entity (*millet*) during the Tanzimat reform period. Proselytising by missionaries, however, is against the law in modern Turkey, and these churches serve only their own communities or foreign refugees, of which Istanbul has an increasing number.

Mystic sects of Islam

Despite Mohammed's doctrine of Islamic unity, the early Ottoman Empire had nearly as many religious divisions as the Christians. Those acceptable were orders established by sultans, with lodges supported by *vakıfs*, and clearly defined rights and ceremonies. They usually settled in cities and drew their clergy from the upper ranks of society. Then there were the secret orders of wandering dervishes who shunned public display, organisation and symbolism, had no links with the state and usually operated through the guilds, among them the Kalendaris, Haydaris, Hurûfis, Abdals and Hamzavis; these latter known collectively as Malâmis, or "blameworthy". They tended to evolve amongst social classes opposed to the government, were often linked to Turcoman tribes and frequently persecuted. Most were Shi'ite, though this in itself did not constitute a radical movement until the 16th century. Over time, the Bektaşis, followers of a Muslim mystic, Haci Bektaş Veli (1209–71), absorbed a number of the Malâmis and achieved legitimacy through association with the Janissaries, the élite Ottoman army unit whose members were originally Christian converts. Turkey's famous comic philosopher Nasreddin Hoca was a Bektaşi, and one-fifth of the population of Istanbul was considered to belong to this sect at the beginning of the 19th century. Today they have a community in central Turkey, famous for its wine which they may have learned from Christian monks who settled nearby. They also employ practices of non-Muslim origin, including baptism, the celebration of the Zoroastrian festival of light, Nevroz, as Ali's birthday, and the recognition of Allah, Mohammed and Ali as a holy trinity. More wordly than Sufis, their primary ethic is truthfulness.

Ecstasy

Sufis also practise forms of worship which combine elements of pre- and early Christian practice, Buddhism, and neoplatonism and resist the legal regulations of Islamic orthodoxy, believing devotion to be a purely spiritual matter. Dancing, music and the use of fire have all been employed in the pursuit of a trance or ecstatic state – some tried howling, levitation, or eating red hot embers. In Ottoman times, the Sufi brotherhoods formed *tekkes* or lodges, which resembled early Christian monasteries. Each was led by a *sheikh*, or religious guide, and the novices (*murit*) were attached to a fully fledged dervish. The most significant community was the Mevlevis, who followed the 13th-

SHI'ITES, SUNNIS AND "REDHEADS"

The first four successors to Mohammed as "Caliph" or leader were (and are) accepted by all Muslims. After the death of the fourth, a revolution broke out against the succession and the caliphate went to the Omayyids, and then to the Abbasids in the 8th century, later to be taken by the Ottomans in 1517.

While most Muslims are Sunni, Turkey has a large Shi'ite community. These so-called Alevis have little in common with the Shi'ites in Iran, as Alevism was mainly a response to the Messianic revolution led by the Shi'ite Shah Ismael of Persia in the 16th century. Alevis were mostly Turcoman nomads who resisted the centralizing tendency of the Ottomans and wished to follow their own laws as well as some shamanist and dervish mystic traditions. The term "redhead" (kızılbağ), deriving from the headgear of these tribes, is used as a pejorative term for Alevis in Turkey today.

Distinctive Alevi traditions include a system of travelling holy elders (*dede*) and a relaxation of the Qur'anic ban on alcohol. Women do not wear veils and they pray along with men in *cemevis*, which have no minaret and are essentially meeting houses rather than mosques, leading the prejudiced to accuse them of orgies and incest. Their leftist political inclinations have also been at the root of continuing mistrust, mainly among Sunni fundamentalists.

century mystic poet and saint Mevlana (lord) Celâleddin Rumi. The sect had great appeal to Ottoman intellectuals. In the early days of the Republic it was banned as a secret order, but has now resurfaced, in some cases, as a "new age" response to modern Islam which attracts many young and foreign followers in Istanbul. During their religious ceremony, the dervishes twirl to the steady beat of drums and strains of mystical music, enacting the death and ultimate union of Mevlana with Allah (*see page 205*).

Nevroz

Kurds may be devout Sunni, Alevi, or Zaza, a form of Zoroastrianism. However, the Persian, Zoroastrian festival of fire and light has been practised by Kurds and many Central Asians for centuries. In recent times it has been taken over as a rally for political and cultural identity in the east leading to tensions and bloodshed. In order to defuse the political tensions surrounding Nevroz, it has now been declared a Turkish national holiday, celebrated by all.

Headscarves and high schools

The formation of the modern Turkish Republic and the sweeping reforms of Atatürk abolished the sultanate and caliphate and replaced Islamic Shari'a law with international civil, trade and criminal codes. Today, despite ongoing Islamic insurgence amongst a small minority, Turkey remains a steadfastly secular country, whose religious leaders are paid civil servants – a measure also instituted to curb their influence. Any political parties calling for a return to Islamic law are banned under the constitution.

However, most Turks consider themselves Muslims, if for no other reason than that it is written on their identity cards, and at least acknowledge the five duties or Pillars of Islam: – the statement of the creed ("There is no God but Allah and Mohammed is his Prophet"); prayer; the giving of alms to the poor; fasting during the holy month of Ramazan (for many in Istanbul, an excuse to go on a diet or give up alcohol for the month); and the not-so-obligatory pilgrimage to Mecca.

A contemporary artist may address the 99 attributes of God in abstract paintings as an old

man works his prayer beads waiting for the bus, a simple operation for the reinstatement of virginity in young women before marriage has become a common practice and more and more baby boys are being circumcised in hospital after birth rather than awaiting the dreaded *sünnetci*'s scalpel at the age of eight or nine. Most Istanbullites also celebrate New Year with the trappings of the Western Christmas, including a turkey, a tree, candles and gifts, leading the more devout to ban it in the mistaken belief that these trimmings are Christian rather than secular or even pagan. In this way Turkey has managed to combine Westward-looking capitalist

ideals with the practice of a moderate Islam that rarely contradicts Mohammed's *Icma*.

Even amongst those considering themselves "born again" Islamisists, girls wearing long, tight, pastel skirts slit up the side, a figure-hugging top, three-inch heels and a daintily fitted designer silk head scarf are not hypocritical, nor is the middle-aged rural matron in shalwar, floral cotton scarf and a loud T-shirt reading: "let's party!" To be contradictory is to be Turkish, and therein is its blessing, bearing little resemblence to Islam as practised in Iran or Saudi Arabia. A recent book of "Special Fatwahs" for Turkish family life has okayed looking at "indecent" photographs in news-

LEFT: at prayer in the Mihrimah Mosque, Üskudar.
RIGHT: most young women in Istanbul wear Western clothes, and many smoke, drink and party.

papers, magazines and films because "they are not real but imaginary, thus looking at them is not comparable to looking at the real body of a woman and therefore not a sin." But it is still a sin to see the privates of your partner, even in marriage.

The secular stamp

There are times when the restraints on religion – such as the continuing debate over the ban of headscarves in universities and government offices – can seem repressive to outsiders.

HIGHWAY WOMEN

The 16th-century Ottoman poet Baqi had the right spirit, writing: *"If ladies when they go abroad/ Are always veiled, appears it strange?/For highway robbers shroud the face/When forth in quest of prey they range…"*

government offices it is important that identities can be made. As to the eight-year mandatory education programme, which means children are not allowed to be sent to religious schools until secondary school age, unhappy former graduates of the Imam Hatip lycées have admitted they would have had more power of resistance over their parents' orders at the age of thirteen, as opposed to the age of eight. As to Islamic resurgence movements and the closure of the religious party

In 1999, a female deputy who refused to take off her scarf while being sworn in to parliament lost her seat. Likewise, recent changes to the educational system raising the age limit for entry into religious training schools, and the closure of Islamist political parties, may seem undemocratic. But a close look at Turkey's fundamentalist or totalitarian neighbours may help explain the risks to the secular constitution of liberalisation. As to veiling, there are practical reasons – in universities, well-covered sisters have been known to sit each others' exams, and most of the controversy has arisen when students demanded that their identity cards carry veiled photos. Likewise at polling stations and

which won an extremely slight parliamentary majority in 1996, Turkish voting patterns reflect a protest against corruption in the mainstream centre-right parties far more than a support for a return to Shari'a law.

Without any strong socialist alternatives (a legacy of the 1980 military coup), the religious parties have shown themselves to be unfailingly populist, the only ones who listen to the needs of the poor in a city which attracts up to 500,000 rural migrants a year and the first to organise aid for the earthquake victims of 1999. ❑

ABOVE: Islamic women wear the black *chador*, or simply a long coat and headscarf.

Cops and Robbers

For its size, Istanbul has one of the world's lowest crime rates. Most Turks are scrupulously honest when it comes to other peoples' property. Only in the bazaars is bargaining a battle of wills, but that isn't cheating – it's just business.

You may, in part, thank the chilling film *Midnight Express* for Turkey's lack of drug-related crimes, for, though drugs may be channelled through the country, penalties for possession or "association" (being with someone in possession) are stiff. Discounting garden variety Beyoğlu drunkenness, the only drug-related upset you are likely to encounter is ragged street children addicted to paint thinner. Huddled in doorways, dressed in filthy rags, most are hopelessly brain damaged and, though they beg and follow you, they are not dangerous. The Sokak Çocuğu (street children's) Foundation provides food, shelter and medical assistance – children frequently sell cards on the street in aid of this charity. Shoe shine boys are a different matter – clever little ragamuffins who are horribly persuasive in several different languages.

Petty crime is a particular menace in "Conference Valley" (near the Hilton) and other areas where business travellers are likely to sport fat wallets. The most common ruse is a feigned street fight which causes momentary chaos as someone bumps against you – leaving a strange lightness in the region of your billfold. Don't stop and stare if you see trouble, and keep your passport and valuables well concealed under your clothing.

Of all the irritations tourists listed in a recent survey, taxi drivers' swindles topped the list. Make sure the meter is on before you set off – the rates from 7am–midnight (*"gündüz"* on the meter) begin at less than US$1. After midnight the price goes up by a third, and reads *"gece"* – night rates. A standard trick is to put the night meter on during the day. Taxi drivers do honestly get lost, but some simply pretend they know where they are and drive you in circles for hours. Your best ammunition is to point out exactly where you want to go on a good Istanbul map. Make sure you understand Turkish currency before unravelling a wad of notes in front of the driver – if you ask him to make the selection himself, expect the worst. That being said, most Istanbul taxis offer great value.

RIGHT: Turkish police can be very helpful, as long as you haven't caused the trouble.

The police emergency number is 155, and there is a Tourist Police Station (tel: 212-527 4503 or 528 5369) in Sultanahmet, opposite the Yerebatan Cistern, which deals with everything from overcharging to bag snatches and sexual harassment. They show little sympathy however for those lured into the Beyoğlu dens of iniquity, and there are increasing reports of travellers accepting drinks from strangers and waking up 12 hours later relieved of all personal possessions. A majority of the perpetrators have not been Turkish, but it is catching on. If a stranger tries to interest you in a night on the town, just say no.

As ever, women face a variety of hassles. In

Turkey these are rarely dangerous, but can be infuriating. Most common is a quick "grope" on crowded streets or buses. It is a waste of time to get the law involved, but a firmly placed elbow or step back onto the villain's toe has a pleasing effect. Make sure you have an audience, or the assailant may attempt to hit back. More public harrassment is often carried out by teenage boys on a dare. Getting a hand up extremely short skirts, in particular, is considered a challenge, so keep micro-minis for the nightclubs, not the Covered Bazaar. If it happens anyway, don't hesitate to make a scene. Merchants in touristic areas will be only too happy to sort out the upstarts – it hurts their business too. ❑

THE GATE OF LIGHT

From the superb Byzantine mosaics to the flamboyant Art Nouveau architecture
in Pera, Istanbul has been a powerhouse of artistic achievement

The history of the arts in Istanbul is contentious. Though there were highly developed cultures in the neolithic and Hellenic cities of Anatolia, the location of Istanbul itself at the crossroads of Europe and Asia has meant a continuous clash of spiritual and social trends which often originated elsewhere but met head-on in the metropolis. In Byzantine Constantinople, a dispute on the human versus divine nature of Christ lasted nearly 500 years, and focused closely on the adulation of icons and spilled over into the Iconoclastic Wars over pictorial representation. For Ottoman Muslims, the late medieval invention of the printing press was seen as virtually satanic, an insult to the word of God which could only be written by calligraphers. Polemics remain heated in contemporary Istanbul, as people argue the merits of modern or traditional, Muslim or Christian, borrowed or indigenous, global and local style. It is, at all times stimulating, the curious legacy of a 2,000-year-old urban tradition.

Divine right of emperors

Early Christians were an ascetic and persecuted minority, and the little visual symbolism they employed was both crude and abstract so as not to attract perilous political identification. The Byzantines seem to have brought the taste for luxury, ritual, idolatry, sumptuous home décor and high-fashion clothing with them from the Graeco-Roman tradition. They wanted the new Christian capital, where they could now build permanent, non-secretive places of worship, to reflect a splendour and dominion that would impress the world. However, Constantine had inherited a city with numerous pagan religions still entrenched, and he found it expedient to incorporate many of those idols, symbols and artefacts into the new religion. In one forum statue, he fused his own image with that of the Sun God, Mithra/Jupiter/Helios/Apollo, just as

PRECEDING PAGES: folk dancers in their finery.
LEFT: art installation in the Yerebatan Sarayı.
RIGHT: concert in Aya Irini during the Istanbul Festival.

7th-century rulers were to mint coins with their portraits on one side, and Christ on the other.

In order to confirm their own leadership as divinely designated, early Byzantine emperors liked to bestow on new churches those relics and ceremonial goods most likely to leave the masses in awe.

Light was considered the first-created element, the conqueror of darkness, and thus gold, as well as all else that glittered, was considered heavenly. Free-standing pagan statuary gave way to mosaics far excelling the stone floor decorations of the Romans – these were of semi-precious stones or luminous glass cubes backed in gold, designed to look their best on the walls and ceilings of churches where large congregations gathered, often in shimmering candlelight. Along with church art, illustrated manuscripts, luscious silk brocades, metalwork, jewellery and carved ivory figures were manufactured in profusion. The emperors alone had the money to commission the best, and, with a strong currency and assurance of continuous demand, the palace workshops attracted the finest talent from around the world. Individual artists of the period – including architects – remain largely anonymous and were known to have lived modestly, considered little more than the civil servants of God.

Justinian

Under Justinian I, 6th-century Constantinople was considered the art capital of the world, but part of the reason for the flurry of activity was dire political need. Paganism had largely been eliminated and Roman laws codified with

Christian principles, but the originally religious Nika riots (*see page 151*) threatened to rupture the empire. The emperor saw church construction and celestial interiors as a method of gently imposing and demonstrating spiritual and social unity at a time of crisis. This is most notable in the spectacular redesign of Aya Sofya's vast dome, an architectural feat never again repeated and which Procopius pronounced to be as terrifying as it was beautiful, given the apparent weakness of the structure which made the dome seem suspended from heaven on a chain.

Justinian's grand plans did not outlive him, however, and were followed by a legacy of debt, high tax, inept government and invasions.

Additionally, the rising tide of Islam had begun swallowing up Christian territories in the Levant and North Africa, a threat which led to the brief 8th-century victory of the Iconoclasts. As long as relics and icons, like ventriloquists' puppets, were seen to work their miracle cures and interventions, in tandem with the political and campaign victories of the emperors, they were sanctioned and glorified. If, however, the emperors failed, as was the case in 602 when a military coup put the centurion tyrant Phocas on the throne, it was easiest, as well as cheaper for state coffers, to blame the worship of icons and take them out of production. Even the smallest church mosaics absorbed several million cubes of glass or semi-precious stone, putting a serious strain on an economy depleted by war. Thus, during the reign of Leo III and his fanatic son Constantine V, Byzantine art went into a decline that would last nearly a century. Later, the gradual influence of the Islamic east, notably the Baghdad Caliphate, were to send Byzantine aesthetics off in a different direction which reached its peak in the 9th century, though mass production once again took its toll on the state treasury.

As to other Byzantine art forms, there is little record, although court banquets were opened with a complex ritual "dance" (stylised procession) of military officials and different divisions of the active political parties (namely the Blues and the Greens), recognisable by their coloured garments and other symbols. The people, then as now, preferred the vaudeville acts and chariot races of the Hippodrome. By the end of the 11th century, the fire had gone out.

Islamic purity

Muslims had no such internal debates over imagery – it was strictly forbidden, though individual sultans may have indulged a passion for certain western art fashions. Mehmet the Conqueror is known to have enjoyed Italian painting and sculpture, especially works by Bellini, who was specially commissioned to paint erotic frescoes in the sultan's private rooms. Mehmet was also the first to have his portrait painted. His liberal outlook was not shared by his dour heir Beyazıt II who later sold or destroyed most of these works.

Figurative painting was still largely forbidden in the 17th and 18th centuries, and thus most extant images of Ottoman court or daily life were made by European "embassy painters" and went to collections abroad. Until recent times there were no serious art collections in Istanbul and a native pictorial tradition did not begin to develop until the 19th century.

Contact with Persians inspired a royal taste for miniatures, and the tile factories at İznik produced works now considered the pinnacle of ceramic manufacture, although the sultans considered them inferior to Chinese imports.

The single art form perfected and revered by the Ottomans was calligraphy, primarily made up of Qur'anic inscription. Its greatest master was considered to be Hamdullah al-Amasi

with little taste for reading, a government too easily threatened by the written word and a bureaucracy obsessed with official stamps.

Mute eloquence

Along with the perceived holiness of calligraphy and the fear of machine printing, the Turkish élite did linguistic somersaults to try and incorporate fashionable Persian and Arabic words within a fundamentally Asian (Altaic) grammatical framework. The impenetrability of the resulting Ottoman language was, until the foundation of the Republic, the primary obstacle to mass literacy and contact with the

(1429–1520), who had a workshop in the palace and instructed the sultans. The "Şeyh Hamdullah" style was to set the standard for 300 years, and Ottoman antique collectors today still value any piece with a *tughra*, the elaborate official seal of the sultan. However, as the Qur'an was considered the literal word of God, to reproduce it mechanically was blasphemous, a belief which retarded the evolution of Turkish literature and science for hundreds of years and can still be felt today in a populace

LEFT: Byzantine icon of the Apostles.
ABOVE: depiction of life in the Topkapı in 1727, by European artist Jean Baptiste Vanmour.

rest of the world. Written in Arabic script, less than half its functioning vocabulary was actually Turkish, and for this reason early Turkic literature, including the campaign records and cosmology of the 8th-century *Orkhon Inscriptions*, the *Manichean* fragments of the Uygur Steppe Empire and the 10th-century epic, *Dede Korkut*, suffered from problems of translation.

After the 1920s, when the Latin alphabet was introduced, Ottoman literature was to suffer the same fate, and today only a handful of scholars can read it. Despite nationalistic attempts to purge foreign words from the vocabulary of the early Republic, "*Yeni Turkçe*" (new Turkish) remains highly susceptible to foreign influence, easy to spot today in amusing phonetic spellings such as *"tabldot"*, *"egzos"* (exhaust) and *"otantik"* which multiply daily.

Divan, or Ottoman court literature, was also given a kick-start by the Conqueror who was the first to have his works "published", but they are not considered to have much literary merit. For the most part Divan poetry is cloyingly romantic as well as starkly antithetical to the political reputation of the writers.

Wandering minstrels

It was the mystic folk poets who "tore the veil" of classical language, talking of love, longing

and union in a way that is often passionate and erotic. Anatolia was the birthplace of many mystic trends, Christian, Muslim and otherwise. Reflecting the lonely sojourner traversing the wide uninhabited spaces under dizzying night skies, the itinerant troubadours paid their way through villages with recitations accessible to the simplest people and their works remain amongst the finest contributions to Turkish literature today. Celâleddin Rumi's 13th-century mystical Sufi poetry was in the more orthodox Persian, and hence Yunus Emre's work, written only slightly later, is easier to assimilate.

"Don't boast of reading, mastering science," he wrote, "or of all your prayers and obeisance.

If you don't identify Man as God, all your learning is of no use at all." The tradition of travelling troubadours (*aşıks*) still exists in Anatolia, though like most folk arts it has suffered greatly since the advent of television and the Internet. Additionally it has long been associated with anti-authoritarian minorities and sects – the 16th–century Alevi/Sufi poet Pir Sultan Abdal was hanged for "provocation" which was to become something of a tradition in Turkey.

Troubadours often accompany themselves on the lute-like instrument, the *saz*. Aşık Veysel, who died in 1973, was considered the last of the "true" minstrels, and at least lived long enough to be recorded. "The soul does not stay in a cage," he sings, "it flies away. The world is a caravansarai where one settles then moves off, the moon goes round, years pass – let friends remember me."

Many Turkish contemporary folk groups have set Turkish mystic poetry to new music and arrangements, and today *saz* musicians hold frequent impromptu "jam" sessions in the the low-budget "eastern" pubs and cafés of Beyoğlu – which are often not at street level but one or two floors up.

In 20th-century Turkish poetry, however, no artist is more beloved than Nazım Hikmet, who died as a communist exile in 1963, caught between continuous imprisonment and suppression in his native country and the faltering idealism and puerile art of the post-Stalin Soviet Union. Written in this political neverland his best works take the tragic, longing tone similar to the mystic poets: "…Some people know all the kinds of grasses, others the fishes/But I the separations/Some people know by heart the names of stars/But I the longings…"

The classical and religious music of the Ottoman courts and dervish orders is plaintive indeed, based on a modal system which predates the Conquest. A product of both Persian and Byzantine influences, it is rigidly formal and heartbreakingly sad. Instruments include small drums and cymbals, various low sounding wind and reed instruments, the zither-like *kanun*, lute-like *oud* and three-stringed violin.

Both types of music were disdained as reactionary in the early years of the Republic, and dervish music was actually banned from the airwaves until the mid-1970s. Fortunately, however, there was much notated source material stretching back to the 15th century. In the 1990s it staged a magnificent comeback and is now being used by experimental groups and widely disseminated abroad.

The *ney* virtuoso Süleyman Ergüner gives concerts worldwide and has been included in many traditional and experimental recordings, notably by American "spontaneous conduction" master Butch Morris who is often in Istanbul.

Art nouveau versus orientalism

A great frenzy of "orientalist" debates began during the 19th-century Tanzimat reform era when the sultans, over-eager to please would-be politically correct objecting to depictions of eastern sensuality as passive, female and indolent in need of domination by the masculine, imperialist, industrialist West, the taste for harem and hamam paintings has endured nearly 300 years. As a much-mimicked chocolate box theme, however, good examples are also hard to come by and terribly sought after, nowhere more than in Turkey itself.

It was over issues of architecture, however, that the headiest debates were to emerge, especially amongst the foreign or foreign-trained architects brought to Istanbul to usher in the new era of construction.

investors in the failing Ottoman economy, handed over great segments of the industrial sector to foreigners. As European art forms flourished in Istanbul, the mysterious world of the Grand Seraglio suddenly swung open to the west, filling the Victorian imagination with a riot of langourous slave girls enveloped in the steam of the bath house. The term "odalisque" derives from the Ottoman word "*oda*", or room, suggesting females lying around waiting for the action, and, despite a century of attack by the

Some believed imported art nouveau styles were "conceived on behalf of Europeans representing the interests of capitalist powers" (as well as the Levantine bourgeoisie and Ottoman élite) and threatened the aesthetic integrity of Turkey. On the other hand, the paşas desperately wanted the country to look modern and native property developers, particularly in Pera, who saw a superb chance to cheat architects by stealing ideas for grand exteriors then using them to disguise otherwise shoddy apartment blocks for which they could extract ridiculous rents from Europeans. Something of this tradition remains in Istanbul today (notably in Cihangir and along the Bosphorus) where

LEFT: Turkish musical instruments in a Galata store.
ABOVE: dervishes whirl in an ecstatic trance in the Yıldız Palace ballroom.

multinational companies fork out extortionate prices for "sea view" properties to house their executives, distorting real market values at the expense of natives. The orientalist argument, however, was quelled by the early 20th century, neo-nationalist sentiment of the Young Turk movement. Here the "Turk Nouveau" style was born, a typically syncretic solution to an ideological rather than practical problem.

Shall we dance?

Many forms of western culture had already taken root in Pera by the turn of the last century, and Atatürk was keen to foster these traditions

is seen by some dance scholars as a "feminist issue" which helped liberate Turkish women from the veil.

During the Russian Revolution in 1917 many ballet dancers fled to Turkey, taking on students and training them for amateur performances, and in the 1930s Lydia Krassa Arzumanova, also a Russian immigrant, established her own ballet school, staging performances throughout the city. The initial performance took place at the Casa d'Italia in 1931.

In keeping with Atatürk's visions for the new Republic, in 1947 Dame Ninette de Valois, a ballerina of Irish extraction and founder of the

in the early days of the Republic. Italians had been watching ballet in Beyoğlu as early as the 16th century, when *St George and the Dragon* was performed in Turkish in front of Sultan Murat III by an army of Christian slaves. The first public theatre, also Italian-run, opened in Galata in the 18th century, staged opera, tragedy and comedy in various languages, and often included ballet sequences.

Giuseppe Donizetti, brother of the renowned opera composer, arrived in Istanbul in 1828 to head the military band and inspired a love of western classical music in the palace. He also brought ballet teachers from Italy to instruct women of the harem. His introduction of ballet

Sadlers Wells Ballet School (now the Royal Ballet), was invited to Turkey to introduce a European standard and help to found the first state ballet school, which later became the Ankara State Conservatory. The Istanbul State Company was established in 1971 and there is a thriving modern and experimental dance movement in the city today.

Opera

Opera was also very popular in 19th-century Istanbul. Quite a few theatres staged operettas, visiting companies from Italy performed almost all of Verdi's operas and some were presented in the palace grounds before the sultan. The

City Opera of Istanbul, established in 1960, is now resident in the Atatürk Cultural Centre (AKM) in Taksim Square as the Istanbul State Opera and Ballet Company (IDOB). But while other events are buoyed by private sponsorship, the state company wings it on a miniscule government budget. Ticket prices remain sufficiently low as to be accessible to all walks of society. Hence, though not as flamboyant as that of a well-funded European company, the 1992 staging of Wagner's *Flying Dutchman* translated into Turkish and Strauss' *Salome*, in German, with a topless soprano, were considered extremely brave by Istanbul standards.

sexes before a play. It was rhythmic and melodic, and, without concern for "purity of origins", embraced a wide spectrum of popular urban music, but particularly that of Istanbul's minorities. *Rembetiko* music came back into fashion in the 1990s after the un-banning of an eponymous Greek film and the re-release of Istanbul recordings made between the 1920s and 1950s. Sadly, however, there are no "folk" performers left – the closest you can get are the musicians who play in Beyoğlu's back alleys, such as Nevizade Sokak, or the Byzantine and Ottoman folk revivalists now popular on the city's stages.

The IDOB currently puts on 175 performances each season in a country where state expenditure on the arts amounts to about 1/3000th of its budget and even that has suffered in the wake of the 1999 earthquake.

New movements

Towards the end of the 19th century a new song form emerged in the city in tandem with the growing popularity of the theatre and was performed by non-Muslim musicians of both

LEFT: dance performance during the Istanbul Festival.
ABOVE: still from the BBC film version of Mozart's *Abduction from the Seraglio*, filmed in the Topkapı.

The speed of light

Contemporary culture is moving at the rate of rockets in the metropolis, in no small part due to the city's exploding youth population who are seeking something uniquely their own. As a result Istanbul today is effervescent with experimental artists and projects rapidly trying to join the threads of two millennia to a future that is thoroughly unique, neither eastern or western but urban, vibrant and thoroughly Istanbul.

The rate of cultural change in the city over the last decade alone can seem terrifying for those caught in the middle and is perhaps difficult to comprehend in the "developed" world where artistic trends have had 500 years to stew. But the increasingly technophiliac, multilingual, impatient and well-informed young will now try everything – from promiscuity and drug abuse to music, dance, and dramatic and film statements which rival New York. And, like any urban centre in the throes of massive change, it is in the cultural sector that questions are both formulated and answered. Unfortunately, the outside world has been the last to catch on, still labouring under the illusion of Turkey as a torpid Islamic camel-culture and ignoring the cutting-edge contemporary art forms emerging daily.

Turkish visual arts have faced the greatest

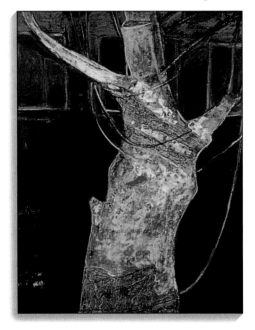

difficulty. Most people will tell you there was no contemporary arts movement in Turkey until the mid 1970s or even later. Technically it's not true – there have been Paris-trained "society" artists in Istanbul since the 19th century, sent by the sultans to imitate what was going on in Europe, and who got – just barely – as far as lukewarm cubism. But even classical abstract painting, a western staple since the middle of the last millennium, does not sell well in the city, and consequently there were few large canvas paintings made before the 1980s. Art merchants claim the Istanbul buyers' taste in home décor and art alike is extremely conservative, and one London-based dealer could not

even encourage the city's richest collectors to purchase original orientalist Picasso and Matisse prints as the tradition of lithography, etching and silk screen was fundamentally unfamiliar to them.

For artists, the core of the problem is the Turkish university system which has always channelled its resources into technical faculties which have a mandatory foreign language programme for those who did not have the benefit of a private lycée. Arts faculties are seen as less important, do not have such programmes and consequently a majority of the city's visual artists do not speak a second language. In turn, this means they cannot apply for international grants or scholarships, organise exhibitions abroad or seek foreign lectureships. Teaching at state schools and universities pays abysmally and artists often feel at the mercy of a handful of dealers, galleries and private collectors who nonetheless remain the only ones who can assist them to show work outside the country. There is some excellent contemporary work to be found, and at a fraction of London and New York prices, but foreigners rarely see it.

Corporate patrons

Curiously, most of the braver Istanbul galleries are corporate, such as the Borusan Cultural Centre on İstiklal which regularly shows seminal work from major international movements of the last century in order to bridge the "missing years" of arts development in Turkey.

Photography, too, long dominated by the "quaint" or disappearing aspects of the city, has been recently wrested into the conceptual sphere by developments in digital processing, and the Pamukbank Gallery of Photography in Nişantaşı has also helped bridge gaps in the evolution of a native style by alternating the works of well known 20th-century foreign photographers with Turkish shows.

Generally considered to be operating on the "image" principle, corporate galleries do not need to worry about sales and often accompany their exhibitions with excellent seminars, publications, videos and performances.

The Istanbul Biennial, organised by the IKSV (*see page 89*), is considered one of the world's top four arts festivals, and the influx of international artists and critics every two years has had the power to overturn many preconceived ideas about the city and is always eagerly awaited.

Speaking out

Private sponsorship has been an enormous advantage in a city which could not otherwise find the funds to present international quality events at prices ordinary people could afford. Yet in keeping with Byzantine and Ottoman paranoia over images and the written word, arts criticism remains weak. The media fears losing advertising revenue or *torpil* (pull) from the country's richest industrialists, so coverage is timid, often beginning and ending with the press release. As a consequence the much needed frisson of cultural debate is reduced to a thimbleful of curators, usually foreign or foreign educated, who alone dare remark on the direction of the arts in Turkey and frequently suffer for it.

In shades of the art nouveau arguments, some believe the wholesale adoption and imitation of art trends from the industrialised west has meant native artists have never had a chance to find their own voice, while others rest assured that cultural development in the metropolis has indeed travelled at the speed of light and can easily take its place in the international arena. In a nutshell, the arts in Istanbul today remain as much of a red hot potato as they were over a millennium ago, ever the scene of political clashes and original compromises.

Sounds magic

It is easier for new music to bypass hoary debates. Though jazz has a long history in the city, dating from the founding of the Atlantic record label in the US by the Ertegün brothers, until recently it has been the preserve of the internationally travelled upper classes. Now, however, from the techno remix of creaking Arabesque star İbrahim Tatlıses to the Balkan Romany musicians joining the Brooklyn Funk Essentials, a fluency of musical experiment soars over the city like a chorus of multicultural angels.

Venues such as Babylon, and events like the Istanbul Jazz Festival and provocative annual *Müzik Şenliği* (Music Festivity) ensure that

> ### CUTBACKS
>
> In addition to the ongoing juggling of event schedules due to shifting Muslim holy days, arts funding in Istanbul is subject to sudden cuts – particularly acute in 2000, in the wake of the earthquake. Visitors may find that some arts events are slimmed down as a result.

Turkish and foreign artists have a chance to hear each others' work and form new syntheses specifically intended to fight back at global pop with something new. It is a phenomenon less than a decade old in Istanbul where domestic labels are only just now being launched for international distribution. The best amongst them is Doublemoon, whose exceptional live studio recordings blend American jazz and blues styles with Turkish Romany groups.

The cutting edge

Despite active backing from Atatürk, film in Turkey has long lagged behind the west, partly because of finance, partly due to a bitter legacy of censorship in the 1970s when film makers such as Yılmaz Güney, whose best known movie, *Yol* (The Road) won a shared Cannes Palme d'Or in 1982, found their works banned and faced jail or exile. Güney spent most of his artistic life writing and directing his films from behind bars before being sentenced to another 18 years on a trumped-up murder charge and escaping to France, where he died in 1984.

Recently, many have opted to solve their problems through joint ventures with European

LEFT: *Milli Reassurans* by a modern Turkish artist, Coülgin Barsırır.
RIGHT: jazz musician Ilhan Erşahin.

companies, though this usually means anodyne content designed to appeal to foreign audiences, such as Ferzan Özpetek's Turkish-Italian *Hamam* (The Turkish Bath) which edited out any modern buildings in the metropolis to provide a romantic backdrop for some gay hanky-panky. Grittier contemporary films about marginal or dispossessed rural people have little hope of international appeal. At the time of writing, the only uncensored foreign films coming into Turkey are those in the Istanbul Film Festival, every spring. Their box office sales, rising nearly 50 percent a year, are bursting the seams of the city's cinemas.

Slippers and television

What do ordinary people do for entertainment? Most do not read anything more taxing than sports results in the newspaper, do not go to concerts or ballet, listen to CDs, seek out the cinema or frequent galleries. The truth is that most Turks are dedicated couch potatoes and the average home has the television on non-stop every night until 1 or 2am. Despite an influx of private and satellite channels, most is either family fare with a lot of singing, news, or melodramatic "Arabesque" films where Romeo goes off to work in Germany for 20 years and comes back rich enough to pay for a life-saving

CHANGING THE FACE OF THE WORLD

"A day will come when the invention of the cinema will be seen to have changed the face of the world more than the invention of gunpowder, electricity or the discovery of new continents. The cinema will make it possible for people living in the most remote corners of the earth to get to know and love one another.

"The cinema will remove difference of thought and outlook, and will be of the greatest assistance in realising the ideals of humanity. It is essential that we treat the cinema with the importance it deserves."

Kemal Atatürk, a believer in all things Western and progressive, was keen to promote a Turkish film industry.

operation and rescue Juliet from an evil stepfather, the mafia, or a forced marriage.

However one genre that deserves mention is comedy, such as the low budget films made by actors Şener Şen, Müjde Ar and Kemal Sunal which alone, like the satirical Karagöz puppets of yore (*see page 237*) help to defuse political and social tensions with satirical sketches widely enjoyed throughout the class strata. Likewise the popularity of "adult" comic magazines such as *Leman* show that humour can still venture where writers fear to tread. ❏

ABOVE: musicians take a break between performances.

The Istanbul Foundation

Over the past decade, the Istanbul Foundation for Arts and Culture (IKSV in Turkish) has been pulling off feats of festival organisation equal to any in Europe, yet it receives only 12 percent of its funding – if that – from central government and private sponsorship now accounts for 70 percent of the festival budget. Founded in 1973 by one of Turkey's most prestigious business families, Eczacıbaşi, it is currently under the flamboyant General Directorship of Melih Fereli, who was on the board of the UK's Philharmonia Chorus before returning to Turkey, receiving an OBE for his contribution to British-Turkish cultural relations.

The ambitious programme includes major annual international film, theatre, classical music and jazz festivals, and the huge Istanbul Biennial (2001, 2003). All of them are attracting unprecedented foreign interest, due to fabulous venues and affordable prices. These festivals are also uniquely free from any state interference or censorship because the Turkish government has long recognised what the Foundation has been achieving for the country's image abroad, light years ahead of expensive promotional campaigns issued from Ankara.

This freedom also gives the Foundation access to the city's most exquisite historic spaces, such as opera and biennial exhibitions in the Byzantine church, Aya Irini, and the Yerebatan Sarayı. There are also plans to present chamber music concerts in Beylerbeyi Palace.

For years, Mozart's opera, *Abduction from the Seraglio*, has been staged live under difficult conditions in the Topkapı and Yıldız Palace. It has now been committed to film in a joint project between BBC Television and Antelope Productions. Set in the actual harem of Topkapı, it also contains documentary sequences illustrating the staging and filming process.

One of the Foundation's greatest problems, however, has been the inadequate size of Istanbul's arts venues. Partly due to the heaving population of under-25s as well as to rapid expansion of the festivals, which broke all attendance records in 1999, state auditoria such as the open air Açik Hava Theatre and the small private clubs used for

the Jazz Festival cannot cope with the crowds. During the International Film Festival it was virtually impossible to walk down İstiklal Caddesi without stumbling over world-renowned directors and fans alike, while cinemas are stuffed day and night. Events are frequently sold out within days of reaching the ticket outlets, leaving many disappointed, and in 1999 the Jazz Festival alone sold nearly a quarter of its tickets via the web, much higher than the world average of 18 percent. The Foundation's new Cultural and Congress Centre in Ayazağa, a US$92 million project on the former hunting grounds of the sultans, was scheduled to open by 2001, with a main auditorium seating 2,500, an

open air theatre, a chamber music hall, two cinemas, a 1,000-seat multipurpose hall, vast outdoor exhibition and event space, a library, rehearsal hall, dance studio and three restored Ottoman buildings. Not only will the new centre greatly relieve Istanbul's existing venues, which are strained to the limit, but offer state-of-the-art acoustics and proper staging facilities for all cultural disciplines. However, the complex is state-funded and has been severely hit by the funding crisis following the August 1999 earthquake, which may delay opening for another year.

Visitors interested in attending the festivals are advised to contact the Foundation's website at http://www.istfest.org for updates. ❑

RIGHT: the main auditorium of Istanbul's new cultural centre – if it ever gets finished.

1,001 NIGHTS

*As the sun goes down, the streets come alive with throngs of people,
some in search of a good time, some determined to provide one*

The first thing you notice, on a hot summer evening in Istanbul, is the crowds. At sunset, a glowing chain of bottlenecked traffic stretches up the Bosphorus from Beşiktaş to Rumelihisarı as the well-heeled head for the better outdoor fish restaurants and nightclubs. Twinkling ferries from the posh outlying suburbs of Erenköy and Suadiye bring hundreds of pierced, tattooed, long-haired or shaven-headed youth into the bowels of the city for heavy metal nights, sailing past the shipyards of Haydarpaşa and the beacon of Kız Kulesi towards the fairy-lit showpiece of Galata Tower which marks the entrance to old Pera.

The streets, too, are jammed – pedestrianised İstiklal Caddesi is packed with bright young things heading for the cinemas, *meyhanes*, and bars that pulse around Taksim Square. The renovated waterfront village houses at Ortaköy are stuffed to capacity with a café society spilling out into the streets, while even the previous garden suburb of Moda has a crammed and classy "bar street" in the old houses of Kadife Sokak

Turkey is foremost a Mediterranean culture, and to "*gezmek*" (stroll around) is as much part of a night out as reaching your destination. Even in the religious neighbourhoods such as Üsküdar and Fatih, veiled women and their extended families trip the light fantastic in swarming teahouses which offer ice cream and live music, usually a *şantör* with a mini synthesiser singing classical Turkish love songs.

The Old City

Nightlife in the Old City, where most visitors stay, is altogether quieter, since there are so many mosques and alcohol consumption is forbidden near them. With the exception of a few bars around Akbıyık Sokak geared towards Antipodean backpackers, and a few upmarket restaurants overlooking the Blue Mosque, the evening in Sultanahmet is a place to relax in an

historic tea garden with old *nargile* smokers. The bright lights most in evidence are those pointing to heaven on the minarets and the nightly Blue Mosque's *son et lumière* show.

"Early to bed" is not a Turkish custom. Into the wee hours most homes have the television on, and teenagers crowd the Internet chatlines

when their parents think they are asleep. From the skyscrapers of Sabanci Plaza in Levent to the famed skyline of domes and minarets in old Stamboul, the city never sleeps, for just as the dawn call to prayer reminds the faithful that holiness is better than a lie-in, the nightclubs are spilling out their bleary-eyed patrons for the long dolmuş ride home and the labourers, hawkers and breakfast-carts have begun to bustle in the streets. Istanbullites have a curious tolerance for noise at all hours, and insomniacs may find earplugs useful.

You also cannot miss the impact of a population largely under 25. In recent years, the raunchy clip joints for which Beyoğlu was so

---

PRECEDING PAGES: Kuzguncuk nightclub.
LEFT: belly-dancing in Beyoğlu.
RIGHT: the dramatically floodlit Süleymaniye Mosque.

justifiably famous have been pushed back away from İstiklal Caddesi as more and more space is taken over by cybercafés, rock bars, bistros and CD shops. An authentic Turkish contemporary identity in music and style has been launched and is all the rage. These are heady times for the cultural self-esteem of young Istanbullites who no longer have to rely on imports and imitation. It also means, however, that the mature visitor looking for such simple traditional entertainment as belly dancing or Turkish folk music can be frustrated, left with the choice of a strictly-for-tourists floor show or a risky venture into Istanbul's demi-monde.

Still, there is something for everyone, and in the city today you will be spoilt for choice regarding evening entertainment. Try Kumkapı, the former Byzantine fisherman's wharf at the back of the Old City, or the streets leading off Galatasaray's Balık Pazar for an outdoor meal of fish and raki surrounded by raucous gypsy musicians, peddlers and Istanbul's colourful marginal communities. There are many more traditional *meyhanes* and sedate, upmarket restaurants in the Beyoğlu area. Brave the coast road traffic along the Bosphorus for the more stylish restaurants and clubs of Kuruçesme, Arnavutköy and Bebek, or content yourself with a little luxury in the knowledge that some of Istanbul's best meals and nightspots can be found in the city's five-star hotels.

Sin City

Upbeat Beyoğlu is still home to some of the most luridly attractive nightlife anywhere – the shamble of dank streets off İstiklal Caddesi and Taksim Square understandably sparks fascination as a quarter historically devoted to "sin" in an otherwise Muslim city. This area was always the foreign quarter of Istanbul, and by the 17th century had become notorious for its taverns and general naughtiness.

Not that the Ottomans themselves were always averse to the pleasures of wine or opium, though they may have forbidden their use amongst their subjects. Even today the ban on alcohol is the Muslim prohibition least observed in Istanbul, with the Ramazan fast frequently used as an excuse to dry out.

Modern Beyoğlu can be a confusing mix of the decidedly upmarket and the strictly no-go, with a lot of in-betweens. There are the low student dives offering a 50p pint of lager and blasting rock music, intel bistros and jazz cafés with sometimes indefensibly high (and well-concealed) cover charges. Gay nightlife is no longer marginalised and is easily found on its own or with the more bohemian elements in bars such as Bilsak 5 and the techno clubs. There are numerous traditional Kurdish cafés where *saz* players offer a song as the mood takes them, and an exceptionally popular (and cheap) Greek wine bar at the back of the Balık Pazar. The famous Pera Palas Hotel bar is loaded with atmosphere while a much cheaper historical option in the Büyük Londres Hotel is a great place to meet locals for a mercifully

HEED THE WARNINGS!

Neither foreign consulates nor the Tourism Police can rescue those foolish enough to fall into the clutches of touts cruising İstiklal Caddesi and Sultanahmet whose job it is to lure male tourists into clubs where they will almost certainly be relieved of their entire holiday budget, with little in the way of legal recourse. These clubs are stocked with whisky dollies ("*konsomatris*" in Turkish) who inevitably land the unlucky punter with a mind-boggling drinks bill. Istanbul tour operators say they are continually shocked by the number of otherwise level-headed visitors who walk into this trap, even after repeated warnings from tour operators and guidebooks.

quiet chat. There is an exceptionally fine city view from rooftop bar of the Etap Marmara.

Techno, rave and jazz

Dance clubs with live music (many off Sıraselviler Caddesi, Taksim) are quite trendy, often alarmingly overcrowded, without visible fire exits, and tend to be populated by intoxicated students given to beer-stealing and the occasional fight. Expect no sympathy from management if you lose your wallet, gold chain or mobile phone here. These clubs are also frequently raided for drugs and under age drinking and it is essential to have your passport on you

One club in Asmalımescit models itself on New York's Knitting Factory, with live world and cutting-edge jazz containing significant Turkish input. Watch posters for concerts, weekend-long techno festivals, Fuji World Music Days or any of the international festivals that are held in summer. For these, at least, private sponsorship can mean very low ticket prices. But there is no escaping overcrowded venues – claustrophobics be warned.

Blondes and belly dancers

Then there are the "*gazinos*" and "*pavyons*". These are a different matter, catering mainly to

for identification or you could land in trouble.

The more highbrow nightclubs are of the rave and techno variety with international DJs and camp theme nights. Expect a hefty door charge for joining the city's most fashionable youth and local celebs on the tiles until 6am. Foreigners complain aboutt the high cover charges, but rarely is anyone turned away for failing to conform to dress codes.

There are several bars which specialise in African music and these are always packed.

LEFT: ultra-modern dance clubs feed Turkish techno to the young, élite and rich.
ABOVE: evening promenade in Ortaköy.

lonely men who will pay a fortune to hold hands with a bellydancer under the spinning lights of a mirror ball and get little in return but some footsie under the table. Likewise, most strip clubs and revue shows are stocked with tall blonde Russian girls to suit Turkish male tastes and pockets.

So where does one go for an "authentic" oriental evening? If your visit is brief, resign yourself to paying US$50+ a head for a night out in a respectable venue in Istanbul where at least the costs are clearly marked and often include food and drink. It is cheapest (and safest) to book with a group through a reliable tour operator. Belly dancing will be included as part of a complete programme. The obligation to spend more by stuffing paper money down the flimsy costume of a dancer is frowned upon in the better houses, but being dragged out on the floor by the bellydancer herself is standard practice, and will be the source of embarrassment for many years to come as your friends or freelance photographers take snapshots of your bare middle-aged midriff and rakı-inflamed face.

Sulukule, along the Old City walls near Kariye Camii and Edirne Gate, provides one authentic alternative, best approached with caution. This is the gypsy quarter, where women dance in their living rooms under the supervision of relatives before any group of strangers willing to pay. While the band of musicians beat and bang on fife and drum, the daughters of the house parade around in swimsuits while the brothers break big bills into smaller denominations for the convenience of the customer, though it is best to have come armed with your own small change. These dancing girls are like coin-operated machines and will stop and start their act according to the cash flow.

A walk on the wild side

In Ottoman times, illicit sexual congress between women and men could prove fatal, but

PUFFING ON A NARGILE

The "hubble-bubble" waterpipe has always occupied a romantic role in orientalist fantasies – references to them in the writings of Balzac indicate a Parisian craze in the early 19th century, and one also shows up in Lewis Carroll's *Alice in Wonderland*. Now they are making something of a comeback in Istanbul's many traditional tea gardens. A good *nargile* is expensive, consisting of a blown glass bowl (filled with water to cool the tobacco), brass fittings and a soft leather tube. The *tömbeki* (compressed Persian tobacco) is hard to find and the pipe requires live coals to light, hence the popularity of hourly rental in tea houses, often shared by a group of friends.

it went on nonetheless, with veiled women perfecting the art of seduction through the eyes and by means of symbols. Trysts often took place in graveyards where single women might be assumed to be praying for the dead. The lure of the secret and forbidden was not lost on foreigners either, and at the end of the 18th century a particularly fine brothel stood next to the British Embassy in Pera.

Homosexual practices amongst the Ottoman élite were also common, and divan poetry is famous for its lyrical love songs composed for the "fawns of Istanbul" – the beautiful Greek dancing boys who worked the Galata taverns and bath houses.

Today, despite outraged denials of Muslim radicals and politically correct anti-orientalists alike, Istanbul's shadow world is curiously relaxed about sexual variety. For the curious, there is no harm in taking a night stroll along the back alleys off İstiklal where flashing neon lights and bouncers in brocade smoking jackets give way to streets lined with black-lit pickup parlours for freelance prostitutes of all varieties. There are copious numbers of police in evidence (and some not in evidence), so if you make sure your wallet and passport are safely secured beneath your clothing, and resist all entreaties to enter dodgy establishments, you can at least appease your curiosity without threat to limb or liberty.

There are some streets full of decidedly suspicious-looking hotels from which pimps march their willowy CIS trade double-file to the nearest *pavyon*, and others where the city's transsexual community makes its living. These are not strictly legal but, like many things in Istanbul, tolerated in exchange for backhanders.

The city's best known legal brothel takes over a warren of streets in Karaköy near the Yüksek Kaldırım (High Steps). It is strictly controlled by the police, with a checkpoint at the entrance, and a major source of tax revenue for the government. Forget any harem fantasies; foreigners are strictly forbidden and the conditions inside sad indeed. Many of these women have been disowned by their families and once inside the *genelev* ("common house") may never get out again; part of the reason for the police check is to frisk for firearms brought in by relatives seeking to vindicate their family honour. Prices are low, geared to poor, unmarried working men, most of the prostitutes are neither young nor beautiful and many use drugs. Though condoms are encouraged and health checks regular, enforcement is lax and disease on the increase.

Bending gender

The transsexual community, by contrast, is independent, feminist and vocal. Once thriving in Ülker Sokak behind the Marmara Hotel, property developers masquerading as moral crusaders have done their best to scatter their

trade and many now do business from private cars and taxis and have branched out into many middle-class suburbs. Prostitution, they say, is not their career of choice but the only one they are allowed to follow, with the exception of the few who have made it as divas and are completely accepted in Turkish society. The most famous is the classical singer Bülent Ersoy, who, as a man in the 1970s, addressed his confused gender identity in a series of romantic films. After a sex change, Ersoy's music was banned for years until he became the first transsexual to be granted a female identity card by President Özal. This is a standard right today. ❑

SWEETS FOR THE SWEET

Perhaps the best remnants of Istanbul's evenings past are to be found in the pudding shops (*pastahane*), many of which maintain their original 1920s décor. It was to these innocent establishments courting couples came to spoon over profiteroles and crème caramel, which helps explain the erotic names of desserts such as Lady's Navel, Lips of the Beloved, and Nightingale's Nests. The *pastahane* is still popular today, for many Turks are teetotal and the bright lighting and glass fronts ensure a visibility approved by religious parents. İstiklal Caddesi offers numerous traditional sweet shops and there are a few left along Divanyolu. Most are open until midnight.

LEFT: quick thrills for middle-aged men and a well-earned tip for the belly dancer.
RIGHT: "Sisi", former king of the drag queens.

THE GRAND BAZAAR

The bazaar is famous today as a tourist trap but, in its heyday, it was one of the world's great financial centres, as influential as Wall Street

The well-worn phrase, "shop 'til you drop" applies literally in Istanbul. The teeming sea of street sellers in Beyazıt and Eminönü alone can take days to explore and the atmosphere is not for the claustrophobic.

Forget Sunday trading laws; only the Grand Bazaar and Spice Market close on Sunday, ruled by Atatürk's Westernising reform laws. For convinced Muslims, however, Friday is still the holy day (note the mosques packed at prayer times) and Sunday, in Turkish, is *Pazar*, bazaar day.

Whatever you want

In Eminönü there are modern *hans* full of quasi-legal imported electronic items where you can see ancient *hamals* (porters) bent like hinges under huge fridges, cookers and TV sets. The Spice Bazaar perfumes the streets with its rich scents of vanilla beans from Madagascar, cloves from Zanzibar, straw baskets from China, and scented oils from Egypt. Most shops stay open as long as there are customers, and many shopkeepers work seven days a week. Even at midnight there are traders on the main pedestrian thoroughfares selling toys, socks, black market CDs and prayer clocks laid out on the ground.

In virtually every part of the city some kind of labyrinth awaits you, be it the alleyways, cul de sacs and winding, dimly lit streets of the Byzantines and Ottomans or the jam-packed hypermarkets and malls of the suburbs. Behind the scenes, in towering skyscrapers, the modern İznik-tiled Stock Exchange and thousands of "*döviz*" (bureaux de change), tense queues of people change ever-devaluing Turkish lira into hard dollars and Deutsch Marks. Shopping is amongst Istanbul's greatest delight and there is no one who will not eventually succumb. Istanbul, World Bazaar, ticks on.

PRECEDING PAGES: rug merchant in the Grand Bazaar.
LEFT: the Western fantasy of an oriental bazaar.
RIGHT: watermelon seller in the Grand Bazaar, photographed in 1885.

Need a cigarette holder hidden in a bottle of dry French champagne, or a mechanical ape that sings when you clap? How about a bottle of Opium perfume for US$25? Walk away from the itinerant merchant and watch the price plunge to $5, for it is a black market fake, as are the $4 Lacoste tennis shirts, the Levis, Calvin

Kleins, Guccis and "Fererra" sunglasses.

Where's the Turkish stuff? Answer: exported. Gön, makers of Turkey's priciest and most fashionable handbags, also manufacture for Coach bags. Paşabahçe crystal, a steal in Turkish outlets, goes by other more European names on the continent. Turkey's fabulous cotton mills produce fashion fabrics and clothing with their German or American price tags already on them, and Mr Benetton has been seen in the cotton-manufacturing regions of the south.

One economist referred to Istanbul as a "virtual economy" since very little is actually produced in the city. Private wealth is tied up in money markets or property and largely goes untaxed due to inflation-related fiddles. This is also why Turkey is unlikely to see a successful Islamic-led government – if the money transferred elsewhere, Istanbul, with 40 percent of the nation's wealth, would sink like a stone.

The world's oldest profession

The historical emergence of the bazaar, predictably, goes back to the dawn of time in the Middle East and Mesopotamia, birthplace of urban civilisation. With the first towns came those quintessential elements of city life – interdependency based on trade and the establishment of a definable market.

the Persians regulated trade in their cities and found the customs of the Greeks barbaric.

The transition from the rigorous design of cities in the Hellenic period to the state of controlled chaos in the orient is in part the victory of the camel and its load over the wheel and wagon. The amazingly evolved network of roads built by the Romans throughout Asia Minor fell into disuse soon after the Muslim conquests of the 7th century. In the cities, a similar transformation occurred – the wide streets, constructed for wagon and chariot traffic with adjacent arcades for pedestrians, slowly disintegrated as wheeled traffic was replaced

Citizens of neolithic Çatalhöyük, near Konya in central Anatolia, used obsidian mirrors, body paint and decorative clothing and appear to have done a roaring trade all the way to Syria and Jericho. However, the agoras of the ancient Greeks and Romans are the best surviving examples of the markets of antiquity. Evidence at Ephesus, Perge and Aspendos suggests that most were large public squares serviced by wide, colonnaded streets, usually leading from the temple or theatre, with awnings hung to protect customers from rain. However, the Hellenistic concept of the free market, so beloved by economists today, appears to be a wholly European invention. Long before Islam,

by the camel, allowing for an uncontained growth of booths and shops in the street itself until the colonnades finally disappeared.

A quest for the exotic

The taste for luxury in Constantinople, of course, predates the Muslim conquest and probably reflects the famous excesses of Rome. In fact the Byzantine city's lust for the sybaritic was an embarrassment to early church fathers trying to preach doctrines of asceticism and self-denial. Benjamin of Tudela laments the silks and brocades worn by anyone who could afford them, the gold and cloisonné jewellery, the grand houses and gold and silver tableware.

Then, as now, the city's location made it the perfect crossroads trading station between Asia, Africa and Europe, whose cold climate increased its jealous demands for spices and other novel riches of the east. Russians brought furs, honey, wax and slaves in return for silk, wine, fruit and gold, and even today trade with Russia and Central Asia is thriving.

> ## MERCHANTS' CODE
>
> "I have never yet been afraid of any men, who have a set place in the middle of their city, where they come together to cheat each other and forswear themselves."
>
> CYRUS THE PERSIAN TO THE GREEKS, FROM HERODOTUS (5TH CENTURY BC).

The Byzantine market

Surprisingly little is known about the market in early Constantinople itself. Some suggest the main commercial district flanked the port around the Mısır Carşı (Spice Market); others that it stood on the present site of the Grand Bazaar, saying the Old Bedesten is a Byzantine structure rebuilt by the Turks, citing an eagle carved in stone above one of the entrances as evidence. Still others maintain that the colonnaded main thoroughfare – today's Divanyolu – was lined with shops which formed the commercial hub of the city. It is known there was a basilica at the Forum of Theodosius where valuables could be stored. Middlemen, especially, had it good. Through them, Constantinople delivered silks, spices, drugs, gold and grains to a hungry world via the quays and customs houses of Neorion (modern Sirkeci), the major port of the city.

The specialisation of labour required an orderly pattern of production, resulting in institutionalised guilds through which the state could easily control supply, price, and profit. Some have called it a "paradise of monopoly and privilege". In fact, as the city was thought to have controlled two-thirds of the world's wealth at its peak, the system seems to have functioned fairly efficiently and great chunks of the guild laws were recycled by the Ottomans. Laws limiting speculation and interest charges were likewise practised by both.

The Silk Road

More than anything else, Constantinople hungered for silk, an addiction which kept the city at the mercy of its ancient rival, Persia, through which caravans on the Silk Road were obliged to pass. The illicit transfer of the silkworm and the discovery of the manufacturing process freed the city of its mundane obligations, but the over-taxation of the peasantry as well as the creation of inefficient state monopolies effectively insured economic decay.

Religion also played a major role in the market – the massive diversion of productivity and wealth to the glory of god may make for good tourism nowadays, but at the time it resulted in

the equivalent of a war economy: it was the icons, not swords, that needed to be turned into ploughshares if the city and empire were to be saved from bankruptcy. The Iconoclastic movement of the 7th century did exactly that, serving the positive and pedestrian function of freeing a large share of church-hoarded wealth for more productive use.

The real commercial flowering of the city, however, owes more to the city-state of Venice than indigenous entrepreneurs. Having been granted trade and tax exemptions and generous port capacity in return for coming to the rescue of Constantinople when the city was attacked by Normans in 1082, Venetian merchants soon

FAR LEFT: street porters manhandle impossible loads.
LEFT: an itinerant perfume merchant.
RIGHT: saddlemaker plying his ancient craft.

put their stamp on the city. Spices, soaps, wax, timber and silks were just some of the commodities in which they speculated, using the city as an entrepôt and trans-shipment point.

Business is good

Today, the bazaar is the main thing that distinguishes the oriental city from its cousin in the occident, a uniquely "Eastern" (or more precisely, Islamic) system of human interaction in commerce that truly sets the two worlds apart. In Islam, there is no unspoken onus attached to business as in medieval Christianity – the most salient Biblical reference to commerce being

the money-lenders whom Jesus evicted from the Temple. Muslims actually encouraged trade. According to pious tradition, the prophet Mohammed extolled good Muslims to seek business as far as China. And they did.

Caravansarais may still be seen along the camel trail trade routes of the Silk Road, with inns built at staging posts along the road for the many merchants who shuttled in security across the vast area of the Islamic cultural sphere, carrying the silks of China, the spices of India, the ebony, ivory and black slaves of Africa and the timber, furs and white slaves of the Caucasus to market cities whose names still give a thrilling tingle to the ear: Samarkand, Baghdad and Aleppo in the east, and Cairo, Fez and Cordoba in the west.

Bazaars were found only in the most important cities, offering merchants local and foreign security for their wares. With great quantities of gold at their disposal, they also operated as headquarters for guilds, stock exchanges and banks, where citizens could store valuables or legal documents under state protection.

The centrepiece of long distance trade was the caravansarai outside the city, and its cousin, the *han* inside. Both consist of an open courtyard surrounded by several stories of rooms, used for warehousing and as hostels – camels below, merchants above.

A civilised affair

The Grand Bazaar was one of the first edifices built by the Mehmet the Conqueror as an essential element of his grand new city. From the start, it was well-regulated. Business opened in the morning with prayers and a firm injunction against cheating, hoarding, and the sale of goods without security. It was all very civilised. The rules – at least in 15th-century Istanbul – were not to be broken without serious consequences. The reasons for enforcing standards were essentially moral; a significant portion of the *bedesten's* profits went on supporting charitable institutions such as mosques, schools, soup kitchens and caravansarais.

By the 17th century, the Grand Bazaar contained upwards of 3,000 shops. If one includes those in the 30 major *hans*, the number totals nearly 4,000. Most were small – tiny by modern standards – and consisted essentially of two

modity, made more so by the sultan's tendency to remove large amounts of the precious metal to his treasury. This in turn led to a value of gold significantly higher in the Ottoman Empire than in the rest of Europe and the development of the bazaar as a major centre of currency arbitrage.

Merchants were virtually assured of a profit of up to 20 percent simply by transporting their gold and silver coins to the lucrative Istanbul market. Thus, despite the steady decline of Venice as an economic power throughout the 17th and 18th centuries, the city never stopped minting sequins for export to Istanbul.

cupboards which could be opened into a street stand during the day and locked at night. Lighting was entirely natural, filtering in through the glass nobs and ventilation shafts on the cupolaed ceiling. There were no advertisements. The wares did the talking, with the merchant perched silently among his merchandise, his feet quite literally in the street. The psychological distance between consumer and the object to be consumed was nil.

Gold, then as now, was a highly valued com-

LEFT: the Grand Bazaar in Ottoman times.
ABOVE: gold is the one form of wealth that Turks trust in an uncertain world of 100 percent inflation.

The merchant classes

Ottoman society had three main social classes – those attached to the palace, such as the military and the clergy; the merchants, who dealt both regionally and internationally; and the craftsmen. Both the latter paid tax, but the craftsmen were additionally subject to a number of market regulations including price control, while the merchants enjoyed almost total *laissez faire* conditions.

There were two kinds of merchants: residents, who traded in the *bedesten*, and travellers, who lodged in the *hans* or caravansarais. The *hans* of Istanbul form a recognisable ring around the bazaar, although several larger and supposedly older *hans* can be found near the Golden Horn. It was in such *hans* that the big money moved.

Transparency, good faith, extended families and cash were the means by which business was conducted. Gold and silver were the usual medium of exchange, with credit accorded only via foreign intermediaries – usually a wealthy Venetian banker. A notable exception to this cash economy was the family-credit network set up by Jewish, Armenian and Greek merchants. The ability to place and send orders over long distances on blind trust played a significant role in successful operations.

Many of these *hans* can still be seen today,

although most are in a rather sorry state of repair, have become sweat-shops or are used for storing plastic shoes and tons of yarn. With luck, however, an obscure door may open a crack to reveal three Turkish should-be schoolboys defying labour laws, two 20-year-old Kurds and one ancient Sephardic Jew, cramped into their respective cubby holes beneath cascades of old yarn, delicately and expertly patching the burns and bruises of time from 100-year-old carpets – some of which have been shipped from England and Argentina to be deftly made as good as new.

By far the best preserved is Zincirli Han, just inside the Mercan Gate of the Grand Bazaar, which, if given over primarily to the sale of carpets and gold, still gives something of a taste of what an intimate *han* used to look like. Other good examples of larger *hans* would include the Büyük Yeni Han, the Büyük Yıldız Han, and the Kürkçü Han – all down the crowded Mahmut Paşa Acclivity Caddesi on the way to the Egyptian Bazaar.

The guilds

Rather like the Byzantine system, the Ottoman market revolved around guilds. These were no mere collections of related labourers or purveyors of certain services, but tightly knit communities of experts, with initiation rights, apprenticeships, cradle-to-grave security, and collective religious habits. Certain guilds were often identified with sufi mystical orders, so that acceptance into a guild meant acceptance into not only a trade, but into a way of life. The textile guild, in particular, did its best to ensure an absolute monopoly, a position which, though

---

THE SLAVE MARKET

The Slave Market, Esir Pazarı, in the Süleyman Paşa Odaları, south of the Grand Bazaar, was officially closed in 1854 due to western pressure, but continued unofficially for some time afterwards. However, the life of an Ottoman slave was not a cruel one, and as no social stigma clung to slave origins they often married well. Some came willingly to Istanbul as a career move. Turkish owners looked after their slaves for life, and the young might be bought by rich Ottoman women who trained them in music, dance or embroidery for healthy resale. The 7th-century traveller William Lithgow, like many early tourists, made a bee-line for the slave market in the company of a 60-year-old French Master Gunner who wished to, "for Conscience and Merits sake, redeeme some poore Christian slave from Turkish Captivity." After inspecting the goods, Lithgow suggested liberating an old man or woman, but the Gunner was set on buying a virgin or young widow "to save their bodies undefloured with Infidels." At 100 ducats he couldn't afford virgins, so selected a widow of 36. Lithgow took them to rooms in Galata, returning early in the morning suspecting "the dissembling devotion of the Gunner to be nought but luxurious lust." His suspicions were confirmed when the woman came out in tears, begging to be returned to her former captivity.

effective in medieval times, could not compete with the growing industrialisation of 18th and 19th century Europe. Once foreign countries were allowed special exemptions for services rendered to the faltering Ottoman state, manufactured goods from the factories of England, France and Germany flooded into the bazaar. It was a case of commercial *déjà vu*, with the Great Powers playing the role held by the Genoese and Venetians in the fading days of Byzantium. Once again Galata, across the Golden Horn, became the preferred place to do business, and banks and trading companies flourished.

FOREIGN EXCHANGE

Don't change all your money at once. With 100 percent inflation, you'll get a few thousand more lira each time you change any hard currency. The *döviz* give better rates (and service) than the banks. Rates also improve as you get closer to the Grand Bazaar.

electronic goods, European-made furniture and anything that looks old as "antique". In theory, anything that is less than 100 years old should pass, but this is not always the case. You should keep all the certificates that an honest merchant gives you – in Turkish and with an official stamp – about the age and origin of your purchases. Most Turkish bureaucrats, perhaps still living in the shadow of the sultans, are overly impressed by official-looking stamps. ❏

The bargain

Today you may well wonder where those old rules against cheating, hoarding, and selling without security have gone, especially when shopping in the streets. It is absolutely true that a majority of merchants see foreigners coming, and will struggle for hours, with all manner of ruses, to get – literally – that extra ha'penny. Appearing to be the winner in the bargaining ritual is a matter of pride, even if the sums are small. Some visitors enjoy the game and some definitely do not. If you do not, go straight to merchants with white beards and beanies – they are the true Islamists who live by the Book, and cheating is not in it.

You must be especially careful with goods that seem a little too cheap. One professional photographer bought up a dozen rolls of astonishingly cheap brand-name films to discover they had three exposures each. Clothing is often "*defolu*" (substandard), so check carefully for holes and rips. Fakes of every description abound, from designer labels to "antique" furniture. Elsewhere you have been warned to avoid touts as you will pay more (their commission) and there are virtually no carpets made today with strictly vegetable dyes, no matter what those big brown eyes may claim.

Shipping large objects out of the country is also risky – officious bureaucrats at the clearing points have been known to impound personal

IN SEARCH OF THE TUGHRA

There are no orientalist collectors as keen as wealthy Turks, and though they veer away from the egregiously erotic, even items kitschy and ostentatious enough to rival Dolmabahçe Palace attract high prices in Istanbul auction houses. Strict laws govern the exportation of Ottoman art, however, and only pieces with iron-clad proof of ownership and origin can even be released onto the Turkish market. But there are loopholes, and if you plan to invest, visit only reputable auction houses to ensure accurate documentation and evaluation on anything you buy, or risk leaving it to the poisonous whim of customs officials. See *Travel Tips* section for listings.

LEFT: tiny workshops such as this quiltmaker's are a fascinating addition to the back streets of the bazaar. **RIGHT:** pots and pans for sale.

PILES OF PATTERNS

Turkish carpets are among the most beautiful, intricate and luxurious
in the world – but buyers need to be discriminating

I t is a rare visitor who won't allow him or herself to be seduced into the cool interior of one of Istanbul's hundreds of carpet shops. No obligation to buy. Sit back and drink tea in tulip glasses or a demitasse of thick black coffee as the friendly merchant rolls out rug after luscious rug. Big rugs, small rugs, square

rugs, runner rugs, rugs for your walls and rugs for your table tops, silk rugs, wool rugs, shag rugs, worn rugs, dear rugs, cheap rugs, good rugs, bad rugs...

Turkey is justifiably famous for its exquisite carpets, which have been sought by collectors worldwide for many centuries. Today, however, the sheer quantity of what's on offer may stun the first time visitor. From the Caucasian-style thick, shaggy piles of the Çanakkale area to the sumptuous carnation motifs of Milas, hard-edged geometric patterns of Cappadocia, stylised figurines of Turkoman rugs, from the region near the Persian border, and wild floral and arabesque designs created at Hereke to

grace the Ottoman courts, no one can help but succumb to their sumptuous diversity.

The minimalist will find spare contemporary designs, and at least one enterprising manufacturer specialises in room-size reproductions of paintings by Kandinsky, Miró and Klee. Country cottage pastels are now produced for those of Laura Ashley persuasion, with bleached cream and beige on offer for those after something simpler. Many shops also stock embroidered Central Asian tent hangings (*suzani*), and woven silk "*ikat*" garments or home furnishings which are easier on the weight allowance.

Do your homework

The best shops are usually the least pushy, with older owners who know their stock, will listen to your specifications and refrain from inundating you with totally unsuitable options. It is important to take your time over the inevitable Turkish coffee or tea on offer, ask plenty of questions and shop around. The better dealers know this and will not rush you, for they are well aware that as you educate your eye you may soon find that what caught your fancy at first can look tawdry later, and that you may deem it worthwhile to spend more money on a higher quality piece than you'd planned.

Those seriously interested in historic carpets should first have a look at those on display in the Museum of Turkish and Islamic Arts in Istanbul (*see page 156*). What one most notices about the older Turkish carpets is the greater variety of colours, including a rich purple, brilliant saffron yellow and pine green rarely seen today, though Bergama and Yağcıbedir rugs do still bear some traces of the old tradition. A glance through a few books to look at regional styles will also help you plan in advance, and it is probably worth taking a few fabric or paint samples and the measurements of the available floorspace in your home.

Bargaining is taken for granted, even with those merchants who say they don't – carpets are coded on the back as a guide to how low the dealer can drop without losing out, and the classic formula of beginning at half the initial offer and arguing upwards still holds true.

Picking a winner

In the past, every village had its own techniques and patterns that made the finished carpet as distinctive as fingerprints. The nomads of the Taurus mountains, for instance, still weave the lustrous Dösemealtı rugs, while their settled cousins in the Yahyalı region have been weaving their own version of Ladik carpets since the 14th century, notable for their dark, rich indigos, greens and walnut-gold. Designs, colours, quality of wool and style of weave help in

play. Many regional styles are in danger of being lost. Some dealers also beat or intentionally fade their goods to create fake antiques or soften garish colours.

The buyers' quest for authenticity in the face of this activity has created a boom market in the vivid *kilims* and *sofras* (mats for the family meal, eaten on the floor) produced in the eastern provinces of Hakkâri and Van. Little valued until about 20 years ago, they escaped the direct influences of the marketplace and are now prized for their bold but simple abstract design. Prices have risen steeply, but they are still significantly cheaper than pile carpets.

attributing textiles to their place of origin, although design is perhaps the least reliable indicator these days. Intermarriage, resettlement, and other influences mean that designs change more quickly than colours or style of weaving, while modern carpet merchants are instructing villagers to mass-produce popular designs and colour schemes tailored to foreign tastes. The end product has little bearing on local tradition, and, together with the increased mobility of the population, means that it is difficult to disentangle the various influences at

LEFT: rug seller in Istanbul.
ABOVE: rugs hanging in the streets of the old city.

SKIRTING THE MINEFIELD

In every corner of the Old City there will be those waiting to lure you into a carpet shop by means both fair and infuriating. Less visible or famous establishments may resort to all manner of trickery such as planting touts, generally handsome, slick young males, at popular tourist attractions, to offer "free" guide services or, at worst, shameless flirtation which can sadly deteriorate into outright abuse if you don't show willing.

Don't mistake business for friendliness; if you've been caught by a carpet tout you can expect to pay considerably over the odds – and you'll be wasting valuable holiday time.

Counting the knots

The quality of a carpet or flat weave kilim is generally determined by the density of its weave – if you compare the backs of most, it is quite easy to see which are the better made by the clarity and tightness of the design. Cheaper carpets and kilims often have a cotton warp (the lengthwise threads) which can be seen easily when examining the fringes. The best quality pure wool or silk knotted pile carpets are the most expensive. Also look out for *cicims*, which combine embroidery with weaving, and *sumaks*, often from Azerbaijan or Iran, where patterns of animals and other symbols have been inserted with threads wrapped around the warp. Pure silk Hereke carpets, first manufactured for the Imperial court, cost nearly three times the average, with more knots per square inch than any in the world.

Sun-dried for subtlety

Until this century most households had their own looms, the thread for which was handspun from locally produced wool, goat hair, cotton or linen. Few households had the capacity or skill to dye self-sufficient quantities of wool, thus each district had its own specialist dyer or relied on itinerant dyers. The colours themselves were

ANTIQUE CARPETS

Mass production of knotted pile rugs is thought to have begun in Konya in the 12th century. However, the Turkic tribes who settled in Anatolia discovered there was already a thriving indigenous tradition of flat-weave kilims whose ancestry may stretch back to neolithic times. The oldest carpet fragment found in Turkey is over 2,000 years old.

The survival of many early Turkish carpets is thanks to the custom of presenting them to mosques as pious gifts, and they were well looked after as Turks wear shoes neither in their homes nor places of worship. Cast an eye over the carpets during any mosque visit, though the rarest have probably been put away for safe-keeping.

From the 14th century onwards Turkish carpets were exported to Europe in large numbers and many can be seen in European paintings, which remain an important source of information about 14th–17th century carpets. King Henry VIII of England was an avid collector, posed for Holbein on a Turkish rug, and was only too happy to seize the large carpet collection of his favourite, Cardinal Wolsey, when the latter fell from favour. Although the contemporary inventories note that about half of his 800 carpets were Turkish, like many a subsequent collector he did not look after them and they rotted away on the damp flagstones of Hampton Court Palace – sadly not one survives today.

traditionally obtained from various indigenous plants. Madder root produces shades from a brickish red to orange and even pinks and deep purple. It was a lucrative export crop as one of the only reliable red dyes until chemical stabilisers were introduced in the 1860s. Other important dyes were indigo for blue, saffron for yellow and walnut for browns.

It's pretty easy to spot chemical dyes – they don't look natural, and have often begun to run even before they hit the market. Vivid pinks and oranges give themselves away, but the bitumen traditionally used to make black can be harder to spot and more dangerous, since it rots the wool over time. In addition those pastel shades developed for Western tastes are often chemically dyed then chlorine bleached or left out in the sun, which will seriously reduce the carpet's longevity. A simple comparison of the colour on the back and front of the carpet will usually tell you what you need to know.

Quality control and commitment to heritage is one of the reasons carpet cooperatives such as the DOBAG Project in western Turkey have been set up, in order to reacquaint women with traditional designs and vegetable dyes.

Patterns and symbols

Turkish carpet and kilim motifs (*nakih*) have traditionally been handed down from mother to daughter, though specifically local designs are being lost through commercial production. Each of the Turcoman tribes who migrated to Anatolia had a *damga* or tribal mark, often a bird or beast, and survivors of these forms can be detected in some of today's designs. In accordance with Islamic tradition, animal and human motifs are preferably abstract.

Amongst Turkish nomads, the *"elibelinde"* or arms-akimbo motif represents good luck while flocks of birds may stand for homesickness. Triangles on their own can represent the talismans containing prayer scraps worn by many nomadic people. The tree of life is a classical spiritual symbol, though a representation of the beech tree is specifically thought to relate to Central Asian shamanist beliefs. An eight-pointed star can represent Fate, or the Wheel of Life. Prayer rugs (*namazlik*) frequently show the *mihrab* (prayer niche) in the mosque, the tip of which is to be pointed towards Mecca, with the forehead of the worshipper bowing accordingly; a mosque lamp hanging from the arch denotes divine light. Funereal carpets, brought to cemeteries for graveside worship, may contain images of cypress trees, headstones, and blue skies above the *mihrab* representing paradise. The pattern of two triangles, tips touching, often represents a girl, and may be used in a "dowry" kilim for luck after marriage. The carnation motif so often seen in Milas rugs is particularly Turkish, and one of the flowers favoured by the Ottoman court. ❏

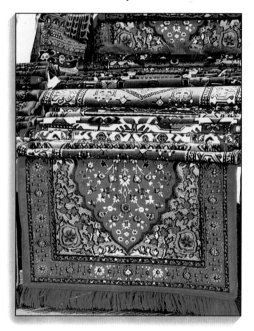

GETTING IT HOME

It is virtually impossible to find a carpet or kilim over a century old – most older pieces are 30–60 years old and thus not really classifiable as antique. However, as Turkey has strict laws on the exportation of antiques, always get a certificate of authenticity just in case. Most reputable shops will willingly supply this.

Many shops offer to ship your carpet home, but unless you know the merchant well, this can be risky. Some travellers have found that what they received was not what they paid for; it will almost certainly mean paying more import duty and you can knock a surprising amount off the price by refusing the "free" postage.

LEFT: choosing a carpet generally involves a great deal of time, tea and bargaining.
RIGHT: cheap machine-made carpets in the bazaar.

TURKISH DELIGHTS

Ottoman food was once considered one of the finest cuisines in the world, and the modern version is filled with delicious surprises

Turkish people take food very seriously. They are convinced their cuisine has no equal, disdain foreign dishes or flavours and can spend hours planning or describing meals. Housewives still usually buy all their ingredients fresh on the day, though recent skyrocketing demands for frozen or prepared foods in the metropolis indicate those days may be coming to an end.

Food rules the day. At dawn you hear the first *simit* and *poaça* sellers calling out their wares from trundle carts – these small pastries are the perfect breakfast on the run for the busy, late for work, and labourers. The first is a sesame seed ring, the second a rich savoury bun which may contain cheese or spiced potato.

A proper Turkish breakfast, however, is a sumptuous spread of goat's cheese, olives, cucumber and tomato, butter, various jams and perhaps some salami or a boiled egg, served with fresh bread and washed down with copious quantities of sweet, strong, black tea. Foreigners often find the savoury element of the Turkish breakfast strange to the palate at first, but as a healthy start to the day it is unequalled.

Lunch is usually soup based on red lentils, (*mercimek* or *ezogelin*) and *sulu yemek* ("juicy food"), stews of meat and vegetables served cafeteria-style with rice, and best at the crack of noon when they are freshest. Later in the day, after they have been left to sit, they are a common source of traveller's tummy. The best antidote and preventative is yoghurt, which comes in many forms. *Cacik* is a cold yogurt soup containing salt, grated cucumber and mint, and in most places outside the metropolis, lots of garlic, though in Istanbul you may well have to request it specially. Garlic also helps eliminate unwanted bacteria from the system.

A touch of spice

Except for the occasional use of mint, cumin, oregano, red pepper and (rarely) garlic, most

Istanbul food is not heavily spiced. The city's yuppie classes disdain spicy food, which they associate with Anatolian peasants. You may find ground, purplish *sumac* on the table or in some foods, which gives a slight sour taste, and you can usually get *pul biber*, dried red pepper flakes, if you ask. Likewise, *sarımsaklı* (garlicky) or *acı*

(peppery) food must usually be requested, for its inclusion is the exception rather than the rule. Fresh lemon juice is used as a common dressing for salads and *mezes*.

In the evening, restaurant menus, especially in touristic neighbourhoods, can get repetitive, so it is well worth seeking out the *meyhanes*. These Turkish-style tavernas in back alleys, full of rakı-drinking males, include many minority-run establishments offering Armenian, Greek, Kurdish or Russian specialities. Most *meyhanes*, especially around Beyoğlu and in Kumkapı, are boisterous establishments with gypsy bands, bums and famous film stars rubbing shoulders in a common purpose: intoxi-

LEFT: cook takes a break. **RIGHT:** sellers with trays of bagels (*simit*) are a welcome sight at breakfast time.

cation, which may lead to singing and dancing as the night wears on. The main dishes may sometimes disappoint, but the *meze* selection is usually superb.

The *meze* platter

There is a decidedly sensible Mediterranean belief that it is damaging to one's constitution to drink alcohol on an empty stomach. *Mezes* will be brought to the table on an enormous tray, from which you make a selection. This is particularly convenient for foreigners as written descriptions of the dishes often don't do them justice or are eccentrically translated (to wit:

"cigarette pie" for *sigara börek*). *Koç yumurtası* (ram's eggs) are testicles, and sheep's brain salad speaks for itself. You can also go back to the kitchen and have a look. Cold *mezes* are usually vegetable dishes in olive oil, but you can choose hot options such as *börek* (fried pastries with cheese or pastrami fillings, also a popular lunch snack), sautéed lamb's liver with onions (*arnavut ciğer*), or fried kalamari (squid). You will also no doubt find *haydari* (white goat's cheese blended with yoghurt and thyme), a variety of pickles, *kısır* (bulgar, onions, pepper and parsley), marinated octopus or squid and roast red peppers in garlic.

DINING IN

Most Turkish housewives take huge pride in making everything by hand, the more complex the better. If you are invited to a traditional Turkish family meal, the proper thanks to the cook is "elinize sağlık" meaning "health to your hand!". When plied with food beyond your capacity, say "doydum, sağol." ("thanks, but I'm stuffed."). Sweets and pastries are the customary gift as they can be enjoyed by the whole family. Amongst the upper middle classes, where women have professional jobs or simply spend all day at the health club, more are cheating, and mixing mezes from the deli counter with a few home additions, although they won't admit it.

Aubergines (*patlıcan*) feature in many forms, including *imam bayıldı* or "the cleric fainted," so called for an Islamic prayer leader who keeled over in ecstasy after eating this delectable combination of aubergine stuffed with onions, tomatoes and garlic. *Patlıcan salatası* (aubergine salad) may come as a purée or in chunks with other vegetables, as well as in fried slices with courgettes and garlic yoghurt. All are eaten with bread.

Dolma ("stuffed things") are also popular, and can be made with courgettes, aubergines, peppers, vine leaves, cabbage leaves, tomatoes, mussels or artichoke hearts filled with a mixture of rice, pine nuts, currants, herbs and spices. It is also well worthwhile keeping a lookout for less common regional *meze* delicacies such as *çerkez tavuğu* (Circassian chicken), a dish of steamed, boned and shredded meat smothered in a rich sauce of garlic, lemon, breadcrumbs, walnuts and oil. A popular Armenian *meze* is *topik*, an interesting mix of meat, raisins and spices covered in a layer of bean paste.

Mezes are delicious and few *meyhane* owners mind if you stick to them and

SACRED CRUMBS

Bread is sacred to older, religious Turks and dropping it on the ground is strictly taboo. You are meant to set old bread on rooftops for the birds, and may notice that many people still make a habit of rescuing dropped bread from the streets, tut-tutting as they go.

Barbecues are a safe way to avoid germs, and may include succulent lamb chops, *şiş kebabı* (beef or lamb), *beyti* (minced meat with lots of spice; the Adana kebab is similar) or chicken, chunks or wings, sometimes marinated in a spicy sauce. Urfa kebabs are huge *şiş* with spiced mince packed between fat slices of aubergine or other vegetables, and may include pine nuts. The traditional accompaniment is *ezme salatası*, a spicy relish made with finely

never bother to order a main meal – assuming, of course, that you continue to drink. Be on the look out for unordered dishes, but, if they urge you to try a freshly made house speciality, don't pass it up.

Barbecues

Meat cooked over coals is called *izgara*, and the best *meyhanes* have their own barbecue (*mangal*) in the middle of the floor, bearing witness to the Central Asian nomadic tradition.

LEFT: colourful café in the middle of the Grand Bazaar.
ABOVE: tempting trays of *sulu yemek* ("juicy food") offer a welcome change from kebabs.

chopped tomatoes, cucumbers, onion, parsley and peppers. In the best *meyhanes* you can watch chefs deftly make their own on the spot with an enormous hatchet – all fresh, no tomato paste, and sometimes with the eastern addition of pomegranate syrup.

Seafood

While *meyhanes* tend to attract the richest and poorest extremes of society, when dining out with most middle-class Turks you will usually be asked if you would like a proper meat or fish restaurant. Alcohol is usually available, but they are less boisterous than the *meyhanes*. Some restaurants offer both meat and fish, but you are likely to get the best selection at those which specialise. Fish is usually eaten at a table set alongside the water (preferably with *rakı*), and most Turks are well aware of quality. There are five separate names for the bluefish alone, from *yaprak* (bay leaf) to *çinaköp* or *lüfer*. Age is all important – many fish are considered to be at their prime in autumn.

Starters in fish restaurants are likely to include mussels stuffed with rice, pine nuts and spices; fried kalamari and shrimp; *balık köftesi* (hot fish-cakes); or cured fish with fresh dill and vinegar and even caviar.

When ordering your main fish meal, it is well

Mediterranean lobster are usually available in season, though pricey even then.

Carnivore's choice

In addition to *izgara*, a meat restaurant may also offer *tandır*, roast lamb baked in a pit, or imaginative traditional specialities such as lamb cooked in a clay pot, on a brick tile, spit-roasted over coals, or in a "*sote*" with tomatoes and other vegetables. *Yahni* is the generic name for meat cooked by indirect exposure to fire, and usually contains a lot of onions – *kuzu yahni*, for instance, is cubed pieces of lamb boiled tender, strained, rolled in flour, sautéed in butter,

to be cautious and ask the price by weight since fish can be as expensive or cheap as the season or restaurant dictates. Some of the most delicious dishes include *kiliç balığı*, swordfish skewered with peppers and tomatoes; *kalkan*, turbot served with lemon wedges, and *karides güveç*, a casserole of shrimp, hot peppers, tomatoes and cheese. Vegetarians should note that a similar dish made with mushrooms (*mantar*) is often available. You may also find *barbunya* (red mullet) or its smaller cousins *tekir*, *lüfer* (bluefish), and *palamut* (bonito). Perhaps the simplest, tastiest, and often cheapest dish is *hamsi*, a Black Sea speciality of anchovies fried crisp in corn flour. Giant shrimp and clawless

and returned into a broth of onions, herbs and spices. Vegetables such as potatoes, tomatoes, green beans, peas, okra or pulses are added to make such creations as *ayva yahni* (quince yahni). Bursa's speciality, the Iskender kebab, is made up of luscious slices of döner meat spread over *pide* bread (like pitta), smothered in yogurt, tomato sauce and hot butter.

Your meaty main course will probably come accompanied by rice. Turkish *pilav* (rice) can be simply cooked with butter and meat broth or richly seasoned with pine nuts, currants, herbs and liver, and is delicious by itself. You will also find *bulgur pilav* and *kuskus*, egg dough made into small pellets and dried.

Something to drink

Ayran is a cold, frothy yoghurt drink whipped with water and salt, and the finest thirst quencher on offer. Even Turkish branches of McDonald's are obliged to include *ayran* on their otherwise standard menu.

Fresh-squeezed juices are widely available, best in winter when the citrus season is in full force in the south. You may also find carrot juice, banana milk and apple juice. Black tea in "tulip" glasses will be served any time you are asked to sit and wait, or go visiting, but there is also a strong tradition of herbal teas, some of which (like sage or even fresh oregano) are unusual to the western palate but very good.

Ihlamur (lime flower) tea is considered a good remedy for colds and flu. *Boza* and *sahlep* are popular drinks in winter, the former made from mildly fermented millet and tasting rather like eggnog, *sahlep* served hot with a sprinkle of cinnamon and often sold by street vendors or on public ferries. It is made from the pulverized tubers of the wild orchid.

The hard stuff

Even though Turkey is a Muslim country, it has a relaxed attitude to alcohol. Those in search of something with a kick can't go wrong with Turkish beer – they are all good. Efes and Tuborg are the most common, and the former now comes in dark and light versions. Turkey was the cradle of the sultana raisin and its wine production is prolific, although the quality does not match up to that in Europe. It is also relatively cheap – the better wines rarely exceed US$6 in the shops, double that in the *meyhanes*, and a bit more on the tourist trail. Typically you will be offered fruity white Çankaya, or the drier Villa Doluca which comes in white or red. Two other popular reds are Yakut and Dikmen, but there are new "noble" varieties entering the market all the time.

The more courageous can try the local aniseed-based tipple, *rakı*, called "lion's milk" by the Turks, which goes well with fish. Be careful, however – it packs a mean punch, and after one or two you are advised to "polish" the *rakı* with beer. Serious *rakı* drinkers take a glass of fresh-squeezed lemon juice (*limon suyu*)

every two or three drinks – it is claimed to be a hangover preventative, and if you request it most waiters will know why.

Dessert

Traditionally, in Istanbul, rich desserts do not figure much after a full meal. Instead, you will usually be offered a selection of seasonal fruits – citrus and bananas in winter, in spring green almonds and plums (the latter served with salt, which is generally an acquired taste for foreigners), strawberries in May, cherries in June, melons in July and August and apples, pears, grapes and pomegranates in autumn. Melon and

white goat's cheese go well together, usually enjoyed lingering with drinks after a meal. And the whole meal is topped off with tiny cups of ultra-sweet, bitter Turkish coffee.

Pudding shops

Turks are notorious sugar lovers, and the heavier sweets and pastry are a custom unto themselves, frequently an indulgence of the mid-afternoon, the Turkish answer to a rich cream tea. The *pastahane*, or pudding shop, attracts families and courting couples and many of the best have kept their original interiors, whether from the 1920s or '50s. Here you will find such luxuries as figs stuffed with almonds,

LEFT: Istanbullites take their food seriously.
RIGHT: irresistible *baklava*, feather-light layers of pastry drenched in syrup and stuffed with nuts.

apricots bursting with cheese and pistachio paste or sugared pumpkin with cream.

Muhallebi means pudding, and *sütlaç* is a sumptuous milk and rice confection baked in an earthenware cup. You can find the sweet sesame slabs called *helva*, *baklava* made of buttered, see-through thin layers of unleavened dough made with pistachio (*fıstıklı*), hazelnut (*fındıklı*) and walnut (*cevizli*). Profiteroles, supposedly an Istanbul invention, are very popular, as are crème caramel, and *aşure*, a traditional celebratory dish made from all 40 different ingredients supposedly left in the ark's kitchen after Noah sighted Ararat.

These days, however, the traditional pudding shop is giving way to the Parisian-style bistro and a café society patronised by Istanbul's artsy and well-off. These bistros, of which there are many around İstiklal, Teşvikye and Ortaköy, come complete with racks of newspapers on the walls, classical music and jazz on the sound system and expensive *latte*. They also serve alcohol, and some do European-style cakes and light meals as well.

Frequently, the more upmarket you go, the more bland the food. Bistros tend to offer mild pasta dishes and salads, but the current fad amongst the new rich is "California cuisine" complete with imported cigars, imported drinks, and gimmicky themes. English-style pubs and fish-and-chips restaurants are all the rage in the upper-middle-class suburbs – with imported cod.

Fast food

Istanbul has many native outlets briskly competing with the Golden Arches and its numerous brethren. The best, by far, are the fish sandwich merchants around the harbours – especially Eminönü, where they ply their trade from fake caïques and wear Ottoman gear. The fish, usually the oily palamut, is either grilled or fried and stuck into half a loaf of bread with onions and tomatoes. It is filling and delicious.

In Beyoğlu and Sultanahmet, *gözleme* restaurants are everywhere, and easy to find, because there are usually women dressed up in peasant gear sitting in the window making them. *Gözleme* is a wide, coarse pancake which can be rolled up with a variety of fillings, and is very cheap. *Lahmacun* is a Kurdish speciality and the staple of many underpaid workers – a cheeseless pizza of ground meat, onions and peppers which are rolled around fresh onions and parsley. *Pide* takes a little longer as it is baked in a clay oven with rich cheese, pastrami or *sucuk*, a spicy salami, sometimes topped with egg. Stuffed mussels with rice, fried mussels with tartar sauce, and baked potatoes with a variety of stuffings are also popular, though grilled lamb's intestines (*kokoreç*) are not for the faint-hearted. Another quick, cheap meal is *menemen* – scrambled eggs to which cheese, tomato, pastrami or sausage may be added.

Raisins and dried seeds or nuts (*leblebi*) are eaten at any time or at social occasions, and the little shops that sell them are frequently open late into the night. Roasted hazelnuts and unshelled black sunflower seeds are the favourites, with powdery dried chickpeas filling in for weight.

Hot stuff

A thoroughly Turkish custom is the all-night *işkembe* or tripe soup parlour, frequented early on by families and after midnight by drinkers lining their stomachs. *Işkembe* is considered medicinal after a night on the town, with crushed garlic, red pepper, oregano and vinegar to taste. There are also soups made from sheeps' heads and hoofs. The less brave can play it safe with roast chicken.

Istanbul's best restaurants

Eating out in Istanbul is almost always a treat, but there are a few truly special places to look out for (*detailed listings are given in Travel Tips*). **Hamdi's** in Eminönü is one of the city's best kept secrets. Overlooking the ferry docks (and a bus terminal) this simple *meyhane* specialises in Eastern Turkish cuisine which includes the use of *nar ekşişi* (pomegranate juice), peppers, garlic and does a "clay pot" kebab if you order it in advance.

Most of the restaurants on **Nevizade Sokak**, behind the Balık Pazar, are good, but as a rule of thumb those which pay the least attention to

Four Seasons in Tünel also does international cuisine in high style.

For fish, Kumkapı, in an earthy section of old Istanbul, is right on the fishermen's quay, and you will find no shortage of gypsy musicians or colourful characters. **Kör Agop** is one of the oldest restaurants in the area – in season, it offers 20 varieties of fresh fish and the house speciality is fish soup. In Sultanahmet, **Balıkçı Sabahattin** has been in business since 1927 and has an excellent selection. The more upscale fish restaurants are mainly sited along the Bosphorus. Among the most famous are **Garaj**, in Tarabya and **Hristo**, on the same

décor serve the best food. There are always gypsy musicians here as well as the indefatigable Madame Anahit whose out-of-tune accordion will leave you no peace unless you grease her palm. **Boncuk** is one of the most reliable, and has a few Armenian specialities.

In Beyoğlu, **Kallavi 20** does an excellent "all in" set meal, with all you can drink and live music (booking essential). **Rejans** is a wonderful Russian restaurant in an alley off İstiklal. Borscht, stewed duck and pork cutlets can be washed down with neat lemon vodka. The

street, which serves Greek seafood specialities. The specialities of **Yeni İskele** in Yeniköy include stuffed kalamari. On the Asian side, **İskele** in Çengelköy has a garden with a fabulous Bosphorus view.

For meat, **Beyti** in suburban Florya is one of the longest established and best restaurants in the city. For Ottoman dishes, **Asitane**, near the Kariye Cami, **Darüzziyafe** in the Süleymaniye complex, and **Haci Abdullah** in Beyoğlu all rate very highly, although you should note that the last two do not serve alcohol. If money is no object and you wish to impress, then **Yirmidokuz (29) Ulus** has a spectacular view, gourmet food and a French chef. ❑

LEFT: perfectly stuffed courgettes.
ABOVE: feel the buzz at a Beyoğlu *meyhane*.

FROM TOPKAPI TO TOWER BLOCKS

Istanbul's legacy of sumptuous architecture lives on, though you may have to search beneath the skyscrapers and radio masts to find it

It is not only Byzantine churches and Ottoman mosques for which Istanbul is famous, though these may be the first to catch the eye. The remains of Byzantine palaces, towers, waterways and prisons, as well as the markets, *hans* and domestic interiors of Ottoman life, such as the interior of the Topkapı harem, pictured above, have intriguing tales to tell – of love, fear, commerce, jealousy, brutality and social change – and especially of women's lives. More than any art form, secular architecture reveals the practical and economic aspects of daily functions, where everyone from the peasant to the nobleman had to wash, shop, cook, sleep, dress and work, where affairs of state were discussed, coins minted, grievances heard, prisoners punished, bread baked and animals stabled. Istanbul has been built over so frequently, and in such a concentrated area, that it can sometimes be hard to picture original functions of the different strata of remains. But humans, from millennium to millennium, are essentially logical, and life one thousand, two thousand years ago went on much as today, in the city's roads, houses, shops and cafés, with only the technology changing.

▷ **BEAUTY IS SKIN DEEP**
Pretty on the outside, but art nouveau facades in Beyoğlu were often used to disguise poor internal planning and extract high rents from foreigners.

◁ **GREEK HERITAGE**
The imposing remnants of Istanbul's Greek past in Balat. Most such buildings keep a low profile today.

△ **BOSPHORUS YALIS**
The Sadberk Hanim Museum is housed in one of the finest of the beautif• wooden mansions which line the Bosphorus.

◁ GUARDING THE EMPIRE
The Walls of Theodosius managed to repel would-be invaders for a thousand years, but in the end succumbed to Ottoman determination.

△ LUXURY PRISON
This stunning Ottoman building, now the exclusive Four Seasons Hotel, used to be a prison where writer Nazım Hikmet was jailed.

ALL FRILLS AND FASHION

Though disapproved of by the Muslim clergy, effete Baroque extravagance was a passion of many sultans. However, it was during the break up of the empire in the 19th century that excess truly overtook good sense, as in the "closet horror" architecture and furnishings of the Dolmabahçe, Yıldız, Beylerbeyi and Ihlamur Kasri.

Retreating into a navel-gazing paranoia, the last sultans looked west to architectural fashions emerging in Europe, importing them, their architects and technology wholesale and untempered to Istanbul, with scant regard to good taste, sensible planning, or aesthetic harmony. Even today Istanbul's antique showrooms show a taste for ostentation neither eastern nor western but quintessentially Turkish.

It is nonetheless worth taking a deep breath and peering through the fug of fussy detail for the many fine individual examples of ornamentation which are otherwise almost obscured by excess.

△ CONCRETE BLOCKS
Most Istanbullites prefer new box-like highrises to the problems of restoration and lack of amenities in older properties.

◁ OTTOMAN STYLE
This delightful restored fountain at the gate of the Topkapı is just one of many around the city, showing the respect accorded fresh water supply.

PLACES

*A detailed guide to the entire city, with principal sites
clearly cross-referenced by number to the maps*

Arriving at the congested Atatürk Airport and embarking on a hectic taxi ride into the heart of megacity Istanbul, the first-time visitor can be forgiven for wondering where the harems and camels have gone. The urban area spreads like a snake along the shores of the Bosphorus and Sea of Marmara for more than 50 km (30 miles) and is still growing apace, swallowing former villages and shanty towns and replacing them by luxury highrises and satellite developments. Passing the vast five-star hotels along the Marmara coast to the right and the tower blocks of Ataköy on the left, you will see a skyline of skyscrapers, cranes and building sites long before you see the famous domes and minarets around the Topkapı Palace. Istanbullites, you soon learn, prefer the purpose-built and efficiently modern to Roman walls, wooden houses and caravansarais, and you may have to dig through the débris of overcrowded and insalubrious neighbourhoods to find the remains of the visions of splendour which have stunned visitors for 2,000 years.

Nonetheless, some areas have managed to keep their original character and architecture. The "old city" is studded with magnificent churches and mosques echoing the Byzantine and Ottoman eras, when separation of religion and state was unthinkable, while the Topkapı Palace itself exudes an aura of the intrigue and absolute power wielded by the sultans. Across the Golden Horn, the jumble of Art Nouveau buildings in Beyoğlu, now the city's entertainment quarter, is often referred as the "new" city, but it is not new at all. Pera reached its peak in the early 20th century but has been a settlement of foreigners since Byzantine times and even now remains non-Muslim in flavour. Likewise, the gently elegant Rococo palaces and wooden mansions of the Bosphorus reflect the days when these former villages were aristocratic summer residences.

On the Asian side, the swanky suburbs from Kadıköy to Bostancı were virtual empty space before the 1960s. Today, the business heart of the city is in the spaghetti junctions of Mecidiyeköy, Levent, and Etiler, but even these are strained at the seams and vast high-tech business complexes are springing up at the furthest edges of town. The media groups deserted Cağaloğlu for Ikitelli less than a decade ago, the stock exchange is in İstinye, and upmarket designer residences are mostly found in satellite cities like Büyükçekmege and Beyköz. If you find it all confusing, you know that you have arrived, for such are the contradictions of this great city. Whether Greek *Byzantion*, Byzantine *Constantinople*, Ottoman *Islambol* or modern *Istanbul*, it remains the crossroads of the world. ❑

PRECEDING PAGES: the Süleymaniye Mosque from across the Golden Horn; view from the top of the Galata Tower; a local bakery.
LEFT: sweeping the steps of a mosque.

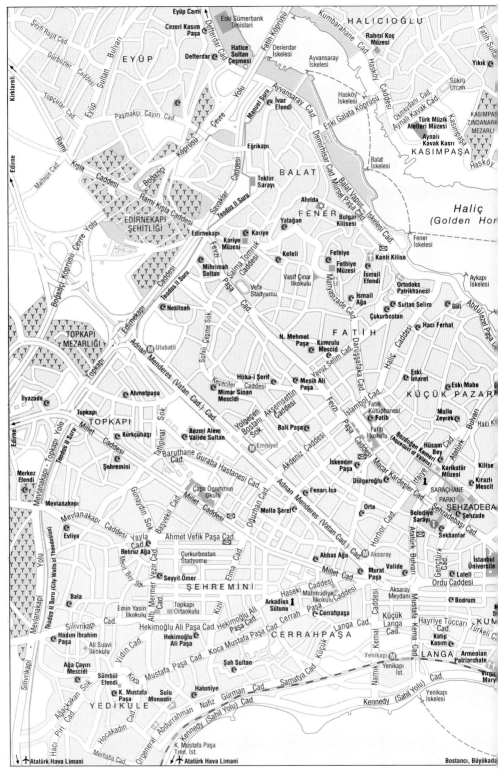

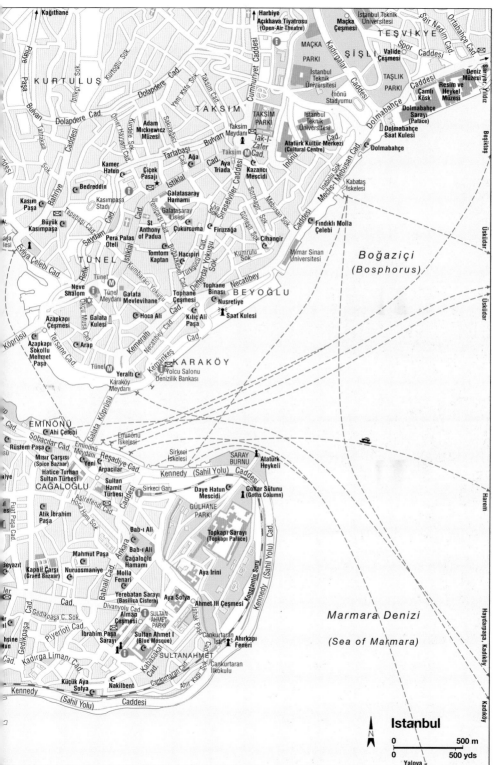

Kağıthane

Harbiye
Açıkhava Tiyatrosu
(Open-Air Theatre)

İstanbul Teknik Üniversitesi

Şair Nedim Cad.

Ortabahçe Cad.

Maçka Çeşmesi

TEŞVİKYE

MAÇKA
PARKI

ŞİŞLİ

Valide
Çeşmesi

Spor
Caddesi

KURTULUŞ

Pilâve
Paşa

Dolapdere Cad.

Yeni Yuva Sok.

Taksim Sok.

TAKSİM

İstanbul
Teknik
Üniversitesi

TAŞLIK
PARKI

Resim ve
Heykel
Müzesi

Deniz
Müzesi

Sarıyer, Yıldız

Dolapdere Cad.

Ömer Hayyam Cad.

Kurdele Sok.

Adam Mickiewicz Müzesi

TAKSİM
PARKI

İnönü
Stadyumu

Çamlı
Köşk

Beşiktaş

Bahriye

Tarlabaşı

Sıraselviler Caddesi

Ağa

Tak-I-
Zafer

Atatürk Kültür Merkezi
(Cultural Centre)

Dolmabahçe
Sarayı
(Palace)

Dolmabahçe
Saat Kulesi

Dolmabahçe

Kamer
Hatun

Çiçek
Pasajı

İstiklâl

Taksim
Meydanı

Aya
Triada

Kazancı
Mescidi

Kabataş
İskelesi

Üsküdar

Bedreddin

Kasımpaşa
Stadı

Galatasaray
Hamamı

Galatasaray
Lisesi

Kasım
Paşa

Büyük
Kasımpaşa

Saydam

Pera Palas
Oteli

St
Anthony
of Padua

Çukurcuma

Firuzağa

Cihangir

Fındıklı Molla
Çelebi

Evliya Çelebi Cad.

TÜNEL

Tomtom
Kaptan

Hacıpiri

Kumrulu
Sok.

Mimar Sinan
Üniversitesi

Boğaziçi
(Bosphorus)

Üsküdar

Refik

Tünel

Neve
Shalom

Tünel
Meydanı

Galata
Mevlevihane

Tophane
Çeşmesi

Tophane
Binası

Nusretiye

Necatibey

BEYOĞLU

Azapkapı
Çeşmesi

Galata
Kulesi

Hoca Ali

Kılıç Ali
Paşa

Saat Kulesi

Köprüsü

Azapkapı
Sokollu
Mehmet
Paşa

Arap

Tersane Cad.

Kemeraltı

Cad.

Tünel

Yeraltı

Yolcu Salonu
Denizilik Bankası

KARAKÖY

Karaköy
Meydanı

EMİNÖNÜ

Ahi Çelebi

Sobacılar Cad.

Rüstem Paşa

Mısır Çarşısı
(Spice Bazaar)

Hatice Turhan
Sultan Türbesi

CAĞALOĞLU

Yeni

Arpacılar

Eminönü
İskelesi

Eminönü
Meydanı

Reşadiye Cad.

Galata Köprüsü

Sultan
Hamit
Türbesi

Sirkeci Garı

Sirkeci
İskelesi

SARAY
BURNU

Atatürk
Heykeli

Kennedy (Sahil Yolu) Caddesi

Harem

Fuat Paşa Cad.

Atik İbrahim
Paşa

Aşirefendi Cad.

Hoca Hanı Sok.

Daye Hatun
Mescidi

Goller Sütunu
(Goths Column)

GÜLHANE
PARKI

Bab-ı Ali

Topkapı Sarayı
(Topkapı Palace)

Mahmut Paşa

Bab-ı Ali

Beyazıt

Kapalı Çarşı
(Grand Bazaar)

Nuruosmaniye

Cağaloğlu
Hamamı

Molla
Fenari

Aya İrini

Konstantin Sütu

Kennedy (Sahil Yolu) Cad.

Haydarpaşa, Kadıköy

Cad.

Gedikpaşa C. Sok.

Babıali Cad.

Yerebatan Sarayı
(Basilica Cistern)

Aya Sofya

Ahmet III Çeşmesi

Divanyolu Cad.

SULTAN
AHMET
PARKI

Marmara Denizi

(Sea of Marmara)

Piyerloti Cad.

İbrahim Paşa
Sarayı

Alman
Çeşmesi

Sultan Ahmet I
(Blue Mosque)

Cankurtaran
İsk.

Ahırkapı
Feneri

Kadıköy

Gedikpaşa Cad.

Kadırga Limanı Cad.

SULTANAHMET

Kabasakal
Cad.

Cankurtaran Cad.

Ahır Kapı

Cankurtaran
İlkokulu

Kennedy

Küçük Aya
Sofya

Nakilbent

Cankurtaran Cad.

(Sahil Yolu)

Caddesi

Istanbul

0   500 m

0   500 yds

Yalova

IN THE NEIGHBOURHOOD

Like most megacities, Istanbul is a series of joined up villages, many of which have managed to keep their original character and architecture

Map on page 134

F ew tourists stray beyond the confines of the Old City and the quaint neighbourhoods along the Asian shore of the Bosphorus – the neighbourhoods which have suffered least from modern redevelopment. Medieval street plans, fortunately, are unaccommodating to heavy traffic, and since mosques cannot be knocked down, these oldest neighbourhoods have by and large been spared the rampant building that has turned the outer suburbs into a wasteland of anonymous, crumbling tower blocks.

However, if you don't explore further, you could be shortchanging yourself and missing some of Istanbul's liveliest – and most historic – quarters. What is usually described as the "new" city in guidebooks (the Taksim area across the Golden Horn from Aya Sofya) is not new at all; Pera reached its peak at the turn of the 20th century, and has actually been settled since Byzantine times. The really new business heart of the city is further out, in Mecidiyeköy, Levent and İstinye, while the "des res" neighbourhoods are increasingly in satellite cities such as Büyükçekmege and Zekeriyeköy.

The Imperial City

Seraglio Point **❶**, the grand hill overlooking the Marmara Sea, the Bosphorus and the Golden Horn, is at it its best seen from a distance, when the domes, minarets, palaces and other grand architecture of emperors and sultans are displayed to magnificent advantage in the city's world-famous skyline. This area has been the watchtower of the world's crossroads for 2,000 years. Most of it is taken up by the vast bulk of the splendid Topkapı Palace. Sadly, most of the grand gardens which ran down to the sea and around the hillside have now been given over to a railway, a main road, poor housing and tourist kiosks. What remains is the decidedly downmarket Gülhane Park, the haunt of poor families and penniless soldiers. But a walk up behind the seedy funfair, towards the Archaeology Museum, Aya Irini, and the Imperial Mint may give a taste of the peace of times past, as do some of the wooden houses in this area, now lovingly restored as upmarket pensions for rich tourists.

Sultanahmet **❷** takes up the rest of the peninsula. This is where the city's famous sites cluster around Aya Sofya and the Blue Mosque. Beyazıt **❸**, next door, is the home of the Süleymaniye Mosque, and famed as an international trading centre crammed with people and goods from all over the world. It is also a student haunt with the Istanbul University at its heart. An always crowded tram line runs through its heart, from the Eminönü docks to the neighbourhoods of Bayrampaşa and Esenler and the central bus garage.

LEFT: catching up with the gossip.
BELOW: book bazaar in Beyazıt.

Colourful essential oils on sale in the Spice Market – for blending your own perfumes.

The market place

High rents have pushed many of the original spice dealers out of the Spice Bazaar in **Eminönü** but they aren't lost, they've just moved to the area at the back and to the right of the Bazaar in **Tahtakale ❹**. Here is the flavour of the souks of yore, the heady scent of ground coffee, cinnamon, cumin and myrrh, and the clanging of hammers from the copper merchants. The goods are a bit tacky but there is almost nothing you can't find here, from plastic kitchenware to camel bells, rush-seated furniture and hand-turned bowls.

The Byzantine fisherman's harbour at **Kumkapı ❺** has always been a little rough, home to kind of carousing you associate with sailors, but fishermen still work here and its seafood restaurants are famous. Sadly, Kumkapı has been on the tourist trail for decades and the touting gets wearisome. It offers a wild night out, but guard against pickpockets and always check your bill carefully.

Aksaray ❻ offers some good and inexpensive hotels, but is largely the realm of "suitcase traders" from the former Soviet states – even most of the shop

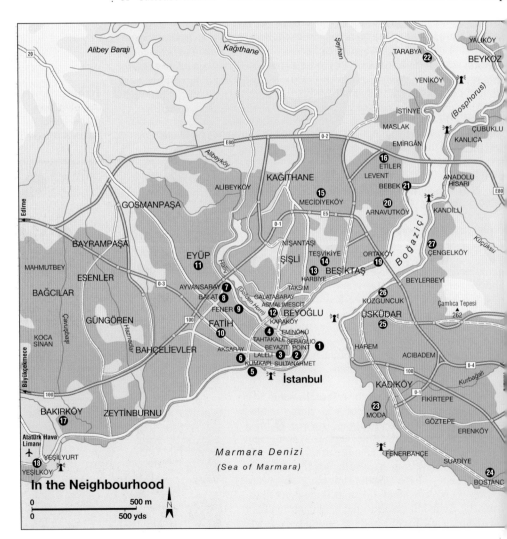

In the Neighbourhood

Marmara Denizi
(Sea of Marmara)

0   500 m
0   500 yds

signs are in Russian. There's not much to interest tourists, but there is of course the irresistible lure of the **Grand Bazaar**. Central Asian sellers squat all around the bazaar, hawking cheap Caucasian carpets.

So-named for the Ottoman breeding grounds and stables which once thrived here, **Ayvansaray ➐** is best reached after a visit to Kariye Camii. Follow the old city walls downwards towards the Golden Horn and you can easily picture sleepy Istanbul a century ago, full of huge plane trees and old wooden houses. **Balat ➑** has been a Jewish neighbourhood since Byzantine times, and though the community has dwindled, many historic synagogues remain. **Fener ➒** was home to a large Greek community and the Greek Orthodox Patriarchate is still here, along with many other lovely churches.

Don't look for a cold beer in **Fatih ➓** or **Eyüp ⓫**: the number of women wearing the full black *çarşaf* should tip you off that these are religious neighbourhoods and you should behave (and dress) respectfully.

The "new" city

Across the Golden Horn, the area surrounding the **Galata Kulesi (Tower)** has many buildings of historic interest – this was traditionally the foreigners' enclave, and after World War I it was occupied by the British. Today, however, the area is locked in a cultural tug-of-war between the east Anatolian poor, the Islamic municipal government, illegal lamp factories (who bribe the municipality to continue their toxic trade), and a group of artsy, "intellectual" Galata residents dedicated to preservation and restoration of the old buildings.

Across the bottom of Tünel Meydanı, a beautiful passage filled with cafés, antique and art shops leads to **Asmalımescit ⓬**, a neighbourhood with at least

Map on page 134

BELOW: Beyazıt Square throngs with street traders.

40 artists' studios and a few small galleries. Trendiness and high rents are driving the poorer artists out, but it is still where they come to drink and play *tavla* in the little restaurants that line Jurnal and Şeyhbender streets.

On a Saturday night it can be hard to walk from Galatasaray to Taksim due to the crowds – this is the focus of Istanbul's nightlife. The elegant passages of old Pera now house fashionable eateries, bars and theatres. But be careful if you stray from İstiklal Caddesi – drinking to excess is a popular local pastime, clip joints abound and bag snatches are common. Off Turnacıbaşı Sokak, in Galatasaray, is **Çukurcuma** famed for antique stores and old junk dealers.

New money

Valikonaşı Caddesi begins at the right hand fork past **Harbiye** ⓭ and marks the start of one of Istanbul's prime and most expensive shopping districts. With their antique showrooms, designer clothes boutiques and interior décor shops, the areas of **Teşvikiye** ⓮ and **Nişantaşı** are where the old money traditionally resides. A peek into the shops and galleries at ground level reveals high style.

The modern business district is centred in the traffic snarl of **Mecidiyeköy** ⓯, stretching outwards to **Etiler** ⓰, and also Levent,which are more residential. Made up mainly of modern highrises, these areas have little appeal for the short-term visitor, but it's worth knowing that this is where you'll find many of the city's most fashionable restaurants, catering for international business clientele.

Green shores

Bakırköy ⓱ and **Yeşilköy** ⓲ ("copper village" and "green village" respectively) are old-fashioned suburbs on the Marmara near the airport which have

BELOW: view from the Galata Tower.

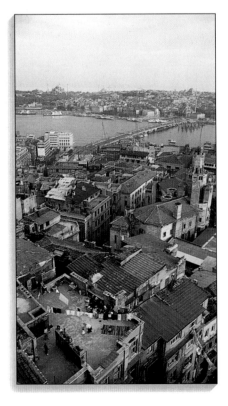

THE BIGGER PICTURE

The view from Galata Bridge provides a classic photograph of the city's skyline, although that perfect Golden Horn skyline of minarets is best viewed from the top of Galata Tower at sunset. At the back of Topkapı Palace, the Mecidiye Köşk (site of the Konak restaurant) provides a superb view over the Sea of Marmara. While for the brave, the view from the middle of the Boğaziçi or Fatih suspension bridges over the Bosphorus is literally breathtaking

Beyazıt Kulesi, the spire at the centre of Istanbul University, was used as a fire watch-tower when the old palace was here. Built in 1828, this structure still provides a bird's-eye view of the city. In fact, you get a marvellous vista from the rooftop bars and restaurants of most major hotels, such as the Hilton, the Ceylan Intercontinental and the Marmara. Bilsak 5th Floor, an artsy club at Soğanc Sokak in Cihangir (near Taksim) is also famed for its view

On the Asian side, the top of Çamlıca Hill has a delightful early 20th-century café and tea garden (currently under the control of the Islamic municipal government, keeping prices low and alcohol out), from where you can enjoy more splendid views.

The Walls of Theodosius are best viewed from the towers at Yedikule.

some excellent seaside restaurants and hotels perfect for short stays. The coastal villages on the European side of the Bosphorus, meanwhile, have been spared vicious development because of their historical past and because the roads connecting them are so narrow; and though property is like gold dust, most retain their village feel due to preservation orders on the old wooden mansions.

The harbour area in **Ortaköy** ❶ is now a bustling enclave of cafés, clubs, and shops especially busy on Sunday, street market day. **Arnavutköy** ❷ is dominated by Robert College and the University of the Bosphorus, the city's most prestigious schools, and has a number of rather offbeat bars, cafés and restaurants. In **Bebek** ❸ the feel of money gets more serious – it is one of Istanbul's classiest neighbourhoods. Likewise **İstinye**, once a seaside village, is near the city's effervescent new Stock Exchange building, and soaring upmarket as a result. **Tarabya** ❹ and **Rumelihisarı** are two of several Bosphorus villages famed for their posh fish restaurants.

The Asian suburbs

Most visitors feel a noticeable change in atmosphere once they step off the boat at Kadıköy. The coastal area from **Moda** ❺ to **Bostancı** ❻ is decidedly upper-middle class, modern, liberal and lacking the tension between poor migrants and old Istanbul money palpable elsewhere. There are many private language schools here and foreign teachers remark, ironically, how "European" it is – from the café streets around Miralay Nazım Sokak to the bars in the old restored houses of Kadife Caddesi in Moda. Prices get higher and shops flashier the further down the 6-mile (10-km) long Bağdat Caddesi you go.

Üsküdar ❼ is a traditional religious neighbourhood with plenty of Ottoman

Map on page 134

BELOW: coffee and cards in Üsküdar.

Map on page 134

buildings but no nightlife to speak of – which is pretty much the case all along the Asian shores, and part of its appeal. Alcohol is hard to find, but Üsküdar in particular has some truly excellent traditional restaurants and the historical waterfront teagardens of **Kuzguncuk** ❷ and **Çengelköy** ❷ are calming.

Local markets

Street markets generally provide a greater variety of goods than shops and at better prices. You can taste a huge range of cheeses and olives, or find village bread or unusual salad ingredients such as sorrel. Indian-made clothes have caught on, and you can also find cut-price fabrics like linen. You can't miss the street sellers in **Eminönü** – they are everywhere from Yeni Cami to the back of the Süleymaniye mosque and around the Grand Bazaar itself. A farmers' market, beside the Spice Bazaar, is one of the best in the city, and at weekends **Beyazıt Square** fills up with Central Asian traders who sell carpets and lovely embroidered silks among other things.

The market area near Fenerbahçe Stadium in **Kadıköy** covers over a square mile on Tuesdays, making it the biggest in the city. Half of it is devoted to fruit and vegetables and half to cheap clothing and household goods. There's a smaller market on Fridays and at weekends; on Sunday you can pick up anything from pricy antiques to junk and the inevitable plastic kitchenware. By contrast, in **Ulus**, an upmarket neighbourhood near Etiler, the Thursday market is famous for designer clothes straight from the factories. An excellent vegetable market is held on Wednesdays in **Yeşilköy**, and on Sundays the restored harbour area at **Ortaköy** is taken over by a craft market with lots of jewellery, locally made clothing, books and antiques. ❑

BELOW: local boys at the Çinili Cami, Üsküdar.

Sporting Istanbul

Many people would claim that the authentic spirit of Istanbul is found not in the Grand Bazaar or Taksim Square, but in a football stadium. **Football** is a national passion that reaches its apogee in Istanbul, home to the three most significant, successful and glamorous clubs in the Turkish Premier League: *Galatasaray* (red and yellow), *Fenerbahçe* (blue and yellow), and *Beşiktaş* (black and white).

It's difficult to avoid the latest results and rivalry. Every weekend evening in season (Aug–May), the big matches are shown live on cable TV, and people gather in bars and tea-houses for 90 minutes of animated viewing, followed by rowdy celebrations with tooting cars and flag-waving supporters.

As a tourist, choosing allegiance and wearing a hat or scarf guarantees you friends and conversation, and a match is an enjoyable way to experience a genuine slice of Turkish life. It's usually safe (Turkish fans don't get drunk), and cheap and easy to get a ticket. The atmosphere is electric. Floodlit matches are highlighted by coloured flares and fireworks, streamers, confetti, chants and songs (often obscene – it's probably better not to understand them!) and frantic scarf-waving.

Basketball is another popular national sport and the one in which Turkey enjoys the most success. Efes Pilsen won the European Radivoj Korac Cup in 1996 – the country's greatest achievement in a team game. Most domestic Turkish clubs, such as *Efes Pilsen*, *Ulker* or *Fenerbahçe,* are privately sponsored and wealthy, and women's basketball is also well supported.

It's thought that **horse-racing** has existed in Anatolia since the 1300s, and a visit to the races is still an entertaining afternoon (every Sat, Sun, Mon and Tues in summer). Betting is taken seriously and if you're unfamiliar with the system, anyone will be happy to explain it – and offer their own tips!

Away from the mainstream, Turkey takes great pride in its heritage of traditional sports. Most famous is **oil wrestling**, or *yagli*

gures, where men wear nothing but black leather breeches and cover their bodies with olive oil to wrestle. Apart from the big annual festival in Kırkpınar (*see page 245*), smaller festivals are held in summer throughout Turkey, some around the Istanbul area.

Camel wrestling is an intriguing winter sport, in which two camels try to overbalance each other. It isn't as cruel as it sounds; male camels fight in the wild. These festivals last all day with music, dancing, eating and drinking – and around 80 camels who fight in pairs in the arena. The closest bouts to Istanbul are held in villages around Çanakkale from December to March.

Cirit is a sport common to east Turkey, a dramatic team game of horseback javelin. For the last few years, Kagithane Belediye (municipality) has organised a competition in northern Istanbul in June (*see Travel Tips*).

Watching sport makes an unusual break from sightseeing. Whether it's 22 men kicking a ball or two camels trying to overbalance each other, it will give you an insight into the modern Turkish way of life. ❏

RIGHT: "Futball" fanaticism starts young in Istanbul, home to three top teams.

SULTANAHMET – THE OLD CITY

Map
on page
144

*Since 650 BC, this tiny peninsula has been the heart of
powerful kingdoms and empires, and the site of fabled palaces,
magnificent churches and mosques*

It can be extremely difficult to visualise Byzantine Istanbul in Sultanahmet as you see it today. So much of Constantine's New Rome has been taken over by Islamic buildings and tourist facilities that remnants of the gold-studded palace walls, mechanical birds, voluptuous gardens, elegant fora and mosaics are scant indeed and may lead one to imagine the whole thing was a fairytale invented for visitors. It is only with a vivid imagination and a bird's-eye view that something of the structure of this mythical city – which was very much real – can begin to be mentally reconstructed.

Byzantion

When Constantine founded his New Rome in AD 326, he quickly sought to fill it with the treasures of the ancient world, and reconstruct the buildings of old Rome. The result was a unique blend of classical paganism and the more recent Christianity, even though this did not become the official state religion until the reign of Theodosius I, some 60 years later. St Jerome, who believed that "celibacy populates heaven", fumed that Constantinople was now "clothed in the nudity of every other city" as the emperor ransacked the remains of the empire for temple statues, even including Anatolian fertility goddesses in the trawl. Yet Constantine had not arrived to empty fields – the city was already nearly 1,000 years old, and he was unquestionably able to incorporate a great deal of what was already there in his grand new design.

In the 7th century BC, the city of **Byzantion** is thought to have covered the area of Seraglio Point and beyond, surrounded by walls considered amongst the strongest in the Greek world. The Sirkeci area, today bustling with trams, ferries, cars and a railway station, was the ancient harbour. The area surrounding Gülhane Park, the Archaeology Museum, and up into Cağaloğlu was the site of temples, bath houses, a gymnasium and stadium. One statue of Venus was reputed to embarrass young women pretending to be virgins by tossing up their skirts as they passed.

The acropolis, on which stood the royal palace of Byzantion as well as temples dedicated to the entire Greek pantheon, was located where the second court-yard of Topkapı Palace is now. This may explain why the Byzantine emperors built their own palace on the slopes of the Marmara and not on today's Seraglio Point – the ancient buildings of the acropolis were still in use. The Greek necropolis stretched out along Divanyolu Caddesi while the city agora was situated at Ayasofya Meydanı, built around a column of the Thracian god Zeuxippos. However, Constantine did replace this statue, with one of his mother, Augusta Helena, whom he sent to Jerusalem to look for cart-

PRECEDING PAGES:
minarets and
domes of Islamic
Istanbul.
LEFT: obelisk and
Blue Mosque.
BELOW: Constantine
founding the city.

Sultanahmet

| 0 | 200 m |
| 0 | 200 yds |

Map on page 144

...ads of relics. During her hunt for suitable trophies, she managed to "discover" many of the world's holiest sites, including the Holy Sepulchre. She returned triumphantly with cartloads of trophies, in particular a fragment of the True Cross, ...ssuring that new Byzantium would capture the market for Christendom.

Central square

...ith 2,500 years of history to consider, take a deep breath and a moment's ...eflection before you set out on your sightseeing journey around Sultanahmet ...r you risk walking right past the remains of New Rome without recognising it.

The faded, tomato red walls and gigantic dome of **Aya Sofya ❶** (*see page ...46*), have dominated the city for more than 1,500 years. This is your guiding ...andmark. **Ayasofya Meydanı**, the square in front of the great church, is today ... parking lot for tour buses, filled with souvenir vendors and newspaper kiosks. ...ut throughout Byzantine times and earlier this was the agora, called the ...ugusteion, a porticoed ceremonial courtyard containing the senate building and ...illared statues.

Stand with your back to Aya Sofya and imagine that before you stretches the ...reat Palace of Constantinople, which once covered all of Sultanahmet, from ...he Hippodrome (At Meydanı) to the Church of Saints Sergius and Bacchus ...now the Küçük Aya Sofya Cami; see p. 146). It included the Magnaura Palace, ...he remains of which can be found in the heart of the backpacker neighbour-...ood, between Akbıyık Caddesi, and the Sea of Marmara.

The Imperial Palace

...he entrance to the palace complex, at Chalke Gate, was roughly along today's ...abasakal Caddesi, the street that leads from Aya-...ofya Meydanı to the Yeşil Ev Hotel and the **Mehmet ...fendi Medresesi** (Istanbul Crafts Centre). This gate, ...f which nothing remains, was once topped with a ...iant mosaic of Christ, with Emperor Maurice ...582–602) and family beneath, receiving divine bless-...ng. It was destroyed by the iconoclast Leo III in 726, ...rovoking a riot led by the soon-to-be "St" Theodosia ...nd an army of angry women. Behind you, what is ...ow Babıhümayun Caddesi was a major thorough-...are running through the gates of what became **...opkapı Sarayı (Topkapi Palace) ❷** (*see page 161*), ...ver the acropolis and down to the sea. Down the ...lope to your left are the walls of the Marmara shore. ...he colonnaded street for royal processions, the Mese, ...vas off to your right, roughly following Divanyolu ...addesi through modern Beyazıt, along the route of ...he crowded tram which runs out to the city's main ...us terminal and beyond. This street led to the mag-...ificent circular Forum of Constantine and on to the ...olden Gate, with luxury shops at ground level and ...tatues above. All that now remains is a rather unim-...ressive piece of stone which was once the "Milion", ... structure representing Point Zero from which all ...oads leading out of the city were measured.

Most of the Great Palace now lies beneath the even ...ore famous **Sultan Ahmet I Cami (Blue Mosque) ❸** ...*see page 154*), and there are few records which

Guidebooks on sale in Ayasofya Meydanı, tourist heartland of the city.

BELOW: the face of old Istanbul.

describe its interior in any detail. One exception was the record of improvements made by the 9th-century Emperor Theophilus, who added many ceremonial halls and pavilions to the palace. He leant towards oriental tastes with names such as "Pavilion of the Pearl" and the "Chamber of Love" and is thought to have been inspired by descriptions of the Abbasid Caliph's capital in Baghdad. He also impressed visitors with mechanical devices such as bronze lions that wagged their tales and roared, golden birds that sang on silver trees and a throne that rose into the air, to the astonishment of one visiting ambassador.

Last vestiges of glory

The closest glimpse you are likely to get of the palace interior today is behind the Arasta Bazaar, at the **Mozaik Müzesi (Mosaic Museum)** (Arastı Çarşısı; open 9.30am–4.30pm; closed Tues; entrance fee) which shows part of the vast courtyard floor thought to have been built by Justinian in the 6th century. This courtyard probably connected the royal apartments to the residential Palace of Daphne and the *kathisma*, the imperial box at the Hippodrome, providing a convenient escape route for the royal family as sports-arena hooliganism is nothing new. Its exquisite mosaics depict wild or domestic animals and hunting scenes and are considered to show the Roman-Hellenistic tradition at its finest.

The remains of the **Bukoleon Sarayı (Bucoleon Palace)** , which bordered on the emperor's private harbour, are sadly difficult to view today as trains from Sirkeci Station follow this route and the area is a bit rough – women are not advised to walk here alone. You can still reach them by taking the paths under the railways at Cankurtaran Caddesi or Nakilbent Sokak and walking along the coast road of Kennedy Caddesi, following the ancient sea walls. But all that remains are three high, marble-framed windows and the corbels of a vast balcony that must have commanded a breathtaking view of domestic caiques and naval vessels protecting the city from invaders. Just to the east of the windows is the ruin of a Byzantine lighthouse, the **Pharos**.

A little west of the Bucoleon Palace, the **Küçük Aya Sofya Cami** (Church of SS Sergius and Bacchus; Küçük Ayasofya Cami Sokak, open at all times except during prayers) was built by Justinian and Theodora in 527. Its mosaics are gone, but the dark green and red marble columns and carved frieze are original. The Greek inscription on the frieze mentions the founders and the saints after whom the church is named, Roman centurions who converted to Christianity and whom Justinian credited with saving his life through a dream. It became a mosque in around 1500.

Aya Sofya

Aya Sofya (Haghia Sophia, the Church of Divine Wisdom; tel: 212-522 1750; open 9.30am–4.30pm, closed Monday; entrance fee) is not only the main Byzantine building still standing in Istanbul but the most spectacular religious edifice in the city, a vast domed structure whose atmosphere is dense with nearly 1,500 years of human faith and prayer. So powerful is its impact that when Mehmet the Con-

When it was finally sacked by crusaders in 1204, the Great Palace was described as containing 500 interconnected halls and 30 chapels decorated with sumptuous gold mosaics, depicting biblical scenes and the heroic feats of emperors.

BELOW: the massive courtyard mosaic, last remnants of the Great Palace.

Map on page 144

ueror took Constantinople in 1453 he ordered his soldiers to desist from pillaging the church while he prayed, dedicating it to Allah. Indeed very little amage was done to the structure but for the removal of some of the relief rosses. The fact that it is a museum today, which leaves out the troublesome uestion as to which religious community it rightfully belongs, does nothing to essen its spiritual power. Members of all beliefs may easily engage in silent evotions as they walk beneath its dark, lofty dome, disturbed only by the rauous appreciation of school tour groups.

Consecrated in 537, during the reign of Justinian, the current church was the iird to be built on the site, and until the conquest was the greatest ceremonial hurch of the empire. The first church burnt in 404, while the second, built by heodosius in 415, was torched during the Nika riots of 532. The present structure, whose dome has inspired religious architecture ever since, was designed y two Greek mathemeticians – Anthenius of Tralles and his assistant Isidorus f Miletus, who were able to apply to architecture the enormous strides that ad recently been made in geometry.

Unfortunately, part of the dome collapsed during an earthquake a mere 21 ears later, revealing a fault in the original plans – the dome was too shallow and he buttressing insufficient. New buttressing was frequently added over the next 00 years, but most of the interior reflects the original 6th-century design.

Borrowed glories

Most of the columns inside are thought to have been taken from pagan temples round the Mediterranean. Eight of green serpentine, under the arches of the ave, are thought to have come from the Temple of Diana in Ephesus, while the

BELOW:
Aya Sofya, one of the architectural wonders of the world.

Temple of the Sun at Baalbek provided the eight red ones of Egyptian porphyry on either side of the nave. The mosaic work in the narthex and the Vestibule of the Warriors dates from the 6th century but other figurative work was destroyed during the iconoclastic period between 729 and 843, so most surviving mosaics belong to a later date.

The public entrance is now through the nine-arched narthex that contains the Imperial Gate; in the past this was reserved strictly for Byzantine royalty and, at the time, popularly thought to be made from the wood of Noah's Ark. Above it is a late 9th-century mosaic featuring Christ with Emperor Leo VI kneeling possibly seeking forgiveness for enraging the Patriarch after too many marriages – he was banned from the church on several occasions. Off to the left is the "sweating column" where Justinian was said to have cured a migraine by resting his head against the stone. Centuries of visitors touching the spot have resulted in a deep dent, now framed in brass and called the "holy hole". Women in search of a husband are meant to put their thumb in the worn hole and twist their hand round 360°. To the right, over the exit, is a mosaic of the Virgin with Constantine and Justinian. Ahead of you, in the conch of the apse, is a particularly fine mosaic of the Virgin and Christ, thought to have been the first figurative work executed after the restoration of icons in 843.

Staffing Aya Sofya was no mean feat, requiring 60 priests, 100 deacons, 40 deaconesses, 90 subdeacons, 110 readers, 25 singers and 100 door keepers. This was expensive, and the church met its costs by keeping a monopoly on the burial business.

A reflection of heaven

The dome rises to 56 metres (183 ft) and rests on four enormous piers joined by equally huge arches. The church's awe-inspiring size was meant to reflect the realms of heaven, and the interior of the nave is indeed celestial in scope – thin marble panels absorbed and reflected the light of thousands of candles and lamps, which illuminated the entire building so well that it could be seen at sea like a lighthouse. The acoustics are staggering, making even the chatter of crowds seem like the murmuring of angels.

Of all the mosaics, the easiest to see are those in the galleries, which were used for worship by women in a way similar to mosques today. In the west gallery a green disk marks the spot where the empress' throne stood, and in the north gallery is a mosaic of the Emperor Alexander holding a skull. The south gallery holds the finest mosaics, including the *Deesis* (intercession) mosaic of Christ Pantocrator, John the Baptist and the Virgin Mary. In the last bay of this gallery is also the crude and curious mosaic of Christ with the Empress Zoë and her final husband, Constantine IX Monomachus, holding a money bag. It is commonly supposed that the empress' string of husbands was responsible for the changing face of the emperor in the mosaic as well as the inscriptions below, however the faces of Zoë and Christ have also been altered

Ottoman additions to Aya Sofya include the huge wooden shields emblazoned with gilded calligraphy of Qur'anic verses, which were added in the mid-19th century, the *mihrab* (niche) indicating the direction of Mecca, and the *minbar* (pulpit) put in by Murat III in the 16th century. Next to the *minbar* is a patterned piece of marble called the **coronation square**; the emperor's throne or omphalos, the official centre of

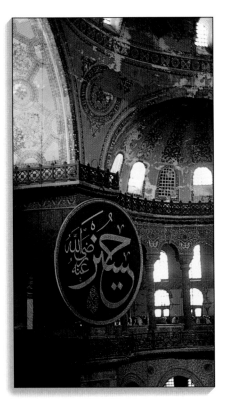

BELOW: Qur'anic inscriptions converted Aya Sofya to a mosque.

he world, was thought to have stood nearby. The loge of the sultans was added
•y the Fossati brothers, Italian-Swiss architects who undertook major restora-
ion for Sultan Abdülmecid in the mid 19th-century. In most senses, however,
he Ottomans generally, left well enough alone, and the mosaics were simply
vhitewashed over, which actually helped to preserve them. They were only
ıncovered again during renovations in the 1930s when Atatürk converted Aya
;ofya into a national museum.

As you leave, don't forget to turn around to catch the Donor mosaic, show-
ng Constantine and Justinian handing the city and the basilica to the Virgin
.nd Child. The structure on the left was the original church's baptismal rooms,
onverted by the Ottomans to tombs for sultans and princes.

ıya Irini

:he Ottoman willingness to recycle Christian monuments for their own use is
)art of the reason so many Byzantine churches remain standing today. They
.lso fared much better than the Imperial Palace in resisting the ravages of west-
•rn, Christian crusaders and time.

Aya Irini ❼ (Church of St Eirene), tucked inside the first gate of the Topkapı
'alace complex, is the oldest Christian site in the city. An old black and white
nosaic on the floor may have belonged to a temple of Aphrodite which previ-
)usly occupied the spot. The original structure, dedicated in 360, was the cathe-
lral of Constantinople until the construction of Aya Sofya, though the current
:hurch dates from the 6th century. Never converted to a mosque, Aya Irini was
ised as an arsenal by the Ottomans and is now a venue for concerts and visual
ırts events, primarily during the Istanbul Biennial festival. Striking in its

Map
on page
144

The gilded Sultan's
Loge was a flourish
added to Aya Sofya
in the late 19th
century.

BELOW:
mosaic of Jesus
Christ and John the
Baptist in Aya Sofya.

simplicity, the huge gold and black mosaic cross above the apse dates from the iconoclastic period in the early 8th century, while below is the only surviving *synthronon* (tiers of seats for bishops) in Istanbul. Unfortunately, however, Aya Irini is not officially a museum and many visitors to Istanbul manage to miss it as its opening times are erratic.

TIP

The Archaeology Museum (tel: 212-520 7740) opens from 9.30am–4.30pm; the Museum of the Ancient Orient opens 9.30am–noon, and the Tiled Pavilion from 1–4.30pm; all are closed on Monday. One ticket covers admission to all three sections.

BELOW: the Alexander Sarcophagus.

The Archaeology Museum

The courtyard behind the church was the resting place of the sarcophagi of Byzantine emperors until their removal to the imposing **Arkeoloji Müzesi** (**Archaeology Museum**) **8**, which can either be approached via a lane behind Aya Irini or from Gülhane Park. The **Çinili Köşk (Tiled Pavilion)** **9** and the **Eski Şark Eserleri Müzesi (Museum of the Ancient Orient)** **10** are also part of the complex.

The Archaeology Museum occupies a space that was once a playing field for the very old sport of *cirit*, a rougher version of today's polo, beloved by many sultans. The museum was founded in 1881 by Hamdi Bey, the son of a grand vizier and an artist with a keen interest in ancient history, whose first act was to put a stop to the export of antiquities from the Empire. The centrepiece of the museum is the collection of sarcophagi found during his excavations at the royal necropolis of Sidon in the Lebanon. Of them all, the finest is the superb **Alexander Sarcophagus**, built for a Sidonian king but depicting the victory of Alexander over the Persians in high relief. It was these finds that necessitated the building of the current museum, which now houses one of the finest collections of classical and pre-classical artefacts in the world.

Inside the entrance, you are greeted by the contorted face of the Egyptian

od Bes, who was meant to scare away evil spirits. Other exhibits include the world's oldest known peace agreement, the *Treaty of Kadesh*, made between the Egyptians and the Hittites in 1269 BC; the mummy of an Egyptian king; a number of Roman statues; remnants of Byzantine Constantinople such as one of the snake's heads from the Serpentine Column in the Hippodrome; lions from Bucoleon Palace; and a rare 7th-century mosaic which survived the iconoclastic era, found during excavation of the Kalenderhane Mosque.

One room is devoted to the mysterious Phrygians, including an 8th-century BC tomb with its grave goods intact, items from excavations at Troy, a copy of the facade of the Temple of Athena at Assos and some 3rd century BC figures of chubby boy temple prostitutes from a shrine of of Aphrodite in Cyprus. The **Museum of the Ancient Orient** displays Hittite finds as well as those from Mesopotamia and Egypt, and friezes from the Ishtar gate in Babylon. In the tile-clad **Çinili Köşk** are tiles and mosque lamps from the finest years of İznik ceramic production.

Map on page 144

Ceramic lion from the Ishtar Gate.

The Hippodrome

The famous **At Meydanı (Hippodrome)** ⓫, once the fire-breathing core of Constantinople, is now a public park. Nothing remains of the stadium itself, which used to hold up to 100,000 people. However, the street surrounding the green, which runs from Ayasofya Meydanı to Üçler Sokak and around to Divanyolu Caddesi, is thought to follow roughly the chariot race tracks beloved of the city at large and the root of many violent disruptions.

The importance of the Hippodrome is indicated by the three monoliths which remain of the many that once graced the arena. The **Dikilitaş** (Obelisk of

BELOW: the Serpentine Column, looted from Delphi.

FOR GOD AND THE TEAM

By the mid-4th century, popular interest in theological disputes reached such a pitch that one bishop remarked that if he complained about the price of bread, the baker would tell him the Father was greater than the Son, and if he asked the maid about his bath water she would reply that the Son was created out of nothing.

Early Byzantine beliefs had a social dimension that even affected the playing fields – chariot team supporters generally fell into groups based on the neighbourhoods in which they lived, and these differences led to tensions of a religious and political nature. The "Greens" tended to be the Monophysite lower classes, annoyed that the emperor was of a different persuasion, and the Blues, the Orthodox bourgeoisie, were hostile since Empress Theodora was a Monophysite and thus influenced Justinian.

According to the historian Procopius, Constantinople was full of gangs behaving like hooligans over religion. The anger that erupted during a match in 532 deteriorated into a mass riot of looting and burning known as the Nika Revolt, which went on for five days, inflamed by general hostility to high taxes imposed by the autocratic Justinian. The mercenary soldiers hired to quell the riots massacred an alleged 30,000 people and Aya Sofya was burned.

*Head of Medusa,
from a pagan temple,
recycled to build the
Yerebatan Sarayı.*

BELOW: the many
columns of the
superb Sunken
Palace.
RIGHT: Ottoman
minarets soar
skywards.

Pharaoh Thutmose III), dating from the mid 15th-century BC, was brought b
Constantine from Karnak in Egypt – its heiroglyphs extol the Pharaoh's victorie
on the Euphrates. It stands on a 4th-century base showing Constantine'
successor, Theodosius I and family, watching a race from the royal box. Th
sides depict the new emperor crowning victors and receiving tribute from cap
tives and the erection of the obelisk itself. Nearby, the **Yilanlı Sütun** (Serpen
tine Column) is another of Constantine's imports, this time from the Temple o
Apollo at Delphi. It was originally created as an offering of thanks to the go
by the 31 cities who defeated the Persians at Plataea in 479 BC and was mad
from the shields captured as booty. Three snakes' heads once supported a golde
tripod holding a golden vase, but the gold was gone before Constantine gc
hold of it and the heads were knocked off in the 18th century. One is in th
Archaeology Museum. Little is known about the last monument in the Hippc
drome, referred to as the **Ormetaş** (Column of Constantine VII Porphyrc
genitus), though it was thought to have been cased in bronze by the 10th-centur
emperor and inscribed with the deeds of his grandfather. The bronze, howeve
was carried off by the crusaders and the monument later used for scaling prac
tice by Janissary recruits under the Ottomans.

The Sunken Palace

The royal palace complex's considerable water supply came from the fabulou
Yerebatan Sarayı (Basilica Cistern) **⓬**, directly across the tram line o
Ayasofya Meydanı (Yerebatan Caddesi, open daily 9am–5pm; entrance fee
Popularly known as the Sunken Palace, it was begun by Constantine an
expanded by Justinian in 532. Today, it provides a unique attraction, an eerily

lit underground chamber, with a vast cathedral-like ceiling supported by 336 columns. It still contains a few feet of water over which bridges and walkways have been constructed, with classical music played to enhance the atmosphere. It has been used as a film set, for concerts and for audio-visual installations during the Istanbul Biennial Festival. The giant Medusa heads, one on its side, were undoubtedly recycled from pre-Christian ruins, as were most of the other columns.

The area around another Byzantine cistern, the Byzantine **Binbirdirek Sarnıcı** ⓭, or Cistern of 1,001 Columns (Klodfarer Caddesi; currently closed for renovation), is now a bazaar. Thought to be the work of Anthemius of Tralles, the daring architect of Ayasofya, this astonishing cistern predates the Yerebatan Sarayı by several hundred years.

Map
on page
144

Islamic Istanbul

Mehmet the Conqueror had no wish to see Constantinople ravaged by pillage and massacre when he took the city in May 1453, for he regarded it as the linchpin of his own dominion and freely acknowledged the city's religious importance. Islam regards Jesus as an early prophet and Christians as "people of the book". Fatih Mehmet thus sought to enrich, not destroy what was already there.

After the obligatory three-day pillage, allowing soldiers to reap spoils of their victory as reward, the sultan set about making the city as beautiful as it had been 900 years before, but this time in the name of Allah and his prophet Mohammed. With the help of the undisputed genius of the architect, Mimar Sinan, he began to create the famous skyline of minarets and domes that lends Istanbul an atmosphere of story-book splendour.

BELOW: the towering domes of the splendid Blue Mosque.

Designed to prove the superiority of Islam, the Blue Mosque remains symbolic to Muslims, and is occasionally the site of fundamentalist-led protests at state intervention in religious affairs – such as a recent obligatory education programme limiting religious instruction for children under twelve.

BELOW: steps and courtyards lead the faithful to prayer in the Blue Mosque.

Western scholars have traditionally failed to pay due attention to the splendid architecture of Istanbul. Some suggest it is due to "guilt" suffered over the abandonment of the once-Christian capital to the Muslim invaders, but when the Conqueror broke through the walls, Constantinople was a dilapidated city of no more than 50,000 people, thanks mostly to the ravages of the western, Christian crusaders. The classical statues had been stolen or sold, the lead roof of the Great Palace melted down for coins, and the once-great empire shrunk pathetically to a few coastal districts and the Peloponnese islands.

The Blue Mosque

The most famous, if not necessarily the most beautiful, mosque in the old city is the **Sultan Ahmet I Cami** or **Blue Mosque** (always open except prayer times), which faces Aya Sofya across Sultanahmet Meydanı, its domes and minarets echoing those of the older church. The complex is entered through a massive ceremonial gate off the Hippodrome, roughly where the royal box for the chariot races must have stood. The entrance to the mosque itself is to the left.

The imposing Sultan Ahmet Camii was clearly designed to compete with the glory of Aya Sofya, its interior walls clad in the exquisite blue İznik tiles which give the building its nickname. It was constructed between 1609 and 1616 by the architect Mehmet Ağa, a student of the great architect Sinan. The mosque contains 260 windows, once glazed with Venetian glass, as well as a *medrese*, hospital, caravansaray and soup kitchen (a *külliye* or "complete social centre" in the Islamic sense). Its six minarets caused a major controversy since this was as many as on the great mosque in Mecca; the Sultan had to donate an extra minaret to Mecca to quell the row.

STRUCTURES OF GOD

To look at the architectural design plans of mosques is to see something of the mysticism once associated with geometry, for these are drawings of great beauty, with their symmetry radiating outwards like a giant sunwheel or mandala. In Islam, the abode of Allah has no defined physical space and the mediation of Pope or priest is deemed unnecessary, thus there is no seating or altar, no place for procession, font or holy icon. A metaphor of Islam could be the desert, a place of great search and longing, undertaken in solitude and silence. Desert nomads needed fixed points of orientation as well as oases with shade and water (described as aspects of paradise in the Qur'an). The mosque fulfilled the role of this oasis.

The prayer hall is designed with minimum encumbrance. The *mihrab*, the conical niche pointing out the direction of Mecca, suggests the abstract and unknowable in a kind of negative space, and the cupola, floating lightly at the summit, is a symbol of transcendence. The cupola also had its secular uses in shedding sand, keeping interiors cool and improving acoustics. The wall holding the mihrab is the *kibla*, and to the right while praying, the *minbar* (or *mimber*) is the steep staircase topped by a conical pulpit from which the imam leads the prayers.

When the mosque was commissioned, Sultan Ahmet was only 19, though he had been on the throne throughout his teen years and roundly criticised for the amount of time he spent with his harem. If he meant the building of the new mosque to be an act of atonement, however, it failed, for he was admonished by the *ulema*, the religious directors, for the time and expense it incurred. The site was occupied not only by the remains of the Great Palace but by that of the palace of Sokollu Mehmet Paşa, which had to be purchased and demolished at great expense. But the young sultan got what he wanted, including the satisfaction of his passion for tiles, of which there are 50 different kinds, putting such dreadful pressure on the İznik manufacturers that it is thought to have contributed to the deterioration of their art. Sultan Ahmet himself dug the first turf in 1617, only to die of typhus a few years later. He and his notorious wife Kösem Sultan (strangled in 1651) are buried here, together with three of his sons.

Just looking...

The Imperial Pavilion at the back of the mosque, once the entrance to the loge of the sultans, now houses the **Hünkar Kasrı** (Museum of Turkish Carpets and Kilims; open 9am–noon, 1–4pm; closed Sat and Sun; entrance fee). This small but inspirational collection of antique carpets is a good place to familiarise yourself with Turkish style and quality without pressure. If you are inspired to buy, the **Haseki Hürrem Hamamı ⓮**, built as a bath house by Sinan in 1556, for Süleyman the Magnificent's wife Roxelana, is now home to the state-run **Turkish Handwoven Carpets Exhibition** (Ayasofya Meydanı; open 9am–5pm; closed Sun and Mon). It has expert staff and reasonable prices, though it smells sadly of damp – which is what you might expect putting wool carpets in a hamam.

Map on page 144

Some of the fabulous İznik tiles which give the Blue Mosque its nickname.

BELOW: the Blue Mosque's elaborate ceiling.

Map on page 144

Anatolian nomadic exhibition at the Museum of Turkish and Islamic Arts.

BELOW: painted wooden ceiling, Museum of Turkish and Islamic Arts.

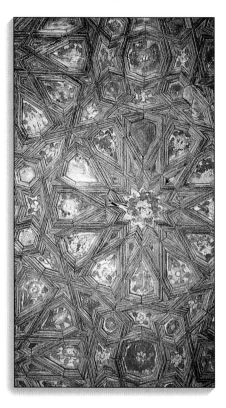

The **Sokollu Mehmet Paşa Cami** ⑮ (Şehit Çeşmesi Sokak; always open except prayer times) is one of Mimar Sinan's architectural triumphs, and is undoubtedly among the most beautiful mosques in the city. It was built from 1571–2, when the architect was 80 years old and was seeking to resolve certain design problems that had previously plagued him. Sokollu Mehmet Paşa (assassinated in 1578) was grand vizier to Selim II and considered one of the most refined and capable diplomats of his time. It is thought that Sinan wished to design a mosque reflecting the character of its benefactor, with colour highlighting certain symbolic functions. In this mosque, as in no other, light refracted from 206 windows dominates the interior, a suggestive metaphor of Islamic paradise. The cupola has 24 windows. The *kibla* around the carved *mihrab* and the top of the *minbar* are entirely covered in blue and green İznik tiles, especially in the *majolica* (the central part of the *kibla* around the *mihrab*) as is the door opposite the *mihrab*.

An essential visit for history lovers is the **İbrahim Paşa Sarayı** ⑯, the palace opposite the Blue Mosque, which today houses the **Museum of Turkish and Islamic Arts** (At Meydanı 46; open 9.30am–5pm; closed Mon; entrance fee). This is considered to be one of the best museums in the country as well as one of the finest extant Ottoman residential buildings in Istanbul. Originally built in 1524 for one of Süleyman the Magnificent's grand viziers, the quality and location of the structure points to a man of great wealth and power who ruled as second in command for 13 years before Roxelana, who perceived him to be a threat to her own power, persuaded her husband to have him strangled. The museum contains more than 40,000 items dating back as far as the earliest period of Islam under the Omayyad caliphate (661–750). It specialises in religious artefacts and historic carpets. The exhibition on the ground floor shows the evolution of the Turkish domestic interior from nomadic tent to a modern Turkish home.

Bath time

In a small street situated on the other side of Divanyolu Caddesi, the 300-year-old baroque **Cağaloğlu Hamamı** ⑰ is definitely worth a stop even if you don't want a Turkish bath (Prof. Kazım Ismail Gürkan Caddesi 34; tel: 212-522 2424; open 8am–8pm for women, 7am–10pm for men). This is the only *hamam* with a bar, is rather Moorish in design, and used to be all the rage with reporters up until the early 1990s – when Cağaloğlu was still the principal journalistic quarter of Istanbul. The baths were built by Sultan Mahmud I in 1741 and its architecture is unique. Prices today are strictly for tourists.

Back on Divanyolu Caddesi, several sultans are buried in the the octagonal **Mahmud II Türbesi** ⑱ (Tomb of Mahmud II; open 9.30am–4.30pm daily), built in 1848, which has a shady cemetery and atmospheric teahouse.

Nearby, the traditional **Çemberlitaş Hamamı** ⑲ (Vezirhan Caddesi 8; tel: 212-522 7974; open 6am–midnight) was constructed in 1583 to a plan by Sinan. It has separate sections for men and women – and reasonable prices. ❑

Turkish Baths

Taking your first plunge into a Turkish bath can be a daunting experience, but don't let concern over what to expect put you off one of the finest and most sensual experiences on offer. Cleanliness is an essential part of Muslim belief, and Turks took to Roman/Byzantine public baths with enthusiasm, believing them to be an ethereal medicine which would help to free the body of toxins, open up the pores, cleanse the skin and rejuvenate the spirit. For women, they also provided an opportunity to laugh and gossip free of the veils and strictures which bound their lives in the outside world. Only a few *hamams* from the golden age of Ottoman architecture still function in Istanbul, but these are worth seeking out for sheer aesthetics alone.

Until the 1920s, *hamams* were owned by *vakifs* or pious foundations. Built as part of mosque complexes before indoor plumbing became standard, they were open to the public and inexpensive. Now, as then, there were either exclusive sections for women and men or separate hours, but whatever the system, strict segregation was enforced in Ottoman times, and breaking the rules was an offence punishable by death. Today "mixed" bathing is available for tourist groups but it is not the authentic *hamam* experience, and is considerably more expensive. But women should not expect to be offered the services of a male attendant.

Most legitimate *hamams* display prices for various services in the reception; in traditional family establishments the full whack including massage is less than US$10 but in touristic *hamams* can rise to $50. It is a good idea to bring your own soap, shampoo and towel, but a *pestemal*, a piece of cloth worn around the waist for modesty, will be provided.

You prepare for your bath in a changing cubicle, *camekân*, where you can lock up your valuables. The main part of the bath is the *hararet*, or steam room, which is surrounded by marble basins. To begin, you can wash yourself or let the attendant *(tellak)* massage

your scalp before taking you to the *göbektasi* or navel stone, a flat, hexagonal marble platform beneath the central dome. Here, you will be scrubbed with a coarse mitt or *kese* to remove layers of dead skin, lathered with a lacy cloth and then massaged. Your *tellak* will slide you around the *göbektasi* and let you know when to turn over. Men sometimes complain of rather rough pummelling, but the women's massage is usually quite gentle, more like the memory of bath day with mother. Later you can relax with tea or other drinks in the cold room or *soğukluk*.

The biggest question is what to wear in the bath. Men are expected to keep their *pestemal* on. Although total nudity is common enough in the women's section, many Turkish women wear briefs, and they can be a little shocked that personal shaving customs among Europeans are different to their own.

You should allow at least an hour (and preferably much more) for your bath, which can be an effective antidote to heat, fatigue or a hangover. Recommended *hamams* are listed in Travel Tips. ❑

RIGHT: rooted firmly in the Roman tradition, the Turkish bath is a social occasion.

11

TOPKAPI PALACE

*For 400 years the Topkapı Palace was the sacred
source of all power within the Ottoman Empire, and the
stage for the rise and fall of sultans*

Map
on page
162

Visitors in the past, as today, could not help but notice that the Topkapı's numerous low pavilions (*köşk*), spread over a series of open courtyards, resembled nothing so much as a tented camp. Given the nomadic origins of the Central Asian Osmanlı (Ottoman) dynasty, such taste should come as no surprise. But Mehmet the Conqueror had legends of sybaritic Byzantium to compete with, and immediately set about making manifest the vision of himself as the "Shadow of God in this world and the next". He filled his court with European scholars and artists, enquiring as to the fashions in royal courts abroad. By the time of Süleyman the Magnificent, the Topkapı was synonymous with grandeur of fairytale proportions. The sultans loved putting on a show for the people, from the gilded imperial caiques moving up and down the Bosphorus to the wedding and circumcision celebrations in the Hippodrome. Yet there was no bourgeoisie or "court society", for the palace was self-contained, and later observers noted the absence of a "civilised" middle class within the city.

It is popularly thought that the empire began its decline after the Conqueror's great-grandson, Süleyman the Magnificent (*see pages 168–9*) decided to consolidate the administrative seat of the empire and his royal residence, harem included, in the Topkapı, but the period of his rule (1520–66) also marks the "golden age" of the Ottomans as seen in the expansion of frontiers, economic stability and its greatest cultural and architectural achievements.

PRECEDING PAGES: the Imperial Hall. **LEFT:** imperial officials gather for a gossip and a snack. **BELOW:** grand processions were once a regular part of court life.

Location, location, location...

Set at the confluence of the Bosphorus, Golden Horn, and the Sea of Marmara, the palace is exceptional in terms of beauty of situation and naval advantage. The current complex, however, built over the acropolis of the pre-Roman city, is considerably smaller than the original, which stretched down to the Sea of Marmara until the Sirkeci Station and railway lines to Europe were completed in 1871.

Trams now clatter down **Alemdar Sokak**, which marked the edge of the outer courtyard. From here, the **Bab-ı Ali (Sublime Porte)** led to the greater offices of government from the late 16th century onwards, though the current rococo gate was built in 1843. Across the street is the **Alay Köşkü** (Parade Pavilion), from which the sultan could spy unseen on comings and goings at the Porte and have a ringside seat for official and military processions. One 17th-century scribe described the colourful Parade of the Guilds, each section dressed in the costumes of their trade along with tumblers, mime actors and other circus acts.

Gülhane Parkı, which now houses a family funfair, was part of the imperial gardens. Its entrance is at the bottom of **Soğükçeşme Sokak**, a steep cobbled street

The Topkapı is open 9am–4:30pm. Closed Tuesday. Entrance fee. Allow the best part of a day to visit the palace. As soon as you enter buy a ticket for the Harem which is visited by guided tour only. These tours frequently sell out by the afternoon. The last tour leaves at 4pm.

BELOW: restored wooden houses on Soğükçeşme Sokak (street) are now a tourist pension.

of restored Ottoman houses, including one which has been converted into an upmarket pension. A righthand turn halfway up leads you to the **Cafer Ağa Courtyard**, once a *medrese*, where there is an inexpensive and shady tea garden surrounded by craft shops.

The outer court

The entrance to the Topkapı is at the top of the street, behind Aya Sofya. The **Fountain of Ahmet III**, built in 1728, marks the **Bab-ı Hümayun** (Imperial Gate), through which tour buses squeeze within an inch of their paintwork to get to the parking lots inside. This gate is one of the Conqueror's original fixtures and is marked with his *tuğra*, (imperial monogram). The first court, or **Court of the Janissaries**, housed offices and buildings of a more public and practical nature. It was an assembly point for those petitioning the Divan in the second court, as well as for the élite *devşirme* soldiers, and to cope with the crowds a rule of silence was imposed.

On the left are the Byzantine church of Aya Irini (*see page 149*), which was used as an arsenal, and the **Darphane-i Amire** (Imperial Mint), now leased to the progressively-minded History and Economics Foundation for exhibitions. Near the ticket office and gift shop stands the **Cellât Çeşmesi** (Executioner's Fountain), which was used to wash blood off swords and hands after a beheading. The sight of it may have helped enforce silence in the court – white pillars nearby held the detached heads of important offenders, such as grand viziers, many of which were stuffed to prolong shelf-life. The heads, tongues or noses of lesser criminals were stuck in niches on the outside of the Imperial Gate.

The inner palace complex consists of three primary courts, each progressive

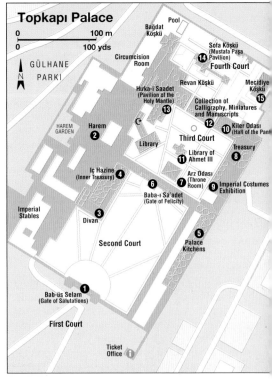

Topkapı Palace

0 — 100 m
0 — 100 yds

GÜLHANE PARKI
N

Pool
Bağdat Köşkü
Circumcision Room
Sofa Köşkü (Mustafa Paşa Pavilion) ⑭
Fourth Court
Hırka-i Saadet (Pavilion of the Holy Mantle) ⑬
Revan Köşkü
Mecidiye Köşkü ⑮
Collection of Calligraphy, Miniatures and Manuscripts ⑫
HAREM GARDEN
Harem ②
Library
Third Court
Library of Ahmet III ⑪
Kiler Odası ⑩ (Hall of the Pantry)
Treasury ⑧
İç Hazine (Inner Treasury) ④
⑥
Arz Odası ⑦ (Throne Room)
Imperial Costumes ⑨ Exhibition
Baba-ı Sa'adet (Gate of Felicity)
Imperial Stables
Divan ③
Palace Kitchens ⑤
Second Court
Bab-üs Selam ① (Gate of Salutations)
First Court
Ticket Office ⓘ

y more exclusive and sacrosanct. These led to other courtyards, pavilions and
halls connected by a maze of gates in the spirit of the Kremlin or Beijing's
Heavenly City – a city within a city, complete with dormitories for the various
guards, craftsmen and gardeners, who all wore their own distinctive garb,
colour-coded for easy reference. Like a tent city, each pavilion served a sepa-
ate purpose and each new sultan added his own according to whim, fashion, or
necessity. It is estimated that, at any one time, no less than 5,000 people lived
and worked in the Topkapı grounds.

Map on page 162

Several major fires did little to preserve whatever architectural unity might
have existed, and the only buildings left from the time of Mehmet II are the Raht
Hazinesi (Treasury Building) and the Çinili Köflk (Tiled Pavilion), now home
to the Museum of Turkish Porcelain (see page 151). This was not a residence.
The Byzantine palace was still standing here at the time of the conquest and the
Conqueror's original palace sat where Istanbul University is today, which
explains why so many of the city's major sites are concentrated in Beyazıt.
Rather, Mehmet II used this pavilion as a place to relax from administrative
pressures, the tiled walls providing respite from the heat.

Inscription over the Gate of Salutations, welcomes visitors to the palace.

The inner sanctum

The palace proper begins at **Bab-üs Selam** ❶ (the Gate of Salutations; other-
vise known simply as **Ortakapı**, the Middle Gate). This opens onto what was
a splendid garden full of exotic birds and animals and trickling fountains, where
ceremonial processions and state banquets were held. Four paths radiate from
the centre. The path on the far left leads to the **Harem** ❷ (*see page 166*), where
you are advised to go immediately to purchase a ticket for the tour, which leaves

BELOW: modern performers still do displays of Janissary drills.

SOLDIER-SLAVES

Devşirme or "gathering" was an invention unique to
the Ottomans. Intended to ensure racial alloys in the
palace and empire, it consisted of a levy of boys (usually
Christians from the Balkans) who were circumcised and
converted to Islam. The most promising were trained in
the Palace School to become pages, officials and soldiers.
Some even became grand viziers. Rulers believed that
the system helped integrate the diverse peoples of the
realm, and encourage competition between various ethnic
groups – thus discouraging any cultural solidarity which
could threaten the state. Although technically slaves, many
of the youths were happy to join the *devşirme* or harem as
a step up in the world – Bosnian Slavs even demanded to
remain eligible after their conversion to Islam.

The Janissaries were an élite military corp entirely
made up of *devşirme*, who wielded enormous power and
influence. By the end of the 16th century, however, the
system of "gathering" had broken down as sons of
Janissaries joined the ranks and paşas tried to save on
household expenses by recruiting their own servants.
Insurrection and arson became the tools with which
Janissaries could blackmail the state, and, after a final
bloody revolt, the institution was abolished in 1826.

every half hour. Next comes the **Kubbe Altı** or **Divan** (Hall Under the Dome), where the Imperial Council met four times a week, reclining on cushioned benches (divans), until it moved to the Sublime Porte in the late 18th century. The **Iç Hazine (Inner Treasury)** ❹, where the Janissaries were paid, is now home to an exhibition of arms and armour which includes swords, bows and arrows, and 15th-century chain mail.

The path on the far right leads to the vast **Kitchens** ❺, once able to provide food for 12,000 people. They now house the palace's stunning collection of Chinese and Japanese porcelain, brought to the empire via the Silk Road. Here you can see one of the world's finest collections of Ming and Ch'ing dynasty porcelain. Sultans, when not supping directly from silver or gold plates, would only use porcelain – İznik pottery was considered common, fit only for servants and Janissaries. Celadon, an early form of Chinese porcelain, was made to resemble jade and thought by wary sultans to neutralise poison.

The Gate of Felicity

The **Baba-ı Sa'adet (Gate of Felicity)** ❻ was guarded by the White Eunuchs who lived above it, and leads to the **Arz Odası (Throne Room)** ❼, where the sultan sat during ceremonial occasions and received viziers after sessions in the Divan. The canopied throne on display dates from 1596, but there are others in the **Treasury** ❽, one of the highlights of the palace, which is home to the Ottomans' coruscating collection of jewels and precious metals. Security is tight for the staggering display which includes a diamond-encrusted suit of chainmail, the 1741 **Topkapı dagger**, originally intended as a gift for the Shah of Persia, and the 84-carat **Spoonmaker's Diamond**, fifth largest in the world.

At the peak of the empire the Divan was one of the most powerful policy-making centres of Europe, where patriarchs, ambassadors and ordinary citizens could lodge grievances and petition for favours. The sultan listened from behind a curtain, so that the viziers never knew if he were there.

BELOW:
the Gate of Felicity.

The exhibition of **Imperial Costumes** is nearby, in what was the Hall of the Pages who looked after the royal wardrobe. Early Ottoman robes were quintessentially Asian of the long-sleeved, side-buttoning variety, made from the bright, sumptuous silks for which the Empire was justifiably famous.

Map on page 162

Next to the Treasury is the **Kiler Odası (Hall of the Pantry)** ⑩, which was used by the 30 pages who prepared the sultan's meals. It once contained an elaborate selection of drugs (mostly antidotes for poison); rare and expensive spices, aromatics and perfumes; huge candles to light the Selamlık, Harem and mosques; vast quantities of sweets, preserves and jams; and "great pieces of ambergris sent by the paşa of Yemen which was one of the ingredients of a favourite variety of sherbet".

Just behind the Throne Room is the **Library of Ahmet III** ⑪. Early scribes observed that some of the books may have been of Byzantine origin, and that most were ornate, intended for show rather than to be read. The Topkapı collection of **Calligraphy, Miniatures and Manuscripts** ⑫ is at the back, with some works dating to the 12th century. There is also an exhibition of European **clocks** which were gifts to the sultans over the years. Since most Muslims marked the time of day by the five calls to prayer, western clocks were a novelty in Istanbul and owned only by the most wealthy.

A golden crib, made for a sultan's son, one of the dazzling treasures on display in the Topkapi.

Sacred relics

The extraordinary **Hırka-i Saadet (Pavilion of the Holy Mantle)** ⑬ contains some of the most holy relics of the Muslim world. Most were brought back by Selim the Grim (1512–20) after his particularly bloody acquisition of Egypt and Syria and his self-appointment as Caliph, or leader of Islam. Of particular veneration for Muslims is the **Holy Mantle** itself, a present from the Prophet to a poet convert whose work so moved him that he had a cloak woven for him in his own harem. Under the Ottomans, this mantle was only displayed to the royal family and favoured high officials on the 15th day of Ramazan. The ceremony involved soaking the garment in water then squeezing the excess into crystal bottles which were sent to city dignitaries as a talisman against plague. The Holy Mantle and **Sancak Şerif** (Sacred Standard) are kept in ornate gold caskets near two of Mohammed's swords and a seal which can only be viewed from an antechamber. Other relics on display include hairs from the Prophet's beard, a Holy Tooth, and a Holy Footprint.

BELOW: fountain in the Library of Ahmet III.

The fourth courtyard was primarily a garden with small "summer house" pavilions and stunning views. The Revan and Baghdad Pavilions were built in the 1630s to commemorate victories of Murat IV, and the Sofa Köşkü ⑭ (or Mustafa Paşa Pavilion) stands in the gardens of the Tulip Period during the reign of Sultan Ahmet III. The intricately tiled Sünnet Odası (Circumcision Hall) and the Iftariye Pavilion, a baldachined marble terrace built for royal fast-breaking dinners during Ramazan, were built by Ibrahim "the Mad". The **Mecidiye Köşkü** ⑮, the last structure built in the palace, is now an excellent restaurant, with panoramic views.

The harem

Of any part of the palace, often it is the harem that intrigues visitors the most, their imagination perhaps fuelled by images of odalisques and slaves reclining on divans waiting for the sultan's pleasure. But the stuffy reality of harem life was probably closer to a convent school, with constant vigilance for misconduct. The harem's unromantic purpose was to provide a reserve of male heirs to the throne by slave mothers who could not make legal demands of inheritance. The only men allowed in were the princes, black eunuchs and, during emergencies, the so-called *Zülfülü Baltacılar* ("Firemen of the Lovelocks"), who wore exaggeratedly high collars to screen their prying eyes. Daily life must have been a squalling racket of babies, spoiled children, competitive mothers, scheming grannies and harassed servants.

The harem entrance is through the quarters of the Black Eunuchs – up to 200 Sudanese slaves who governed the sultan's household, as they were considered more trustworthy than the white slaves. From 1574 until 1908, the chief black eunuch was one of the most powerful men in the palace, keeping the harem accounts, and overseeing entrance and discipline.

On the guided tour you pass the *hamam* (baths) and the **Cariyeler Dairesi** (Courtyard of the Concubines) before reaching the luxurious **Chambers of the Valide Sultan**, strategically located between the apartments of the Sultan and his higher ranking favourites. The *Valide Sultan* (Mother of the Sultan) often selected the concubines for her son. A slave girl's primary goal was to catch the sultan's eye, perhaps by demonstrating musical or dancing abilities in the **Hünkar Sofrası (Imperial Hall)**. She was then bathed, perfumed, dressed up in royal lingerie, and sent a gift wrapped in a handkerchief before being led to

Much Ottoman family law was designed to fill loopholes in Islamic law. Technically, as slaves, the Sultan's four chief "wives" were not wives at all, only "mothers of sultans".

BELOW: Ottoman miniature of bathtime in the harem.
RIGHT: elaborately decorated harem doorway.

his chamber in the utmost secrecy so as not to arouse jealousies. If she gave birth to a boy, she acquired the elevated status of *Haseki Sultan*.

Map on page 162

This was far from the den of unfettered sex and perversion conjured up by shocked Victorians, though boredom and sexual frustration must have been rife. By the 18th century order in the harem, which contained anywhere from 400 to 800 women, seems to have broken down, and the weary sultan was obliged to service them on a regular rota basis – one girl was executed for selling her "turn" to another. There are more than 300 rooms, of which only 40 are open today, but it is enough to give a taste of the claustrophobic breeding pens of the Ottomans. Those seeking fantasy fodder will be disappointed.

As the Empire declined the complex became more and more overcrowded. By the mid 19th century there were over 800 odalisques incarcerated in the harem. These women were virtual slaves and often war booty from various foreign campaigns and they lived for the most part in squalid conditions.

Yet true love did occur; Süleyman's passion for Roxelana (or Hürrem Sultan, "the laughing one", as she was known in Turkish) is well documented in letters. And there were others: Selim II and Nurbanu; Ahmet I and Kösem Sultan; and the 17th-century Sultan Abdülhamid I and a harem favourite, testifying, if nothing else, to the triumph of monogamy. Abdülhamid left the following letter:

"My Rühhah, your Hamid is yours to dispose of. The Lord of the Universe is the Creator of all beings, and would never torment a man for a single fault – I am your bound slave, beat me or kill me if you wish. I surrender myself utterly to you. Please come tonight I beg of you. I swear you will be the cause of my illness, perhaps even of my death. I beg you, wiping the soles of your feet with my face and eyes. I swear to God Almighty, I can no longer control myself". ❑

BELOW: miniature showing a birth in the harem.

SILKEN CORD AND GILDED CAGE

The Ottoman dynasty's rules of succession were muddy, leading to fratricide on a hideous scale. Mehmet the Conqueror had decreed that whichever of his sons should inherit the throne, it behoved him to kill his brothers "in the interests of the world order". In the four centuries of Ottoman rule, 80 princes were killed by strangulation – the preferred method for royal assassination. Murad III sired 103 children, and at his death 20 sons survived him. But when the eldest, Mehmet III, succeeded to the throne, his first act was to murder his 19 brothers and dump seven concubines pregnant by his father into the Bosphorus.

At this point the courts became concerned about the extinction of the dynasty, and in 1607 fratricide was replaced with the institution of the *Kafes* or Cage, where superfluous heirs were held in sequestered luxury unless needed, kept busy with crafts and sterile concubines. Much has been written about the effect that this imprisonment had on the minds of future sultans – it is blamed for the pathological paranoia of Ibrahim the Mad, whose reign is best remembered for the 280 concubines he ordered drowned in the Bosphorus upon hearing rumours of a harem plot. Fate proved Ibrahim's fear of strangulation was justified – he ended up a victim of the silken cord.

SÜLEYMAN THE MAGNIFICENT

Süleyman reigned from 1520 to 1566 – the Golden Age of the Ottomans. He excelled as a conqueror statesman, legislator and patron of the arts

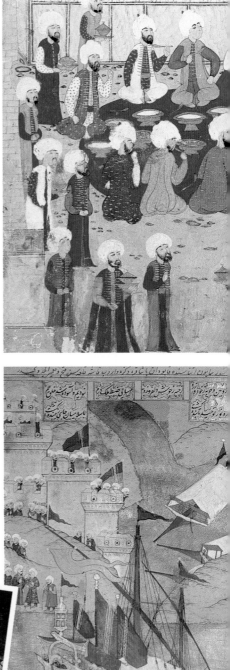

Süleyman inherited the throne at the age of 26 and reigned for 46 years (1522–66).

Portraits of him vary greatly, but memoirs and historical records are more consistent about his appearance. He was "tall, broad-shouldered", had a "long graceful neck...aquiline nose...dark hazel eyes...fair skin, auburn hair, beetling eyebrows...long arms and hands".

The young sultan immediately proved himself to be a man of many parts – and many titles. The Europeans dubbed him "the Magnificent" even during his reign; he preferred the title "Kanuni" ("Lawgiver"). His ground-breaking Codex Süleymanicus synthesised Islamic and secular law to establish a comprehensive judicial system with the concept of "justice" as the cornerstone, a guarantee of equal justice for all and a measure of leniency in the penal code.

As Caliph and ruler of Islam's holiest places, Süleyman consolidated the Sunni Supremacy over Shi'a, while his skill as a military strategist more than doubled the size of his Empire.

At home, he was a great patron of the arts. Architecture, painting, calligraphy, illumination, weaponry, tiles and textiles, woodwork, metalwork and literature all flourished during his reign. He himself was an accomplished goldsmith and a fine classical poet whose collected works furnished many proverbs.

▷ **AGE OF KINGS**
Henry VIII and Elizabeth I of England; Ivan the Terrible of Russia; François I of France; and Holy Roman Emperor Charles V: these great monarchs were all Süleyman's contemporaries.

◁ **ARTISTS' PATRON**
Twenty-nine painters (half of them Europeans) worked in the Palace Studio, producing many albums of miniature paintings depicting Ottoman military campaigns and court life.

▽ **CLOTH OF GOLD**
Even the clothes worn by the royal family were works of art. They were made of silk, lavishly embroidered with gold and silver thread.

A DEVOTED FAMILY MAN

Until Süleyman, Ottoman Sultans traditionally did not marry, enjoying themselves instead with the women of the harem. But this father of eight sons and one daughter fell in love with and married one of his concubines, Roxelana, later known as Hürrem. It is thought that Süleyman was faithful during their 25-year marriage.

Hürrem was clever and ambitious, the first of many generations of harem women to involve themselves in palace politics. Some of Süleyman's sons died young, but she was determined to keep the path clear for her own son, Selim, who later proved a disastrous ruler.

To this end, she persuaded Süleyman to order the execution first of his heir apparent, Mustafa, a favourite of the armed forces, his son Beyazıt and Beyazıt's four sons. All of these unfortunates were strangled with a silken bow as it was illegal to shed royal blood.

◁ **EMPIRE BUILDER**
Süleyman's navies dominated the Mediterranean as his fearsome armies swept east, west and south across three continents.

▽ **MONUMENTAL GLORY**
Süleyman's architect, Sinan, designed some of Turkey's greatest buildings, including the superb Süleymaniye Mosque.

BEYAZIT AND THE GRAND BAZAAR

Map on page 174

From the battered ruins of Constantinople, Mehmet the Conqueror conjured a glorious new vision of a great Muslim city funded by the world's largest bazaar

W hen Mehmet the Conqueror and his immense army of Janissaries breached the walls of Byzantium in 1453, there was not much left of the fabled "Queen of Cities". Political and religious strife, class warfare and ravaging by crusaders had left Constantinople with an empty treasury, a debased coinage, an army composed of mercenaries and even its crown jewels pawned to Venetian bankers. From a peak of half a million, the population had shrunk to 50,000. The city had become a collection of scattered villages debilitated by plague and whose inhabitants, according to one observer "go continually about the city howling as if in lamentation". Shunned by Catholic Europe, even its churches were in ruins – Hagios Polyeuktos had been shattered by an earthquake and ransacked by the crusaders; one of the holiest shrines in Byzantium, Our Lady of Blachernae, had burned down and never been rebuilt; and the Church of St. Theodosia was witness to the last Byzantine Emperor, Constantine XI Dragases, praying with a throng of terrified, relic-waving believers before fighting to the death as the Turks swept into the city.

PRECEDING PAGES: entrance to the Grand Bazaar. **LEFT:** chai seller in Beyazıt Square. **BELOW:** mending antique carpets.

The Conqueror *(Fatih)* did not want to destroy the coveted city, but he did want his reconstruction of Istanbul to have an Islamic character in accordance with the dictates of Shari'a, holy law. At the city centre were to be mosques and *medreses*; charitable institutions *(vakıf)* such as hospitals and hospices for the poor; and a commercial centre or *bedesten* to finance the *vakıfs*. It was an interlocking system that integrated the commerce of the city with its religious, educational and social needs. At its core was the Fatih Cami complex *(see page 187)* which once had eight *medreses*, a huge library, a *hamam*, hospital, caravansaray and leather workshop.

Fit for an emperor

The sultan's love of classical allegory (such as his identification with Alexander the Great) and his belief in dynastic destiny made sure that the new "Domain of the House of Osman" reflected his personal ambitions as well as the word of Islam. Some churches were converted to mosques, some given back to the Christian community. He ordered artisans, merchants and people of rank from all over the Empire to settle, trade and build. After starting construction on his first palace at Beyazıt, the *bedesten* (bazaar) was quick to follow, uniting merchants of all nationalities under a strictly regulated system which included price and production control, and functioned much as banks and stock exchanges do today.

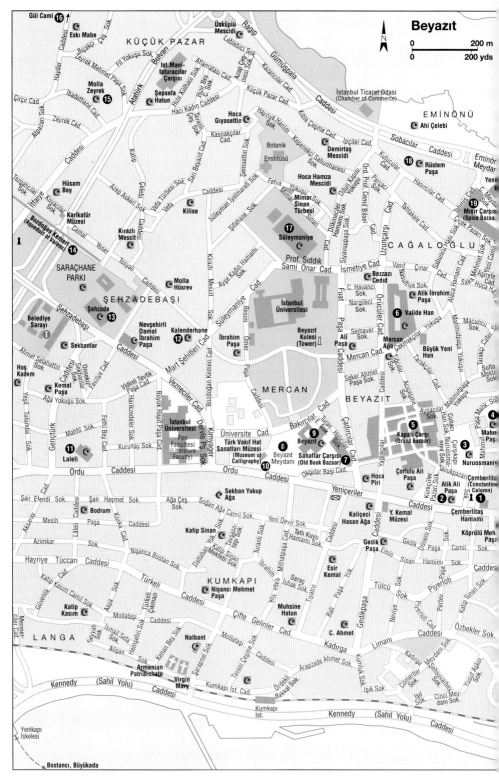

Beyazıt

Mehmet's original palace stood on the spot now occupied by Istanbul University, purposefully adjacent to the ancient Forum of Theodosius, which was traditionally considered to be the city centre. Sixty years later, the royal household gradually began moving to the Topkapı, and the old palace was used as a place to put widows, ageing harem slaves and servants out to pasture.

Map on page 174

Still trading

Today's Beyazıt is cluttered with tourist shops, hawkers, restaurants and trams, and, with prices totally unregulated, it may seem a far cry from what it was 500 years ago. But the effervescent atmosphere of international trade remains the same, and the sheer quantity of goods is dizzying. Laleli and Aksaray are bursting with the commercial activity of "luggage traders" from post-Soviet countries, where there is still a shortage of many basic goods and cheap clothing is in great demand. In contrast, some of the exquisite antique carpets and textiles in the Grand Bazaar are priced for serious collectors only. There are also so many mosques, Byzantine churches, shops, old caravansarais and historical tea gardens that if your time is limited you might have to choose between history and piety or pure self-indulgence. The district takes in the busy ferry docks of Eminönü, the Mısır Çarşısı (Spice Bazaar), the open markets of Tahtakale and Uzunçarşı, the Grand Bazaar, the enormous Süleymaniye Mosque complex and the Aqueduct of Valens.

Little remains of the **Forum of Constantine**, which was near the Forum of Theodosius except for the forlorn metal-banded remains of the porphyry **Çemberlitaş (Constantine's Column)** ❶, once topped by a statue of the sun god Jupiter/Helios or Apollo. It is commonly thought to have been designed by Constantine to synthesise his own holy sovereignty with that of a still fashionable pagan god, and numerous Christian relics were buried at the base. The Byzantine historian Anna Comnena (1083–1153), however, indicates that it may have been pre-Christian in origin and simply renamed by Constantine, as local people always referred to it as *"Anthelios"*. In any event, the emperor seemed imperturbed when it blew down in a gale and declined to take it as a bad omen, saying, "I know of one Lord of life and death. The collapse of images, I am sure, does not induce death". The forum itself was surrounded by a two-storey portico, and contained the senate building along with various Christian and pagan statues, all about 2.5m (8 ft) below the current ground level.

Before leaving Yeniçeriler Caddesi, look for the **Atik Ali Paşa Cami** ❷. It is hard to see due to the high walls around it. This is one of the oldest mosques in the city, built in 1496 during the reign of Beyazıt II by his eunuch grand vizier. Its tea garden specialises in "mystic water pipe smoking" – the traditional Turkish *nargile* (*see page 96*). Behind it, on Vezirhane Caddesi, are two other mosques worth a detour. The **Nuruosmaniye Cami** ❸, begun in 1748, was the first to display baroque features, which were disapproved of by the clergy at the time. The gate behind the complex leads in to the Grand Bazaar. The **Mahmut Paşa Cami** ❹ was built in 1462 by Mahmut Paşa I, a

Constantinople's population reached nearly one million in the 9th century. Daily life focused on the fora, which were used as civic and trading centres. They were also rallying points for news bearers, agitators, and those wishing to repudiate a spouse or expose a cheat.

BELOW: barber shop near the Nuruosmaniye mosque.

The tomb of Mahmut Paşa I, grand vizier to Mehmet the Conqueror.

BELOW:
"Main Street" in the Grand Bazaar.

highly respected Byzantine aristocrat who converted to Islam and ultimatel; became grand vizier to Mehmet the Conqueror. In the heady times to follow however, he fell out of favour, a victim of court gossip, and was executed i 1473. Fortunately his beautiful tomb had already been constructed. Adorne with simple turquoise, dark blue and green tiles from early İznik kilns, it is on of the mosque's most attractive features. Part of the original complex, th **Mahmut Paşa Hamamı**, has now been incorporated into a *han*.

Back on Yeniçeriler Caddesi, just before the Grand Bazaar, is another *nargil* smokers' tea house, in the Çorlulu Ali Paşa courtyard, named for yet anothe executed grand vizier whose family interred his head in the tomb nearby.

The Grand Bazaar

The **Kapalı Çarşı (Grand Bazaar) ❺** (open 9am–7pm Mon–Sat) began trad ing as the Conqueror's fortress-like İç Bedesten, which now stands at the centr of a vast complex radiating outwards to include 64 "streets", over 3,000 shops 22 entrances, 25,000 employees, four fountains and two mosques. Howeve rents have become very steep and, sadly, the goods are growing increasingly les exotic as shops come to rely on the rapid turnover of less expensive items. Nev ertheless, if you take the time you should still be able to find treasures – fror carpets to copper, silks to leather.

Kalpakçilar, the main vaulted street in the bazaar, shimmers with gold ea rings, bracelets, rings and chains worked into intricate designs that appeal t Middle Eastern tourists, who like their gold with the stamp of the Prophet on i Simpler bracelets and earrings are for the local market, where gold has long bee regarded as an instantly convertible dowry and a hedge against divorce or infla tion. Pious Muslims, too, prefer dealing in gold to su lying their hands with interest-bearing bank account:

The centre of goldsmithing is the **Cuhaza Har** which contains over 300 ateliers, as well as nine gol smelting forges and scores of wholesale outlets. Th market maintains a rigorous system of control ove quality, which ranges from the standard 14 carat fc earrings to 20 carat for light rope-chains and up to 2 carat for heavy bracelets. When buying gold, be sur to check for the stamps showing the number of cara and identity of the goldsmith. Studios in **Zincirli Ha** to the right of the Mahmut Paşa Gate, creates custor designs, and many jewellery merchants of both silve and gold make large reductions for bulk purchase

Behind the bazaar, the **Valide Han ❻** (corner c Çakmakçılar Yokuşu and Tarakçılar Caddesi; ope 9.30am–5pm Mon–Sat) was built by Kösem Sulta in 1651 and was the centre of Persian trade in the cit By 1700, several thousand people, most of them fror Azerbaijan, were living here, which explains the pre ence of the Shi'ite mosque at its centre. Traditionall animals and goods were stored at ground level whi itinerant merchants and craftsmen stayed above, bi today the *han* has been taken over by weavers. Furth down the street, the baroque **Büyük Yeni Han** h; three levels of shops, joining many more hans ar craftsmen's alleys. **Süleyman Paşa Han** was former the slave market (*see page 106*).

Just beyond the Grand Bazaar, a gracefully ornamented gateway, **Hakkaklar Kapısı** (Gate of the Spoon-Makers), leads to an area frequently overlooked in the overwhelming hurly-burly, known as the **Sahaflar Çarşısı** . This has been the market of secondhand booksellers' since the 18th century. Before literacy was commonplace, any scrap of paper bearing Ottoman script was considered to have come from a religious book and was therefore holy.

Thousands of literary pleasures, treasures and eccentricities await visitors in this exotic but dwindling world. You may find a fragile remnant of handsome paper from a 450-year-old Qur'an, preserved with egg-white and with 22-carat gold leaf motif decorations in the margins; a four-volume black leather-bound 1876 edition of *Les Misérables* or *Gone With The Wind* in a 1938 British edition. Sadly, however, most of the 40-plus bookshops in this peaceful tree-shaded courtyard now deal in secondhand paperbacks and blackmarket students' textbooks (printed locally).

Elif No. 4 is the best-known shop in the Sahaflar Çarşısı. It is widely recognised that owner Mr. Aslan Kaynardag's knowledge of Turkish books – both old and new – is unsurpassed. If the book exists in Turkey, he is said to be the man to find it for you.

Across the way at No. 27 is Güzen Kitap Ve Yayınevi, run by brothers Ünal and Sinan. Started over 30 years ago by their father, they usually obtain their books from library closings in Europe and Turkey or buy them from estates being settled. After you've seen what the shop offers, ask one of the brothers to take you across the courtyard to the upstairs storeroom at No. 2. It's perfectly safe and there you will be pleasantly surprised to discover 5,000 more volumes, including unexpected Greek religious texts, hidden in storage.

Maps on pages 174 & 177

TIP

It is worth seeking out the working goldsmiths in the bazaar because these days much of the jewellery on sale in shops is imported from India and elsewhere.

BELOW: kitsch souvenirs include belly dancing and Aladdin costumes.

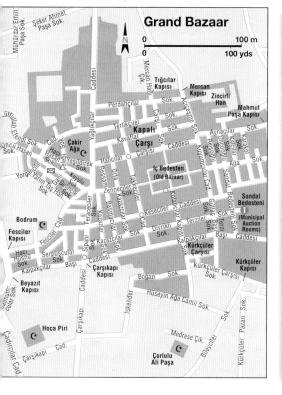

Grand Bazaar

N

| 0 | 100 m |
| 0 | 100 yds |

Beyazıt Square

The back of the market leads to **Beyazıt Meydanı** , the once splendid **Forum of Theodosius** (built in AD 393), which had a statue of a bronze bull at its centre and huge triumphal arches. Its columns, some carved to represent peacock feathers, were either used in the Yerebatan Sarayı, or are lying along the tram tracks on Ordu Caddesi. Fragments of the **Column of Theodosius**, adorned with reliefs of the emperor's campaigns against the barbarians, can be seen in the foundations of the **Beyazıt Hamamı**, now converted to shops. Nearby are the imposing gates of **Istanbul Üniversitesi** (University). In the sprawling outdoor market along the Beyazıt mosque wall, a motley group of people sell everything from antiques to old coins and stamps while students eternally discuss urgent academic and political questions. Other vendors of all descriptions in the background show off their diverse wares (electrical tools, plastic toys and antique or cheap pocket watches) while the old men seated in chairs along the periphery laugh and relate the latest news of the day.

The **Beyazıt Cami**  is the oldest surviving imperial mosque in Istanbul, completed in 1506 as an adjunct to the old palace. Sultan Beyazıt II, the son of Mehmet the Conqueror, was considerably more conservative than his father, ordering the Bellini royal portraits and erotic frescoes broken up and removed from the palace immediately upon accession. This mosque is thought to reflect his austere and pious nature, but also to have marked the beginning of a distinctive Ottoman architectural style, both subtle and symmetrical. The 20 verdantique, red granite and porphyry columns, however, are probably much older.

Pious Beyazıt may have been, but a quick strangling with a bow string might have been fairer treatment of his brother Cem, who was kept 14 years as a

BELOW: the Aqueduct of Valens, still in use in the 19th century.

"guest" in the Vatican and various European courts under the illusion that his request for aid in pursuit of the throne was being taken seriously. Meanwhile, Beyazıt "the Saint" was supplying backhanders to his brother's "hosts" through a Genoese merchant in Galata. Cem Sultan died in Naples, probably poisoned.

At the eastern end of Beyazıt Square, the mosque's *medrese* is now the **Türk Vakıf Hat Sanatları Müzesi (Museum of Calligraphy)** ⓾, an excellent exhibition of this quintessentially Islamic art, with displays of tools and a tableau of an early workshop (open 9am–4pm Tues–Wed; entrance fee). Works shown here are from the archives of the Turkish Calligraphy Foundation.

Map on page 174

Baroque extravagance

A detour of under 1 km (1,100 yards) to the left along Ordu Caddesi brings you to the city's most lavish baroque mosque, **Laleli Cami (Tulip Mosque)** ⓫, completed in 1763 and famous for its lush use of coloured marble. It was built by Mustafa III, whose tomb stands next to that of his son, Selim III, who was hacked to pieces in his rooms by Janissaries after an ineffectual anti-corruption drive. The enormous bazaar in the basement, a unique feature, is now packed with post-Soviet luggage traders buying up Turkish clothing.

Otherwise, continue along Şehzadebaşı Caddesi to **Kalenderhane Cami** ⓬ (16 Mart Şehitleri Caddesi), formerly the 9th-century Monastery of Maria Kyriotissa, which began life around 400 as a Roman bath. Excavations in the 1970s revealed a 7th-century mosaic of the Presentation of Christ in the Temple, one of the oldest extant Byzantine works from the city, thought to have been hidden here during the iconoclastic era, and a mid 13th-century fresco of the life of St. Francis – both are now in the Archaeology Museum. Original Byzantine features include the marble work in the prayer hall and the remains of a fresco in the entrance way. Nearby, the **Şehzade Cami (Prince's Mosque)** ⓭ was built by Sinan for Süleyman the Magnificent's much-mourned son Mehmet who died of smallpox at the age of 22. With this complex, Sinan succeeded in enclosing the maximum space with the minimum visible support. The attractive garden of tombs (open 9am–5pm, Tues–Sun), arranged around that of Şehzade Mehmet, was designed to reflect the garden of Paradise. The buildings incorporate unique early İznik tiles and exquisite stained glass.

Brilliant engineering

The Şehzade complex is at the southern end of the **Bozdoğan Kemeri (Aqueduct of Valens)** ⓮, a superb feat of Byzantine engineering. It was built in AD 375 and was still functioning at the end of the 19th century. Originally 1 km (1,100 yards) long, it brought water from mountains up to 200 km (120 miles) away which flowed into a nymphaeum at the Forum of Theodosius (now Beyazıt Square). Today about half of it remains, towering over the busy traffic on Atatürk Bulvari.

Just to the north, with a commanding view over the Golden Horn and Galata, the virtually ruinous but still imposing **Molla Zeyrek Cami** ⓯ (the former Monastery of St. Saviour Pantocrater; Idabethane Sokak; closed to visitors) was an early 12th-century

BELOW: the Zeyrek area is targeted for restoration once the earthquake has been paid for.

monastic complex of three churches founded by Empress Eirene and her husband John II Comnenus. It was one of the richest monasteries of the Byzantine period, with 700 monks, a hospital and a mental asylum. In 1437, the north church was described as "richly adorned in gold mosaics", though none have survived. At the centre of the complex is the Church of the Archangel, the mausoleum of the Comnenus and Palaeologus dynasties, which boasts a richly patterned marble floor. Until the devastating earthquake in 1999, it was due to be renovated; now it must wait a little longer.

Towards the harbour, the **Gül Cami**  (Church of St. Theodosia; Mektep Sokak) was built in the 9th century by Basil I. The original dedication to St Euphemia was quickly overshadowed by the popularity of the martyred St. Theodosia,who had led the mostly female riot against iconoclast Leo III when he smashed the icon of Christ above the gate of the Great Palace. It was here that the last Byzantine Emperor, Constantine XI Dragases, uttered his final prayers the night before the Conqueror broke through the city walls. The Ottomans used it as a naval storage depot until the 17th century, when it was converted in to a mosque.

Sinan's crowning glory

Just north of Istanbul University, the **Süleymaniye Cami (Mosque)** ⓱ and surrounding complex is one of the most magnificent and atmospheric sights in Istanbul, Sinan's finest and biggest masterpiece. More astonishingly, it was completed in only seven years, a testimony to the resources and wealth of the Empire. Süleyman the Magnificent and his beloved wife Roxelana had already moved to the Topkapı, so nearly half the imperial gardens of the old palace

BELOW: the huge Süleymaniye Cami is one of Sinan's finest creations.

were requisitioned, in particular the crown of the hill overlooking the Golden Horn. The 24 columns in the courtyard are thought to have been salvaged from the Byzantine royal box at the Hippodrome. The tilework and stained glass are exquisite, and the calligraphy in the domes and pendatives was done by one of the finest artists of the period. In the cemetery are the tombs of Süleyman the Magnificent and his wife, Roxelana, and of the architect Sinan himself. It can take some time to see all of the Süleymaniye complex. Also fascinating is the neighbourhood behind – a warren of old Ottoman houses and marketplaces now given over to student accommodation and cybercafés. It is worth noting the **Darüzziyafe Ottoman Restaurant** (Şifahane Caddesi 6; see Travel Tips), previously the mosque's soup kitchen and the banqueting hall of the original complex, and the **Ikram Teahouse** in a sunken garden surrounded by high walls, which comes as a merciful relief after a long day's sightseeing. Note, however, that this is a religious neighbourhood – which means no alcohol is served.

Map on page 174

The water's edge

You can reach the Golden Horn from here, heading down the maze of streets that lead to Küçük Pazar and the Galata Bridge, through a lively local market. The small **Rüstem Paşa Cami** ⓭ (Hasırcılar Caddesi) is one of the loveliest mosques in the city. It was commissioned from Sinan by Süleyman the Magnificent's favourite daughter, Mihrimah in 1561, in memory of her husband, the grand vizier Rüstem Paşa. Rüstem Paşa has not been remembered favourably by history – he and Mihrimah conspired with Roxelana (Hürrem Sultan, Mihrimah's mother) to get both the previous grand vizier, Ibrahim Paşa, and the likely heir to the throne strangled, neither replacement being to the

BELOW: the lavish interior of the Süleymaniye Cami.

SINAN

Mimar Sinan (1489–1588), the greatest of all Ottoman architects, influenced religious and civic architecture during his lifetime and for centuries after his death. Born into the Greek Orthodox faith, this youth from the Karaman was selected under the *devşirme* system for Janissary training in the imperial schools. He rose rapidly through the ranks, serving in the Household Cavalry, as a Captain in the Royal Guard and later as Commander of the Infantry Cadet Corps. The aptitude he displayed as a designer and builder of fortifications and other military constructions brought him eventually to the attention of Süleyman the Magnificent who appointed him *Darüs-saadet*, Architect of the Abode of Felicity. He was 50 when he completed his first civil building. For the next 40 years Sinan devoted himself to a prodigious output of architecture. In addition to minor works like aqueducts, fountains and granaries, he was involved in the design and construction of 34 palaces, 79 mosques, 33 hamams, 19 tombs, 55 schools, 12 caravansarais and 7 *medreses*. He regarded the Şehzade Cami as the work of his apprentice days, the Süleymaniye, as the work of his maturity and the Selimiye Cami in Edirne as his *chef d'oeuvre*. He is buried in a simple tomb in the triangular garden northwest of the Süleymaniye mosque.

Map on page 174

Colourful heaps of spices perfume the air of the Spice Bazaar.

BELOW: feeding the birds at the Yeni Cami.

RIGHT: pots and pans for sale.

advantage of the future Empire. Rüstem Paşa was, however, good at filling the imperial coffers, and unusually died of natural causes while still in office. The mosque is lavishly decorated with the finest İznik tiles, which are worth studying individually in detail; some of their colours were never again reproduced in İznik kilns. Many of the best are in the galleries.

Continue a short way down Hasırcılar Caddesi and you hit the famous **Mısır Çarşısi** ⑲ (Spice Bazaar; open 8am–7pm Mon–Sat) built in 1660 to pay for the **Yeni Cami** in front of it, known to locals as the "pigeon mosque" for reasons that are immediately apparent. *Mısır*, in Turkish, means both corn and Egypt, as it was from Egypt that spices, grains, pulses, coffee, incense and henna came in great abundance, arriving annually in a convoy of galleons to great fanfare, accompanied by warships which protected them from pirates. Syria was famed for its soap. Between them these two countries provided a third of the Empire's wealth. Today's Spice Bazaar, alas, is increasingly full of touts and tourist junk, but there are nonetheless a handful of the old spice sellers left and their array of goods is astonishing.

If the hassle gets too much, simply follow the streets – and your nose – along Hasırcılar Caddesi and Tahtakale Caddesi, where many of the less famous spice sellers, *kahvecis* (coffee grinders) and *pastırma* (dried, spiced beef) makers have moved. Further out towards Uzunçarşı Caddesi is a warren of streets inhabited by craftsmen, coppersmiths, wood-workers and more, with an old Istanbul ambience you won't find elsewhere. The **farmer's market** at Tahmis Caddesi is one of the best in town, and if you walk along the front of Kalçın Sokak, where the shops face the sea (and the bus station) you can find **Hamdi's**, one of the city's most authentic (and cheapest) eastern Turkish restaurants (*see Travel Tips*). ❑

PARADISE FLAWED

Istanbul has always produced strong reactions in its visitors. William Lithgow travelled here several times between 1614 and 1632, and wrote a vivid account of the city in *Rare Adventures and Painfull Peregrinations*. "Truly, I may say of Constantinople, as I said once of the world, in the Lamentado of my second pilgrimage:
A painted whore, the mask of deadly sin,
Sweet fair without, and stinking foul within.
For indeed outwardly, it hath the fairest show; and inwardly, the streets being narrow, and most part covered the filthiest and most deformed buildings in the world. The reason of its beauty is, because being situate on moderate prospective heights, the universal tectures afar off yield a delectable show, the covertures being erected like the back of a coach after the Italian fashion, with guttered tile. But being entered within, there is nothing but a stinking deformity, and a loathsome contrived place without either internal domestic furniture, or the external decorations of fabricks extended like a palace. Notwithstanding that, for its situation, the delicious wines, and temperate climate, the fertile circumjacent fields, the Hellespont sea, and pleasant Asia on the other side; it may truly be called the paradise of the earth."

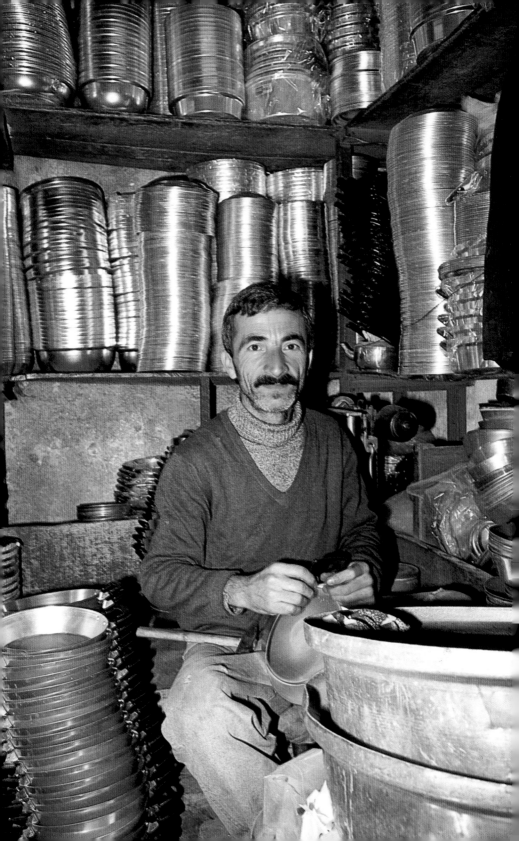

THE GOLDEN HORN

*The Greek and Jewish quarters, city walls and cemeteries
are only some of the hidden treasures along the shore
of the now sadly polluted ancient harbour*

Map
on page
188

The great **Fatih Cami complex** , on Islambol Caddesi, was built by Mehmed the Conqueror in 1463, only 10 years after he had breached the walls of Constantinople. "True art is to create a glorious city", he said at its founding. Built on the site of the 6th-century Church of the Holy Apostles, from which it borrowed its columns, the mosque was at that time the Ottomans' greatest architectural feat, intended to rival Aya Sofya. The architect is said to have been executed for failing to make the dome as large as that of the great Byzantine church. Nevertheless, the sultan chose to be buried in this great mosque, which became the spiritual heart of the city.

At any one time, its *medreses* housed a thousand students who would later become the clergy or judges of the empire – a forerunner of Istanbul University. It was also a model of charitable works which was copied all over the empire, with nearly 400 employees, a *han* (inn), hospital and soup kitchen for the poor and travellers. It was only to be outshone by Sinan's masterpiece, the Süleymaniye complex, a hundred years later. Most of the complex was destroyed by earthquake in 1766, but the *medreses*, the northern entrance portal to the courtyard, and the Qur'anic inscriptions above the lower outside windows, by master calligrapher Pir Yahya as-Sufi, are original.

PRECEDING PAGES:
Christ with Adam
and Eve, fresco in
St Saviour in Chora.
LEFT: reading the
Torah, Balat
Synagogue.
BELOW: Fatih Cami,
the Conqueror's
Mosque.

Fener and Balat

Nearer the Golden Horn, the dreamy, old-fashioned neighbourhoods of Fener and Balat are an atmospheric part of the city, still relatively undisturbed, largely due to pollution and stench from the shipyards, abbatoire and tanneries on the closed-in waterway.

"Balat" is a corruption of the Greek *"palation"* (palace) and refers to the presence of Blachernae (*see page 191*). Fener derives from the Greek *"phanar"*, meaning lighthouse. Most of Istanbul's Jewish community are Sephardic, welcomed to the city after their expulsion from Spain in 1492. However, there have been synagogues and a Jewish settlement at Balat since Byzantine times. During its "golden age" in the 18th and 19th centuries, Balat had six synagogues. The oldest and most significant of these is the **Ahrida Sinagogu** ❷ (Gevgili Sokak; open by prior arrangement or as part of Jewish Heritage tour), which was built by Jews from Ohrid in Macedonia before the Conquest, though the current ceilings and walls are baroque. The altar, shaped like Noah's ark, contains rare holy scrolls.

In 1665, Sabbatai Sevi, a Jewish merchant from Izmir, declared himself the Messiah. Preaching a doctrine of free love, he filled the Ahrida with believers, until they were forced by the authorities to choose between death and conversion. Newly Muslim, he

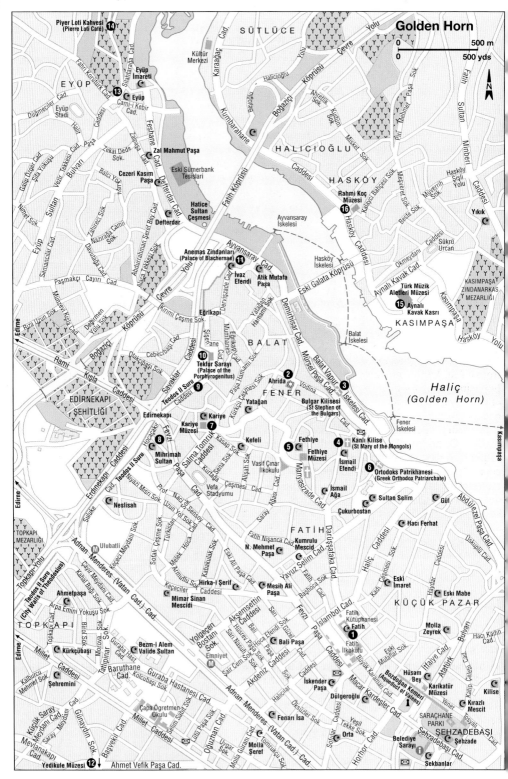

Golden Horn

Piyer Loti Kahvesi (Pierre Loti Café) ⑭

0   500 m
0   500 yds

N

SÜTLÜCE

Kültür Merkezi

EYÜP

Eyüp İmareti

⑬

Eyüp Cami-i Kebir Cad.

Eyüp Stadı

Zal Mahmut Paşa

HALICIOĞLU

Cezeri Kasım Paşa

HASKÖY

Eski Sümerbank Tesisleri

Hatice Sultan Çeşmesi

Rahmi Koç Müzesi ⑯

Defterdar

Yıkık

Ayvansaray İskelesi

Hasköy İskelesi

Anemas Zindanları (Palace of Blachernae) ⑪

İvaz Efendi

Atik Mutafa Paşa

Türk Müzik Aletleri Müzesi

Eski Galata Köprüsü

Aynalı Kavak Kasrı ⑮

KASIMPAŞA ZINDANARKASI MEZARLIĞI

Eğrikapı

BALAT

Balat İskelesi

KASIMPAŞA

Tekfur Sarayı (Palace of the Porphyrogenitus) ⑨

⑩

Teodos II Suru

Ahrida ②

Vodina

③

Haliç (Golden Horn)

EDİRNEKAPI ŞEHİTLİĞİ

Teodos II Suru

Edirnekapı

Kariye

Yatağan

FENER

Bulgar Kilisesi (St Stephen of the Bulgars)

Fener İskelesi

Kariye Müzesi ⑦

⑧

Mihrimah Sultan

Kefeli

Fethiye ⑤

⑥ Fethiye Müzesi

Fethiye ④

Kanlı Kilise (St Mary of the Mongols)

İsmail Efendi

⑥ Ortodoks Patrikhanesi (Greek Orthodox Patriarchate)

TOPKAPI MEZARLIĞI

Neslisah

Vasıf Çınar İlkokulu

Vefa Stadyumu

İsmail Ağa

Sultan Selim

Gül

Çukurbostan

Hacı Ferhat

Ulubatlı

FATİH

Fatih Nişanca Cad.

Kumrulu Mescid

N. Mehmet Paşa

Eski İmaret

KÜÇÜK PAZAR

Ahmetpaşa

Hirka-i Şerif

Mesih Ali Paşa

Eski Mabe

TOPKAPI

Mimar Sinan Mescidi

Fatih Kütüphanesi

Fatih ①

Molla Zeyrek

Kürkçübaşı

Bezm-i Alem Valide Sultan

Bali Paşa

Fatih İlkokulu

Hüsam Bey

Bozdoğan Kemeri (Aqueduct of Valens)

Karikatür Müzesi

Şehremini

Emniyet M

İskender Paşa

Dülgeroğlu

Kilise

Kırazlı Mescid

Çapa Öğretmen Okulu

Fenari İsa

Yeşil Tekke Sok.

Orta

SARAÇHANE PARKI

SEHZADEBAŞI

Şehzade

Molla Şeref

Belediye Sarayı

Sekbanlar

Mevlanakapı

Yedikule Müzesi ⑫

Ahmet Vefik Paşa Cad.

was treated well, but then took to mixing Judaism with Islam. A few of his followers, the *Dönme* ("returned"), still exist, as Muslims who practise certain Jewish traditions.

Map on page 188

Small Christian colonies survived throughout the Ottoman period and this area also has several fine churches, such as the extraordinary pre-fab **Bulgar Kilisesi ❸** (Church of St Stephen of the Bulgars; Mürsel Paşa Caddesi 85; open 9am–4pm daily) which was entirely cast of iron in Vienna in 1871, shipped to the Golden Horn and assembled on the spot for the Bulgarians who had just split from the Greek Orthodox Patriarchate. It is still in use. The 13th-century **Kanlı Kilise ❹** (St Mary of Mongols; Tevkii Cafer Mektebi Sokak; open 9am–5pm daily) is the only surviving Byzantine church to remain under the control of the Patriarchate, given immunity by the Conqueror himself. Amongst other icons of note, it contains a superb 11th-century mosaic of Theotokos Pammakaristos (All-Joyous Mother of God).

Engraving at the Greek Patriarchate, still the symbolic headquarters of the Orthodox church.

Orthodox headquarters

The Church of the Virgin Pammakaristos, now **Fethiye Cami ❺** (Fethiye Caddesi) is one the best kept secrets of the city, as it contains 14th-century gold-backed mosaics considered equal to those of St. Saviour in Chora, though they are kept in a side chapel and you need special permission from Aya Sofya to view them. After the Conquest it served for 100 years as the Greek Patriarchate but was later converted to a mosque. The Greek Patriarchate has had its headquarters in Fener since 1601. The **Church of St George (Ortodoks Patrikhanesi) ❻** (Sadrazam Ali Paşa Caddesi 35; open 9am–5pm), which dates from 1720, houses numerous early sacred relics, including the coffin of St Euphemia, an ivory-inlaid throne associated with the 4th-century St John Chrysostom and various icons and mosaics.

BELOW: children play below a doorway.

In theory, the Ecumenical Patriarch heads the world's Orthodox churches, though this is largely symbolic today. In practice, its rule has always been contentious. Gregory V's rally to overthrow the Ottomans, at the beginning of the Greek war of Independence in 1821, led to riots and tension that has survived to the present day. The Patriarchate is under strict security, though guided tours are available.

The pretty, secluded **Selim I Cami** (Yavuz Selim Caddesi) was built in 1522 beside what was once the Byzantine Cistern of Aspar. The gardens make a quiet place to sit after a long walk and there are excellent early İznik tiles in the porticoes and prayer hall. Many of the fixtures are original.

Kariye museum

The undoubted star of the neighbourhood is the superb 11th-century **Church of St Saviour in Chora**, now the **Kariye Müzesi ❼** (Kariye Cami Sok.; open 9.30am–4pm; closed Wed; entrance fee), which has over 100 of the finest Byzantine mosaics in the world. "In Chora" has a double meaning: both "in the country", as the church must have been, but also "in nature" or life, alluding to the humanity of Christ.

The early 14th-century statesman and theologian

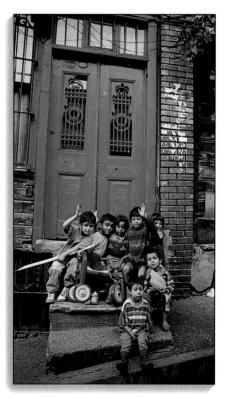

Head of Christ, one of many gilded mosaics in the spectacular church of St Saviour in Chora.

BELOW: St Saviour in Chora has one of the world's finest collections of Byzantine mosaics.

who commissioned the spectacular mosaics and frescoes, Theodore Metochites, wanted to relate to the common people "how the lord himself became mortal on our behalf," by depicting dozens of Biblical scenes from the genealogy of Christ to the Annunciation of Mary and the Last Judgement in about as controversially populist a style as one could then get away with. The frescoes, in particular, almost resemble comic-book religious tracts – they were meant to be accessible to all. Recent restorations were undertaken by the Byzantine Institute of America, and it is worth joining a tour group or purchasing a guide book in order to understand the works in their proper chronological order.

The area around the museum, including the Kariye Hotel and Asithane Restaurant, was renovated by the Turkish Touring and Automobile Assocation under the indefatigable Çelik Gülersoy.

Just before you reach the walls, near the Edirnekapı, is the **Mihrimah Sultan Cami ❽**, which was built by Sinan in 1565 for Süleyman the Magnificent's favourite daughter. It was made light and airy by the use of delicate stained glass and the many windows which pierce the dome.

Building for an empire

The **Edirnekapı** is one of the most important of eleven gates and 192 towers along the magnificent **Teodos II Suru (City Walls of Theodosius) ❾**, which extend for more than 6 km (4 miles) from the Marmara Sea to the Golden Horn. They successfully protected the much-coveted city of Constantinople from invasion for over 1,000 years. Unfortunately, since they are difficult to reach (being pierced by motorways and surrounded by some insalubrious neighbourhoods), the walls are frequently only seen by visitors when they are trav-

elling by taxi to or from the airport. Fewer still "walk the walls" from end to end. Along the northern stretch of the walls, in the neighbourhood of **Ayvansaray,** the remains of the **Palace of Blachernae** and **Tekfur Sarayı**. These are the best of the surviving Byzantine imperial residences, sufficiently out of the way to have escaped being levelled for apartment blocks, and still surrounded by huge plane trees and traditional wooden houses. In recent years, the Golden Horn was so badly polluted that locals said their eyes burned, and the smell of sulphur saturated the air; property, therefore, has not been at a premium.

The closer of the two to Edirnekapı is **Tekfur Sarayı** ❿ (Palace of the Porphyrogenitus; Şişehane Caddesi), thought to have been an annexe to Blachernae during the 14th-century Palaeologic dynasty. The upper storeys were the living quarters, looking out onto an open courtyard. There are still coloured glass fragments in the topmost window arches. After the Conquest, the palace was used to house exotic animals such as giraffes, panthers and elephants, which sultans showed to visiting dignitaries – hence the area's name Ayvansaray ("Animal Castle"). In the 18th century, the few remaining İznik potters used the grounds as a workshop.

Blachernae

The **Anemas Zindanları (Palace of Blachernae)** ⓫ (Dervişağa Sokak, behind the Ivaz Efendi Cami) was originally something of a retreat for early Byzantine royals, the first palace having been built in around 500, near the ancient sacred spring, the Ayazma of the Blachernae. It wasn't used as a permanent residence until the final glory years of Constantinople under the Comnene dynasty in the 12th century, when it was enlarged and rebuilt to true imperial standards. One visitor described walls and pillars clad in gold, heroic frescoes everywhere, and a gold throne and crown studded with diamonds. In 1204, all this glory was stripped and looted by the rampaging crusaders.

Some effort was made at restoration under the Palaeologi, the final Byzantine dynasty, in 1261, but by the beginning of the 15th century it was again derelict. Today, the only remains are the towering facade, a rather dangerous and deep stairwell leading to the bottom of the walls and the highway below, and the **Prison of Anemas**, named after the Anemas brothers who imprisoned here for life after plotting to murder Emperor Alexius (1081–1118).

If the **Ivaz Efendi Cami** is open, be sure to have a look – though tiny, it purports to be a work of the great Sinan and contains some lovely İznik tiles.

The sacred **Ayazma of Blachernae**, a short way down Dervişağa Sokak on the right, does its best to frustrate visitors. Like many extant Greek shrines, it keeps a low profile, comprising part of an unassuming modern chapel with grumpy caretakers. This is probably the sanctuary that Anna Comnena refers to as the Theometor (Mother of God), where an icon of the Virgin – supposedly painted by St Luke – was venerated in a solemn annual Byzantine ritual. Some suggest that the icon was hacked up by the Janissaries in the initial raid on St Saviour in Chora; others are still searching for it. Given the obsessions and

Map on page 188

The Anemas prison tower was popular for the incarceration of unpopular Byzantine emperors. One such was Isaac Angelus (1185–95), who sided with Saladin in Jerusalem against the Christians in the 3rd Crusade – leading to the infamous sacking of Constantinople by the 4th Crusade.

BELOW: it took 1,000 years to breach the walls.

BELOW: Eyüp Cami, one of the holiest places of Islam.

violence that have always surrounded icons, perhaps the caretakers are justified in trying to discourage strangers.

Yedikule

The run-down areas of **Samatya** and **Yedikule**, near the sea at the southern end of the walls, were once important parts of the city as they were near the Golden Gate, through which newly crowned or victorious emperors processed in triumph, and where important state visitors were received.

The **Imrahor Cami** (Imam Aşir Sok. 9) began life as a 5th-century Studite monastery which had 1,000 monks at its peak as well as an especially holy relic – the head of John the Baptist. By the 8th century it was a major centre of Byzantine scholarship, known for its mass transcription of books, and for its hot debates on the pros and cons of iconoclasm; it later housed the University of Constantinople. At the time of the Conquest, however, with the city's population greatly reduced, Samatya was an independent community which surrendered to the Muslims and escaped pillage. It remained a Greek neighbourhood until recent times.

The fortress of Yedikule was famously feared for its Seven Towers – two of which were explicitly dedicated to the imprisonment, torture and execution of high-ranking offenders, including the last Greek Emperor of Trebizond, one unpopular teenage sultan and numerous unfortunate foreign ambassadors. The **Fountain of Blood** washed decapitated heads and gore out to sea, while the **Tower of Inscriptions** (Yazılı Kule) contains still-visible names and laments in many different languages carved into the wall.

It is certainly worth making a special trip by taxi to see this powerful castle,

now the **Yedikule Müzesi** (9.30am–4.30pm, closed Mon; entrance fee); the view from the top of the walls is spectacular.

Map on page 188

Eyüp

Further up the Golden Horn from Fener and Balat, **Eyüp** is a thoroughly Muslim holy village surrounding the shrine of Eyüb Al-Ansari, who is believed to have been a standard bearer of the Prophet Mohammed killed during the first Arab siege of Constantinople in 688. Eyüp was founded as a separate town outside the walls of Constantinople by the Conqueror, and settled by people from Anatolia and Bursa attracted by the holy mausoleum. The Eyüp Mosque vies with Damascus and Kerbala to be the fourth most important place of pilgrimage in the Islamic world – after Mecca, Medina and Jerusalem. The neighbourhood is extremely solemn and devout as a result, so visitors should be careful not to offend local sensibilities.

The Haliç (Golden Horn) is a flooded river valley and great natural harbour. Its name comes from its curved shape and because it is said to be filled with gold and treasures thrown in by panicking Byzantines during the Conquest.

The current **Eyüp Cami** (Cami-i Kebir Caddesi) is baroque, built by Selim III in 1800. The shrine of Eyüp himself is lit up in green, the holy colour of the Prophet. On Sundays it is fun to watch the boys arriving dressed to the nines for their circumcision ceremonies while newlyweds come to the mosque after their legal but dull secular wedding to be blessed by the imam. Note the way very religious brides blend eastern and western customs by wearing the classic white dress but with a more serious veil covering their hair. Nearby is the **Tomb of Sokollu Mehmet Paşa**, designed by Sinan. He also built the **Zal Mahmut Paşa Cami** (Zalpaşa Caddesi) for the murderer of Süleyman's son Mustafa. There are a number of interesting tombs at Eyüp, and the **Cemetery** overlooking the Golden Horn is also extremely beautiful, with fascinating Ottoman gravestones telling the history of the empire.

Above the cemetery, you can take a well-earned rest at the **Piyer Loti Kahvesi (Pierre Loti Café)** (Gümüşsuyu Balmumcu Sok 1, open 8am–midnight), which commemorates the late 19th-century romantic French naval officer and writer whose works lament the Europeanisation of Istanbul. The view from its cheerful terrace is stunning.

Crossing the Horn

The upper reaches of the Golden Horn were the picnic grounds and hunting lodges of the royals in times past. **Hasköy**, directly across the water from Balat, was a Jewish settlement and Ottoman shipping centre. **Aynalı Kavak Kasrı** (Kasımpaşa Caddesi; open 9am–5pm; closed Mon and Thurs) was an 18th-century sultan's playground, used in particular by Selim III, an accomplished musician, when taking time out for composing; it contains an excellent display of historic Turkish classical instruments.

The **Rahmi Koç Müzesi** (Hasköy Caddesi; open 10am–5pm Tues–Sun; entrance fee) presents a fascinating collection of mechanical and scientific gadgets relating to steam engines, aviation, shipping and other types of engineering, in a beautifully renovated 19th-century factory. There is an excellent and reasonably priced French restaurant on the premises, open for lunch and dinner. ❑

BELOW: Sunday afternoon at the Pierre Loti Café.

Grave Rites

I n 1717 Lady Wortley Montague noted that the cemeteries around Constantinople were outstripping the city itself.

"Tis surprising what a good deal of land is lost this way in Turkey", she wrote. "On no occasion will they remove a stone that belongs to a monument". And thus it is in Istanbul today – with a population passing 12 million – that grave space has become alarmingly limited, and may not be reused, just as mosques may not be deconsecrated.

For Muslims, graveyards are not places of sadness, in fact a great deal of courting went on in them as they were one of few places in which women were allowed to walk freely. The city has over 100 cemeteries, many of them open air "museums," steeped in history, which provide fascinating social commentaries on the incredibly diverse, multi-cultural legacy of the city.

A good starting point for a tour is **Eyüp**, the huge burial ground which winds its way up the hills on the western shore of the Golden Horn outside the city walls. On the lower levels of the cemetery, tombs are closely clustered in walled gardens with poetic names such as "the Valley of the Nightingale." The older tombs consist of two upright gravestones – the one at the foot end shorter – and a stone slab over the grave, in which the deceased would be placed facing Mecca. The grave must also be big enough for the deceased to sit up respectfully when quizzed on the Day of Judgement by the angels Munkar and Nakir.

Reading the stones

In Ottoman times, the headstones of the graves were decorated with turbans, the variety and number of folds indicating the social rank and occupation of the deceased – whether he had been a paşa, dervish or eunuch. A turban a little to one side of the gravestone indicates death by decapitation. When the turban was banned in 1828, the fez took its place. A woman's headstone bears a rose for each child born to her.

Other headstones are humorous and inspiring testaments to those who joyously pursued life's pleasures until the end. For instance, on an elaborate tombstone with the relief of an almond, cypress and peach tree is the lament, "I've planted these trees so that people might know my fate. I loved an almond-eyed, cypress maiden and bade farewell to this beautiful world without savouring her peaches".

Or what can create a more vivid image than the following epitaph: "A great pity to good-hearted Ismail Efendi, whose death caused great sadness among his friends. Having caught the illness of love at the age of seventy, he took the bit between his teeth and dashed full gallop to paradise".

Other graveyards are also worth a visit. **Karaca Ahmet** in Üsküdar is said to be the largest Islamic cemetery in the world. Among the rows of ornate graves, near the central crossroads, is the mausoleum of Sultan Mahmut I's beloved horse, his hoof prints visible in the stone slab. **Rumelihisarı** cemetery enjoys an excellent location on a hill overlooking the Bosphorus. One most unusual grave, off the main road, is that of Rona Altınay, a young stewardess who died in an air disaster, whose tomb is marked by a detailed miniature plane crashing into the stone slab, in a tiny, and somewhat bizarre, recreation of the original tragedy.

Visiting the saints

Individual *türbe* (tombs) of saints, usually called *Baba* (father) or *Dede* (grandfather), are to be found throughout the city and are visited by the faithful who leave flowers or small presents as symbolic offerings. Poorer pilgrims leave a piece of their clothing as an intimate reminder of their personality. They believe that the holy man in paradise will be reminded of them every time the rag blows in the wind and will answer their prayers.

Traditional families often put newborn children under the saint's care, obliging the children to make periodic visits to the shrine throughout their lives.

Most saints are thought to have curative

powers. Telli Baba, the most famous, is supposed to have communicated with the Prophet Joshua, and his tomb is always decorated with the gold and silver ribbons worn traditionally by brides. Oruç Baba, in Topkapı, is currently popular and many of the faithful visit his tomb to break their fast and make a wish during Ramazan.

Horoz Dede (Grandfather Rooster), buried in Unkapanı, received his nickname during the siege of Constantinople when he made the rounds each morning, crowing loudly to wake the troops. He was killed in the final battle and Mehmet the Conqueror was among the mourners. The grave is very popular among women, whom he is said to help find husbands.

Those wishing to find work should go and see Tezveren Dede in Divanyolu Caddesi. If you have lost something, pay a visit to Abdurrahmani Sami, who lost his head in battle while a standard bearer of the Arab Sultan Eyüp. His casket, covered in emerald green velvet, is on display in a small building next to the Yeşil Konak Hotel. ❑

LEFT: a quiet place for a snooze in the peaceful Eyüp cemetery.
RIGHT: detail of gravestone in Eyüp cemetery.

BEYOGLU AND TAKSIM

Map on page 201

The "New City" has always been Istanbul's foreign enclave, famous for its lively debauchery in the late 19th century, and still the place to party

Pera, which simply means "the other side" has been the cosmopolitan area of Istanbul since Byzantine times. Jewish merchants seem to have been the first to settle on this stretch of land along the Golden Horn, directly opposite the imperial capital, using their international trade links to satisfy the city's passion for silk. In the 14th century, the area became a free trade zone for the Genoese as their reward for helping the Comnene Emperors to evict the crusaders. It was they who built the Galata Tower as a look-out point.

At various points in history, Pera has been virtually a city unto itself, with its own ships, windmills, churches, walls, *bedesten* and, occasionally, its own laws. In the 16th century, when Istanbul was the largest city in Europe, non-Muslims made up a third of the population; the Ottomans desperately needed European contacts and expertise, and this is where they settled. The only thing Christians were not allowed to do was ring their church bells, lest it interfere with the *muezzin* chanting the call to prayer.

Infidel debauchery

Pera was the heart of Constantinople's international trade, but also its debauchery. According to 17th-century travel scribe Evliya Çelebi, there were "200 taverns and wine houses where the Infidels divert themselves with music and drinking... I saw many hundreds bareheaded and barefooted lying drunk in the street". The taverns also seemed to offer dancing boys and girls as a lure to men of all persuasions; in one notable incident a riot between locals and Janissaries ensued over possession of a 14-year-old boy. It went on for three days and left 50 dead. Despite almost every new sultan's determination at the beginning of his reign to close the bars and brothels, the good intentions never lasted long.

In 1717, the wife of the British Ambassador, Lady Mary Wortley Montague, was a well known socialite in Pera. Blessed with a lively and inquiring nature, she was able to witness first hand, as well as to admire, the sensuality of Ottoman daily life. Alexander Pope was inspired to tease her with the following verse:

Lastly I shall hear how the very first Night you lay in
Pera, you had a vision of Mahomet's Paradise, and happily awaked without a Soul. From that blessed instant
the beautiful Body was at full liberty to perform all the agreeable functions it was made for.

The complete Europeanisation of Beyoğlu, which now incorporates the area from the Galata Tower to Taksim Square, really began in the early 19th century when international trade developed into diplomatic

PRECEDING PAGES: view from the Galata Tower. **LEFT:** view of the Galata Tower and old Pera. **BELOW:** Pera girls knew how to party 100 years ago.

Femmes turques chez eux.

relations and foreign embassies sprung up on or near the "Grande Rue de Pera" (today's İstiklal Caddesi). The commercial centre of the capital shifted from the old Bazaar district to Galata and Pera, which meant that the Ottomans had begun to hand over economic power to foreigners, and that the death of the Empire was nigh.

Increasing numbers of secret meetings between grand viziers and foreign ambassadors took place at the Sublime Porte, honorary consulships were sold, and spies were everywhere. The great foreign and multinational banks – Credit Lyonnais, Ottoman Imperial, Bank of Salonica – had their offices along the Grande Rue. The stock exchange was also set up in Galata: daily rates were reported in journals published in Pera in several European languages. The Ottoman debt grew until the treasury went bankrupt in the 1880s, and was placed under the receivership of international commissions.

High culture

Bad times for the Ottomans, perhaps, but Beyoğlu was at its swinging peak. Opera arrived in 1847, shortly after Giuseppe Donizetti, the brother of the opera composer, was brought to the imperial palace to instruct young Abdülmecid I in Western music. His presence as the head of the military band and music master to the palace led to an increasing interest in Western music, opera and ballet in the city. He brought ballet teachers from Italy to instruct the women in the harem. Outside the palace, the company of Naum Efendi, a Catholic Arab, staged the operas of Bellini, Meyerbeer and Berlioz – sometimes even before they appeared in Paris. The first public theatre in Pera was Italian-run, and staged opera, tragedy and comedy in various languages.

BELOW: Istanbul's oldest lift, still working in the Pera Palas Hotel.

ART NOUVEAU IN PERA

Not all Europeans in Istanbul were simple colonialists. Writers such as Pierre Loti lamented the "petty, practical and utilitarian" fashion for Art Nouveau which was sweeping Pera. Claiming the whole district had become a "lamentable pastiche of a European city", he removed himself to the strictly Muslim district of Eyüp. He blamed the fashion-mad Levantines, non-Muslim descendants from Galata's old "foreign" community, but Muslim students showed little interest in the architecture faculty in the newly opened Academy of Fine Arts, and the Ottoman élite were mad for works "à la Franka".

Unfortunately, most of the Art Nouveau buildings of Beyoğlu looked spectacular from the outside, but were disasters within. They were built of cheap materials and by cheap labourers after the (often unpaid) architects had submitted their designs. However, some of the grander buildings were optimistically "signed" by the architect – one, in a fit of futurist optimism, called himself *Yenidünya* (New World). It took the nationalist movement, inspired by the Young Turks from 1910 onwards, to develop a "Turk Nouveau" style that survived until the early days of the Republic, when the capital was moved to Ankara. Its leading exponents were Kemaledden and Vedat Tek.

By 1854, the district had emerged as an informal municipality, with the gas-lit Grande Rue, a centrepiece for its shimmering nightlife, famed for its theatres and ballrooms – a little piece of Paris in the middle of a Muslim city. Boulevards and streets took names such as "Rue de Venise" and "Passage d'Europe". French was the language of preference, top hats and tails were required in the now boisterous Çiçek Pasajı and grand ballrooms attracted the westernised sons of Ottoman nobility who waltzed with the dispossessed Russian princesses arriving in droves after the Bolshevik revolution. Many of these refugees were also ballet teachers who survived by taking on students and training them to put on amateur performances.

And education

When the Orient Express was completed in 1889, new arrivals were taken by horse-drawn carriage to the newly opened Pera Palas Hotel. This was followed by others, including the Grand Hotel de Londres, its now shabbier and cheaper cousin on Meşrutiyet Caddesi. Commercial expansion was accompanied by its educational counterpart. Englishmen and Americans, Jesuits and Lazarists, Jews and Armenians opened up their own schools, some of which continue to excel today as the leading schools of modern Turkey. In 1868, the Turkish government joined the trend by establishing the Imperial Lycée of Galatasaray, modelled on French public schools, with lessons conducted in French. Its monumental cast-iron portals opening onto a tree-lined courtyard, flanked by two fountains of sculpted marble, still dominate Galatasaray Meydanı.

At the turn of the 20th century, Constantinople was two distinct cities, as in many ways it still is today. The decaying medieval warrens of Muslim Stamboul,

Vintage trams creak nostalgically along İstiklal Caddesi.

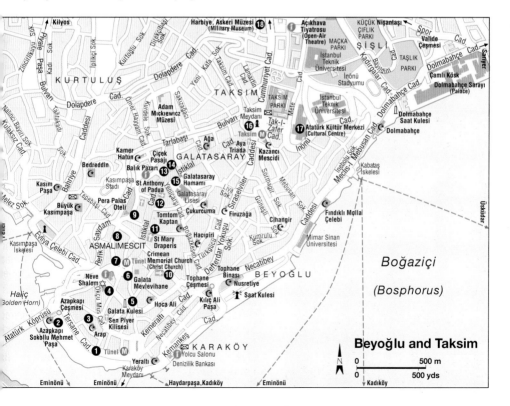

epitomising the last days of the Ottoman Empire, contrasted strongly with the extravagant, egregious wealth of European Pera. Not only did foreigners have control of the economic sector, but also construction, and their architects were given a free hand in "ushering in the new era", which was often at odds with the character of the city.

Ultimately the pleasures of Pera were also to attract a westward-leaning and hard drinking young officer named Mustafa Kemal who was so impressed by the ballets, operas and theatre evenings he attended there that he made the continued development of European culture paramount during his reforms in the new Republic of Turkey.

Flyposting for clubs and concerts, on İstiklal Caddesi.

Troubled times

By the 1970s, Beyoğlu had fallen on troubled times, the scene of armed conflict between political dissidents and government forces in the lead up to the 1980 coup. Even today, Taksim and İstiklal Caddesi are the main focal points for political marches and the sight of riot squads (generally greatly outnumbering demonstrators) and Panzer tanks is not unusual. Until a makeover in the mid-1980s, when İstiklal Caddesi was pedestrianised, the area was considered a shadow world of brothels, strip clubs, and organised crime.

Since 1990, however, the street has gone more upmarket, becoming the Grande Rue once more. If you look carefully through the crowds of trendy young people on their way to bars and cinemas, you can still find remnants of the smart past with its Art Nouveau architecture and elegant passages, where caryatids beckon you inwards to what are now the cafés, antique shops and alternative record stores of the city's thriving, élite youth culture.

BELOW: İstiklal Caddesi, heart of Istanbul's shopping and entertainment district.

Churches and synagogues

Begin at Karaköy, where **Tersane Caddesi ❶** (Perşembe Pazar) is crowded with traffic and best known as the place to buy ship fittings, toilets, tools and tiles. In centuries past, however, it was a significant part of the city – just to your left, at Galata Bridge, are the Zulfaris Synagogue, the old Rüstem Pafla Caravansarai and the Galata Bedesten. Next to the Atatürk Bridge, the **Azapkapı Sokollu Mehmet Paşa Cami ❷** is one of the last mosques to have been built by Sinan – in 1578. It has a beautiful fountain dating from the early 18th century. At Yolcuzade Sokak, **Yanık Kapı** ("Burnt Gate") is the only surviving piece of the 14th-century Genoese walls which once surrounded Galata, with a coat of arms and the Cross of St George carved into it. **Arap Cami ❸** (Kalyon Sok 1) is named after the Moorish refugee who joined the flight of Jews from Spain in 1492. Originally it was 14th-century church of **SS Paul and Dominic,** and the square belfry makes a rather unconventional minaret.

Back at Karaköy, the **Yüksek Kaldırım** ("High Steps") lead up from Bankalar Caddesi. The first thing you notice, on your left, is the **Camondo mansion**, home of a rich banking family which has been renovated as an apart-hotel. Count Albert Camondo was born in Ortaköy, and helped found the first Jewish

Map on page 201

school. After running into trouble with the city's more conservative rabbis for daring to include Turkish and French lessons in the curriculum, he moved to Paris. On the street parallel to your right is the large **Aşkenazi Synagogue**. However, modern **Neve Shalom** ❹ (Büyük Hendek Caddesi, just west of Galata Tower) is used more often by Sephardic Jews. Most of this neighbourhood was Jewish, some of them from the Karaite sect and; a stroll around the hillside reveals many beautiful old Jewish buildings in a sad state of neglect.

The **Galata Kulesi (Tower)** ❺ (open 8am–9pm daily; entrance fee) was built by Genoese settlers in 1348 to defend their colony, which had been granted free trade and a semi-independent status after the city was liberated from the Latin occupation. Take an elevator to the top where the restaurant, nightclub (with cabaret) and balcony all offer a fabulous, sweeping view of the city. At the bottom are several friendly teahouses. The Dominican **Sen Piyer Kilisesi** (Church of SS Peter and Paul; Galata Kulesi Sokak), on the descent from the Tower toward the sea, dates originally from the 15th century, but was rebuilt by the Fossati brothers in 1853. Gravestones show the large Maltese community of Istanbul adopted it in the mid-19th century. **Galip Dede Sokak**, up to your right, is Istanbul's musical instrument centre, where you will find everything from rock equipment to classical instruments and CDs.

In a spin

The most interesting sight in this area, is the **Galata Mevlevihane** ❻ (Galip Dede Sokak 15; open 9.30am–4.30pm; closed Mon), the former *tekke* of the Whirling Dervishes – the Muslim equivalent of a monastery. Those belonging to the sect, founded in 1231, devote themselves to the contemplation and

In 1900 the total Jewish community of Istanbul was 300,000, most of whom were of Sephardic origin. Today it is little more than 20,000 – most have emigrated to Israel.

BELOW: floodlights and neon of Taksim Square by night.

celebration of the deity, including the trance-inducing spinning ritual. Dervish orders were considered reactionary and banned in the early days of the Republic, so, officially, the monastery is now the **Divan Edebiyatı Müzesi**, a museum of classical Ottoman poetry and musical instruments. But the Whirling Dervishes are still there, and perform their ritual dance (*sema*) for visitors on the last Sunday of each month at 3pm and 5pm (more often in summer), in return for a small donation. They also perform regularly during the Mevlevi festival around 17 December. This particular Dervish is rather "new age" – most of the members are young, and women dance alongside men. The music accompanying the ritual is hauntingly beautiful and CDs can be purchased on the premises.

Advanced engineering

At the top of Galip Dede, the **Tünel** ❼, the smallest and one of the oldest underground railways in the world, meets the old-fashioned tram that runs along İstiklal Caddesi to Taksim. Built by the French in 1875. Tünel takes passengers from Karaköy to İstiklal, saving them the steep walk uphill. Across from the Tünel tram stop, the **Passage du Tunnel** is one of many Belle Epoque shopping arcades in Pera which still reveal their architectural grace through the accumulated grime of a century. This one specialises in art and antique shops.

At the back of the passage, you enter Sofyali Sokak, and Istanbul's artist quarter of **Asmalımescit** ❽, a shadowy half-mile crosshatch of streets such as Şeyh Bender and Jurnal Sokak where there are currently more than 40 artists' studios and a few small galleries and restaurants. On Şeyh Bender, there is a small, progressive music venue called **Babylon**. On the corner of Minare Sokak, the Art Nouveau mansion of the sultan's stovemaker has been renovated and turned into

BELOW:
Karaköy Square.

restaurant and cybercafé. To the left, on Asmalımescit Sokak, just past Yakup restaurant, is the house which was the home of Donizetti Paşa, founder of the Ottoman Imperial Band (which replaced the traditional Janisaary *mehter* band), and elder brother of the famous opera composer Gaetano Donizetti.

The most famous landmark of old Beyoğlu is the grand century-old **Pera Palas Oteli ❾**, which still has its original 19th-century furniture and fittings. It was created in tandem with the Orient Express train service from Paris to Istanbul, and for many years was the only place in Istanbul where foreigners could stay – hence its reputation for intrigue. Its many famous guests have included Trotsky and Mata Hari; but its greatest notoriety came after the mysterious disappearance of English crime writer, Agatha Christie, who was eventually found to have been staying here while the police searched at home.

Back at Tünel, a turning on the right, Şahkulu Bostanı, leads to the **Crimean Memorial Church ❿** (Christ Church; Serdar-i Ekrem Sokak). Built in the mid-19th century by George Street, who also designed the London Law Courts, it was dedicated to the British soldiers who died in the Crimean War. It lay in ruins for a number of years until discovered in the 1980s by an Anglican priest whose parishioners helped renovate the building.

The diplomatic quarter

Old and very grand embassy buildings abound nearby. Essentially, they are palaces of distinctive, if pompous, architecture set in shady gardens. Heading along İstiklal Caddesi, from Tünel, the first on your right is the **Swedish Embassy**, built in the late 17th century. Its central location reflects the fact that the Swedes (and Poles) were important allies of the Ottoman Empire due to

Map on page 201

BELOW: dervish whirling for Allah.

SUFI RITUAL

Sufis are Muslim mystics. Numerous orders (*tarikats*) developed around charismatic leaders, one of the greatest of whom was the poet and teacher, Mevlana Mohammed Celaleddin-i Rumi, who founded a sect in 13th-century Konya. The dance ritual of the Whirling Dervishes represents man's spiritual journey to enlightenment. The *semazen*'s headdress symbolises a tombstone, the wide skirt a shroud. The *sema* ritual is in five parts. It starts with an eulogy to the Prophet, which is followed by a drum beat symbolising God ordering creation. Next comes the *taksim* (distribution), an instrumental improvisation on a reed flute (or *ney*). In the fourth part, semazens greet each other in a thrice-repeated circle, accompanied by a piece of music called the *peshrev*, representing the salutation of souls. At the end are four salutes, or *selams*. The first is man's perception of God and subjection to Him. The second expresses the rapture of man witnessing the splendour of creation in front of God's greatness and omnipotence. The third salute is the rapture and sacrifice of the mind to love, an ecstatic state of unity, and the fourth is the Semazen's coming to terms with his destiny, and his return to his task in creation. The ritual ends with a reading from the Qur'an.

their common enmity toward Russia. Right next to it is the lavish Art Nouveau **Botter House** (note the projecting iron daisies, reminiscent of propellers) designed in 1900 by a leading Italian architect, Raimondo D'Aranco for Abdül-hamid II's personal tailor. Next comes the **Russian Embassy**, followed by a Catholic church, **St Mary Draperis** ❶, built by Franciscans, which dates from 1789. It is possibly the only Catholic church in the world whose inscription commemorates a Muslim Monarch – Abdülhamid. The **Dutch Embassy**, like the Russian, was built in the 1840s by the Swiss-Italian Fossati brothers (who also undertook the first great renovation of Aya Sofya in modern times). There is a Dutch Reform chapel, now called Union Church, whose services in English are somewhat more conservative than the Crimean Memorial Church.

The **French Embassy**, off Postacılar Caddesi, pre-dates the rest, as France was the first European nation to be befriended by the Ottomans. The present building was erected in 1831 after fire destroyed the original 16th-century palace (and much of Pera), though the Chapel of St Louis dates from 1581, a pretty example of French Renaissance architecture. Very close to the Maison de France is the **Palazzo di Venezia**, which became the Italian consulate after the unification of Italy. The present building dates from 1695. Also nearby, on a very steep and narrow alley that climbs up to İstiklal Caddesi, is the now disused **Spanish Embassy**, containing a chapel dedicated to Our Lady of the Seven Sorrows. Originally built in 1670, the present structure is a 1871 reconstruction.

Behind Odakule, a modern highrise office block on the left, is the Armenian Catholic church, Surp Yerortutyun. Beyond that, another Greek church, the **Panaghia**, built in 1804, sits in a narrow cul-de-sac off İstiklal Caddesi. Opposite, the Italianate **St Anthony of Padua** ❷, dating from 1914, probably has the largest congregation of any of the Catholic churches.

Galatasaray

You are now in Galatasaray, the main intersection with the eponymous lycée on the right, and to your left, down Meşrutiyet Caddesi, the **British Embassy** (now a consulate), built in 1845 by Sir Charles Barry the architect of the Houses of Parliament in London. The imposing building may be Italianate in style, but the garden is typically English and plays host to an annual fête for the British community and guests. The former Corpi family residence, on the same street, is now the **US Consulate**.

If you go down the hill to the right of the British Consulate, you can find the Greek Orthodox church of **Aya Triada** and the **Kamer Hatun Cami**, an example of the Turk-Nouveau style by the nationalist architect Kemaleddin, built in 1911.

Beyond this is the gaping scar of the Tarlabaşı motorway, an eyesore which basically chopped Pera in half when it was built. Houses were pulled down to make way for it and some inhabitants made homeless. Life beyond the motorway went downhill as fast as that in Beyoğlu went up. Most of the houses are in dreadful repair. The area can be dangerous for petty thievery, but in the region of Sakızağacı Caddesi a number of Greek, Armenian and Syrian Orthodox churches are hiding amongst the slums.

BELOW: woman making *pide* (pitta bread) in a restaurant window.

Alleys and passages

Istanbul's famous fish market, the **Balık Pazarı** , opposite the British Consulate, contains a few remnants of Beyoğlu's European past, such as the *Sütte* delicatessen, which sells pork products (a rarity in the city). Within the lively, smelly market, a well-hidden doorway leads to the largest Armenian church in town, **Surp Yerortutyan** (another Holy Trinity), which dates from 1838. The recently renovated, statue-lined **Aynalı Pasajı** (Passage de l'Europe), which connects Meşrutiyet Caddesi and the fish market, is now full of gift shops.

The splendid Cité de Pera is now better known as the colorful tavern-alley of **Çiçek Pasajı** ⑭, where cheap restaurants and roving street musicians vie for attention in one of Istanbul's busiest and most entertaining restaurant quarters. In an alley to the back of the main bazaar, the restaurants on **Nevizade Sokak** give a more raunchy flavour of times past, while restaurants such as *Boncuk* still serve traditional Armenian specialties.

İstiklal Caddesi's old passages retain their architectural charm, though many have become home to alleycats and shops selling cheap jewellery. The passage just before the Paşabahçe glassware shop specialises in cheap designer-imitation clothing. Others to watch for include **Syrian Passage** (No. 346 on İstiklal Caddesi), built in 1908 by a former governor of Syria; **Aleppo Passage** (No. 138); **Emek Pasajı** (No. 124) which earlier housed the exclusive club of Cercle d'Orient; and **Cité Roumelie** (No. 88), built by Ragip Paşa, a palace chamberlain, who was one of the small number of Turks who trickled into the area at the beginning of the 20th century. The majestic exteriors of two theatres, **Alkazar** (at No. 179 İstiklal Caddesi) and **Alhamra** (No. 258, near the church of St Anthony) also convey an aura of the epoch, though today both are cinemas.

Map on page 201

TIP

At the back of the fish market, at the corner of Kalyoncu Kulluğu Caddesi, is the old Paniyoti Greek Wine Bar. Recently renovated, with its original casks on show, it attracts a good age and ethnic mix, and puts on Greek music.

BELOW: Çiçek Pasaji offers Istanbul's most entertaining meals.

Map on page 201

The Independence Memorial in Taksim Square.

BELOW: skyscrapers are changing the Istanbul skyline.
RIGHT: early evening traffic near Taksim Square.

Opposite the Galatasaray Post Office is a narrow alley leading to Turnacıbaş Sokak. In this alley is a small bistro/bar, which was a charming Art Deco Jewish patisserie in its first incarnation. However, the back walls, uncovered during restoration, appear to be Byzantine. Turnacıbaşı runs to the **Galatasaray Hamamı** ⓑ, built in the 1570s. Follow this street around to the left and you find yourself in **Çukurcuma**, where there are a great many junk shops and antique dealers. Continuing up İstiklal Caddesi, on the left is the 16th-century **Ağa Cami**. **Imam Adnan Sokak** (left) and **Büyükparmakkapı** (right) are both bursting with bars and clubs of all descriptions, and at Meşelik Sokak is an imposing late 19th-century Greek church, **Aya Triada**. The last building of note at Taksim is the old **French Consulate**, now the French Cultural Centre, which started life as a plague hospital in 1719.

The new "new" city

You are now at **Taksim Meydanı** ⓖ, a large modern square with an imposing Independence Memorial; at the time of going to press it was dominated by building work for a new underground rail link to the suburb of Levent. North of the square are the **Atatürk Kültür Merkezi** ⓗ, the city's main concert hall, and "Conference Valley", which includes the Hilton Hotel and the Açikhava Tiyatrosu (Open Air Theatre). Down Gümüşsuyu Caddesi are several hotels and bars.

In nearby **Harbiye**, the one sight worth a stop is the **Askeri Müzesi (Military Museum)** ⓘ, which has displays of cannons, weaponry, and elaborate costumes (open 9am–5pm Wed–Sun; entrance fee). Particularly impressive are the embroidered tents from Ottoman military campaigns. In summer, Janissary bands play in the museum between 3 and 4pm. ⃞

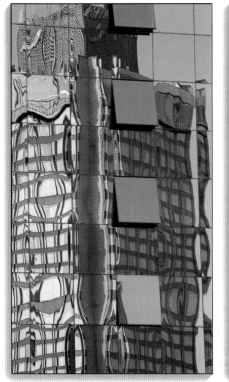

The Orient Express

The mysterious Orient Express of Agatha Christie and Graham Greene is deservedly famous, for it opened at a moment of massive change in both Ottoman and European history. For most foreigners, late 19th-century Constantinople was a shimmering pipedream of luxury, debauchery, and political intrigues, and without question many tourists came just for a peep at the previously forbidden, gazing in awe at the minaret-spiked sky of sultans and harems.

The seat of the decaying sultanate was now at Yıldız. The state was in such irrecoverable debt that even the embroideries of the Topkapı throne had been melted down to provide revenue for industrial progress and reforms. Pera had suffered a devastating fire and was being rebuilt in the latest Art Nouveau fashion to suit the interests of the rich foreign residents taking control of the economy. The shores below the old Topkapi Palace were cleared of their *köflks* and woodlands to make way for the legendary train from Paris to Constantinople which would attract an élite clientele of crowned and deposed royalty, maharajahs, moguls, *femmes fatales* and spies in fact and fiction.

Instigated by the Belgian entrepreneur Georges Nagelmakers, under the sponsorship of King Leopold II, it was completed by an Austrian contractor. The first train ran from Paris to Istanbul in 1889. Service on the route continued up to World War I and resumed with a vengeance in the 1920s – a period in which the train most lived up to its reputation for intrigue, with shady deals in the smoking lounge and assassination plots in Balkan tunnels.

What fact did not offer, fiction soon provided, and numerous literary creations began stalking the handsome wagons. Graham Greene's first successful novel, *Stamboul Train*, took place entirely aboard the Orient Express and the station platforms along the way, and there are few English-language readers who are not familiar with Agatha Christie's *Murder on the Orient Express*.

RIGHT: the book and film of *Murder on the Orient Express* assured the train a place in legend.

Characters – both real and imaginary – were taken by carriage across the Golden Horn to the Pera Palas or Park Hotels; the latter, especially during World War II, was a veritable nest of spies. But the wrecker ball has taken the Park, and espionage in Istanbul today must now be conducted in less evocative venues such as the Hilton or Hyatt.

With the advent of commercial airlines, the classic pullmans and heavy oak diners were absorbed into other lines in Europe or banished to railway graveyards, and in 1977 the last few decrepit wagons were put on the auction block. The tracks still exist, but attempts to renovate the old luxury cars and begin through trips to Istanbul for nostalgic jetsetters have been scuppered by war in the Balkans. The existing train is depressing indeed, running from Munich through the no man's lands of the Greek and Bulgarian borders to Istanbul and famous now only for robberies and corrupt officials trying to extort dollars from the unwary. In its heyday, the Orient Express was truly the "Train of Kings" but now it is no more than a glorious legend. ❏

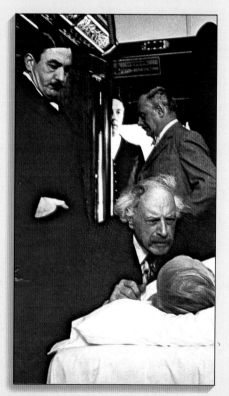

PAVEMENTS MADE FOR PLEASURE

The quantity of sunshine enjoyed by Istanbul encourages the outdoor life, distinguishing this Mediterranean culture from northern nations

Despite the impression some may have that a predominantly Muslim culture is, at least for women, cloistered and inward-looking, Turks are first and foremost a gregarious people who love to stroll, shop, picnic, gossip or simply hang around on street corners. Occasionally the city's religious local authorities attempt to ban outdoor seating in cafés, bars and restaurants "in deference to the poor", but such measures have had limited effect since people across the entire social spectrum vote with their bottoms to retain the right to alfresco rest stops on hot days. The streets, *meyhanes*, markets and tea gardens of Istanbul continue to swarm, and even the poorest family groups express atavistic nomad roots by grilling *köfte* and boiling tea in public parks, often beneath signs specifically forbidding it. The shores of Üskudar are thronged with scarved women, some even holding hands with their sweethearts, while the middle classes storm the fish restaurants and nightclubs of the Bosphorus or cram the European cafés and espresso bars of high density shopping districts.

Nearly all Turks prefer to buy their fish and vegetables from open markets, just as all socialise with their neighbours from stoops and balconies. Of course, some live outdoors due to homelessness rather than choice, but even these prefer the streets to being confined, as most of Istanbul's socially concerned will affirm.

▷ **WATERFRONT HEAVEN**
There is something sybaritic about sitting in a Bosphorus seafood restaurant, with a plate of fresh kalamari. Thousands of Istanbullites flock to them each evening.

△ **TOUGH AT THE BOTTOM**
Islam encourages charity as a sacred duty; many homeless have a regular circuit of places they go for food, drink and cigarettes.

▷ **FAST FISH**
The best "fast" food on sea or land – barbecued mackerel sandwiches with plenty of onions sold along the Bosphorus.

△ **CHERRY RIPE**
Locals prefer to taste before buying from markets and street vendors.

▷ **HUBBLE BUBBLE**
The Istanbul experience is not complete without a hypnotic taste of the *nargile* (water pipe) and endless cups of sweet black tea.

ROCKING WITH THE ROMANIES

For centuries, Romany musicians have been serenading drinkers and diners in every corner of the globe, and Istanbul is no exception – although they have long dispensed with the bandanas and gold earrings in favour of dress suits or old cardigans.

Streets of dancing girls still ply their trade in family surroundings along the walls of Theodosius, while competing musicians trawl the back-alley *meyhanes* of Beyoğlu. Many now receive professional international esteem, joining contemporary musicians on the "world music" circuit. Istanbul's Romany families have produced generations of fine musicians playing a unique blend of Balkan and eastern melodies, with virtuoso clarinetists often stealing the show. Veteran musician Barbaros Erkose has been performing and recording with New York trombonist Craig Harris with CDs such as the Doublemoon release *Nation of the Imagination*.

◁ **BREAKFAST ON THE RUN**
Simits (sesame seed rings) and other cheap pastries sold by street vendors are popular snacks among busy Istanbullites.

▽ **PACKMAN**
Hamals (street porters), who carry an astonishing amount on their backs, move around easily in areas too crowded for vehicles to manoeuvre.

THE BOSPHORUS

*This narrow strait between the Black Sea and the Sea of Marmara
is the most romanticised, most documented, most coveted and
most fought-over waterway in the world*

Map
on page
216

The Bosphorus is one of the redeeming glories of a city choking on an over-large population and urban sprawl. Its magnificent shores are lined by many beautiful buildings, from opulent palaces to fabulous wooden *yalıs*, yet this is also one of the world's most important waterways. The narrow shipping lane through the Dardanelles, Sea of Marmara and the Bosphorus is the only connection between the Black Sea and the Mediterranean. Throughout history, soldiers, statesmen, monarchs and emperors – Alexander the Great, Julius Caesar, Constantin, Mehmet the Conqueror, Queen Victoria, Czar Nicholas I, Winston Churchill, Atatürk, Hitler and Stalin – have all realised that the fate of nations and empires hinged on the possession and control of the straits.

Free for all

The Black Sea is 35 cm (13 inches) higher than the Sea of Marmara and has a far larger drainage basin than the Mediterranean, setting up complicated two-way currents through the Bosphorus, with low salinity water cascading out to the south, while high salinity water is forced back into the Black Sea at a lower level. These powerful, complex currents, together with the narrow width of the straits mean that navigation can be hazardous. Large vessels are required to change course 12 to 13 times, while the narrows at Kandilli force them into a tight 80°-turn in a stretch of water only 672 metres (735 yards) wide. Wrecked and burning tankers occasionally force the safety issue onto the front pages, but attention soon fades.

Bringing in any real safety measures is virtually impossible, for the Bosphorus is unique politically. Under the terms of the 1936 Montreux Convention, it is an international waterway (legally much the same as the high seas), even though bordered on both sides by Turkey. Ships enjoy free passage through the straits, and Turkey is permitted to police only vessels flying its own flag. Istanbul is the only place in Europe where a ship without protection and indemnity insurance can approach within half a kilometre of a major metropolis. This legal loophole explains why a Lebanese ship which foundered in 1992 rests on the floor of the Bosphorus with her cargo still aboard. No insurance – no salvage.

A collision near Istanbul in March 1994 between the tanker *Nassia* and the bulk carrier *Shipbroker*, both Greek-Cypriot registered ships, came near to being an urban nightmare. The *Nassia* drifted and foundered ashore. Her 19 million gallons of crude oil burned for a week, 28 seamen were killed in the collision and explosion, and several firefighters needed hospitalisation for smoke-related injuries. Only the fact that the accident occurred at the Black Sea entrance to the

PRECEDING PAGES: *yalıs* on Bosphorus waterfront. **LEFT:** Bosphorus Bridge at night. **BELOW:** Turkish flags fly over the international waterway.

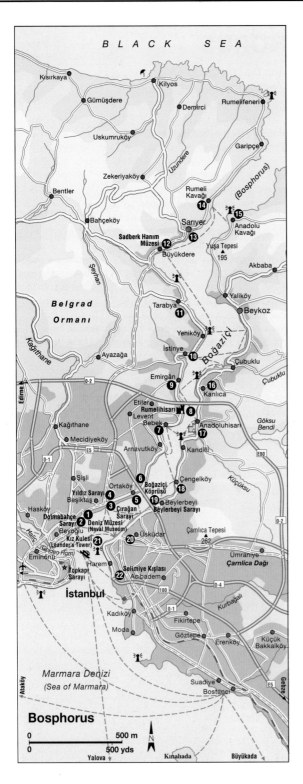

Bosphorus spared any further catastro phic effects. Had the collision taken place a few hundred metres furthe south, the current would have carried the burning vessel into the heart of the city

Overcrowded

Supertankers did not exist and traffic through the straits was minimal when the Montreux Convention was signed in 1936. Sixty years ago, there was an average of 17 ships a day, most carry ing grain, and weighing about 13 tons Today, the situation is very different Around 137 ships passed through the straits every day in 1998, some weigh ing as much as 200,000 tons, many car rying oil, gas, chemicals, nuclear wast and other hazardous materials.

Now, with the imminent prospect of supertankers from the Central Asia oilfields regularly ploughing throug the Straits, the probability of a seriou environmental disaster is real. Th Turkish government is backing th

ANCIENT APPRECIATION

Even the ancients recognised th beauty of the Bosphorus: Herodotu wrote that Darius, the King of Persi "*came to that place in his march from Susa where the Bosphorus was bridge in a territory of Calchedon, went aboar ship and sailed to the Dark Rocks, whic the Greeks say formerly moved; there h sat on a headland and viewed th Pontus (Black Sea), a marvellous sigh For it is the most wonderful sea of all.*

Darius's bridge did not survive. I pillars were used by the Romans to buil a temple to Artemis. Sadly, nothin remains of this either, as all traces (ancient temples at the entrance to th Bosphorus lie buried under th foundations of the great Ottoman fort However, it's easy to find the midwa point that Herodotus wrote of as a like bridging point; it's called Kandilli – th narrowest part of the passage at 67 metres (735 yards).

Map on page 216

building of a pipeline from Baku to Ceyhan in an effort to cut down sea traffic. It would certainly be effective but with so much money at stake, the Russians and Iranians are both insisting on their own routes and, for now, negotiations are deadlocked.

Meanwhile, regulations are being tightened. But it is a nerve-wracking sight to see tiny fishing boats bobbing between tankers as big as the Dolmabahçe Palace and crowded commuter ferries zipping beneath their giant bows. A fully laden gas supertanker exploding in the middle of Istanbul could, potentially, be as destructive as the appalling earthquake in 1999.

CRUISING THE BOSPHORUS

There are a great many ways to cross the Bosphorus. The simplest way is to cross one of the two bridges: there are numerous buses to such Asian districts as Kadıköy, Bostancı, Pendik, or Beykoz from Taksim, Beşiktaş and Mecidiyeköy.

However, by far the best way to experience the Bosphorus is by taking one of the numerous ferries, which means that you can avoid the continuous traffic that clogs up the coast roads. Skilled pilots weave between tiny fishing boats and giant container ships, battling with fierce currents all the way. The main ferries – from Eminönü, Karaköy or Beşiktaş across to Üsküdar or Kadıköy – run every half hour until 10.30 or 11pm. There are also public commuter ferries from Bosphorus ports into Eminönü in the morning and back up the Bosphorus in the evening, some as far as Anadolu Kavağı. Other ferries follow a circular route, from İstinye to Yeniköy, Beykoz and Çubuklu, and back to İstinye. Every landing has a schedule posted for all the lines.

Sea buses are faster than the old-fashioned ferries, but sitting in a closed

According to legend, the Bosphorus (the "Ford of the Cow") gained its name when Zeus had an affair with the beautiful goddess, Io. Jealous Hera sent a swarm of gnats to irritate Io who, for some inexplicable reason, turned herself into a heifer to swim the channel and escape.

BELOW: laden ferry on the Bosphorus commuter run.

When travelling away from the city centre, it's best to try and keep plenty of small change to hand. Some shops and small restaurants may have difficulty in changing large notes should you wish to buy only a bottle of water or a snack. There are ATM machines outside the Dolmabahçe Palace, if you need a top-up.

BELOW: Eminönü harbour, near Galata Bridge.

deck, you see little of the charm of Istanbul. Most people use these for longer journeys, such as from Bostancı to Bakırköy (out near the airport) or from İstinye down to the centre of town in Beşiktaş.

Tourist boats

The best option for sightseeing up the Bosphorus is to take one of the inexpensive city-run circular cruises, which leave from the main **ferry dock** in Eminönü (Pier 3 – look out for the sign *"Boğaz Hattı"*) at 10.35am, 12.45pm and 2.15pm during the week, and at 10am, noon, 1.30pm and 3pm at weekends (times do alter, so you should check on arrival in Istanbul: call 212-522 0045). These same boats dock at Beşiktaş 15 minutes after leaving Eminönü. The trip takes two hours in each direction (with time for a leisurely lunch at a fish restaurant in Anadolu Kavağı).

Other, more expensive Bosphorus trips are run by private companies such as **Plan Tours** (tel: 212-230 8118), which offer dinner cruises. The Bosphorus tours touted on the waterfront by small companies and individuals can sometimes be less pleasant as you may find yourself bombarded to loud, bad music and unable to escape.

Private ferry operators

Some cross-Bosphorus routes are catered for by private operators running small, sometimes noisy boats. The main lines for simple crossings are between Eminönü or Beşiktaş and Üsküdar, with the Beşiktaş line running until around 1.30am at weekends. Another private route, at the northern end of the Bosphorus, crosses from Yeniköy to Beykoz. With jetties right next to the harbour on either side of the strait, these little boats do not run late at night, nor do they run on schedule – but they do run. One more line runs from just south of İstinye to Çubuklu, although we hesitate to recommend it because its schedule seems wholly at the whim of the captain of the day; it is even sometimes pressed into service by the exclusive restaurants on the Asian side.

THE EUROPEAN SHORE

For thousands of years, the Bosphorus was lined by tiny agricultural villages, most belonging to non-Muslim minorities such as Jews and Armenians. In the halcyon days of the 1720s, and in the decades that followed, it became fashionable for the Ottoman high society to retire to the *yalıs* of the Bosphorus in summer. The Sultans built their own lavish *yalıs*, before moving into their new permanent residence, the Dolmabahçe Palace in 1853.

During the reigns of Abdülmecid (1839–61) and Abdül Aziz (1861–76), half a dozen baroque and neo-classical palaces, several bright mosques, imposing administrative halls and innumerable kiosks and gazebos improved the visual grace of the Bosphorus under the direction of the Balyan family of imperial architects.

The waterway became associated with a somewhat illusory end-of-the-century lifestyle of gentle refinement and cultivation which combined an imagined Oriental tranquillity with idealised European manners – an ivory *köşk* that grew only more gracious as the Empire's economy collapsed and the state disintegrated around it.

In the late 20th century, reality returned, first with the apartment blocks of the wealthy of a less aesthetically inclined age, then with the proletarian shanties that claimed a giant share of the once-wooded hills. Nevertheless, some traces of a bygone beauty remain and the modern mansions of the newly ultra-rich have added another layer of architectural interest to the waterfront.

Map on page 216

Palace of the last sultans

As the boat leaves behind the unforgettable skyline of Istanbul, the first major landmarks along the European shore are the Museum Naral and the graceful, white Dolmabahçe Palace.

The **Deniz Müzesi (Naval Museum) ❶** was first established in the Dolmabahçe Palace mosque, but now has its own building just across the ferry landing in Beşiktaş (İskele Caddesi; tel: 212-261 0040; open 9am–5pm Wed–Sun; entrance fee). The museum has some old weaponry, oil paintings and engravings, and a 16th-century map of the Americas drawn by the illustrious Ottoman cartographer Piri Reis. The favourite of most tourists, however, is the large collection of imperial caiques, the boats used to carry the sultans up and down the Bosphorus. There's nothing like seeing these lovingly restored boats to understand the indulgent royal lifestyle that so typified the Bosphorus.

The magnificent **Dolmabahçe Sarayı (Palace) ❷**, built in 1853, belongs to a different era from the Topkapı; its style has a greater affinity with Versailles than with the domed and arched labyrinth of the older palace. Mahmud II

Golden jug in the Dolmabahçe Palace.

BELOW: stunning waterfront façade of the Dolmabahçe Palace.

BELOW: the grand crystal staircase in the Dolmabahçe Palace.

(1808–39) had already abandoned the Topkapı for various Bosphorus residences (which no longer exist), but it was his son, Abdülmecid, who was responsible for constructing the Dolmabahçe. The young sultan was quite the romantic Victorian gentleman: he suffered the love of various European ladies; wept to the music of Chopin; and appropriately died of consumption. He wished to make a clean break with the oppressive, bloodsoaked memories of his ancestors, and determined to remould his palace in a "civilised" European image.

Billion dollar fantasy

The result sums up the dreams and paradoxes of an age. The palace is a self-conscious reaction to the Ottoman past, and an affirmation of the faith and will to revive the Empire in a new form. Its opulence is spectacular, if sometimes overbearing, doing full justice to a final bill equivalent to a billion dollars at today's prices. The artistry is masterful, and at times eccentric. In addition to 16 external pavilions, the palace has 285 rooms, no fewer than 43 toilets and 6 hamams, including one carved out of pure alabaster. The throne room is the largest in Europe, with a dome 35 metres (115 ft) above the floor, carrying a 4-ton crystal chandelier – reputedly the heaviest in the world. The staircases have crystal balustrades, and much of the furnishings would have pleased Louis XV.

The harem is less ostentatious than the state rooms, but still fascinating. For all its Western architecture and lifestyle, it still has separate sections for the official wives and concubines, with a central meeting room for tea and embroidery. Atatürk died here in 1938; his bedroom and office remain as he left them.

This last, fantastic display of Ottoman glory was also the setting for the end of its 620-year long saga. It was from here that the last sultan, Mehmed VI

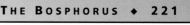

Vahdeddin, fled at dawn on 18 October 1922, making his escape by rowing boat to a British frigate that would take him to asylum in Europe. His palace remained as the symbol of a brief era of hope that went sour, an experiment that failed to take root, as he was repudiated both by diehard conservatives and the radical Republic.

Map on page 216

The more the merrier

Two other imperial residences of the same age are located a short distance from the Dolmabahçe on the European shore. The gutted edifice of the **Çırağan Sarayı** ❸, weathering the elements since it was destroyed by fire in 1910, has now been turned into Istanbul's most luxurious hotel. If you can't afford to stay there, the Tuğra is one of Istanbul's best restaurants while summer nights pass delightfully with live jazz and blues at the hotel's waterfront Q Bar.

For a time, the palace halls served as residence, then prison-cell for the demented Murad V (deposed in 1876 after a brief reign), while his brother, Abdülhamid II (1876–1909) kept a paranoid eye on him from the **Yıldız Sarayı** ❹ (tel: 212-259 4570; open 9am–3pm; closed Mon and Thur; entrance fee). Here, one can admire the creations of that tragic character, the last of the great Sultans, who became, amid his self-imposed solitude, one of the most accomplished carpenters of his empire. The **Şehir Müzesi (City Museum)** first opened in 1939 in the Beyazıt Medrese, moving to its present home in the Fine Arts Hall of Yıldız Palace in 1988 (Barbaros Bulvarı; tel: 212-258 5344; open 9am–4:30pm; closed Thurs; entrance fee). It shows the life of Istanbul through 18th and 19th-century paintings, glassware, porcelain, textiles and metalwork.

Gilded throne in the Yıldız Palace

BELOW: sentry on duty at the gates of the Dolmabahçe Palace.

The 19th-century kiosks in the vast **Yıldız Parkı**, surrounding the palace, once catered only to Abdülhamid serving for the customary strolls he took to relieve his obsessive fear of conspirators. From the declaration of the Republic until 1995, they provided favourite spots for Istanbul lovers to hold hands and exchange secret words, far away from the strict attentions of father, brother, sister, spouse, neighbour and policeman. Now they have been lovingly restored by Istanbul's restoration champion, Çelik Gülersoy – along with the imperial park and pavilions at Emirgân, further upstream, the graceful patisserie on Çamlıca Hill, and the new developments at Fenerbahçe, on the Asian side – and the lovers have to find more secluded corners of the park.

Ortaköy

A short way up the shore from Yildiz, **Ortaköy** ❺ is graced by a little pearl of a mosque, sprightly and mannered, created by the Balyans at the same time and in the same spirit as Dolmabahçe. In recent years, the pleasant quayside square next to the mosque has become a haven for artists, bohemians, Bosphorus University students and sundry irregulars of Istanbul. Its open-air cafés and fish restaurants meanwhile are now becoming distinctly yuppified. Popular community events include an outdoor Sunday crafts market, with plenty of food stalls, and the city's only open-to-all New Year's party.

The spectacular **Boğaziçi Köprüsü** (**Bosphorus Bridge**) ❻, spanning the skies above Ortaköy, surprisingly contributes to the beauty of the spot. This was completed in 1973, as the fourth-longest suspension bridge in the world. The breathtaking views it offers from the driveway (pedestrians unfortunately are not allowed on it) are matchless. At all costs, try to avoid the rush hour crush which has necessitated the construction of a new bridge 6 km (4 miles) upstream.

The hill above Rumelihisarı is crowned by the campus of the former Robert College, built in 1863 by Yankee missionaries, and later grew into one of Turkey's best academic institutions. Nationalised in 1971 and then renamed Bosphorus University, it still retains its dignity and traditions.

Poetry and tulips

Arnavutköy is one of the most picturesque of the Bosphorus villages. By contrast, **Bebek** ❼ is distinguished by a conspicuous concentration of wealth, with side-effects like fancy shops, cafés, and gleaming white yachts. Its attractions include the superb Art Nouveau **Consulate of Egypt**, which was once a summer residence of the Egyptian royalty; Bebek Badem Ezmesi, an unprepossessing Turkish delight and pistachio fondant shop which makes the best marzipan in the world; and the long roadside strand teeming with fish and fishermen from August onwards (rod and line available on the spot).

To fully appreciate the beauty of Afliyan and Rumelihisarı, which occupy two flanks of the hill north of Bebek, take a long stroll up their narrow cobblestoned streets, through tranquil cemeteries and past lilac-bedecked villas overlooking the Bosphorus. The **Aşiyan Müzesi** (Aşiyan Yokuşu, Bebek; open 9am–5pm; closed Mon and Thur; entrance fee) is a shrine to the Edebiyat-ı Cedide (New Literature) movement, housed in the former home of the poet Tevfik Fikret, built in 1906. Now on the campus of **Boğaziçi Üniversitesi** (Bosphorus University), the museum is a charming period piece of late Ottoman

BELOW: Mehmet's key to Istanbul, the Rumelihisarı.

THE TWO HISARS

L ying at one of the narrowest points of the Bosphorus, the two forts of Rumelihisarı and Anadoluhisarı have perfect command of the waterway, a fact mirrored by the nearby placement of modern ship traffic control towers. Asian **Anadoluhisarı** was built by Yıldırım Beyazıt (Beyazıt I; 1389–1402) for use in an unsuccessful siege of Constantinople in 1394–1402. After the fall of Constantinople, the fortress was simply allowed to fall apart and was quarried for building stones.

Rumelihisarı, the mightiest fort ever built by the Ottomans, was built by Beyazıt's great-grandson, Mehmet the Conqueror, in 1452, the year before he conquered Constantinople. He used his new creation to cut off grain supplies from the Black Sea – the final nail in the Byzantine coffin. After 1,000 years, the once-great Empire had been driven back within its city walls. The massive fort was finished in a mere four months, showing the kind of manpower at Mehmet's disposal. It consists of three main towers – each named after the paşa who oversaw its construction – 13 bastions and connecting walls. After 1453 the main tower was used as a prison, until the whole complex was restored and turned into a museum for the 500th anniversary celebration of the Conquest in 1953

literary life. It has photographs of the movement's participants, personal belongings of Tevfik Fikret and of the woman poet, Nigar Hanım, and two oil paintings by Abdülmecid II. At **Rumelihisarı** , the shore is dominated by the stupendous **fortress** built by Mehmet II in 1452 as a prelude to the conquest of the city (tel: 212-263 5305; open 9.30am–5pm; closed Mon; entrance fee). Plays and concerts are regularly staged at its open amphitheatre, an experience not to be missed.

Map on page 216

Emirgân ❾ offers a lively tea garden in the village square, and the fabled tulip gardens in the hilltop (formerly imperial) park, from where a specimen of that exotic flower first travelled to Holland in the 17th century. The village is named after the Persian prince whose scandalous liaison with Murad IV was the talk of Istanbul in the 1630s. A small adjunct of his erstwhile palace, the graceful *yalı* which later belonged to Sherif Hüseyin (an Ottoman MP from Mecca who in 1916 became the leader of the Arab revolt, and whose descendants reign in Jordan), can be seen on the coast road. Nearby, the **Atlı Koşk** (Equestrian Villa Museum; opening times not available at the time of going to press), was once the property of a wealthy industrialist, Sakıp Sabancı, who donated it, together with all its antiques and his incomparable collection of Ottoman calligraphy, to the new Sabancı University, situated just east of Istanbul.

A haven of wealth

After Emirgân you pass the impressive harbour of İstinye ❿, home of Istanbul's new Stock Exchange. On the coast road, just before rounding the bend into İstinye, a turnoff leads to the **Sarı Kasrı** (**Yellow Lodge**), where the breathtaking views from the courtyard of the restored villa evoke the grace of the old life here. A few wealthy individuals still enjoy the old style, as you may realise upstream at **Yeniköy**.

This area of the Bosphorus shoreline is off-limits to the casual visitor, with military properties, private homes and diplomatic summer residences leaving little room for exploration. To either side of the bay in **Tarabya** ⓫ extends a row of 19th-century summer residences belonging to various European embassies, with their magnificent parks and superbly preserved examples of old Istanbul wooden architecture. The Austrian consulate is an exception, being used year-round and built in solid teutonic brick. It might pay to be brazen and try to get past the forbidding gates of one of them: it may be your tax money that keeps the place running, unless you are British, in which case your money went up in smoke. The British summer consulate burned down in the 1920s and was never rebuilt, though a few consular employees enjoy homes on the site. Tarabya itself is distinguished by a gigantic state-owned hotel, and a row of lively if somewhat showy and overpriced restaurants whose outdoor tables clog the street and the quayside on summer evenings. Stopping by for a 2am spread of fruit, *rakı* and *meze* is still an Istanbul classic.

Another choice is to visit the area in daylight hours and also head a little further up the coast to the charming **Sadberk Hanım Müzesi** ⓬ (Piyasa Caddesi No. 25–29, Büyükdere; tel: 212-242 3813;

BELOW:
time for a little
peace and quiet.

open 9am–3pm; closed Wed; entrance fee). Housed partially in the restored Azaryan Yalısı, this delightful museum commemorates the wife of Turkey's first great industrialist, Vehbi Koç, who spent her life collecting the handicrafts which form the core of the collection. The Koç family later added the collection of Hüseyin Kocabaş, a great collector of antiquities and close associate of Sadberk Hanım. Pieces range from an 8,000-year-old ceramic figure through Assyrian cuneiform trade tablets and Hittite coins to textiles and home furnishings from the 19th century. Together, the buildings and the collections that they contain make this one of the jewels of Istanbul.

Sarıyer , a first stop for trawlers returning from the Black Sea, boasts a colourful fish market and some of the best fish restaurants in town. The alley extending from the market contains several "authentic" fishermen's taverns, serving the freshest fish and strongest liquor on rickety seaside tables, with a fiddle player and the occasional drunken brawl providing spice after midnight. The alley has been marked for development; but the visitor should be consoled by the presence of similarly delightful establishments in the fishing village of **Rumeli Kavağı** , and **Beykoz**, opposite Sarıyer on the Asian shore.

THE ASIAN SHORE

The northern end of the Bosphorus is a restricted military zone. One happy effect of this arrangement has been the preservation of **Anadolu Kavağı** . This village is cut off on all sides, and is normally accessible only by water on the tourist ferry or shuttle boat from European Rumeli Kavağı (although it is possible to drive in from Beykoz). Consequently, it has virtually no motor traffic, the hills have not been invaded by apartment blocks, land prices have not skyrocketed, and the place has kept its bucolic charm, with colourful fish restaurants built on wooden stilts and flocks of ducks competing for the diners' leftovers. The massive Genoese **fortress** looming above is no longer off-limits, and it offers a stupendous view over the mouth of the Black Sea – well worth the long, steep walk.

BELOW: the central staircase of the Beylerbeyi Palace.

The section of the Asian shore further south, between **Kanlıca** and Çengelköy, is arguably the most picturesque stretch of the Bosphorus. It is best appreciated by renting a motorboat from Kanlıca, and cruising very close to the coast. Before leaving, taste the fresh yoghurt that has made the village famous, or dine in the Art-Nouveau luxury of the Khedive's Palace, Hidiv Kasrı in **Çubuklu**, another summer home of the Egyptian ruling family.

There is a string of original *yalıs* along the shore between Kanlıca and Anadoluhisarı. These include the 18th-century **Safvet Paşa**, named after a prime minister who held office in the 1870s; the **Amcazade Hüseyin Paşa** house, a dilapidated little gem built for the powerful grand vizier who ruled in the 1690s; the home of Count Ostrorog, an important figure of the Russian-dominated 1830s, and the *yalı* of the Cypriot Mehmet Emin Pafla, who was prime minister three times in the 1850s.

After disembarking from your boat, take a stroll around **Anadoluhisarı** , where a peaceful lagoon

Map on page 216

lugs a storybook 14th-century **castle** (open access; *see box, page 222*) The village itself has steep narrow streets and balconied houses. At **Kuleli**, the imposing edifice of the military lycée stands on the site of the Byzantine Empress Theodora's convent for repentant prostitutes.

Çengelköy ⓲ is graced by the classic beauty of the **Sadullah Paşa Yalısı**, named after a brilliant young diplomat of Abdülhamid's reign but built much earlier. Several other local *yalıs* still belong to families of the original owners. The village got its name from a Byzantine anchor *(çengel)* found here. The pleasant waterfront tea garden offers sweeping views all the way to Topkapı and the Galata Tower, while the village square has a Greek monastery (its church services open to the public) a baroque fountain, and majestic plane trees. This is one of the few places that retain the flavour of old Istanbul, but is also famous for a couple of the best fish restaurants in the city, the Iskele and Kordon (*see the Travel Tips section*).

The cream-cake **Beylerbeyi Sarayı** (**Palace**) ⓳ (open 9am–4pm; closed Mon and Thur; guided tours only; entrance fee), like the smaller Küçüksu Palace further up the coast, dates from the great mid-19th century imperial building binge. It epitomises an ornate rococo style. In fact, the human scale of the architecture makes Beylerbeyi an altogether more enjoyable palace to tour than its bigger cousin, the Dolmabahçe. Note the inlaid stairs of the Fountain Room, the hand-decorated doorknobs and the single-block carved table of the harem, and try to imagine the gilded prison in which a raging Abdülhamid II, deposed in 1909, turned out his final carpentry masterpieces in walnut and rosewood.

Haydarpaşa Station on the Asian shore links Istanbul with the rest of Turkey.

BELOW: the Kız Kulesi at sunset, symbol of Istanbul.

The other Istanbul

Üsküdar ⓴ is an old residential district, once a Muslim "middle-class" abode, with countless little mosques, tranquil cemeteries and nostalgia-laden streets. At least five of the principal mosques in the area were built for imperial mothers or daughters, in a noticeably "feminine" style.

Salacak, the seaward bluff below Üsküdar, offers some of the most spectacular panoramas of central Istanbul across the Bosphorus. Sunset at the Huzur (Arap) Restaurant here is an unforgettable visual and gastronomic experience. The **Kız Kulesi** ㉑, known in English as Leander's Tower, presents its coquettish profile only 150m (500 ft) off shore. This picturesque symbol of Istanbul is associated with the mythical Leander, the lover who braved the waves every night to meet his imprisoned sweetheart. Actually a Greek watchtower, converted to a lighthouse in the 12th century, it has recently been leased to a business consortium which plans to renovate it and open it to tourists. To the east, the huge **Selimiye Kışlası** (**Barracks**) ㉒ dominates the hill. It is now a state prison but has an important past: it was here that Florence Nightingale invented modern nursing, during the Crimean War of 1854. Nearby, the small **Florence Nightingale Museum** (Selimiye Kışlası, Üsküdar; tel: 216-343 7310; open only on Saturday) is dedicated to the world's most famous nurse. ❏

THE BOSPHORUS – CONTINENTAL DIVIDE

Ever since Jason first battled up it in search of the golden fleece, the turbulent Bosphorus has been the stuff of romantic dreams

As late as the 1960s, one author described Istanbul as a "big collection of villages". The typical urban hub consisted of a quaint square, flanked by the local mosque (or church or synagogue) and a market street of rickety shops shaded by plane trees and vines and surrounded by a maze of residences. This structure not only imparted distinctly human proportions to the urban environment. Each village was a community in microcosm, complete with its prominent rich houses, shop and poor-man's back alley, giving the city a markedly different look to the more broadly segregated Western cities.

Under the onslaught of mass immigration and development, predictably, much of this structure has been swept away. Often all that remains are the old village name which now designates an arbitrary city bloc – several hundreds of them within the Old City alone – and Istanbullites' habit of specifying an address simply by the name of the neighbourhood. Where the villages of Istanbul do preserve something like their original charm is in the outskirts, notably along the winding shores of the Bosphorus.

Bosphorus villages have long been semi-rural settlements and were inhabited during Ottoman times mainly by the Christian and Jewish minorities that supplied the capital's fresh produce and fish. Arnavutköy was popularly known for its aromatic strawberries; Çengelköy specialised in sweet cucumbers; while the Jewish gardeners of Kuruçesme held the market in artichokes.

△ FRYING TONIGHT
With stocks dwindling throughout the Mediterranean, Istanbul's small fishing fleet struggles to stock the fish markets.

▷ A PLACE TO PLAY
With ts shores lined with charming villages, palaces, cafés and esplanades, the Bosphorus has long been Istanbul's favourite summer playground.

△ BRIDGING THE GAP
This graceful suspension bridge was the first permanent structure to cross the Bosphorus and link the two continents.

◁ EAST MEETS WEST
The Bosphorus is the official boundary between Europe and Asia. The metropolis of Istanbul is built on both sides of the divide.

△ STRATEGIC VICE
The line of castles, towers and strongholds along the shores of the Bosphorus a proof of the Straits' strategic importance over several thousand years.

GINGERBREAD MANSIONS

As local aristocrats took up residence on the Bosphorus, a new style of architecture evolved. Their wooden waterfront mansions – called *yalı* – were distinguished by an elegant simplicity of form, graceful cascades of eaves and balconies; from the mid-1800s, intricate ornamentation became a feature, too. The oldest *yalı* in the city is the Amcazade Hüseyin Paşa Köprülü Yalısı, built in 1698 .

The Asian shore of the middle Bosphorus was especialy rich in *yalıs*, but some of the finest have been destroyed. In his book, *The Bosphorus*, John Freely points out that "these old *yalıs*, many of them half-ruined and some abandoned… were once brightly painted and embowered in lush and brilliant gardens." Byron, one of the first travellers to mention these houses, writes in Canto V of *Don Juan* that "Each villa on the Bosphorus seems a scene…"

Those lucky few who live in restored *yalıs* enjoy a unique way of life, with a lingering hint of the charm of life in Ottoman times.

△ SHIPSHAPE
As one of the world's busiest shipping lanes, the Bosphorus is also home to several dockyards providing essential maintenance to local and passing trade.

◁ SWEET WATERS OF ASIA
By the late 18th century, the Bosphorus was becoming a fashionable aristocratic playground, with palaces and pleasure gardens over-looking the busy waters.

THE OUTER LIMITS

As Greater Istanbul sprawls ever outwards to link up with other towns along the shores of the Sea of Marmara, new areas open up to the more inquisitive tourist

Map
on page
232

Istanbul has been growing so quickly over the past couple decades that it is difficult to draw the line around its outer limits. In certain places to the northwest you can see the line of development stop quite clearly – there are apartment blocks, a final street, a wire fence, and then fields begin. In the main directions of development, however, roughly following the shoreline of the Sea of Marmara, the buildings simply never stop. They may thin out a bit here and there, but Greater Istanbul now stretches from Gebze in the east all the way across the Bosphorus and past the Atatürk Airport to Tekirdağ.

Airport district

Yeşilkoy ❶, on the Marmara coast near the airport, was established as a summer resort in the late 1800s. It is now a commuter town, yet retains much of its fin-de-siècle charm, with a village centre chock full of restored Victorian houses, antique shops, restaurants and café-bars. This village street scene is precisely the effect aimed at by such all-new developments as the exclusive Kemer Country Club, but which of course escapes their grasp. Here is the real thing, replete with shoe repair shops, electricians, plumbers and the like.

Those who cannot bear to miss any museum should take a short taxi ride to Yeşilyurt ❷. This is also an attractive village, though not as gentrified as Yeşilkoy, and therefore less pleasurable for shoppers. However, for aviation addicts, it is home to the **Aerospace Museum** (Hava Harp Okulu Komutanlığı; open 9am–5pm; closed Mon and Tues; entrance fee). To get there, look for the gleaming blue tower of the Polat Renaissance Hotel, (built to accommodate visitors who favour easy access to the airport) or the huge **Dünya Ticaret Merkezi** (CNR World Trade Centre).

Nearby **Florya** ❸ appears to be a somewhat dowdy old residential district, but its high, ivy-covered walls hide several grand estates, including one belonging to the President of Turkey, Süleyman Demirel. There are also some fine tea gardens and good, unpretentious restaurants on the waterfront.

Skyscraper city

A little way north of Taksim, Levent and Maslak can be reached very easily by dolmuş from behind the Ceylan Inter-Continental. You can also hop on anywhere along the line, such as in Beşiktaş. A new metro linking these northern suburbs to the city centre is currently under construction. **Levent** ❹ grew in the mid-1950s as a residential area for those wishing to escape the apartment blocks of Şişli. Early residents tell of hearing wolves howl at night. Those same people today look out to see skyscrapers towering over

PRECEDING PAGES: Büyükada, the largest of the Princes' Islands. **LEFT:** giving the bank a facelift. **BELOW:** Istanbul's new look in modern Maslak.

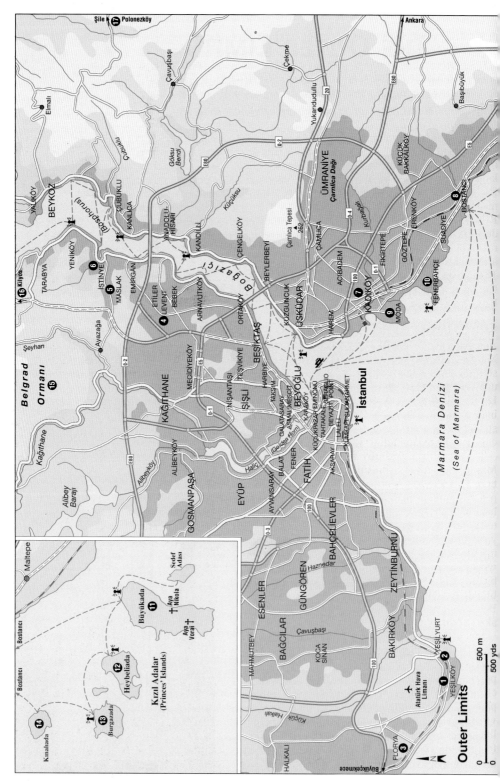

Şile 17 Polonezköy

Ankara

Çavuşbaşı

Çekme

Elmalı

E80

Yukarıdudullu

20

E80

O-2

Çubuklu

Göksu
Bendi

ÜMRANIYE
Çamlıca Dağı

KÜÇÜK
BAKKALKÖY

E5

YALIKÖY

BEYKOZ

(Bosphorus)

ÇUBUKLU

KANLICA

Küçüksu

ANADOLU-
HISARI

O-4

Kurbağalı

BOSTANCI

8

Çamlıca Tepesi
262

ÇAMLICA

ACIBADEM

ERENKÖY

Klyos 16

TARABYA

YENIKÖY

İSTINYE
6

EMIRGAN

KANDILLI

CENGELKÖY

BEYLERBEYI

KUZGUNCUK

ÜSKÜDAR

FIKIRTEPE

GÖZTEPE

SUADIYE

10

FENERBAHÇE

MASLAK

ETILER
LEVENT
4

BEBEK

ARNAVUTKÖY

ORTAKÖY

KÜÇÜK

KADIKÖY
7

9

MODA

B o ğ a z ı ç ı

Şeyhan

Avazağa

0-2

KAĞITHANE

MECIDIYEKÖY

NIŞANTAŞI

PEŞIVIKYE

HARBIYE

BEŞIKTAŞ

E5

TAKSIM

ŞİŞLİ

0-1

Belgrad
Ormanı
15

İstanbul

BEYOĞLU

KARAKÖY

TAHTAKALE SERAGLIO
POINT

İstanbul

M a r m a r a   D e n i z i
(Sea of Marmara)

Kağıthane

ALIBEYKÖY

Alibey
Barajı

ALIBEYKÖY

GALATASARAY

ASMALIMESCIT

KÜÇÜKPAZAR EMINÖNÜ

BEYAZIT
LALELI

SULTANAHMET

AKSARAY

E80

EYÜP

Haliç

AYVANSARAY

BALAT

FENER

FATIH

O-3

100

BAHÇELIEVLER

GOSMANPAŞA

GÜNGÖREN

Haznedar

ESENLER

ZEYTINBURNU

BAĞCILAR

Çavuşbaşı

BAKIRKÖY

YEŞILYURT

KOCA
SINAN

100

2

MAHMUTBEY

1

Atatürk Hava
Limanı

YEŞILKÖY

FLORYA

HALKALI

Küçük Halkalı

Büyükçekmece

Outer Limits

N

0   500 m
0   500 yds

Maltepe

Bostancı

Bostancı

Sedef
Adası

Büyükada
11

Aya
Nikola

Aya
Yorgi

Kızıl Adalar
(Princes' Islands)

Heybeliada
12

Burgazada
13

14

Kınalıada

their modest plots, and must compete for parking with thousands of office workers. Levent has many fashionable restaurants and shops, but no museums.

From here, the road to Etiler passes the **Akmerkez Shopping Centre**, an urban mall equal to any in Europe. Fast food is juxtaposed with fine jewels and fashions, highlighting the tremendous wealth of Istanbul's upper middle class. A little further on, you reach **Bosphorus University** (*see page 222*).

Map on page 232

Corporate jungle

Büyükdere Caddesi, the main road to Maslak, is lined by rows of corporate headquarters, from Roche and Eczacıbaşı to the giant Sabancı towers, and the large campus of **Istanbul Technical University**. Maslak ❺ has grown from a few farmhouses into one of the city's major axes of development, linked by main roads to the Bosphorus at Sarıyer and İstinye, the Belgrade Forest and Kilyos. Each of these arteries has spawned a patchwork of luxury housing developments, from the small and exclusive to the vast and sprawling. On the road to **İstinye ❻**, the ultramodern **Istanbul Stock Exchange** houses its own art gallery. Also in Maslak is the **Maslak Mansions Museum** (tel: 212-276 1022; open 9am–3pm; closed Mon and Thur; entrance fee), while the **Maslak Cultural Centre** is set to open in 2000. Meanwhile, **Orman Parkı** (Forest Park) hosts concerts and fairs throughout the summer.

TIP

One way to get an eagle-eye view of the outer limits is to take a trip to the summit of **Çamlıca**, the tallest hill in Istanbul. Regular bus services run from Üsküdar. The best time for photos is in the early morning.

Continental divide

Across on the Asian side, the main thrust of development follows the Sea of Marmara. **Gebze** is considered to be the edge of the city, as it is literally the last stop for the commuter trains. However, the level of development continues unabated towards the industrial area surrounding **İzmit**. This city was at the epicentre of the devastating earthquake in August 1999 which destroyed great swathes of apartment blocks and set off a fire at the country's largest oil refinery.

The area from **Kadıköy ❼** stretching along the Marmara Sea towards **Bostancı ❽** has scenes of great beauty and some historic interest. In years gone by, people living on the European side of Istanbul would have summer homes out here. Many still do, though today fully a third of the city's population lives here year round, in the vast residential sections stretching inland and along Bağdat Caddesi, the one-way avenue which runs parallel to the Marmara coast, and is lined by shops most of the way. Here you can find every brand name known, from Marks and Spencers to Benetton, Lacoste and BMW. The coast road itself is almost entirely residential.

Many people here commute daily to Europe, by ferry or across the Bosphorus bridges, but the main highway inland is fast sprouting its own array of corporate headquarters. Asian Istanbul is by far the cleaner, greener, better organised and more modern part of the city. For this reason, it holds little for the visitor seeking the exotic Orient – though the shoreline has a number of historic *yalı* along it and several fine 19th-century homes are tucked in amongst the high rise apartment buildings.

BELOW: Kadıköy market, one of Istanbul's largest.

Buy a return ticket
from Sirkeci to
Büyükada on either
the ferry or seabus
and you can stop off at
the other three islands
on the way back into
Istanbul. They are all
included in the price.

BELOW: holiday
crowds at the ferry
port, Büyükada.

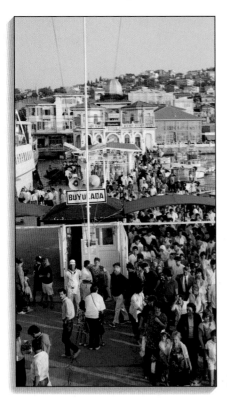

Fashionable suburbs

Just up the hill from Kadıköy's ferry landing, in a now trendy suburb called Moda **9**, a former mayor of Istanbul decided to reclaim the shoreline for the people, much to the chagrin of those with waterfront property. Thousands of loads of landfill have built up a new waterfront, with a wide esplanade for walking and biking. From Kadıköy to the Moda Yacht Club, the path has been landscaped and dotted with inexpensive cafés and charming tea gardens. The development begins again on the other side of the Fenerbahçe peninsula, but here leaving several marinas and yacht clubs and military recreation centres with their access to the water intact. They proved to have too great a concentration of wealth and influence for even a popular mayor to overcome. Meantime, Moda's backstreets are still full of beautiful homes and gardens, though they are fast disappearing under the impetus of rocketing property values.

Take a dolmuş or taxi to check out the **Fenerbahçe 10** area. On the shore, in **Kalamış**, Kalkedon (Chalcedon) is one of Istanbul's only outdoor dance clubs. From there you can walk past the Kalamıfl Marina, ogling the fantastic yachts towards **Fenerbahçe Park**, a beautiful small headland, with abundant kiosks and gazebo cafés, set in an area carefully planted with grand trees and flowering shrubs. The western half of the shoreline belongs to several clubs, including the eponymous **Fenerbahçe Club**, home to one of Turkey's top football teams (*see page 139*). The main park and all the eastern shore is given over to public pleasure. From there, you have to walk around the military centre before regaining access to the seaside esplanade. This runs for about another 16 km (10 miles) through Bostancı to the shipyards of **Tuzla**, lined for much of the way by expensive apartment buildings, all new, save for a few 19th- and early 20th-century mansions.

The Princes' Islands

The Princes' Islands, in the Sea of Marmara, just a few miles off the Asian shore, are clearly visible from this esplanade, but they are truly a world apart. Above all, they have no cars. It is essential to visit them to get a real sense of their dignified serenity.

The nine islands are known as the Princes' Islands because of their regular use as a handy place to keep potential Ottoman usurpers under house arrest. Others too, have tasted exile here, the most famous of them being Leon Trotsky.

Ferries run regularly from Sirkeci on the European side and Bostancı on the Asian side, to the four main islands: Kınalıada Burgaz, Heybeli and Büyükada. Boats from Sirkeci take about 50 minutes to reach the first island, then 15 minutes to each of the next three. Faster catamaran seabuses serve the same four islands from Kabataş on the European shore, just downstream from the Dolmabahçe Palace.

Büyükada 11 is the largest of the islands, and the one "must see" for tourists. A showcase of late 19th century gingerbread houses, the island is also richly forested with pine trees. On arrival, walk a few metres uphill from the landing to Carriage Square and hire horse-drawn cab for a tour of the island. The cab inevitably take you to the top of the peak. From there you can either continue on a longer tour around the peak, or hop off and make the short climb to St George's, a rather standard Greek Orthodox church with incredible views of the Sea of Marmara. Looking out to sea you can imagine yourself on just about any Greek island, but turn around and the one and only Istanbul fills the horizon. There is a small café-restaurant next to the church.

Many people choose to walk back down to the harbour. It only takes about 20 minutes and leaves plenty of time to examine the architecture and gardens. There are many restaurants back in town, along with a few hotels for those who want to prolong their stay.

Map on page 232

Greek heritage

Historically, **Heybeliada** ⓬ was a centre of the Greek community; look for the theological seminary that dominates one of its three hills. There are six other churches and monasteries as well, the most notable being the **Panaghia**, a well-preserved Byzantine work dating from 1431. This now stands within the grounds of the Naval Academy, which also occupies the former residence of Patriarch Karadjas, built in the 1770s. A distinctly Aegean atmosphere still pervades the very pleasant harbourside promenade, lined with sprawling cafés shaded by large umbrellas and ancient plane trees.

Burgazada ⓭ has a smaller more select population, with Jewish families having replaced the earlier Greek majority. The dome of the Greek Church still overlooks the harbour, however, and the charming little monastery of St George, set among cypresses on a bluff, rivals the best in Greece. This island also boasts some extremely pleasant streets. The two hotels have very reasonable rates, while the local swimming clubs offer day rates priced just high enough to

LEFT: ornate gingerbread trim on a Büyükada *yala*. **BELOW:** with no cars, horses are the islands' only form of transport.

Map on page 232

Sunbathing at Kilyos on the Black Sea coast, one of the nearest sand beaches to Istanbul.

BELOW: misty woods near Polonezköy.

deter the hundreds of Istanbul day-trippers from spoiling their calm and chic.

Kınalıada ⓮ is not forested like the others, and somewhat less desirable for a summer home. It was bought by some Armenian dreamers in the 19th century, who tried to establish an utopian community. The project went bust and the planners sold off the land in small parcels. The Greek convent on the saddle between two hills is now an orphanage.

Of the remaining five Princes' Islands, two are privately owned, one belongs to the military and two are uninhabited. **Sedef Adası**, accessible by boat from Büyükada, has a very pleasant settlement, whose beach and restaurant are open to outsiders. Protected from the north wind by its larger neighbour, the island has an almost semi-tropical climate.

Black Sea beaches

Back on the European shore, the road inland from Büyükdere takes you north towards the Black Sea coast. The first stop is amongst the birch and oak of the **Belgrad Ormanı (Belgrade Forest)** ⓯ – named after a Serbian colony set up here in the 16th century to manage the reservoirs supplying water to Istanbul. The omnipresent Mimar Sinan designed and built the graceful aqueducts, some on Byzantine foundations, which vault across the valleys. Picnic grounds and impromptu restaurants line the road and the area fills with nature-starved city dwellers at weekends. (Some of them actually do bring the kitchen sink; the nomadic past still lives in the heart of the Turkish soul.) On the coast, **Kilyos** ⓰ is an old fishing village with miles and miles of sandy beaches. The whole area is being developed at great speed, with the addition of apartment blocks, a huge country club and the new campus of Koç University. It gets very crowded on hot summer weekends, but there are more than 160 km (100 miles) of undeveloped beaches to the north.

On the Asian coast of the Black Sea, the landscape is similar. A long, curvy drive from Beykoz takes you to **Şile**, which has clean air, tall cliffs, good fish restaurants and many hotels and pensions. Even in winter it is exciting to see the great waves rolling in from the Black Sea and smashing into the rocks, sending water spouts 40 and 50 metres into the air.

A touch of Poland

A detour en route to Şile leads to **Polonezköy** ⓱, or Pole Town. In the 1850s, the exiled nobleman Adam Czartoryski set up a village here for Polish refugees who fought against Russia in the Ottoman Army during the Crimean War. The sultanate granted land on the condition that it could never be sold to outsiders.

The community kept to itself, setting up dairy farms and cherry orchards and raising pork for sale in the city – a rare commodity in a Muslim country. Electricity arrived only in 1973 and there is still no bus service to the village. The people here were left untouched until they came into contact with state authorities in the 1920s, when they acquired Turkish citizenship. The village still retains a remarkable Polish character, though this has somewhat lessened with the passage of time and the construction of newer housing and a five-storey hotel.

Karagöz

The striking similarity between the translucent oilskin Turkish Karagöz shadow puppets and those of Indonesia are not a coincidence, for the tradition is likely to have come from early Arab trade with Java, arriving in the early Ottoman capital of Bursa in the 14th century via a network of caravan trade routes. Though their antics are not dissimilar to those of the rough and tumble Punch and Judy, the stock characters of the original Turkish shadow puppets are thought to have been based on a blacksmith named *Karagöz* (Black-eye) and *Hacıvat*, a mason, who were employed as construction workers on the Orhan Gazi Cami in Bursa. Notorious for distracting workers and holding up completion of the mosque with their quarrels and comic disputes, they were executed by an angry Sultan Beyazıt. The facts are uncertain, but the names of Karagöz and Hacivat are said to be recorded on the building registry and their graves are in Bursa.

The first historic reference to Karagöz in Turkish history, however, describes Sultan Selim I's delight in a shadow play depicting the hanging of the last Mamlûk Sultan of Egypt in 1517, perhaps an indication it had become a common Ottoman amusement. Certainly Karagöz was well established as court entertainment by the end of the 16th century – there is a lengthy description of shadow plays performed by Arabs during the marathon 55-day circumcision celebration for Murad III's son Mehmet III at Topkapı in 1582. More often, however, the puppet performances at the palace were comic and/or pornographic private shows for the sultan and his favourite concubines.

Amongst the people, and especially in Pera where there was a permanent Karagöz theatre, the shows were noted for being lewd and licentious in the manner of the Italian *commedia dell'arte*, and foreign witnesses expressed shock that women and children were allowed to sit through performances. In the tradition of Priapus, Karagöz himself was often endowed with an unwieldy, detachable

phallus. Gradually, however, puppet theatre also became known for biting political satire. By the first half of the 19th century, it had become true agitprop, at a time when censorship was rigid and popular entertainment the safest form of political criticism. As recently as 1968 the late Turkish left-wing satirist Aziz Nesin won a competition for new Karagöz texts. Today, the satirical tradition has been taken up by "adult" comic books such as *Leman*, as it is still easier to be critical in Turkey by means of the visual image than the written word.

Older Turkish people may best remember Karagöz as family entertainment during the long nights of the Ramazan fast. It is this tradition that the Çelikkol family in Bursa hope to resurrect in their annual international Karagöz festivals, which take place in the autumn and include seminars and training. The new Karagöz theatre in Çekirge is across from the graveyard where the original blacksmith is said to be buried. A Karagöz training school has also been opened in Istanbul as part of the Children's Foundation.   ❑

RIGHT: one of the quarrelsome tradesmen on whom the Karagöz tradition was founded.

AWAY FROM THE CITY

*East officially meets west here, with European Thrace and Asian
Marmara facing each other from opposite shores of the
Dardanelles and the Sea of Marmara*

Both important areas of Turkey, Thrace and Marmara attract a large number of visitors each year. Those in search of history find a land of ghosts – from the many thousands who died in horrific battle at Gallipoli, to the warriors at ancient Troy who fought for the heart of a beautiful woman. Though physically close to Istanbul, the people here are very different and feel intense pride in their own history and rich local traditions.

Thrace

The European area of Turkey, **Trakya** (**Thrace**) occupies the extreme southeastern tip of the Balkan peninsula. It is a windswept region of fertile farmland, melancholy bogs and vine-covered hills that gently descend to the sea. The E-80 motorway bisects Thrace: the successor to the Roman Via Egnatia, it is Turkey's main roadlink with Europe.

According to the philosopher Xenophanes (active *circa* 570–478 BC), the ancient Thracians were a blue-eyed, red-haired people very much like the images of their gods. They were known for being quarrelsome, so much so that Herodotus said they would have been invincible, if only they could agree with one another. But the Macedonians and Romans found that they made excellent soldiers. Thracian women also had a fearsome reputation – unable to agree on which one of them would have Orpheus, they tore him to pieces. Strabo, more kindly, praises the Thracians for their musical skill.

Modern Thracians are bluff, shrewd and tenacious, maintaining the reputation of their ancestors for being good fighters. The standard of living here is higher than in much of Anatolia, shown by the neat, well-kept houses of the towns and villages. The climate varies a good deal – bitterly cold in winter, hot and sunny in summer. Farmers produce tobacco, root crops, maize and wine. The last is set to take on new significance as big investors from Istanbul and Europe upgrade the vineyards with world-class grape varieties such as merlot, pinot noir and chardonnay.

Edirne

The principal city of the province is **Edirne ❶** (population 210,000), which took over from Bursa as the Ottoman capital for a time. Standing within a few kilometres of the border with Greece and Bulgaria, Edirne has a busy, cosmopolitan air and one of the finest mosques in the world.

The first settlement at this strategic junction of the Meriç and Tunca Rivers dates back to the 7th century BC. Under the Romans, the then Hadrianopolis (or Adrianople) became a garrison town with a thriving armaments industry. During the reign of Diocletian

PRECEDING PAGES:
market trading is
an art form in
Turkey.
LEFT: a quiet backstreet in Bursa.
BELOW: Sinan's
masterpiece, the
Selimiye Cami.

(285–305), it became capital of one of the four provinces of Thrace. It was attacked by Avars in the late 6th century, by the Bulgars in the 10th, and sacked twice by crusaders before falling to the Ottomans in 1362. Renamed Edirne, the city became the forward base for Ottoman forays into Europe, serving as the empire's capital from 1413 until the conquest of constantinople in 1453. Süleyman the Magnificent liked to hunt locally, returning home only when the croaking of the marsh frogs made sleep impossible.

By the early 19th century, Edirne had become a quiet provincial backwater, but its tranquillity was not to last. It was captured by the Russians in 1829, again in 1879 and, briefly, by the Bulgarians in 1913. Retrieved by Enver Paşa later that year, it was taken by the Greeks in 1920 and held by them until 1922. Not only was Edirne the scene of occupation, hardship and privation, it became a safe haven for thousands of refugees from the European provinces of the Ottoman Empire, its population fluctuating wildly in those troubled times.

The master's masterpiece

The **Selimiye Cami** Ⓐ towers over Edirne. Considered by many to be the highest attainment of Ottoman architecture, it was built between 1569 and 1575 by master architect Sinan and completed when he was 79 years old. The enormous complex, comprising the mosque itself, *avlus* (courtyard), *külliye* and *medrese* (religious school), is approached through a pleasant garden. The *arasta* (arcade) where souvenirs and religious objects are sold is the work of Sinan's pupil, Davut Ağa. The Selimiye epitomises Sinan's great mosque design plan: a succession of 18 small domes lead the eye to a great central dome framed by four slender minarets. Soft red Edirne sandstone has been used extensively and effec-

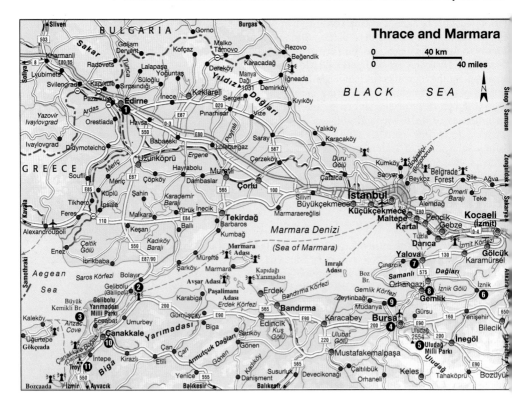

tively in decorative details, particularly over the arches in the courtyard. Inside, one is awed by the extraordinary sense of space and light conveyed by the great floating dome supported by eight giant, stately pillars. The mosque's rectangular plan is cunningly masked by the arrangement of the side galleries – those on the lower floor open to the outside while those on the upper floor open inwards. The lower part of the *mihrab* and the sultan's loge are clad in fine İznik tiles and there is a beautifully carved marble *mimber* (pulpit).

Maps:
Area 242
City 244

The *medrese* behind the mosque is now the **Türk-İslam Eserleri Müzesi ⓑ** (Museum of Turkish and Islamic Arts; open daily 8.30am–5.30pm, to 5pm in winter; entrance fee). Its collection includes an embroidered satin tent used by Ottoman viziers, stone inscriptions, copies of the Qur'an, weapons, glass, photographs and records of the oil wrestling matches held nearby (*see page 245*). The **Arkeoloji ve Etnografya Müzesi ⓒ** (Archaeology and Ethnography Museum), nearby, has among its treasures Thracian ceramics, bronze fibulae, marble busts, jewellery, Greek, Roman and Byzantine coins, embroidered costumes, carpets and kilims, and an arsenal of weapons from scimitars to bows (open Tues–Sun 8.30am–5.30pm, to 5pm in winter; entrance fee).

Architectural detail on the portal of the Eski Cami.

Heavily guarded treasure

The restored **Eski Cami ⓓ** in the city centre was constructed between 1403 and 1415. Modelled on Bursa's Ulu Cami, it is a square building divided into nine domed sections. Its upkeep was paid for by revenues from the **Bedesten ⓔ** built in 1418 to store and sell valuable goods; according to the 17th-century Turkish traveller, Evliya Çelebi, 60 night watchmen guarded its treasures. Nearby are two of Sinan's buildings: the great **Caravansarai ⓕ**, built for the

BELOW: courtyard of the Selimiye Cami.

grand vizier Rüstem Paşa, and the **Semiz Ali Paşa Arasta** **G** (market). Shop here for books and Edirne's speciality soaps, shaped like fruit and vegetables.

Across the road is the **Üçşerefeli Cami** **H** (Mosque of the Three Balconied Minarets). Built between 1438 and 1447, in the reign of Murad II, it represents a stylistic innovation in early Ottoman architecture, using a massive circular dome over a rectangular floor plan for the first time. The architect evidently had some difficulty with the dramatic concept; the dome is supported by massive pillars with awkwardly wedge-shaped areas filled by turret-like little domes at the sides. Yet the interior breathes strength and reassurance, while the exterior has beautiful decorative details and a courtyard festooned with arcades of pillars. Each of the balconies is approached by a separate staircase within the same minaret – an engineering marvel.

Near the Üçşerefeli Cami is Sinan's **Sokollu Mehmet Paşa Hamamı** **I** (still a bath, open daily to men only, 6am–10pm), with a fine dome and plasterwork. Sadly, its İznik tiles have disappeared. Behind the *hamam* stands the castle of Edirne which was built on the foundations of the Roman fort. Today, the sole surviving tower is used as a fire station.

On a hillock a short distance east of the Archaeology Museum, the **Muradiye Cami** **J** was built by Murad II in 1435 as a lodging for the Mevlevi dervishes but has since been converted into a mosque. You may have to find someone to open it for you, but the tiled interior is well worth the effort.

A dolmuş from near the Hamam of Sokollu Mehmet Paşa will take you northeast over bridges and dykes out into the countryside, to the gleaming white **Beyazıt Külliyesi** **K**. Built between 1484 and 1485 by Beyazıt II, the complex comprised a mosque, hospital, medical school, soup kitchen, pharmacy

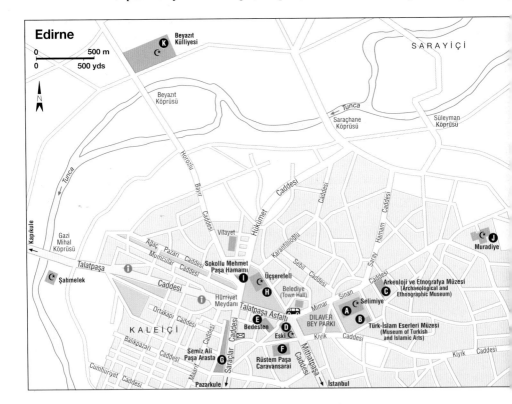

hamam, *medrese*, kitchens and storage rooms. It was one of the great charitable foundations of the Islamic world. The asylum's hexagonal cool white stone treatment room (to the right) had domed alcoves where the patients were soothed by running water, live music and flowers. According to Evliya Çelebi, visits to the tranquil asylum were a favourite pastime of the youth of Edirne.

Maps:
Area 242
City 244

Gallipoli

At the far western end of Thrace the village of **Gelibolu (Gallipoli)** ❷ cuts off the neck of a narrow peninsula overlooking the straits between the Mediterranean and the Sea of Marmara. Like the Bosphorus, these straits are a strategic bottleneck of inestimable value, the site of many a bloody encounter, by far the most horrific of which occurred during World War I.

"Damn the Dardanelles! They will be our grave!" wrote Admiral Fisher to Winston Churchill in a letter dated 5 April 1915. Those words were to haunt the Allied Naval Forces and reverberate through history.

Under the control of Winston Churchill, in his first major role as First Lord of the Admiralty, a combined Allied force of nearly half a million men tried to force a passage through the Dardanelles to Istanbul in order to knock Turkey out of the war. Nine months of fierce and heroic fighting on both sides, which peaked during April and May, left an estimated 500,000 casualties. Some 86,000 Turks and 160,000 Allied troops lay dead. It was one of the bloodiest and most tragic campaigns of the Great War, characterised by hopelessly heroic bayonet charges against trenches defended by machine guns.

General Liman von Sanders, the German commander of the Ottoman armies, could not have guessed what forces he had set in motion when he ceded com-

BELOW: oil wrestling is one of Turkey's most popular indigenous sports.

OIL WRESTLING

Turkish *yagli gures* (oil wrestling) is a summer sport which takes place throughout the country, with the largest and oldest contest held at Kırkpınar ("Forty Springs"), several kilometres outside Edirne.

In 1360, the armies of Süleyman Paşa rested here after a battle and ended up wrestling to pass the time. The finalists continued for many hours, neither willing to admit defeat, and were found next morning locked in a deathly embrace. Since then, a tournament has been held every year, attracting over 1,000 wrestlers from all over Turkey. Some are national heroes with sponsorship deals, such as Ahmed Tasci, champion throughout most of the 1990s; but most are farmers who participate just for honour.

The wrestlers, who wear only black leather breeches, are covered in diluted olive oil, making them difficult to grip. Traditional music is played during the fights, which take place in a grassy meadow watched by a huge appreciative audience. There are nine different classes, the highest and most prestigious being the *Bas Pehlivan*, or Head Wrestler. Modern rules dictate a maximum fight time of 40 minutes, during which a wrestler must get his opponent on the ground or win on a points system, judged by experienced referees.

NAPIER G. A.
NICHOLLS H. S.
NOLAN E. J.
OAKES H.
O'GRADY B. E.
OLIVE W. G.
PARKER E. A.
PAYNE W. H.
PERROTTET B. J.
POWELL B.
READ A. J.
READ C. G. M.
REEVE H. M.
REID T.
RENEHA

*The grim death toll
recorded on the
Australian Memorial,
Gallipoli.*

mand to his junior officer, Mustafa Kemal. Kemal climbed to the summit of the Çonkbayır mountain range from where he could observe the activities of the entire Allied fleet. During one of the many desperate struggles that followed, he gave his exhausted soldiers the historic command: "I am not ordering you to attack, I am ordering you to die". They did so and won the campaign.

Start at the **Kabatepe Military Museum** (open daily 8.30am–5pm; entrance fee), then visit the Lone Pine Cemetery and Anzac Cove, where Australian and New Zealand troops lie – a moving testimony to the waste that is war. The actual battlefields are marked by explanatory plaques.

The Turkish Memorial at **Anzac Cove ❸**, unveiled on Anzac Day, 25 April 1985, bears an eloquent message of reconciliation written by Atatürk:

*There is no difference between the Johnnies and the Mehmets to us,
Where they lie side by side here in this country of ours,
You, the mothers who sent their sons from faraway countries,
    wipe away your tears;
Your sons are now lying in our bosom and are in peace after having
    lost their lives on this land,
They have become our sons as well.*

Every year on 25 April, surviving Anzac and Turkish veterans return here to remember their dead and renew their friendship.

Marmara

In classical times the territory south of the Sea of Marmara (ancient Propontis) was divided into Bithynia and Mysia. According to Herodotus, the Bithynians were a fierce, warlike people who came originally from Thrace. After the expulsion of the Persians from Asia Minor by Alexander the Great they formed an independent kingdom with its capital at Nicomedia (modern İzmit). There is no record of a Mysian kingdom. It was, rather, a geographical term for the area covering the Troad, Aeolis and Pergamon. Before the Romans took control in 129 BC, Mysia had been ruled by the Lydian, Persian and Pergamene kings.

It is an area of great physical variety, from the awesome bulk of Uludağ, near Bursa, to the softly rounded hills of İznik and the great lakes and fertile plain to the west. From the summit of Mt Ida on the southern edge of the region, the gods are said to have watched the progress of the Trojan War. The region's rich and varied produce satisfied the ancients and has only improved with age – great black olives and wine from around İznik; the best onions in Turkey from Karacabey; and prize cattle and horses from the Ottoman stud farm at Hara.

This sadly is also the area at the epicentre of the devastating earthquake in 1999. Many of the small coastal resorts, such as Gemlik and Erdek, Yalova and Gönen – popular seaside resorts amongst Istanbullites but largely unknown to foreigners – suffered heavy casualties. It will be several years before they recover fully. Of the area's monuments, the most famous is also the least visually exciting, the muddy mound of ancient Troy.

BELOW: the Turkish memorial, Gallipoli.

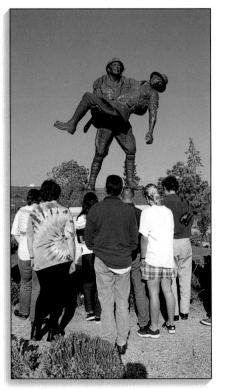

Bursa

Turks used to speak of *"Yeşil"* Bursa – "Green Bursa" – because of the city's sylvan setting on the lower slopes of Uludağ. Today, **Bursa ❹** is the fifth largest city in Turkey and industrial success has produced a certain proliferation of unsightly warehouses and factories, upsetting the symmetry and skyline of this ancient city. Yet the old quarter still presents an unrivalled display of charming early Ottoman architecture.

According to Strabo (*Geography* 12.4.3), the Bithynian king Prusias I Cholus "the Lame" (228–185 BC) founded Bursa and gave his name to the city (but altered to the Hellenistic form, Bithynlan "Prusa"). In 74 BC the last Bithynian ruler, the vicious and ineffectual Nicomedes IV, willed his kingdom to Rome. Prusa prospered under Roman and early Byzantine rule, but suffered greatly from the Arab raids in the 7th and 8th centuries and fell to the Selçuk Turks in 1075. In 1326, Orhan, son of Osman, the founder of the Ottoman kingdom, took the city. Its new rulers lavished money and care on their first real capital. Orhan issued his first coins here in 1327 and set up a trading centre in 1340. The form of the inner city still follows Ottoman lines, with the main area surrounding the mosques and religious foundations built by the first six Ottoman sultans.

Çekirge

The elegant suburb of Çekirge, to the west of the city centre, is probably one of the best places to stay. Mineral water, gushing from the mountainside at temperatures ranging from 47–78°C (116–172°F), is used to treat rheumatism, gynaecological and dermatological problems. The **Eski Kaplıca**, erected on the site of Roman and Byzantine baths, and the **Yeni Kaplıca ❹**, built in 1552 by grand vizier Rüstem Paşa are two of Bursa's many historic spas. Many local hotels also sport their own deluxe mineral baths. The oldest and most luxurious is the **Çelik Palas Oteli ❸**, traditional haunt of kings and statesmen, with a beautiful marble pool, Turkish bath and sauna in its grand Art Nouveau building.

Where there are spas, you always find entertainment. You may be able to catch a shadow puppet play at the **Bursa Karagöz Sanat Evi** (Karagöz Theatre and Museum; Çekirge Caddesi 3; open Tues–Sat noon–5pm; performances at 2pm, 8.15pm).

Also in Çekirge are the **mosque and tomb of Murad IV**, built between 1366 and 1385. Murad, known as Hudâvendigâr, Creator of the World, spent most of his reign at war. Based on the usual inverted T-plan, the mosque has a number of unusual features – sometimes attributed to the work of a captured Italian architect. The ground floor held a *zaviye* (dervish lodging), and the upstairs a *medrese*, perhaps representing a victory of orthodox teaching over heterodox mysticism. The tomb of the warrior sultan lies across the road in a lovingly tended garden. The complex's elaborate toilet, with two washrooms, five cubicles and a central fountain, is still in use.

Heading towards the old city, you reach the **Kültür Parkı ❻**, one of the city's main social centres (Çekirge Caddesi; always open; entrance fee). It has pleasant gardens and walkways, a small boating lake, and a

Maps:
Area 242
City 249

TIP

The Karagöz Antique Shop (in the bazaar at Eski Aynalı Çarşı 1–17; tel: 224-222 6151) has an interesting display of Karagöz puppets, and other traditional artefacts for sale. Ask here about Karagöz puppet performances.

BELOW: forging metal bowls.

BELOW: tomb of Orhan Gazi, Ottoman conqueror of Edirne.

variety of restaurants and nightclubs. At its centre is the local **Arkeoloji Müzesi** (**Archaeology Museum**) ❶, which has some fine Hellenistic sarcophagi, and a delightful tea garden (open 8.30am–noon, 1–5pm; closed Mon; entrance fee).

The Muradiye complex

Just to the south of Çekirge Caddesi is the **Muradiye Külliyesi** ❷ (open daily 8.30am–5.30pm in winter, to 5pm in summer; entrance fee; you may have to tip the doorman to see some parts, which are open in rotation). Built between 1425 and 1426, this complex comprises a mosque, *imaret* (soup kitchen and hostel) *medrese* (religious school), the tomb of Murad II (1421–51) and the sepulchres of various other Ottoman royals. Above the portico, brick patterns highlighted in azure tile depict the heavenly spheres, while thunderbolts in blue glazed tile flash in the marble to the right of the entrance. This mosque is built on the *eyvan* plan of a central covered hall surrounded by rooms, which was borrowed by the Ottomans from the mosques of Central Asia and Iran. Around the *mihrab* are plain blue and white tiles. In the lovely gardens are twelve tombs of differing styles, amongst them that of Süleyman the Magnificent's unlucky son, Şehzade Mustafa, whose tomb is lined with İznik tiles depicting hyacinths, tulips and blossoming shrubs. Accused of treason, he was strangled with a bow string by deaf mutes, in his father's campaign tent at Ereğli.

Across from the mosque is a carefully restored 17th-century **Ottoman house** (open Tues–Sun 9am–5pm; entrance fee), while a couple of streets away is the **Hüsnü Züber Müzesi** ❸, a restored Ottoman guest house with elaborate wood work, built in 1836 (Uzunyol Sok 3, Kaplıca Caddesi; open Tues–Sun 10am–5pm; closed Mon; entrance fee).

From here, climb the steep hill, along Kaplıca Caddesi, to the Hisar (Citadel) and **Osman ve Orhan Gazi Türbeler** ❹ – tombs of the first Ottoman leaders, set amongst the ruins of a Byzantine church overlooking the city walls. There is an excellent view from the terrace.

The market quarter

The **Çarşısı** ❺ (bazaar) – founded by Orhan Gazi in the 14th century and substantially extended by subsequent sultans – is still the commercial centre of Bursa. In the daytime, his busy shopping area is crowded with locals inspecting wares laid out in the narrow alleys lined by small shops. Bursa's traditional products – cotton goods, towels, knives, silk and antiques – are all on display.

At the heart of the bazaar, the bedesten, built by Beyazıt I on the site of Orhan Gazi's earlier building, is an impregnable structure still used for storing and selling gold and silver jewellery and other valuable goods. Its massive doors are locked shut every night. Some of the bedesten's revenues went to aid Orhan Gazi's nearby mosque foundation; the greater part supported Beyazıt's Ulu Cami.

Amid the narrow, bustling streets is a group of *han* built around quiet courtyards shaded by trees and cooled by fountains. Orhan built the **Emir Han** ❻ the earliest example of an Ottoman *han* constructed accordance with the requirements of inner city commerce. Much restored, it had a courtyard, pool and trees surrounded by rooms which could be used as shops, storage area or dwellings. The rather grand, two-storied **Koza Han** ❾ was also built around a courtyard, in the centre of which sits a tiny octagonal *mescid* (small mosque) built over a fountain. Dazzling rolls of coloured silk cascade over the counters of the tiny shops that surround the courtyard. Not far away is the much restored **Orhan Gazi Cami** ❿, built in 1339, with a massive five-bay portico adorned with Byzantine columns and domed central hall.

Map on page 249

Bursa's great mosques

Along Atatürk Caddesi rises the massive bulk of the **Ulu Cami** ❶ (Great Mosque), built by Beyazıt I (1389–1403). He promised before the battle of Nicopolis in Macedonia in 1396 that, if victorious, he would build 20 mosques. He cheated and built one mosque with 20 domes. The Ulu Cami dominates the surrounding area like a great fortress. Windows pierce the walls of rough-hewn blocks of warm yellow limestone, while doors on three sides have carved marble portals. The north door may have been added by Timur when he occupied Bursa in 1402. Five rows of four domes divide the interior space, supported by huge pillars ornamented with inscriptions from the Qur'an in stylised calligraphy. A *şadirvan* (ablutions fountain) sits beneath the central dome.

Window detail of the Yeşil Cami (Green Mosque), Bursa.

From here, walk in an easterly direction to the **Atatürk monument**, known colloquially as the *"heykel"*, from the Turkish for statue, and follow the yellow signs to the **Yeşil Cami** (**Green Mosque**) ❶, built in 1419 by Mehmet I (1413–21). The outside is almost all marble. Its name comes from the green tiles which once covered the roof and the tops of the minarets. Note the delicate

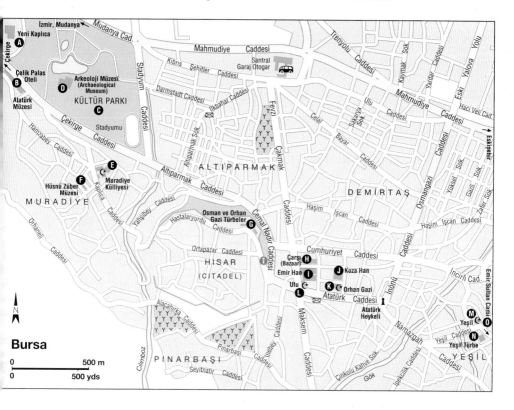

carving and the band of turquoise tiles around the windows. Inside, the decoration overwhelms the eye. Circles, stars and geometric motifs on turquoise, green, white and blue tiles succeed and supplant each other in an endlessly changing composition so harmonious and complex that it can be none other than a representation of the heavens. By the gorgeously decorated *mihrab*, an inscription in Persian states that it is the work of the master craftsmen of Tabriz.

The Yeşil Cami, an *eyvan*-type mosque, has a *şadirvan* in the middle of the central hall and raised prayer halls on all four sides. To the right and left of the central hall, doors open to rooms with elaborate stucco shelving and fireplaces. The rooms may have been dervish quarters or used by government officials. Immediately to either side of the entrance, narrow stairs lead up to the richly decorated sultan's loge overlooking the prayer hall. You may need permission to see the loge.

The local culinary speciality of Bursa, created by Iskender Bey who had a restaurant in the town centre, is the Iskender kebab – slices of meat roasted on a vertical revolving spit laid on flat pide *bread and drenched in tomato sauce, yoghurt and melted butter.*

Green Tomb

Across the road, Mehmet I's **Yeşil Türbe (Green Tomb)** is perhaps the loveliest building in Bursa (open daily 8.30am–noon, 1–5.30pm). Walk slowly around the tomb to enjoy the extraordinary turquoise of the plain tiles and the richness of the patterned tiled lunettes over the seven windows. The inside walls, apart from the decorated *mihrab*, are ornamented with plain turquoise tiles on which are set lozenges of patterned tiles. The elaborate, almost frivolous but empty sarcophagus of the sultan is flanked by those of his close family. Muslim law does not permit burial above ground. The terrace offers a fine view over the city and the plain beyond.

Slightly to the right of the tomb, set among the cypresses of a large cemetery,

BELOW: the interior of the Yeşil Turbe (Green Tomb).

is the **Emir Sultan Cami** . Rebuilt at the beginning of the 19th century in a popular but over-elaborate style, it was constructed originally in the 15th century in honour of Emir Sultan, dervish counsellor and son-in-law of Beyazıt I.

To reach the twice-restored **complex of Beyazıt I**, walk down through a quiet neighbourhood of small houses, then climb a steep slope to the outcrop on which the complex stands. Constructed between 1390 and 1395, it consisted originally of a mosque, an *imaret* (soup kitchen), two *medreses*, a hospital, palace and Beyazıt's tomb (*türbe*). Today only the mosque, *türbe* and one *medrese* remain. After his unhappy captivity as a prisoner of Timur and death at Aksaray, his son Süleyman Çelebi brought Beyazıt's body back to Bursa. Reviled by subsequent sultans for his defeat (Murad IV visited Bursa with the express purpose of kicking the tomb), Beyazıt rests under a plain sarcophagus.

Maps:
Area 242
City 249

Out of Bursa

Just south of Bursa, the richly forested, mountainous **Uludağ Milli Parkı** 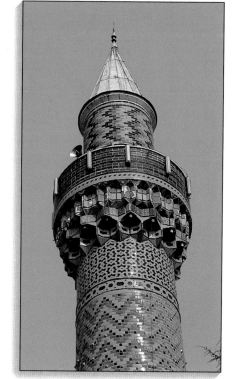 (National Park) claims to be Turkey's premier ski resort. At an altitude of between 1,900–2,500 metres (6,235–8,200 ft), it has hotels and family chalets, ski-lifts, chairlifts, slalom and giant slalom courses and beginners' slopes. The season lasts from December to May.

Climb Uludağ the easy way – by cable car.

In spring and summer, the national park attracts those interested in natural history, with long walks for the fit and eager beside tumbling brooks and across slopes carpeted with wild flowers to the tarns near the summit. Some of the hotels are open throughout the year. *Kendin pişir* ("grill your own") meat restaurants abound, particularly in the Sarıalan picnic area. A cable car leaves several times daily from the city centre, although the service may be cancelled during bad weather. The ascent by road takes about an hour.

BELOW:
minaret of the
Yeşil Cami in İznik.

Nicaea

İznik 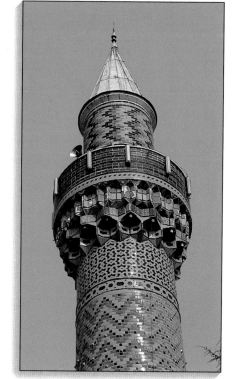 (formerly Nicaea), now a small, pretty lakeside town, 80 km (48 miles) northeast of Bursa, was instrumental in the history of Christianity. In 325, Nicaea hosted the First Ecumenical Council which condemned the Arian heresy and formulated the Nicaean Creed still used by most Christian denominations today. The Iconoclastic controversy was also settled here, by the Seventh Ecumenical Council, held in the Basilica of Aya Sofya in 787.

Occupied by Byzantines, Persians, Mongols and Turks at various times, Nicaea was both refuge and capital for the Byzantine Lascarid dynasty during the crusader occupation of Constantinople in the 13th century. Orhan Gazi conquered Nicaea in 1331, renamed it İznik and turned the basilica into a mosque. Skilled craftsmen brought here from Tabriz in Iran by Selim the Grim (1512–20) set up the ceramic industry which made the magnificent tiles used to adorn the great Ottoman mosques of the classical period. In the 17th century, ceramic production was moved to Kütahya, in central Anatolia.

There are many pleasant walks along the lakeshore, while the ancient walls and four great gates are largely intact. In the ruined Byzantine **Basilica of Aya Sofya** (open daily 9am–noon, 1–5pm; entrance fee) there are sections of the mosaic pavement of Justinian's 6th-century church and part of a 7th-century fresco of the Deisis. During its 57 years as Lascarid capital, substantial additions were made to Nicaea's fortifications and church buildings. The **Hacı Özbek Cami**, built in 1333, is the earliest Ottoman mosque which can be dated accurately. Nearby, the **Yeşil Cami** (Green Mosque), built between 1378–1392 by Candarlı Kara Halil Paşa, has particularly harmonious proportions, but sadly, the original İznik tiles on the minaret disappeared a long time ago and have been replaced by inferior substitutes from Kütahya.

İznik's **Arkeoloji Müzesi** (Archaeology Museum; open daily 8.30am–5pm; entrance fee) is housed in the Nilufer Hatun İmareti. Nilufer Hatun, wife of Orhan Gazi, was a beautiful and distinguished Greek princess, daughter of Emperor John VI Catacuzenos, who remained a Christian after her marriage. Orhan Gazi trusted his wife completely, leaving her in charge of affairs of state during his many military campaigns. In the museum there are some fine İznik tiles, Roman glass, portrait busts, plates and bowls. Note the inscription on the tombstone of an Ottoman lady who expressed a pious wish that there would be plenty of dancing boys in heaven.

Yalova

A historic spa on the southern shore of the Gulf of İzmit, **Yalova** ❼ is popular with middle-class Turkish holidaymakers. The town suffered greatly in the great earthquake of 1999, but the rubble has been cleared, even if the emotional scars have not. The spas themselves were not damaged. It is accessible from Bursa by road and there is a regular ferry service from Istanbul. The excellent Turban Hotel, some 12 km (8 miles) inland, stands at the site of the hot springs. A few

BELOW: the Yalova landscape offers an idyllic rural dream.

ruins attest to Yalova's historic past, while Atatürk's house is now a **museum** (open Tues–Sun 8.30am–noon, 1–5pm; entrance fee).

Map on page 242

Gemlik ❽ (ancient Ciucius) is one the most beautiful small resorts on the southern shore of the Marmara Sea. According to Strabo (*Geography.* 12.4.3.), it was near here that Hercules lost his lover, Hylas, when he sent the boy to fetch water from the spring of Pegae. The nymphs who lived in the spring, overcome by the beauty of Hylas, pulled him under the water to keep him forever. Gemlik's small hotels and pensions are usually full of Istanbul visitors during the holiday season. Unfortunately, industry has so polluted the sea here that one should not swim.

The small town of **Mudanya ❾**, on the coast north of Bursa, is also popular with Turkish holidaymakers. In 1922, the Turkish nationalists negotiated an armistice here with Britain, Italy and France, thus avoiding a fresh war with the Allies, who had occupied substantial parts of the country, including Istanbul and Thrace. Catamaran and ferry services operate daily between Mudyana and Istanbul. Some quaint small fishing ports dot the beautiful coastline to the west of town. There are few hotels in these places, but there are many places where you can camp, with permission. A number of local mosques, including that at **Zeytinbağı**, were formerly Byzantine churches.

Çanakkale

Because of its position, there have been settlements at **Çanakkale ❿** from very early times – control of the Dardanelles brought wealth and power. The straits get their other name from the maiden Helle. With her brother, Phrixus, Helle fled on the back of a winged ram from their evil stepmother, Ino, who wished to kill

BELOW: swimmers relax in Yalova's thermal pool.

Turkish archaeologists at Kırklareli, near the Black Sea, have discovered the foundations of another citadel, much like the one at ancient Troy. They believe that the two cities may have been allied as part of the same political and military system, controlling access to the Dardanelles.

BELOW: a modern wooden horse entices the tourists into Troy.

them. Unfortunately, she fell from the ram's back and drowned in the strait which became known as the Hellespont. Persian King Xerxes built his bridge of boats here, across the narrowest part of the Dardanelles, to land 100,000 troops in Thrace. His planned conquest of Greece ended in defeat at Salamis and Plataea, but the area has remained a crucial control-point between the two continents. Çanakkale became an active trading and transit point between Asia and Europe after Mehmet II built a fortress here in 1452, and was a thriving place right up to World War I.

Although it may not have reclaimed entirely the international status it enjoyed in the 1800s, when it played host to scores of consulates and customs houses, the town has revived its fortunes greatly in recent years, with a fine new seaside promenade. The local restaurants maintain their reputation for serving fresh seafood. Enjoy a glass of tea or a beer in one of the cafés while you savour the bustling activity of the port and its never ending parade of large freighters and fishing boats. From the small promontory at the north end of the town, there is a spectacular view of old Çanakkale, its old Ottoman fortress, the harbour and, beyond, the broad panorama of the Dardanelles. You can also clearly see the giant white figure of Atatürk cut out of the hillside on the European side.

The **Çanakkale Archaeology Museum** (1.5 km/1 mile south of the town centre on the road to Troy; open daily 8.30am–noon, 1–5.30pm; entrance fee), has artefacts, sculpture and ceramics from Troy, including a crystal amulet and crystal lion-head (Troy II), a pot cover in the form of a female head (Troy III), goblets (Troy VI) and beautiful terracottas (Troy VIII). There are also collections of costumes; Roman, Byzantine and Ottoman coins; and a display of Atatürk's military clothing. The garden displays sarcophagi, stelae and funerary urns.

Troy

The name **Troy** ⓫ (open daily 8.30am–5.30pm, to 5pm in winter; entrance fee), conjures up visions of the star-crossed lovers Helen and Paris, of Greek and Trojan heroes, betrayal and revenge, cunning and deceit, of a huge wooden horse, the destruction of a great city and of blind Homer who immortalised them all in two epic poems, the *Iliad* and *Odyssey*.

Did Agamemnon and Clytemnestra, Achilles and Odysseus ever exist? Did these events actually take place? Was there really a siege of Troy? Whether one regards Homer as an early minstrel and wandering entertainer, or as the bearer of history's most profound legends, the adventures of these heroic figures have become an integral part of the world's heritage, and their fates have enthralled and moved countless generations.The debate over the accuracy of Homer's account continues to this day.

What is known is that Alexander the Great came to Troy in 333 BC. He made a propitiatory sacrifice to the spirit of Priam, received a gold crown from a citizen of Sigeum where, it was believed, the Greeks had beached their ships, and exchanged his weapons and armour for some kept in the temple of Athena, thought to date from the time of the Trojan War. Then he anointed his body with oil and, to the applause of his soldiers, ran naked to the mound where Achilles was supposedly buried. His friend Hephaestion did the same at the tomb of Achilles' companion, Patroclus.

Troy was destroyed in about 82 BC, during the Mithridatic War, and rebuilt by Julius Caesar. It received special honours from several emperors as the birthplace of Aeneas, legendary founder of Rome. When Julian the Apostate (AD 361–63) visited *Ilium Novum*, as Troy was then known, he was greeted by the bishop, Pegasios, who offered to show him the sights of the ancient city. Julian was astonished to find a fire smouldering on an altar at the tomb of Hector and the statue of the hero covered in oil. The bishop explained: "Is it strange that they [the people of Troy] should show [their] respect... as we show ours for our martyrs?" The growing importance of nearby Alexandria Troas soon caused the city to decline, a process accelerated by the silting up of the harbour.

Map on page 242

Schliemann's great discovery

Then it all began again... Towards the end of the 19th century, a wealthy German businessman and amateur archaeologist, Heinrich Schliemann, began to excavate at Hisarlık, using the *Iliad* as his guide. Accompanied by his second wife, a beautiful Greek girl named Sophia, selected for him by the Archbishop of Athens, he dug a great trench into the mound he believed to be Troy.

Heinrich Schliemann, the German amateur archaeologist who discovered Troy.

For over four months he led his team of more than 150 workers, while the academics laughed at the mad German who squandered his wealth so foolishly. But Schliemann found gold. First a necklace, then gold cups, daggers, lance heads, silver vases and two extraordinary golden headbands worn, he judged, by royalty. In fact he had not found Homer's Troy, his treasure came from the remains of an earlier Bronze Age civilisation which had existed about 1200 years earlier. Schliemann took the treasure to Germany but it disappeared during World War II, turning up again only recently in Russia.

BELOW: the Temple of Athena, Assos.

Although there are seven cities, each built on top of the previous one, little of the site's fine pedigree is visible, and viewing requires a good imagination. Begin at the massive tower in the great wall of Troy VI. Continue through the east gate, passing the carefully constructed houses of Troy VI, to the scruffier buildings of Troy VII. From the windy summit you look over the plain to Homer's "wine-dark sea". Here you can see the great north-south trench gouged out by Schliemann. He found his treasure trove northwest of the paved ramp against the wall of Troy II. It may have been through the west gate beyond that the Trojans wheeled through the horse statue into the city.

Assos

Forty km (24 miles) south of Troy is Ayvacık, the turnoff point for **Assos**. Renamed Behramkale by the Turks, Assos is the site of the longest stretch of city walls built by the ancient Greeks: 3 km (2 miles) in all. Some of the arches and city gates are masterpieces. The hilltop citadel and temple to Athena offer a superb view of the sea and the Greek island of Lesbos. It is too far for a day trip from Istanbul, but once here, the first siren call of the magnificent Aegaean coast urges you over southwards to the Turquoise Sea. ❑

INSIGHT GUIDES

TRAVEL TIPS

New Insight Maps

Maps in Insight Guides are tailored to complement the text. But when you're on the road you sometimes need the big picture that only a large-scale map can provide. This new range of durable Insight Fleximaps has been designed to meet just that need.

Detailed, clear cartography
makes the comprehensive route and city maps easy to follow, highlights all the major tourist sites and provides valuable motoring information plus a full index.

Informative and easy to use
with additional text and photographs covering a destination's top 10 essential sites, plus useful addresses, facts about the destination and handy tips on getting around.

Laminated finish
allows you to mark your route on the map using a non-permanent marker pen, and wipe it off. It makes the maps more durable and easier to fold than traditional maps.

The first titles
cover many popular destinations. They include Algarve, Amsterdam, Bangkok, California, Cyprus, Dominican Republic, Florence, Hong Kong, Ireland, London, Mallorca, Paris, Prague, Rome, San Francisco, Sydney, Thailand, Tuscany, USA Southwest, Venice, and Vienna.

✺ INSIGHT GUIDES
The world's largest collection of visual travel guides

CONTENTS

Getting Acquainted

Turkey

Turkey is a vast area of 814,578 sq. km. (320,000 sq. miles), of which 3 percent is in Europe and 97 percent in Asia. The two continents are divided by the Bosphorus, the Sea of Marmara, and the Dardanelles in the northwest of the country. To the north lies the Black Sea, to the south, the Mediterranean, and to the west the Aegean; with a total of 8,333 km (5,000 miles) of coast. The country also has land borders with Greece, Bulgaria, Georgia, Armenia, Iran, Iraq and Syria. The capital of Turkey is Ankara.

Language: Turkish is the official language.

Religion: Officially 98 percent are Sunni Muslim, 2 percent are Orthodox, Catholic or Protestant Christians and Jews.

Time: Turkish Standard Time is 2 hours ahead of Greenwich Mean Time. It advances by one hour in

Average Temperature

	(°C/°F) Max	(°C/°F) Min
Jan	8/46	3/37
Feb	9/48	2/36
Mar	11/51	3/37
Apr	16/61	7/45
May	21/69	12/53
Jun	25/77	16/61
Jul	28/82	18/65
Aug	28/82	19/66
Sep	24/76	16/61
Oct	20/68	13/55
Nov	15/59	9/48
Dec	11/51	5/41

summer (Apr–Oct) to GMT +3.

Currency: Turkish lira (TL). This has been so devalued over recent years that it can take millions to buy even a simple meal.

Weights and measures Metric.

Electricity 220 volts AC. Two-prong round plug.

International dialling code 90.

Istanbul

Although no longer the capital, Istanbul was the capital of Turkey from 330–1923 and is still the country's commercial, financial, cultural and historic centre.

Geography: The city is unique in the world because it is divided into two continents; about 60 percent is in Europe and 40 percent in Asia, with the Bosphorus marking the border. The Golden Horn, an inlet of the Bosphorus, further divides European Istanbul into two sections; the old city and the new. The total area of the city is 320 sq. km (143 sq. miles).

Population: 32 percent of Turkey's population (about 65 million) is concentrated in the Marmara region, around Istanbul. The city's population is now estimated to be nearly 12 million, of whom some 90 percent originate in rural Anatolia. Over 300 people per week move here from the country. About 30 percent of Turks are under 15 years old, 5 percent are over 65.

Climate

The best months to visit Istanbul are June and September if you want comfortable warm weather while sightseeing. May and October are lovely if you don't expect a deep tan. July and August can be uncomfortably hot, but there is usually a cool breeze, and the evenings are perfect. It usually snows a little in late January, February or early March, but only for a couple of days. The best feature of Istanbul's climate is that it almost never stays the same for longer than 3 days and the sun shines on more than half the days of the year.

Government

Turkey has a 550-member Grand National Assembly and a multi-party political system which is largely democratic in nature, though changes can seem volatile from the outside. The elections in 1999 brought a new coalition, with the DSP (Democratic Left Party – centre left) forming a majority with the MHP (Nationalist Action Party – extreme right) and the ANAP (Motherland Party – centre right) with Bulent Ecevit (of the DSP) as Prime Minister. The third-biggest party is the FP (Virtue Party – religious right) which grew from the ashes of the disbanded Refah (Welfare) Party. The president of the Republic is veteran politician Süleyman Demirel.

Among other international organisations, Turkey is a member of the UN, an associate member of the EU and member of the EU Customs Union, and a member of the OECD, the Council of Europe and NATO.

Economy

Impressive growth figures, of around 7 percent a year, are countered by 70–100 percent inflation. Turkey has a strong agricultural base (wheat, sugar beat, sunflowers, fruit, vegetables), and the country is a major producer and exporter of tomatoes, hazelnuts, aubergines, watermelons, cotton and wool. Other industries include textiles, leather, food, car manufacturing and chemicals. Tourism makes a significant contribution to the economy, with an estimated 10m visitors a year. The country's largest single investment is the Southeast Anatolian Project (GAP), a series of massive dams, hydro-electric power plants and irrigation facilities on the Euphrates and Tigris rivers in the southeast. The country also hopes to build an oil pipeline from the Central Asian oilfields to relieve shipping pressure on the Bosphorus. Istanbul itself is mainly a trading and service centre, but it has heavy industry along the Marmara.

Planning the Trip

Tourist Offices Abroad

Australia: Room 17, Level 3,
428 George St, Sydney NSW 2000
Tel: (02) 9223 3055
Fax: (02) 9223 3204
E-mail: turkish@ozemail.com.au
Canada: Constitution Square,
360 Albert St, Suite 801, Ottawa,
Ontario, K1R 7X7
Tel: (613) 230 8654
Fax: (613) 230 3683
E-mail: toturcan@magi.com-web
web: www.magi.com/~toturcan
UK: 170–173 Piccadilly (First Floor),
London W1V 9DD
Tel: (020) 7629 7771/7355 4207
Fax: (020) 7491 0773
E-mail:
tto@turkishtourism.demon.co.uk
USA: 821 United Nations Plaza,
New York, NY 10017
Tel: (212) 687 2194/5, 949 0470
Fax: (212) 599 75 68
E-mail: tourny@idt.net
Suite 306, 1717 Massachusetts
Avenue, NW, Washington DC 20036
Tel: (202) 429 9844, 429 9409
Fax: (202) 429 5649
E-mail: TOURISMDC@soho.ios.com

Visas and Passports

Visa requirements are complex and
change quite frequently. The
following information was correct
for end of 1999, but check through
your nearest embassy or tourist
office for up-to-date information.

Visa requirements for entering
Turkey vary substantially according
to your nationality. All travellers
need a valid passport with at least
six months validity. Some European
citizens (Germany, Belgium, France,
Netherlands, Luxemburg, Spain,
Italy, Malta, Switzerland and

Greece) can enter on an official
identity card in lieu of passport,
although it would be sensible to
bring a passport also.

Visa costs also vary depending
on nationality. If your visa is granted
on entry, bring cash in US dollars or
UK sterling to pay for it (usually
$5–$20 dependent on nationality;
USA citizens pay $45).
**Citizens of the following countries
can obtain their 3-month multiple
entry visa at the point of entry into
Turkey:**
Australia, Austria, Belgium, Brazil,
Britain, Hong Kong, Ireland, Italy,
Netherlands, Portugal, Spain, USA.
**The following can obtain a single-
entry visa at the point of entry, for
a maximum of one month:**
Albania, Azerbaijan, Armenia,
Belarus, Czech Republic, Estonia,
Hungary, Jordan, Latvia, Lithuania,
Moldova, Poland, Russia, Slovakia,
Taiwan, Tajikstan, Turkmenistan,
Ukraine, Uzbekistan, Yugoslavia.
**The following can obtain a single-
entry visa for maximum 15-days:**
Albania, Georgia, Guatemala, Sri
Lanka (SL with letter from their Hon.
Turkish Consulate in Colombo).
**The following are exempt from
visas, for maximum of 3 months:**
Argentina, Bahamas, Bahrain,
Barbados, Belize, Canada, Chile,
Denmark, Ecuador, El Salvador, Fiji,

Turkish Embassies

UK: 43 Belgrave Square, London
SW1X 8PA
Tel: (020) 7589 0360, 7589 0949
Fax: (020) 7245 9547
Visa Information: 0891 347 348
(60p per minute at all times)
USA: 3005 Massachusetts Ave,
NW, Washington DC 20008
Tel: (212) 223 2337, 223 2341
Fax: (212) 223 2343

Finland, France, Germany, Greece,
Grenada, Iceland, Iran, Israel,
Jamaica, Japan, Kenya, Korea (S),
Kuwait, Liechtenstein, Luxembourg,
Malaysia, Malta, Mauritius,
Monaco, Morocco, New Zealand,
Norway, Oman, Qatar, Rep of
Maldives, Turkish Rep of N. Cyprus,
Saint Lucia, San Marino, Saudi
Arabia, Seychelles, Singapore,
Sweden, Switzerland, Trinidad and
Tobago, Tunisia, UAE, Uruguay,
Vatican City.
**The following are exempt from
visas, for maximum of 2 months:**
Bosnia & Herzegovina, Croatia,
Indonesia, Macedonia, Romania,
Slovenia.
**The following are exempt from
visas, for maximum of one month:**
Bolivia, Costa Rica, Kazakstan,
Kyrgyzstan, Maldives, South Africa.

Useful Web-sites

www.turkey.org
Republic of Turkey Home Page –
Turkey's shop window on the net.
Contains useful tourist information,
including visa requirements and
government press releases on
news stories concerning Turkey.
www.mfa.gov.tr
Turkish Foreign Ministry
www.embassy.org
Turkish Embassy, Washington
www.turkishdailynews.com
Turkish Daily News Home Page.
Updated six days a week, the
newspaper's electronic arm aims
to be a key source of information
in English about Turkey. Subscribe
online by credit card (current cost
$0.20 per page/area).

www.bilkent.edu.tr
Bilkent University, Ankara. Excellent
site linked to media, art and culture,
academic needs and campus radio.
www.Ataturk.com
Details of the great man's life in
Turkish and English.
www.Turkiye.com
One of the best Turkish American
sites, linked to US-based web pages.
www.turknet.com
An introductory site, with maps,
pictures and links to other sites.
Also worth a try:
www.turkishnews.com
www.turkishodyssey.com
www.fco.gov.uk
Updated travel and general health
advice from the Foreign office.

Drugs

Possession of narcotics is treated as an extremely serious offence; penalties are harsh. You can also be arrested for being with other drug-takers, even if you do not have any yourself.

TRANSIT VISAS

These are not required by passengers continuing their journey to another country by the first connecting flight, providing they hold a confirmed onward ticket and don't leave the airport.

VISA EXTENSIONS

Ask at any police station (tourist police by preference) about visa extensions. They are not granted automatically, especially if the authorities suspect that you have been working. It is technically possible to leave Turkey at one of the land borders for at least 24-hours before re-entering, although immigration police are becoming more suspicious of people who do this repeatedly. It helps if you can show that you have ample money to finance your trip.

Customs Regulations

You are allowed to bring the following into the country duty-free: 200 cigarettes, 50 cigars, 200g pipe tobacco, 5 litres wine or spirits, 1kg chocolate and 1.5kg coffee. In addition, it is possible to buy 400 cigarettes, 100 cigars and 500 grams of pipe tobacco from Turkish Duty Free shops on entering the country, but these tend to be quite expensive.

Cars, valuable electronic equipment (e.g. a laptop computer or mobile phone), any items over $15,000, and antiques may be entered in the owner's passport on arrival, and checked on exit to prevent their being sold in Turkey.

There is no limit to the amount of foreign currency that may be brought into Turkey, but not more than US$5000 worth of Turkish currency may be brought in or out.

EXPORTING ANTIQUES

It is strictly forbidden to take antiques, including antique rugs and carpets, out of the country. Should you buy anything old or old-looking, be sure to have it validated by the seller, who should get a clearance certificate from the Department of Antiquities. Respectable carpet dealers in particular should be familiar with the procedure.

Holidays and Festivals

For national holidays, see box below. Religious holidays are linked to the lunar calendar and move back ten days each year. Secular festivals also move to coincide with weekends and precise dates can change annually. Contact your nearest Turkish tourist office to keep up to date.

During major holidays, shops (including the Grand Bazaar and Spice Bazaar) and businesses are closed. Local shops will usually re-open on the second or third day of the holiday. Museums are closed on the first half-day only.

Ramazan: the holiest festival in the religious calendar. During the holy month, a majority of the population (even non-devout Muslims) fast from sunrise to sunset, which includes the prohibition of intake of water and cigarettes. Civil servants may be asleep at their desks, taxi drivers may put you out as the sunset approaches so they can stop to eat, and many people are extremely irritable. The good news, however, is that until 2004, Ramazan will fall in mid-winter, infinitely preferable to the long hot days of summer. In Istanbul, this makes little difference to tourists as restaurants remain open, but avoid eating at sunset as the restaurants, roads and transport will all be crowded.

Seker Bayram (Sugar Holiday):

three-day celebration at the end of Ramazan, where people, especially childen, are offered sweets wherever they go.

Kurban Bayram (the Feast of the Sacrifice): a four-day holiday celebrating Abraham's sacrifice of his son Isaac (Feb–Mar for the next few years). It involves the ritual throat-slitting of sheep and cows, although rarely in public.

New Year's Eve: this falls during Ramazan for the first couple of years of the century. Celebrations are muted as most people don't drink during this period.

Mirac Kandili: celebrates the Prophet Mohammed's nocturnal journey to Jerusalem and ascension to heaven on a winged horse – though not an official holiday, mosques are often illuminated for it (in March).

Nevruz (the Festival of Light): celebrated on March 21, this is originally thought to have been a Zoroastrian fire festival, but is now associated with Kurdish tradition.

Cultural Festivals

(Check tourist offices for exact dates)

April: Istanbul – International Film Festival; Istanbul – Tulip Festival.

May: Bursa – International Tulip Festival; Edirne – Kakava Festival; Istanbul – International Theatre Festival.

June: Istanbul – International Classical Music Festival; Bursa – International Music and Dance Festival.

Public Holidays

Jan 1	New Year's Day
Apr 23	National Sovereignty and Children's Day
May 19	Atatürk's Commemoration and Youth and Sports Day
Aug 30	Victory Day (final rout of invading forces in 1922)
Oct 29	Republic Day (declaration of Turkish Republic)

Business Hours

Offices are generally open Mon–Fri from 9am–6pm, Sat until 12 noon (mostly) and closed on Sun. Government offices are open from 8am–5pm, closed Sat–Sun. Shops are usually closed on Sunday, although more and more large stores are staying open every day. The large shopping centres and smart clothes shops open later, at 10am, closing between 8 and 10pm. Small neighbourhood stores generally open from 8am–9pm; some stay open much later, often until midnight. Banks are open from Mon–Fri 8.30am–12 noon and 1.30pm–5pm; a few main branches also open Sat morning; all have 24-hour cash dispensers. Post Offices are usually open Monday to Saturday 9am-5pm. The larger garages all remain open 24 hours a day. Museum opening times are listed under individual sights in the Places section.

July: Istanbul – International Jazz Festival; Edirne – Traditional Kırkpınar Grease Wrestling Competitions (sometimes June); Bursa – International Folk Dance Competition.
September: Istanbul – Tüyap Arts Fair.
October: Istanbul – International Arts Biennial (odd-numbered years); Istanbul – Akbank Jazz Festival.
November: Bursa – International Karagöz and Shadow Theatre Festival.

Health Precautions

As a rule, inoculations are not necessary for Istanbul, but it is always wise to be up to date with polio, tetanus and TB when travelling. You should also consider immunisation against Hepatitis A (spread through contaminated food and water). Antimalarial tablets are not necessary. As everywhere else, AIDS and Hepatitis B are prevalent and precautions should be taken.

In the UK, detailed health advice, tailored to individual needs, is available from the MASTA (Medical Advice for Travellers Abroad) dial-up travel service. Tel: (0891) 224 100 (premium rate) Web: www.medicalonline.com.au/medical/masta
Alternatively, ask a British Airways Travel Clinic to find your nearest branch, tel: (01276) 685 040.
Medical insurance, including cover for medical evacuation, is essential, as medical costs in Turkey are high in private hospitals, and EU reciprocal agreements do not apply. Check that a general year-round travel policy, if you have one already, will cover you on the Asian side of the country (some companies use Asia as a threshold).

For medical treatment within Turkey, *see page 274.*

Money Matters

The currency is the Turkish lira (TL), which has one of the lowest unit values of any currency in the world. As this book went to press, it was heading rapidly for the milestone 1 million lira to UK £1. Discussions continue as to whether to knock several noughts off the end of the huge numbers involved, making them easier to handle. The situation is so out of control that most calculators cannot cope because they don't have enough room for all the digits.

Don't change all your money at the beginning of the holiday; the rate of exchange at the change offices (*doviz*) and banks in Turkey is better than anything you could get at home, and with the lira tumbling so fast, it will continue to improve throughout your trip. Rates are worse in hotels and worst of all at airports.

It is easy to change your leftover TL back into hard currency at change offices (not banks) before you leave, though the rate is worse at the airport. You may require your original exchange slip to reconvert money at the airport bank.

TRAVELLER'S CHEQUES

Traveller's cheques can be cashed at the foreign exchange desks of banks, post offices, and some change offices; most charge a commission. You will need your passport.

CASH

It is useful to bring a supply of foreign cash, especially US dollars, pounds sterling or deutschmarks, which can be used directly for larger purchases. Many shops selling carpets, jewellery and leather will accept and even bargain happily in most hard currencies, although the price may vary accordingly.

CREDIT CARDS

Credit and debit cards, including all the major ones such as Visa, Switch, Amex and Mastercard, are accepted by an increasing number of shops, restaurants, hotels and petrol stations.

Credit Card Hotlines

American Express
Tel: (0212) 235 9500 ext 205
Diners' Club, MasterCard, EuroCard and Visa
Tel: (0212) 211 5960

BANKS AND ATMS

Banks are plentiful in Istanbul. The Türkiye Is Bankasi and Garanti Bankasi at Istanbul airport open 24 hours a day; for other opening times see Business Hours above. The city also has many 24-hour cash dispensers accepting credit cards and bank cards with PIN numbers. Use them exactly as you would at home. The machines usually offer you a choice of four or five languages. They can only issue Turkish lira. There may be a few days' delay in the transaction reaching your home account, which can work to your advantage as the commission charge may well be cancelled out by the intervening inflation and drop in the lira's value.

FOREIGN EXCHANGE OFFICES (DÖVIZ)

Foreign currency is in great demand so you won't have to look very hard for a place to change it. Avoid unauthorised dealers as you will not get a better deal from them.
Foreign exchange offices offer much the same rates as the banks but much quicker service. (There are a few exceptions, so always check the rate, which should be clearly displayed.) US dollars and German deutschmarks attract a better rate than less-frequently traded currencies. These offices rarely accept traveller's cheques. They are open Mon–Sat 8.30/9am–8.30/9pm; some, in main tourist areas, also open on Sunday. No commission is charged for cash.

TAX-FREE SHOPPING
See Shopping, page 298–301.

What to Wear

Summer: In summer, light, cotton clothing is essential, a shady hat and sunscreen are useful. Mosquitoes (non-malarial) are found during summer, so it is useful to bring repellent. Plug-in electric antibug devices are available locally.
Spring and autumn: Days are warm but evenings cool, so a light jacket or jumper is necessary.
Winter: Can be cold and damp, with occasional light snow. Warm weather clothes are necessary, especially for evenings. A water-proof jacket/umbrella is useful.
Footwear year-round: Comfortable, sturdy shoes are a must for walking

the uneven or cobbled pavements of the bazaars, streets and sites. Comfortable sandals are good for the summer.
Clothing, footwear, photographic equipment, medications and toiletries are all easily available in Istanbul should you leave some vital item at home.
Dress-code for visiting mosques: Women may be asked to cover their heads when visiting mosques so you should always carry a scarf or hat. Clothing for visiting mosques should be modest. For women this means a longish skirt or trousers, and covered shoulders. For men, shorts and vests are not acceptable. Some of the mosques of tourist interest will offer you material to cover yourself, if your clothing is insufficient. You must remove your shoes or sandals, so ensure your feet are clean.

Getting There

ARRIVING BY AIR

Flight time to Istanbul from London is about 3½ hours; from New York about 9 hours.
There are regular direct or connecting flights to Istanbul's Atatürk International Airport from most major cities in Europe and the US. Turkish Airlines flies to 63 destinations worldwide, including

Main Airline Offices

Turkish Airlines
Turkey: tel: (0212) 663 6363
UK: tel: (020) 7766 9300/33
USA: tel: (310) 646 5214; (305) 374 1956; (212) 339 9650/339 9661; (1-800) 288 2520
web-site:
www.turkishfltbooking.com

British Airways
Turkey: tel: (0212) 234 1300.
UK: central booking, tel: (0345) 222 111
USA: central booking, tel: (1-800) AIRWAYS
web-site:
www.britishairways.com

30 in Europe, as well as Chicago, Miami, New York, Cape Town and Johannesburg.
From the UK, the two main scheduled carriers are Turkish Airlines (THY) and British Airways. *Istanbul Airlines* is a slightly cheaper Turkish carrier with scheduled services twice a week.
At the time of writing, Atatürk International Airport was in the throes of major expansion and renovation to help meet the ever-increasing passenger traffic. The extension was due for completion in 2000. Another airport, currently under construction on the Asian side, will take several more years to complete.

Airport Transfers
From Atatürk International Airport (tel: 212-663 6400, fax: 212-663 6250), the easiest but most expensive way to get into the city is by **taxi**, of which there are many. Although cab drivers may not be that good at finding their way around, if you know the name of your hotel and its area, you will get there. The fare will be registered on the meter and should come to under $16 (£10). Sadly, there are inevitably drivers who do their best to multiply the fare by driving round in circles or simply saying that the meter broke; try and check roughly how much it should be before getting in. (*See Taxis, page 265*). Hotels can arrange transfers, but this can be much more expensive.
The best option, especially for one or two people, is the highly efficient and comfortable **Havas bus**, from Atatürk airport to the centre, operating every 30 minutes between 6am and 11pm, and continuing at longer intervals through the night. Tickets cost around $3 (£2) each. There are stops at Aksaray (alight here for Sultanahmet and take a taxi) and Şişhane, before terminating in Taksim Square.
Going *to* the airport, there is an additional private **minibus** service from Sultanahmet, which costs around $4 (£2.50). It leaves about every hour during the day and will

pick up from your hotel; check with the hotel or local travel agents to book your ticket. This service does not run *from* the airport.

Allow plenty of time for checking in, especially in high season.

ARRIVING BY SEA

During the summer there are car–ferry crossings between Turkey and Venice, Ancona, Bari and Brindisi on the Italian Aegean coast, taking 30-60 hours. Timetables and operating companies vary from year to year, although Turkish Maritime Lines runs a regular summer service. Some routes pass through the Corinth Canal, cutting hours and adding interest to the journey.

Turkish Maritime Lines, Istanbul, tel: (212) 244 0207.

ARRIVING BY RAIL

The last of the old Orient Express trains rolled into Istanbul over 20 years ago. Two years ago an attempt to revive them was scuppered by the Balkan wars, but there are still regular trains from Europe to Istanbul. The **Istanbul**

Express has departures for Istanbul from Munich, Vienna and Athens, with connecting services in Belgrade and Sofia. There are also weekly departures from Budapest, Bucharest and Moscow. Reductions are available for students and people under 26. Turkey is part of the Interail and Eurail networks. (See below for international trains.)

Through-tickets from the UK can be booked through **Rail Europe**; tel: (0990) 848 848; web-site: www.raileurope.com. In the USA, contact **Forsyth Travel Library**; tel: (1-800) 367 7984.

Trains from the west arrive at Sirkeci station in Eminönü. Trains from the east come into Haydarpaşa station on the Asian side.

ARRIVING BY BUS

Bus services operate from major European cities, especially Germany and Austria and from the Middle East and former Soviet Bloc. Buses arrive at Esenler coach station in northwest Istanbul. Bus companies run a free minibus service from there to most areas of the city. For contact details, *see Getting Around, page 264.*

International Trains

Destination	Time of departure	No. of hours
Sophia (Bulgaria)	23.20	12
Athens (Greece)	08.20	24
Bucharest (Romania)	20.45	8
Budapest (Hungary)	23.20	33
Warsaw (Poland)	23.20	40
Prague (Czech Rep.)	23.20	30
Paris (France)	23.20	52
Allepo (from Haydarpaşa) (Syria)	08.25	35

ARRIVING BY CAR

In addition to a valid driving licence, you will need the vehicle's log book and proof of ownership (or power of attorney if you are driving someone else's vehicle), a Green Card (from your insurance company) and suitable insurance (check you are covered for the Asian side of the country). AA Five-Star, or a similar

Airline Offices in Istanbul

Turkish Airlines
Head Office:
Atatürk Airport, Yeşilköy, Istanbul
Tel: Reservations: (0212) 663 6363
Sales: (0212) 663 6300
Fax: (0212) 663 6250
Other branches:
Ataturk Blv, 162, Gul Palas Apt, 6/F, Aksaray.
Tel: (0212) 511 9222/3
Kadıköy, Recep Peker Cad. 27, Kiziltoprak. Tel: (216) 418 44 86
Taksim. Tel: (0212) 252 11 06
Aeroflot
Mete Cad. 30, Taksim
Tel: (0212) 243 4725/6
Air France
Cumhuriyet Cad. Taksim
Tel: (0212) 256 4356
Alitalia
Cumhuriyet Cad. 14, Elmadağ

Tel: (0212) 231 3391
American Airlines
Cumhuriyet Cad. 47/2, Taksim
Tel: (0212) 237 2003/4, 237 2050
British Airways
Cumhuriyet Cad. 10, Taksim
Tel: (0212) 234 1300
Delta Airlines
Hilton Hotel, Taksim
Tel: (0212) 231 2339, 663 0752
Istanbul Airlines
Cumhuriyet Cad. 289
Tel: (0212) 231 7526, 509 2121
KLM
Vali Konagi Cad. 73/7, Nisantaşı
Tel: (0212) 230 0311, 663 0603/4
Lufthansa
Büyükdere Cad. Maya Binasi, B-Blok, Esentepe
Tel: (0212) 288 1050, 288 0855

Qantas
Cumhuriyet Cad. 155/1, Elmadağ
Tel: (0212) 240 5032, 240 7787
Sabena
Cumhuriyet Cad. 6, Taksim
Tel: (0212) 231 2844
SAS
Cumhuriyet Cad. 26/A, Elmadağ
Tel: (0212) 296 6060
Singapore Airlines
Halaskargazi Cad. 113, Harbiye
Tel: (0212) 232 3706, 234 3416
Swissair
Cumhuriyet Cad. 6, Elmadağ
Tel: (0212) 231 2845
TWA
Cumhuriyet Cad. 193, Elmadağ
Tel: (0212) 234 5337
United Airlines
Cumhuriyet Cad. 341/2, Harbiye
Tel: (0212) 231 9321/3

US Tour Operators

ATC Anadolu Travel & Tours
420 Madison Ave, Suite 504,
New York, NY 10017
Tel: (1-800) ANADOLU or (0212)
486 4012.

**Blue Voyage Turkish Tours
& Travel**
323 Geary St, Suite 401,
San Francisco, CA 94102
Tel: (1-800) 81-TURKEY or (415)
392 0146.

Club America
51 East 4nd St, Suite 1406,
New York, NY 10017
Tel: (1-800) 221 4969 or (0212)
972 2865.

Wilderness Travel
1102 Ninth St, Berkeley,
CA 94710
Tel: (1-800) 368 2794 or (510)
558 2488.

insurance package which includes
breakdown cover is advisable.
Drivers may use their national
licence with a Turkish translation for
up to 3 months, but are advised to
take an international licence.

It is possible to drive to Turkey
via Bulgaria or Greece, or via Italy,
with a ferry to Turkey (see above).
The roads leading to or from Russia

are often in a bad state of repair. At
the crossing point you will need to
show the car's registration
documents and your driving licence.
You will be issued with a certificate
for the car which you should keep
with you at all times. You are
allowed six months' tourist use of
your car in Turkey duty-free, and
your car should leave the country
with you. Should you write your car
off during your stay, you need
special papers to certify that the
car has not been sold in Turkey.

Approximate distance between
London and Istanbul is 3,000 km
(1,860 miles). For further details on
driving in Turkey, *see Getting
Around, page 268–270*.

Package Tours

The choice of package and other
holidays now available in Turkey is
enormous, with more than 200 UK
operators offering holidays to the
country. Turkey is now able to
accommodate everyone from the
independent traveller to families to
the sybaritic sunseeker and it's
worth shopping around for the best
deal on flights and hotels. A
package will probably work out
much more economical than
booking independently, particularly
if you want to stay in one of the top
hotels whose rack rates are
ridiculously high.

UK Tour Operators to Istanbul

President Holidays
92 Park Lane, Croydon,
Surrey CR0 1JF
Tel: (020) 8760 055;
24-hr brochure line: 020-8667
1313; Email:
enquiries@presidentholidays.com
Web: www.presidentholidays.com
Istanbul specialist offering a wide
variety of hotels including Special
Licence Hotels (*see page 280*).
Sunquest
23 Prince's St, London W1R 7RG
Tel: (020) 7499 9991.
Simply Turkey
Chiswick Gate,
598-608 Chiswick High Rd,

London W4 5RT
Tel: (020) 8747 1011.
Metak Holidays
70 Welbeck St, London W1M 7HA
Tel: (020) 7935 6961.
Tapestry Holidays
24 Chiswick High Rd,
London W4 1TE
Tel: (020) 8742 0055.
Savile Row Tours and Travel
Savile House, 6 Blenheim Terrace,
St John's Wood, London NW8 0EB
Tel: (020) 7625 3001.
Anatolian Sky
1112 Stratford Rd, Hall Green,
Birmingham B28 8AE
Tel: (0121) 633 4018.

Getting Around

City Transport

Istanbul's public transport does
leave something to be desired.
There is a wide range of options,
including trams and an
underground, but these fledgling
services are all single lines and
often don't connect. The easiest
form of public transport is the huge
fleet of cheap taxis. Best of all,
many of the tourist sights are within
easy walking distance of each other
and with a little careful planning,
you rarely have to look for other
means of transport.

BUSES

City buses run by the municipality
are orange (older) or green (newer),
with the letters IETT on the side.
Bus fares are cheap but journeys
can be slow, and it is advisable not
to travel during rush hours as buses
get incredibly crowded. Bus
services usually end on main routes
at around midnight.

Buy **tickets** in advance either
from one of the many bus-ticket
booths; or from shops, kiosks and
street sellers near bus stops
(street-sellers charge approximately
25 percent extra). *Tam bilet* means
full, ie. a normal adult ticket. Drop
your ticket into a small box as you
board the bus (at the front). Some
longer urban journeys require more
than one ticket.

Most locals use the *akbil* or
"intelligent ticket" which is an
electronic token onto which fares
can be loaded. You buy a certain
number of journeys, and put your
token into the special machine at
the front of the bus, where the fare

is deducted. Bus prices are slightly cheaper with the *akbil*; the token can easily be recharged, and it is far easier and more convenient if you are spending more than a week in the city. There is a refundable deposit for the token itself.

In Istanbul there are also, confusingly, similar but older-looking orange and cream full-size private buses *(Özel Halk Ötöbüsü)* which are in fact retired municipality buses. On these you pay the driver's attendant who sits just inside at the front. The fare is the same as on the public buses.

There are also private minibuses, usually blue and cream, or plain cream, which are faster. Pay the fare (variable according to your destination) directly to the driver, or his assistant. These drivers go fast and furiously, but you can stop them to get on or off anywhere. These buses can get very crowded.

All buses have a directions board at the front and on the side. There are maps of the network at bus stop shelters.

TAXIS

Finding a taxi: Taxis *(taksi)* are bright yellow with a light on top. In Istanbul they are reasonably priced and plentiful at any time of day or night. Most operate independently around a local base, which may be no more than a phone nailed to a telegraph pole. There are few radio-controlled networks. Hotels and restaurants will always be able to find you a taxi.
Fares: Always check the meter is switched on. Night-rates operate between midnight and 6am and

Maps

All tourist offices, and the airport, give a good **free map** of the city, with tourist attractions clearly marked and in several European languages. These are the best maps available, and they are free, so don't bother with maps sold on the street.

cost 50 percent extra. Check the current day and night start-rate as soon as you arrive. If crossing the Bosphorus, the bridge toll (500,000TL or about US$1) will be added to your fare.
Scams: There are a few dishonest drivers, mostly operating from the airport and in the old city, who take advantage of the tourist's confusion with Turkish currency and numbers. It is difficult to argue in Turkish that you handed over a five million lira note when the taxi driver says it was 500,000, or even 100,000, which is a similar colour. Take your time when counting out money. If you have a major dispute with a taxi-driver, ask him to take you to the police station, and usually he will back off.
Finding your destination: Most taxi-drivers will try their hardest to help you, though speaking little or no English. A common "mistake" is for a driver to take you to Topkapı (the district) rather than Topkapı Palace. Ensure he understands where you want to go. It helps to have your destination written down in case of difficulties over your accent, and also because your driver may himself be new to the area. State the area location first, eg "Sultanahmet" and go into detail later. When you get close to your destination, the driver will ask for directions, so locate it on the map.
Tours: For long distances or sightseeing tours with waiting time built in, prices can be negotiable.

DOLMUS

Another method of travelling around the city is by dolmuş (literally "full", sharing the same root as stuffed vegetables). Originally this was a large shared taxi, but now it is a yellow minibus with a "dolmuş" sign on top. They are often as fast as a taxi, and only take 8 people with no standing, so are therefore comfortable and quite cheap. A dolmuş travels along a fixed route for a fixed fare, paid to the driver. At the start of the route, it may not set

Trams

A light rapid rail system links Eminönü, Sirkeci (by the train station), Beyazıt, Aksaray and the western suburbs. Tickets are different to bus-tickets; buy them near the station, or use your *akbil*.

There is also a stately "nostalgic" tram which trundles slowly up and down İstiklal Caddesi between the Tünel and Taksim Square.

off until it is full, which can entail a wait. After that passengers can get on and off whenever they want. A few words of Turkish are necessary to be able to tell the driver when you want to get out: *inecek var –* there is someone getting out; *müsait bir yerde –* at a convenient place. Dolmuşes usually run much later than buses (until 3 am), and are safe for women.

UNDERGROUND

The long-awaited underground is due to be finished shortly, connecting Taksim to Levent in the north, via Harbiye, Şişli and Mecidiyekoy.

METRO

The oldest metro in the world is in Istanbul, a single stop connection up the steep hill between Tünel and Karaköy, built in 1877. This should not be confused with the new Metro, which operates between Aksaray, Bagcilar, Esenler (the inter-city coach-terminal) and Bakırköy.

LOCAL TRAINS

On the European side, local trains run from Sirkeci station along the coastal road to the suburbs of Ataköy and Florya. On the Asian side, they run between Haydarpaşa Station and the suburbs.

Water Transport in Istanbul

Istanbul has the second busiest local sea-transportation system, after Hong Kong, with a busy network of large steamers, small water buses (which operate like dolmuşes), catamarans, seabuses and water taxis. From the main jetties at Eminönü and Beşiktaş on the European side there are **ferries** to Kadıköy or Üsküdar on the Asian side, or up the length of the Bosphorus (*see page 217*). Buy a *jeton* at the *gise* (both pronounced as in French) and drop it in the slot at the entrance to the jetty *(iskele)*. Each jetty serves one destination which is prominently displayed.

The dolmuş **water buses**, called "*motors*", cross at certain points all along the coast. You pay on board. **Water taxis** can be hired privately near the Galata Bridge to go up the Golden Horn. The **hydrofoils** serving the outer suburbs are more expensive; the timings are arranged to suit commuters, so most trips are in the morning and evening, but they can whisk you to the Princes' Islands in 30 minutes.

A **Bosphorus cruise** (tel: 0212-522 0045) is a lovely way to view the elegant waterside mansions or *yalıs* lining the banks of this channel separating Europe from

Boat Rental

Halas M/S
Iltur A.H.
Tel: (0212) 287 1014
An historic restored Bosphorus ferry, redecorated and fitted with 15 cabins, now a luxurious yacht which has hosted royalty and many celebs. Daily and weekly rentals.

Hat-Sail Tourism & Yachting Inc.
Maçka
Tel: (0212) 258 9983
Bosphorus cruises for groups or executive meetings with lunch/dinner and cocktails, also yacht cruises on the Aegean and Mediterranean Seas.

Private Plane Hire

Hiring small jets and helicopters for personal charter is a new and booming business in Turkey.

Bon Air
Orman s. 10, Florya
Tel: (0212) 663 1829
Fax: (0212) 574 0147
Çelebi Air Service
Yeşilköy. Tel: (0212) 663 8700
Gokkusagi
Polis Egitim Merkezi,
Arkasi Ozel Havacilik,
Hangarlar Bolgesi, Sefakoy
Tel: (0212) 541 2917
Fax: (0212) 541 2923.
Güven Air
Florya. Tel: (0212) 662 0362
Mach Air
(same address as Gokkusagi)

Tel: (0212) 541 1423
Fax: (0212) 541 9594
Sancak Air
(same address as Gokkusagi)
Tel: (0212) 541 4141
Fax: (0212) 541 0285
Top Air
(same address as Gokkusagi)
Tel: (0212) 599 0227
Fax: (0212) 599 7910
Pilot Helicopter
Perpa Binasi Heliportu,
Piyalepasa Bulvasi
Tel: (0212) 281 0300
(18 minutes sightseeing helicopter ride, approx $40)
Turk Hava Kurumu (THK)
Yeşilköy
Tel: (0212) 591 7373

Asia. For an almost absurdly small fare, public ferries leave every day from Eminönü jetty number 3 (Boğazhatti) at 10.35am, 12.00, and 13.35 (in summer); with one per day in winter at 10.35. They go all the way to Anadolu Kavağı, where you can take a lunch break before your return journey (*see also page 217*).

Princes' Islands (Adalar): Ferries leave from Adalar Pier, Eminönu, for this group of islands off the Asian shore in the Sea of Marmara (*see also page 234*). The journey takes an hour and stops at all the islands before terminating at Büyükada, the largest.
Departure times: 8.30, 10.15, 11.30, 13.05, 15.00.
Return from the last island: 13.45, 15.45, 17.15, 18.20, 20.15, 23.00
Sunday departures: 8.30, 9.30, 10.00, 11.00, 12.00, 13.00, 14.00, 15.30, 16.30, 17.30
Sunday returns: 12.50, 14.20, 15.20, 16.10, 16.45, 17.15, 17.50, 18.15, 18.45, 19.35, 20.15, 21.30, 23.00

Printed timetable booklets covering the Istanbul water transport system are available at the ticket windows of the jetties, but they do sell out quickly.
The seabuses *(Deniz Otobüsleri)*

have their own separate jetties and timetable.
Fast catamaran sea buses offer services from Kabataş, Eminönü, Beşiktaş, Sariyer, Bostancı, Bakırköy, Yenikapı, Kadıköy, Yalova and the Princes' Islands. Information; tel: (0216) 362 0444/249 1558.

Sightseeing Tours

The tourist office, local travel agencies, hotels and pensions will all be able to offer you, or help you find, a wide choice of worthwhile city tours and trips out of Istanbul. The city has a high number of guides speaking foreign languages fluently: especially, English, German, French, Japanese, Spanish and Italian. It is best to stick to official guides.

Tours of Istanbul vary from half-a-day for part of the city to longer guided tours lasting several days. You can tailor the tour to your needs, and engage a private guide, car or minibus and driver by the day. Most guides will take you to particular shops or restaurants where they may be getting commission, so you should arrange in advance if you wish to stop at a particular place for lunch or to do your shopping.

The classic city tour includes the major places of interest, eg Aya

Sofya, the Grand Bazaar, Blue Mosque, Topkapı Palace etc. A two-day city tour will also take in the Dolmabahçe Palace and Galata Tower. There are half-day and full-day sailing tours of the Bosphorus. Istanbul by night includes dinner and a show, with a belly-dancer and folk dancers. There are also tours to the nearby Princes' Islands.

If you are arranging tours of other parts of Turkey, *shop around* as prices can vary alarmingly.

Out of Town

Travel within Turkey is relatively straightforward: air, bus, boat, train and car hire are all widely available and easy to arrange. Road networks are improving, but there is still some way to go, and Turkey's hilly geography does not make driving particularly easy.

For this reason road journeys can take longer than the distance would seem to suggest on the map –

when planning journeys allow no more than 60 kmph (35–40 mph) in rural areas.

BY AIR

Turkish Airlines and Istanbul Airlines (*see page 262–3*) offer a good network of reasonably priced domestic flights. You need to be flexible as to timing if booking at short notice on a popular

Tour Operators and Travel Agents

Arnika
İstiklal Cad., Mis Sok. 6/5 Beyoğlu.
Tel: (0212) 245 15 93
Daily and weekend tours to the countryside around Istanbul.
Art Tours
Valikonağı Cad. 77/3, Nihantaşı;
Tel: (0212) 231 0487
Fax: (0212) 240 4945
Flight reservations, city tours, car rental and congress organisation.
Fez Travel
Sultanahmet. Tel: (0212) 516 9024
Email: feztravel@feztravel.com
Web: www.feztravel.com
Friendly outfit, geared for backpackers, offering small group adventure, a Black Sea coast bus and an all-in deal for Cappadocia. Unique hop-on, hop-off round-trip bus circuit through popular destinations.
Fotograf Evi
İstiklal Cad., Zambak Sok. 15,
4th floor, Beyoğlu.
Tel: (0212) 251 0566
Photography and travel club, geared for young people, organising nature walks and slide shows.
Gençtur
Yerebatan Cad. 15/3,Sultanahmet.
Tel: (0212) 520 5270
Student travel agency offering discount cards as well as nature tours near Istanbul.
Gezi Evi
İstiklal Cad. 95-99/2, Beyoğlu
Tel: (0212) 245 5886/244 2666
Tours around Istanbul and Turkey.
Grup Günbatmadan
İstiklal Cad., Zambak Sok. 15,
4th floor, Beyoğlu

Tel: (0212) 293 0438
Fax: (0212) 245 6035
Organises trekking trips around the country at all levels.
Meptur
Büyükdere Cad. 26/17, Mecidiyeköy
Tel: (0212) 275 0250
Tailor-made group tours, city packages, corporate travel.
Plan Tours
Cumhuriyet Cad. 131/1, Elmadağ
Tel: (0212) 230 2272/230 8118
Fax: 231 8965
City sightseeing tours, incoming travel, meetings, seminar and congress organisation, ticketing, hotel reservations, car and yacht rentals, hunting trips, Jewish heritage tours.
Setur
Cumhuriyet Cad. 107 Elmadağ
Tel: (0212) 230 0336
Fax: (0212) 230 3219/231 1487
Car rental, air tickets, tours and conference organisation.
Sultan Tourism
Cumhuriyet Cad. 87, Elmadağ
Tel: (0212) 241 3178
Fax: (0212) 230 0419
Conferences, private and group tours, air tickets. Car, bus, helicopter, aircraft hire.
Sunday Holiday
Abdülhamit Cad. 82/2 ,Taksim
Tel: (0212) 256 4156;
Fax: (0212) 256 8808
Tailor-made group tours, hotel reservations, city packages and conventions.
Tour Select
Cumhuriyet Cad. 173/6, Elmadağ
Tel: (0212) 232 4885

Fax: (0212) 232 4889
Conferences and meetings.
Trans Orient
Cumhuriyet Cad. 211/2, Harbiye
Tel: (0212) 233 6822
Fax: (0212) 230 6359
Incoming reservations, group and individual tours, seminar and congress organisation.
Viking Turizm
Mete Cad. 24, Taksim
Tel: (0212) 293 5272
Airline ticketing, corporate and leisure travel, conferences.
Yehil Bisiklet
Lalezar Cad. 8/1, Kardelen Apt.,
Selamiçehme, Kadıköy
Tel: (0216) 363 5836
Cycling club and shop which sells cycling gear, undertakes repairs and organises trips.

Thrace and Marmara
Bursa:
Karagöz Tourism & Travel Agency
Kapalı Çarşı, Eski Aynalı Çarşı 12,
Bursa.
Tel: (0224) 221 8727
Fax: (0224) 220 53 50.
Guided tours of Bursa and the surrounding area.
Gelibolu Hassle Free Tourism & Travel Agency
Anzac House, Cumhuriyet Mey.
61, Gelibolu.
Tel: (0286) 213 5969
Fax: (0286) 217 2906
E-mail: hasslefree@anzachouse.com
Web-site: www.anzachouse.com.
Guided tours to Troy, the Troad, the First World War Battlefields and Ephesus.

connection or at a busy time. Book through any local travel agent; tickets can be picked up and paid for at the airport. You can book domestic flights in your own country, but it is cheaper to pay for them in Turkey. It is also possible to book through the internet.

BY BUS

Buses are the preferred method of long distance travel as they are cheap, reliable, and generally comfortable. All buses are non-smoking and all inter-cities buses are air-conditioned. Competition between companies is intense; the best are more expensive and have more comfortable seats, clean toilets and refreshments as well as the traditional libations of lemon cologne; some play videos.

There is no comprehensive national or local **timetable**, so you have to work out the best route and departure time for yourself. Several companies cover each route. **Tickets** are easy to obtain, although each company has a separate office (they are often next door to one another). As you approach any one, you are likely to be pressurised by touts for the others. Seats are reserved, and unaccompanied women will not be allowed to sit next to a man they do not know. Most long-haul journeys take place at night.

Most long distance buses depart from Istanbul's main bus station, Esenler, which also contains many ticket offices. However it is better to buy your ticket in the centre before heading out to the bus station, as popular routes get very full in high season. Look for a proliferation of ticket offices in Taksim (İnönü Cad.), Beşiktaş, Aksaray and Sultanahmet. All companies organise a free minibus service to take you to and from the bus-station; the ticket office will tell you your nearest pick-up point.

BY TRAIN

Major cities and many places between are connected by the Turkish State Railways (TCDD), but the network is limited and fans out from Istanbul; cross-country connections are virtually non-existent. Although cheap – a first class ticket from Ankara to Istanbul will cost about US$15 (£10) – travel can be very slow and not always comfortable.

The best connections are between Istanbul, Ankara and İzmir. The *Mavi Tren* ("blue train") or *Ekspres* (express) services reach their destinations in times comparable to taking one of the more upmarket bus companies. The *Mavi Tren* between Istanbul and Ankara leaves Istanbul's Haydarpaşa station at 11.50pm,

reaching Ankara at 8am; and has a dining car, couchettes and sleepers.

Purchase tickets and reserve seats or sleepers in advance. You should be able to book a ticket to and from anywhere in Turkey in Istanbul, Ankara or İzmir, where the system has been computerised, but it can prove difficult to do so. Sleepers get booked up, especially over public holidays. Choose between a *küsetli* (pull-down couchette style compartment with six sharing, pillows provided but no bedding); *Örtülü küsetli* (four bunks, bedding provided) or *Yataklı* (first class, two or three bed, linen).

For reservations and enquiries:
Haydarpaşa Station (Asian side); tel: Operator (0216) 336 8020; Information (0216) 336 0475/2063; Reservations (0216) 337 8724/336 4470
Sirkeci Station (European side), tel: Operator (0212) 520 6575; Information (0212) 527 0050

Driving

It is not worth renting a car just for Istanbul; in fact it is a positive liability. However, you may wish to consider it if you plan any trips out of town. Driving in this busy corner of Turkey is only for the confident and experienced. However if you keep calm and drive cautiously you will be perfectly safe. The road network is extensive, with new toll-motorways completed and more under construction. Otherwise there are few dual carriageways, and many three-lane roads where the central lane is used for overtaking.

Surfaces are reasonable, but the overall engineering of the road can be poor, with poor drainage making roads excessively dangerous in rain. Few mountain roads have crash barriers and most have narrow hard shoulders. For added thrills, many overconfident locals seem happy to overtake at high speed on blind corners.

By far the largest number of vehicles on the road are buses and trucks, and very many of the trucks are elderly, overloaded and

Major Inter-City Bus Companies

Kamil Koç (Istanbul, western and southern destinations, Ankara): Taksim, tel: (0212) 252 7223/24
Pamukkale (Istanbul, western and southern destinations): Taksim, tel: (0212) 249 2791; Kadıköy, tel: (0216) 336 5413; Esenler, tel: (0212) 658 2222
Ulusoy (Istanbul, Ankara, Black Sea region, İzmir and the Aegaean, Antalya and the Mediterranean plus international destinations): Head Office, tel: (0212) 658 0270; Taksim, tel: (0212) 249 4373; Kadıköy,

tel (0216) 336 4538; Merter, tel: (0212) 664 0640
Varan (Istanbul, Ankara, western and southern destinations, international): Head Office, tel: (0212) 658 3000; Taksim, tel: (0212) 251 7481; Reservations: (0212) 527 5615; Kadıköy, tel: (0216) 337 2965; Bayrampaşa; tel: (0212) 658 0270

Many others, including **Metro** and **Ülüdağ**, have offices along İnönü Caddesi near Taksim.

underpowered (and often on the wrong side of the road).

Access roads to many of the lesser archaeological sites are single track and made of pitted gravel. They are usually driveable with extreme care in good weather, but rain can cause mud and rock slides, instant waterfalls and fast-flowing rivers, all in the middle of the road. Some sites are simply not accessible in winter, except on foot.

Driving at night is not advisable if you can avoid it as roads are not well lit, nor well-enough signposted. Hazards include unlit trucks and tractors, horses and carts and even flocks of sheep. Main roads between cities are usually well-lit and signed.

RULES OF THE ROAD

Drive on the right and unless signed otherwise, give way to the right, even on a roundabout or multiple junction where you might think you had right of way.

Road marking and signposting is only moderate: it can be good on the new motorways, and on some rural routes, with historical sites clearly marked with yellow signs. At motorway junctions be prepared for traffic coming from unexpected directions, and do not expect to be able to get back onto the motorway easily if you make a mistake. Some dual carriageways have very broad hard shoulders, alarmingly used by locals driving in the wrong direction, to avoid the long distance to the nearest junction.

Traffic lights change straight from red to green. A flashing arrow means you may turn right with care even if the main light is red.

Everyone is supposed to wear a seat belt, and to carry a warning triangle and a first aid kit. Almost no-one does. You will usually see a small cairn of rocks, or similar, in the road to warn of a breakdown, but only at the last minute as they are usually placed very close to the vehicle in question.

There is a total ban on alcohol when driving; even one beer will put

you over the limit.

The traffic police operate control points on the access roads to many cities. Always carry your driving licence, passport, log book, insurance certificate, and vehicle registration, as you may be asked for any or all of them. There may also be seatbelt checks, breath tests, speed traps and checks for faulty vehicles. Most traffic offences are punishable by on-the-spot fines; ask for a proper receipt.

ROAD ETIQUETTE

Although Turkey has much the same highway code as other countries, the population does not obey it. As a result Turkey has fourteen times as many road traffic accidents per number of vehicles as the UK.

Expect the unexpected from Turkish drivers. They will overtake on both sides and cut in without much thought. They may stop suddenly, or pull out or reverse without warning. Indicators are seldom used. Everyone drives very close to one another: if you leave a reasonable stopping distance ahead of you, someone will fill the gap.

No driver ever stops at a pedestrian crossing, in fact they can be positively insulted if you suggest that they should slow down! If you beckon to pedestrians to cross in front of you, they will be confused. By all means pause, but they expect to dodge the traffic.

Some driver signals mean the exact opposite of their UK equivalent. Flashing your headlights, by day or night, means "I am coming through", not "please go first". There is a lot of hooting, mostly to warn that you are being passed, or from behind, to hurry you up. A loud hoot means keep out of the way; two short pips on the hooter sometimes means "thanks".

Do not assume that traffic will stop to let you out of a side turning – you have to push in.

Another surprise, if you are not used to it, is that the driver in front will almost certainly not apply his hand brake on a hill – you will be

wise to leave room for him to roll back until he applies the foot brake. Although Turkey has much the same highway code as other countries, the population does not obey it. As a result Turkey has fourteen times as many road traffic accidents per number of vehicles as the UK.

Expect the unexpected from Turkish drivers. They will overtake on both sides and cut in without much thought. They may stop suddenly, or pull out or reverse without warning. Indicators are seldom used. Everyone drives very close to one another: if you leave a reasonable stopping distance ahead of you, someone will fill the gap.

No driver ever stops at a pedestrian crossing; in fact they can be positively insulted if you suggest that they should slow down! If you beckon to pedestrians to cross in front of you, they will be confused. By all means pause, but they expect to dodge the traffic.

Some driver signals mean the exact opposite of their UK equivalent. Flashing your headlights, by day or night, means "I am coming through", not "please go first". There is a lot of hooting, mostly to warn that you are being passed, or from behind, to hurry you up. A loud hoot means keep out of the way; two short pips on the hooter sometimes means "thanks".

Do not assume that traffic will stop to let you out of a side turning – you have to push in.

Another surprise, if you are not used to it, is that the driver in front will almost certainly not apply his or her hand brake on a hill – it is wise to leave room for the car to roll back until the driver applies the foot brake.

Speed Limits

• 120 kph (70 mph) on motor-ways
• 90 kph (55 mph) for saloon cars on main roads, 80 kph (50 mph) for vans, and 70 kph (40 mph) if towing a trailer or caravan
• 50 kph (30 mph) in urban areas.

BREAKDOWNS

Most commonly, you may lose a windscreen due to grit thrown up or dropped by another vehicle, or puncture a tyre. In case of any breakdown you will find people inordinately helpful. For tyres, you need a *lastikci* (tyre repair man), a small shop where even fairly severe damage will be repaired. For windscreens and other car parts you will need the nearest *oto sanayı*. Even in a small town there will be an area dedicated to motor spares and repairs. Especially if you are driving a local hire car, parts and repairs should be easily available and reasonably priced.

If you break down in your own car, your insurance documents should tell you what to do. British motoring associations have reciprocal agreements with the Turkish Touring and Automobile Association, TTOK; the American AAA does not. Other nationalities should check the position before travelling; however, hired cars always come with instructions.

TTOK national 24-hour emergency breakdown number; tel: (0212) 280 4449.

PETROL

The western half of Turkey is well supplied with petrol stations, mostly open 24-hours, some of which are good places to stop for a meal and a rest, being well equipped and with clean toilet facilities. Most have staffed forecourts so you don't have to fill your car yourself. The attendant will check oil and clean the windscreen, and will appreciate a tip. Petrol *(benzin)* is available in 3-star "normal" and 4-star "süper" grades. Lead free petrol *(kursunsuz)* is available at most petrol stations in western Turkey. Diesel *(mazot or dizel)* is available everywhere. The further east you go, the more infrequent the stations become. Beware of bargain-priced diesel. There has been an influx of cheap fuel from Iraq which is exceptionally dirty. It is usually possible to use credit cards, but in practice, it is much easier to pay by cash.

PARKING

Take heed of "no parking" signs. Although the fines are relatively small, having your car towed away

Car Hire Abroad

UK Central Booking
Avis, tel: (0990) 900 500
Budget, tel: (0800) 181 181
Europcar, tel: (0345) 222 525
Hertz, tel: (0990) 996 699
US Central Booking
Avis, tel: (1-800) 230 4898
Budget, tel: (1-800) 472 3325
Europcar (Dollar),
tel: (1-800) 800 6000
Hertz, tel: (1-800) 654 3131

is extremely time-consuming. On-street parking areas (look for an *otopark* sign) are manned by watchmen who will approach as you park, and either give you a receipt or place a ticket on your windscreen. Charges vary, but are not expensive – around $2 (£1.50) for two hours in central Istanbul. There are also covered multi-storey parks in some places, a few on-street meters and ticket machines, and valet parking at the smartest hotels, clubs and restaurants. It is not easy to find a parking place on the streets anywhere in Istanbul. You can often have your car washed while it's parked: look for *oto yıkama* signs.

Car Hire in Istanbul

Avis
Head Office, tel: (0216) 454 11 11
Istanbul Airport,
tel: (0212) 663 0646/7
Taksim (at the Hilton Hotel entrance), tel: (0212) 241 78 96
Budget
Airport, tel: (0212) 663 0858
fax: (0212) 663 0724
Taksim, tel: (0212) 253 9200
fax: (0212) 237 2919
Europcar
Airport, tel: (0212) 663 0746
fax: (0212) 663 6830
Taksim, tel: (212) 254 7799
fax: (0212) 255 5928
Hertz
Head office, tel: (0212) 234 4300
fax: (0212) 232 9260
e-mail: herzekn@sim.net.tr
Atatürk Airport,

tel: (0212) 663 0807
Harbiye, tel: (0212) 233 1020
Decar
Head office, Istanbul,
tel: (0212) 288 4243
fax: (0212) 288 4245
e-mail: decar@dedeman.com.tr
Thrifty
Istanbul, Kızıltoprak (on the Asian side), tel: (0216) 345 0102

Caravan Hire

Let's
(Cars and caravans for hire)
Istanbul Airport,
tel: (0212) 573 4502
Taksim, tel: (0212) 254 6997
Anadolu Caravan
Istanbul, tel: (0212) 260 1480
Hewa Caravan
Istanbul, tel: (0212) 661 4144

Car Hire

To rent a car you should be over 21 and have held a licence for a year, and you will need a credit card or substantial cash sum for the deposit. Car hire companies have offices in most cities and tourist areas, or you can make arrangements in advance through your travel agent. Car hire in Turkey is quite expensive (minimum $300 or £200 per week inclusive), and there is a huge variation in price, even between the major companies. It is often cheaper to book in advance as part of a fly-drive package, but whatever method you choose, get several quotations before deciding. Basic insurance will be included in the price but you should check that collision damage waiver (CDW) is added; it is worth the extra cost.

If you book in Turkey, small local Turkish hire companies may offer a better deal especially if you are booking out of season. It is worth trying to bargain a little, especially if you suspect business is slack.

Campervans and caravans can be hired locally, but these too are expensive. Motorcycles, scooters and bicycles can all be hired in tourist areas.

Child seats should be available for a small extra charge, but you need to check this when booking.

Hiring through an international company will allow you to return the car to a different point for no extra charge. Local companies will usually allow this only if they have an office at your destination.

Sea Transport

Turkish Maritime Lines (TML): Istanbul, tel: (0212) 249 9222/244 0207 operate an all-year-round service between Istanbul and İzmir, departing Fridays at 3pm and arriving the next morning; returning Sundays at 12 noon, arriving in Istanbul the following morning. The Maritime Lines also serve the ports of the Black Sea region from May–Oct. Departure from Istanbul is on Mondays at 2.30pm, with stops at Zonguldak, Sinop and Samsun on the Tuesday, and Giresun, Trabzon and Rize on the Wednesday. The return is on Thursday with stops at Ordu, Samsun and Sinop, arriving back in Istanbul on Friday at 1.30pm.

Around the Sea of Marmara, there are car and passenger ferries crossing between Darica and Kartal on the northern shore (east of Istanbul), and Yalova on the south-eastern shore, and faster sea buses between Yenikapı to the west of Istanbul, Yalova and Bandırma, on the route to İzmir and the Aegean. There are ferry links between Eceabat on the Gallipoli peninsula and Çanakkale, and between Bandırma and the Marmara islands. Timetables for these services can be found at any of the sea bus or ferry terminals in Istanbul.

Practical Tips

Media

Over the last decade Turkey has enjoyed a media explosion, and there has been a surge in enthusiasm for new technology, which means that Turks can and do publish and broadcast in profusion. But quantity doesn't necessarily mean quality. The radio waves are so crowded with channels that stations have to take turns. There are dozens of regular TV channels, while apartment buildings bristle with aerials and dishes as people tune in to the world's cable and satellite networks.

TELEVISION

From a single state-run TV channel at the beginning of the 1980s, Turkey now has around 30 national channels, most of which are privately-owned and broadcast from Istanbul, and many regional channels. Light entertainment, soaps, game shows and pop music

videos dominate, but some channels also show foreign films (cable channel Cine 5 sometimes shows films in their original language with subtitles), and there are dedicated sport and music channels.

RADIO

Before 1993 only state-run radio stations broadcast. Today Istanbul has many private stations playing Western and Turkish pop and rock, interspersed with news broadcasts, all jostling for air-space. State channel *TRT3* (FM 88.2) appeals to more sophisticated listeners with jazz, Latin and classical music.

NEWSPAPERS AND MAGAZINES

There are now 29 major Turkish newspapers, nearly all with an average daily circulation of over 500,000. Competition is fierce as they chase a relatively small reading public and compete with the growth of radio, TV and the internet.

Sabah and *Hürriyet* are Turkey's best selling national newspapers and are considered to be the leading public opinion makers, with good news coverage and lots of colour. *Turkiye* and *Milliyet* follow not far behind. Left wing *Cumhuriyet*, with a daily circulation of around 50,000, is the most

Local Tourist Information Offices

Government-run tourist information offices *Turizm Danısma Burosu* are marked with a white "i". Most open Mon–Sat 9am–5pm; the one at Istanbul airport is open 24 hours.

The service isn't always enthusiastic but most staff speak English and sometimes German or French, and should have a good collection of city maps, timetables, listings and details of festivals. Some have useful lists of accommodation but will not make bookings.

Atatürk Airport
Yesilköy;
tel: (0212) 663 63 63/663 0793.
Galatasaray
Mesrutiyet Caddesi 57;
tel: (0212) 245 6875/243 3472.
Hilton Hotel Arcade, Harbiye;
tel: (0212) 233 0592.
Karaköy Sea Port
tel: (0212) 249 5776.
Sirkeci Train Station
Istasyon Cad. 24/2, Sirkeci;
tel: (0212) 511 5888
Sultanahmet Square
tel: (0212) 518 1802.

serious newspaper. *Yeni Safak* (30,000) has a religious angle. Nearly all the nationals are produced in Istanbul.

The magazine market is also exploding. In 1990, there were only 20 magazine titles published; by 1997 it had shot up to 83, and subject matter is becoming far more diverse. There are Turkish editions of many international magazine titles, plus countless popular Turkish weeklies and monthlies.

Postal Services

Post offices *(postane)* are marked by a yellow sign with the black letters "PTT". They are usually open Mon–Sat 9am–5pm. Some, like the PTT at Galatasaray, also open on Sundays. Services at the larger PTTs include post restante, foreign exchange bureau, and metered phones. For stamps only, the desk is open 8am–8pm. There are also small PTT kiosks in tourist areas where you can buy stamps, post letters, and buy cards for public phones. Stamps are only available

International Codes

Dial the international prefix 00 and then the country code (listed below), followed by the number you want:

Australia	61
Canada	1
Ireland	353
New Zealand	64
USA	1
UK	44

from PTT outlets. PTT postboxes are yellow, marked PTT and *şeşiriçi* (local), *yurtiçi* (domestic) and *yurtdışı* (international). Use airmail for everything; surface mail is slow and unreliable. Even airmail can take anything from 5 days to three weeks to reach the UK or US. Express post costs more, but is supposed to take no more than three days to arrive. If you are sending a parcel, the contents will be inspected, so don't seal it beforehand.

Telecommunications

TELEPHONE

Huge numbers of Turks have mobile phones and use them constantly. If you have a GSM mobile, cleared for foreign use, you should be able to log onto the local network.

Public telephones are common in most areas. Phone cards *(telefon kartı)* can be bought from PTTs, or news-stands and vendors near phone booths. They are reliable and easy to use and come in denominations of 30, 60 and 100 units. Some public phones also take credit cards – much cheaper than phoning overseas from your hotel. Alternatively, there are metered phones in PTTs (for which you pay after your call; open 8am–midnight) and expensive metered private telephone offices (yellow and black, signed "telephone-fax").

Useful national and international codes and operator services are posted in phone boxes. Instructions in card phone boxes are in English, French, German and Turkish.

English Language Media

TV: TRT Channel 2 broadcasts the TV news in English at 10pm, and has CNN on Mondays at 7.40pm. TRT3 also broadcasts news in English, French and German following the Turkish bulletin at 9am, 12am, 5pm, 7pm and 10pm. Dozens of foreign TV channels, including BBC Prime, MTV, Eurosport and CNN are available on satellite and cable.

Radio: Voice FM (90.6) broadcasts news in English (from Voice of America) at 3pm. BBC World Service can be received on a short-wave radio with a good aerial, but reception is not very clear.

Print: There is one locally published English-language daily paper: the *Turkish Daily News*, which provides coverage of local and international events. It lists cinemas showing English-language films (not always accurate!), the main satellite and TV channel

programming and is also useful for its classified ads, which target the foreign community.

A useful English-language magazine, *The Guide*, is published bi-monthly in Istanbul, offering visitors practical information, arts news, and restaurant and shopping listings. It can be found in major hotels, some bookshops and newsstands in tourist areas. Web: www.theguideturkey.com.

The InterMedia publishing company produces several useful reference books in foreign language editions: guides to eating out in Istanbul, a step-by-step guide to Istanbul, and the indispensable *Almanac*, packed with vital political and economic statistics. Intended for visiting executives, it includes airlines, car hire, travel agents, consulates, as well as company addresses.

Cornucopia is a beautifully

illustrated English-language magazine featuring Turkish arts, history and culture. It is stocked at Turkish bookshops which sell foreign-language publications or you can subscribe on the web at www.cornucopia.net. *Atlas* and *Globe* are monthly quality travel magazines with English text summaries.

Foreign publications: International newspapers (including major European titles) and magazines can be found at newsstands and bookshops in tourist areas and hotels, especially Taksim Square, İstiklal Caddesi and Sultanahmet. Newspapers sometimes come a day late, and most are sold at many times the domestic cover price.

It is possible to find foreign-language books (commonly English, French and German) and most hotel shops stock a few titles. (*See Bookshops, page 300*).

Important Numbers

Calling Turkey (from abroad): 90

Operator numbers
(Only the international operator will definitely speak some English):
Directory Enquiries (Istanbul): 118
Intercity (Turkey) Operator: 131
International Operator/Directory Enquiries: 115
Dial a Telegram: 141
Wake-up Call: 135

Regional dialling codes
Don't dial the area code if calling the area you are in.
Istanbul:
European side 0212
Asian side 0216
(You should use these codes if calling from one side of the city to the other).

Bursa:	0224
Çanakkale:	0226
Edirne:	0284
Yalova:	0226

Collect Calls
It is possible to make a reverse call to most countries in the world. Dial 00-800-your country code-1177 for the following countries; England (BT), USA, Australia, Ireland, and South Africa. For Canada, the last four digits are 6677.

TELEGRAMS AND FAX

Telegrams can be sent from most post offices. The number of words and speed required determines the cost. There are three speeds: normal, *acele* (urgent) and *yıldırım* (flash). This can also be done over the phone by dialling 141, but you will probably encounter language difficulties. Faxes can also be sent from major PTTs, hotels and photocopy shops.

INTERNET

Turks have a passion for new technology, and are currently conducting a love-affair with the internet. Internet cafés in Istanbul, which range from cramped smoky rooms to fashionable places to "hang-out" are springing up all the time, and the cost is getting cheaper as more servers appear and networks get quicker. In mid-99, the cost per hour averaged $2 (£1.50), half the price of the previous year. Most internet cafés are concentrated in Taksim, especially around İstiklal Caddesi, Beyoğlu, Aksaray and Sultanahmet. For useful web-sites, *see page 259*; for internet café listings, *see page 288*.

Foreign Consulates

Although all the embassies are in Ankara, the capital, the consulates in Istanbul handle the majority of visa and passport matters. If you need a visa for somewhere else for your onward travel from Turkey, you will probably be able to get it in Istanbul, although check in ample time. (In popular tourist areas you may find an Honorary Consul – a local person appointed to take on consular responsibilities).
Australia
Tepecik Yolu 58,
Etiler;
tel: (0212) 257 7050;
fax: (0212) 257 7601
Canada (Hon)
Büyükdere Caddesi, 107/3,
Gayrettepe;
tel: (0212) 272 5174,
fax: (0212) 272 3427

Ambulance Services

Istanbul is relatively well provided with ambulances, but the biggest problem is the traffic, which comes to a standstill during the morning and evening rush hour. Such is the drivers' frustration that some vehicles stubbornly refuse to give way to the emergency services.

Ambulance 2000:
Tel: (0212) 222 61 61
Helicopter service with fully

Ireland (Hon)
Cumhuriyet Caddesi 26/A, Harbiye;
tel: (0212) 246 6025
UK
Mesrutiyet Caddesi 34,
Tepebaşı;
tel: (0212) 293 7540;
Consular
tel: (0212) 252 6436;
fax: (0212) 245 4989
USA
Mesrutiyet Caddesi 104, Tepebaşı;
tel: (0212) 251 3602

Bursa
UK (Hon)
Ressam Sefik Bursalı Sokak,
Basak Caddesi No 40;
tel: (0224) 220 0436

Medical Treatment

Istanbul is pretty safe medically, as long as you are reasonably sensible. For health preparations, *see page 261*. **Traveller's diarrhoea** is the main hazard, best avoided by food and water hygiene. Drink only bottled water, wash or peel all fruit and vegetables, and ensure cooked food is piping hot. It's safest to eat freshly prepared local produce. Meat and fish are usually safe if properly cooked through.

Should you succumb, let your system flush itself out, only resorting to treatments such as Imodium if completely necessary. Drink plenty of non-alcoholic soft drinks or black tea, containing rehydration salts (prepackaged sachets are a useful addition to

equipped machinery and staff on board.
General Ambulance Ltd:
Tel: (0212) 541 29 17/19
Mob: (0532) 312 51 29.
Fully equipped air ambulance, jet, and helicopter service.
International Hospital Ambulance:
Tel: (0212) 663 30 00
Istanbul Health Services:
Tel: (0212) 247 07 81/231 11 44
Medline 2000;
Tel: (0212) 280 00 00.

Emergency Numbers

Ambulance (public) 112
Police 155
Fire 110
Emergency 115
Tourism Police (0212) 527 4503

your first-aid kit), eat plain food and avoid oil or dairy products. (A reputed local cure is Turkish coffee with a squeeze of lemon juice!). If the diarrhoea lasts over 48 hrs, seek medical advice.

Heatstroke and sunburn are relatively rare in Istanbul, but be sensible, drink plenty of fluids if hot, and cut down on alcohol intake during the day. If you are **bitten** by any animal, it is vitally important to seek medical attention as soon as possible; you may require vaccination against rabies. While waiting for the doctor, the best first aid is to wash the wound thoroughly; five minutes scrubbing with soap under running water is recommended. Malaria is not a problem here, but you may be bitten by mosquitoes.

TREATMENT

A **pharmacy** *(eczane)* should be your first port of call for treating minor ailments. A rota system ensures one pharmacist in every district stays open 24 hours for

emergencies. This is referred to in Turkish as a *nöbetçi*. The address is noted in pharmacists' windows.

As far as medications are concerned, most drugs are available in Turkey over the counter, without prescription. Self-treatment is not to be recommended, but it is easy to replace routine medication. It is a good idea to show the pharmacist the empty container, to be sure that you are being given the right drug. Remember that generic drugs can be marketed under different names.

HOSPITALS (HASTANESI)

Some doctors and dentists in Istanbul speak English or German and many have been trained abroad to a high standard. Most four and five star hotels have a doctor who can speak some English and/or German on call in case of emergency.

State hospitals are well equipped and much cheaper than **private hospitals**, although they are usually very crowded and chaotic. All hospitals work on a pay-as-you-go basis; requiring payment on the spot, in advance of any treatment, which includes scans and x-rays. This has been known to happen even in extreme emergencies. Keep some cash and a credit card on you at all times (although some state hospitals don't accept cards).

Crime by Tourists

Of the many millions of Westerners who flood into Turkey each year, not all are law-abiding. The Turks take a very dim view of drunken tourists scaling the statues of Atatürk, or being anything other than respectful to their national icons, religion or women. If you do get into trouble with the law, contact your consulate for advice and assistance.

Some **ambulance** services operate independently; others are attached to particular hospitals. For contact details, *see box, below*.

Security and Crime

Istanbul has an enviably low crime record. This reflects Turkish society: low incidence of drug use, respect for law and order, and, most important of all, close-knit communities and family ties. Foreigners and tourists are regarded as guests, so are very well treated. In normal circumstances you can expect the police to be polite and helpful. Tourist areas are regularly patrolled by special Turizm or Tourist Police, who will do their best to help you and speak some French, English, German or Arabic.

Inevitably, however, Istanbul has some crime. Car crimes and break-ins are possible and purse-snatching and pickpocketing are on the increase in crowded places such as the Grand Bazaar, Eminönü and İstiklal Caddesi. Take the same precautions you would at home – don't leave valuables, or your bag, visible in a car; use a handbag with a long strap slung diagonally over the shoulder; take care of bags, wallets and cameras; and don't walk down dark streets on your own late at night. In spite of this, Istanbul at night is far safer for women than most European cities. (*See Women travellers, page 276*).

There have been reported instances of tourists – especially

Hospitals in Istanbul

Private Hospitals
Acıbadem Hastanesi
Kadıköy, (Asian side);
tel: (0216) 326 3336.
American Hastanesi
Güzelbahçe Sokak,
Nisantaşı;
tel: (0212) 231 4050.
Florence Nightingale Hastanesi
Abidei Hürriyet Caddesi 290,
Çağlayan, Şişli;
tel: (0212) 224 4950.
German Hospital
Sıraselviler Caddesi 119, Taksim;
tel: (0212) 251 7100/8.

International Hospital
(ambulance service), Yesilköy;
tel: (0212) 663 3000.
Marmara University Hospital
(Asian side);
tel: (0216) 327 1010.

State Hospitals
Etfal Hastanesi
Etfal Sok, Şişli;
tel: (0212) 231 2209.
Taksim Ilk Yardim
Siraselviler Cad. Taksim
(Emergency)
tel: (0212) 252 4300.

single men – being targeted by a "friendly" local. The victim is taken for a drink which is drugged, and then robbed whilst he spends a day or two asleep.

Also beware of a scam which consists of a tourist being taken to a nightclub or bar by a local and presented with an astronomical bill. Only when it is too late do you realise that the women who have been sitting drinking with you are being paid for their presence. A refusal to pay usually leads to threats of violence and being frogmarched to your hotel or cashpoint machine to get the money. It's useless going to the police to report such incidents after the fact, but the Tourist Police are aware of which bars should be avoided. If in doubt, ask before accepting an invitation. This crime is most common around the Taksim area, and is especially perpetrated upon men travelling alone or with a male companion. (*See 1001 Nights, page 93*).

DRUGS

The film *Midnight Express* was an exaggeration, portraying the Turks in a very negative light, but it is true that heavy penalties are exacted on anyone found in possession of drugs. A foreigner on a narcotics charge can expect long-term imprisonment.

Etiquette

There are few don'ts in Turkey; there is little interference in the personal lives of foreigners as they are regarded as a law unto themselves. Your visit is governed by the rules of hospitality which form a substantial part of the infrastructure of Turkish society. This means that you are truly regarded as a guest and (mostly) to be accorded the utmost help.

Public displays of affection between couples can give offence, as can nudity. Beachwear is worn only on the beach, and topless sunbathing is frowned on. Feet are regarded as unclean – so don't put them on a table, or where someone might sit. Should you be invited into a Turkish home, remove your shoes. In Istanbul, women may wear shorts and sleeveless tops, and men must always wear tops.

MOSQUES

The call to prayer from the minaret comes five times a day between dawn and nightfall.

Non-Muslims should not enter a mosque during prayer time and especially not during Friday mid-day prayers. Both men and women should be modestly dressed (knees and shoulders covered). Before entering remove your shoes. You can leave them outside, carry them or use the plastic shoe covers available at larger mosques. Women may be asked to cover their heads. Take care not to disturb, touch or walk in front of anyone who may be at prayer. The larger, more famous mosques will be open throughout the day from the first prayer to the last one at night. Smaller ones may only open at prayer times; you may have to find a caretaker (*bekci*) or

Photography

Istanbul is hugely photogenic and, taking photographs is perfectly acceptable in almost any context. Turks will generally be pleased to be included in your photograph, and if on holiday themselves will be busily snapping away. However it is polite to ask first, and to respect their wishes if they say no. Some veiled women prefer not to be photographed. Some people may ask for a copy print. If you take their address, make sure you send the pictures. Museums sometimes charge for the use of cameras or video; flash may not be allowed as it can damage delicate paints and textiles. Mosques usually allow discreet flash-free photography but you should be tactful.

wait for prayer time, and enter as the worshippers leave.

TURKISH TOILETS

Turkish toilet facilities can be disconcerting; standards of public lavatories vary hugely from sparkling to revolting. Most are the squat variety, although you will find clean Western-style facilities in the more upmarket hotels and restaurants, main sights and museums and in the swish new American-style shopping malls such as Akmerkez or Carrefour. Arm yourself with wipes and a supply of paper (which goes in the bin, not the hole, as the drains can't cope with it). Special nappy-changing or baby rooms are very rare.

Tipping

It is customary to tip a small amount to anyone who does you a small service; the hotel cleaner, porter, doorman who gets you a taxi and so on. In cinemas it is customary to give coins (eg TL50,000) to the usher who shows you to your seat. For some inexplicable reason small change

Developing and printing is easily available and of good quality; fast photo developing shops (from under half an hour) have sprung up everywhere.

Prices for film and for processing are high and comparable with the equivalent express service at home.

All kinds of films (print, slide, b&w) are cheaper to buy in photographic shops than at tourist sites, which generally carry only a limited supply of print film.

Professional standard processing for b&w and slides is also available. The best and cheapest area for buying, processing and developing films (and any camera equipment) is in **Sirkeci**, opposite the train station.

(bozuk para) is in short supply.

A porter who carries your luggage in a smart hotel should get $2–4. In restaurants, round the bill up by 5-10 percent; if service has been included, leave 5 percent on the table in cash for the waiter. If you've had a snack in a small local restaurant, leave small change. Taxis are the exception: you don't tip taxi drivers and they do not expect it, though you can round the fare up to the nearest suitable figure as change can be a problem.

Women Travellers

Turkish attitudes towards women are liberal in Istanbul compared to the rest of the country. You will see women wearing anything from a full black veil to smart Western-style dress and even high fashion miniskirts or lycra. If you are planning to visit any mosques, cover your knees and shoulders and carry a scarf.

The city is liberal, Westernised and safer than many European countries. Leers and suggestions may be common, but instances of physical attack are rare. Women visitors should not be afraid to travel alone, or to go out at night, though provocative dress may create problems and at night you might feel more relaxed with a companion. You should expect Turkish men to chat you up, often in an outrageously flamboyant fashion, but you can reduce harassment to a minimum by dressing respectably and looking as if you know where you are going. If you are groped by a stranger, speak up loudly; the shame will usually be enough to fend him off and everyone nearby will make it a point of honour to rush to your defence.

Family life in Islam is private, so public displays of affection are not common; religious couples will not even hold hands in the street. On long-distance buses you will not be permitted to sit next to a strange male, but there is no segregation on local transport.

Restaurants often have a designated *"aile salonu"* (family room), and sometimes they'd prefer a lone woman to sit there. You may not be welcome at a traditional coffee or tea room *(kahvehane* or *çayhane)* away from a tourist area, as these are usually considered to be male preserves.

Travelling with Children

Turks adore babies and children, they will be delighted you have brought yours with you, and will undoubtedly make a huge fuss of them.

You will need good sunblock, hats and long light clothes for children in summer. In case of tummy upsets, bring prepacked sachets of rehydration salts such as Dioralyte, although they are also available in every chemist. Babies can take this from a bottle. Disposable nappies and other baby gear such as Johnson's toiletries are easily available, if expensive for imported brands; and there are branches of Mothercare and M&S in Istanbul. You can buy ready-prepared baby food in supermarkets and chemists, some imported from Europe.

City streets are far from buggy-friendly: high kerbstones, steep and uneven surfaces make them almost impossible to push. Buses are often crowded and their entrances are high and awkward. Bring a rucksack-style baby carrier or papoose if possible; most Turkish babies are simply carried in their parents' arms.

DISCOUNTS

Child discounts are different in Turkey from elsewhere: Normally you pay for children over 7 on public transport, but you may not pay for under-13s at museums. It seems often to be at the whim of the attendant. Hotels will offer anything from a third to 50 percent off both room-rates and set meal charges.

HOTELS

Hotels will almost always put up extra beds if there is space in your room. Most places have family rooms, sometimes for as many as six, and even *pansiyons* may have small apartments/suites with a mini-kitchen included at no extra cost. You need to ask in advance if you need a cot.

FOOD FOR CHILDREN

Restaurants rarely offer meals specifically for children. If you would like something plain, ask for *çok sade*, or *acısız*, not peppery hot. *Çocuklar için* means "for the children".

Much Turkish food, however, is sufficiently simple to satisfy even the fussiest child and restaurants will do their best to find something for the children to eat, even if you can't see something obvious on the menu.

There are plenty of plain dishes in Turkish cooking which western children will find acceptable without having to resort to fast food, although pizzas, burgers and chips can be found easily. Dishes children may like include grilled *köfte* (meatballs), *sade pilav* (rice), all kinds of Turkish bread, *pide* (Turkish pizza; be careful of the sort that comes with goat topping), any grilled meat, lamb or chicken *şiş kebabs*, grilled steak or chicken *(tavuk or piliç ızgara)*. Chips are *patates tava*. A plate of plain salad vegetables (lettuce, grated carrot, tomato, cucumber etc) is called *söğüş*. Turkish rice pudding is excellent *(sütlaç)*. You can always ask for a plate of sliced fresh fruit for dessert, melon or ice cream.

FOOD FOR BABIES

Ready-made babyfood is common. Breastfeeding mothers need not feel shy, but as Turks are modest in public, you should be discreet. Wear something loose, or use a large scarf or beach wrap to screen yourself and your baby – this is what rural Turkish women do, and it will come in useful to protect you from hot sun.

SIGHTSEEING WITH CHILDREN

Istanbul can be hard work, but can still be enjoyable with small children. Very little in Turkey is specifically devised with children in mind, although Turkish people are always very friendly and welcoming to them. Palaces can be difficult, as you may have to join a guided tour, which the children will find boring (and the guide's English is often difficult to understand). Istanbul has some great parks and gardens with tea-shops. If you get desperate, head for one of the shopping malls where you will find a children's play area, clean lavatories and fast food.

A few favourite sights include:

Bosphorus ferry (*see page 217*); **Topkapı Palace** (*see page 161*); the **Archaeological Museum** (*see page 150*; this has a children's section, and a mock-up of the Trojan Horse to climb on); **Rahmi Koç Museum** (*see page 193*; which has a number of working models of steam locomotives, engines and mechanical toys); the **Naval Museum** (*see page 219*); **Yerebatan Cistern** (*see page 152*); the **Military Museum** (*see page 208*); and **Rumeli Hisarı** (*see page 222*).

PARKS AND PLAYGROUNDS

Yıldız Park (entrance on the coast road between Beşiktaş and Ortaköy) is great for children and adults, a true oasis of trees and quiet walks in the heart of the city.

There are two restored buildings, Cadir Kösk and Malta Kösk which have large terraces where tea and snacks are served. Malta Kösk has

an excellent buffet dinner every Sunday afternoon.

Emirgân Woods, overlooking the Bosphorus, contains restaurants and cafés, as does **Beykoz**, on the Asian side.

Park Orman in Maslak district, is in the Fatih Children's Woods, it has facilities for children and families, including a swimming pool, picnic area and playground.

Gulhane Park, below Topkapı Palace, is a popular place for families with children.

Tatilya, "The Republic of Fun", Beylikdüzü, 18km west of the airport on the E5 motorway out of the city, is Istanbul's only theme park. It is fairly small, but clean and well run with safe rides for various age groups, plus various eateries and shops – all under a glass bubble.

Darica Bird Paradise and Botanical Garden, Darica, 45km (30 miles) east of Istanbul, off the E5. 70 hectares (150 acres) of gardens and zoo, with a surprising range of species including zebras, kangaroos, penguins and exotic birds. The zoo is acceptably well-kept, and has an excellent play area and several cafés.

Business Travellers

Business travellers are often guests of a Turkish company, and the visit will be governed by the rules of hospitality. You can expect to be whisked from place to place by chauffeured car and thoroughly entertained after hours. Although your hosts may speak good English or German, you may prefer to engage an interpreter of your own. The top hotels are geared to business travellers and will be able to provide office and conference facilities, and can be relied on to receive and pass on faxes and telephone messages in English.

Translation and Business Services
Bayza Diler
Tel: (0212) 244 0793
Çitlembik
Tel: (0212) 292 3032

Gay Travellers

Turkish attitudes to gays, or to overtly gay behaviour, are contradictory. On the one hand they are proud of their home-grown transvestite or transsexual singers; on the other they can be publicly intolerant of gay couples, so gays are advised to be discreet in public. There are gay bars and discos in Taksim, and gay couples should not have any problems in the main "straight" discos, especially in Taksim. (*See 1001 Nights, page 93*).

Travellers with Disabilities

Although there have recently been some improvements, Istanbul has hardly any facilities of any kind for the disabled and even manoeuvring a wheelchair is a strenuous challenge. There are virtually no disabled toilet facilities, and mosques will not usually allow wheelchairs in. However, people are exceptionally friendly and kind and will do their best to help to get you into a museum or building. There are no low-level telephone booths except in hotels, and very few buses have wheelchair access (those that do are listed on bus-maps). The Turkish Tourist Office in London issues a guide to facilities for the disabled in Turkey. **Turkish Association for the Disabled** in Istanbul Tel: (0212) 521 4912. **For information before you travel**:

UK
RADAR (Royal Association for Disability and Rehabilitation) 12 City Forum, 250 City Road, London EC1V 8AF
Tel: (020) 7250 3222
Fax: (020) 7250 1212.
USA
SATH (Society for the Advancement of Travel for the Handicapped) 347 Fifth Ave Ste 610, New York NY10016
Tel: (0212) 447 7284
Fax: (0212) 725 8253).

Religious Services

Turkey is officially a secular state, although 98 percent of the population are Muslim. Greek Orthodox, Jewish and Armenian minorities are practising in the city and there are functioning churches and synagogues. Attending a service can be a way of meeting people who live and work in the place you are visiting; and a way of experiencing the building itself in its intended setting.

MOSQUES

There are hundreds of mosques in the city; some of the most interesting ones include:
Atik Valide Mosque
Üsküdar; built by Sinan in 1583.
Beyazıt Mosque
Beyazıt (see page 177).
Blue Mosque (Sultanahmet Camii)
Sultanahmet (see page 154).
Eyüp Mosque
(See page 192).
Fatih Mosque
Fatih (see page 187).

Kiliç Ali Paşa Mosque
In Tophane, designed by Sinan and built in 1580 on order of Ali Paşa.
Mirhrimah Mosque
Edirnekapı, built in 1555 by Sinan for Mirhrimah Sultan, daughter of Süleyman the Magnificent.
Nuruosmaniye Mosque
Cağaloğlu (see page 175).
Ortaköy Mosque
(See page 221).
Rustem Paşa Mosque
Eminönü (see page 180).
Suleymaniye Mosque
Beyazıt (see page 179).
Şeyhzade Mosque
Şeyhzadebasi (see page 179).
Valide Mosque
Aksaray; begun in 1597 by Davud Ağa, completed in 1663
Yeni Cami (New Mosque)
Eminönü (see page 181).

CHRISTIAN CHURCHES

Protestant
Christ Church (Anglican)
Serdarı Ekrem Sok. 82, Tünel, Beyoğlu (behind the Swedish Consulate, off İstiklal Caddesi)

Tel: (0212) 251 5616
Built by subscription in the 1860s to commemorate those who died in the Crimean War, the church was designed by Victorian architect C.E. Street and is visited by fans of High Victorian and colonial church architecture. This little corner of Gothic splendour has a liberal, international atmosphere. Matins 9am; Evensong 6pm daily; sung Eucharist 10am on Sundays.
St Helena's Chapel
British Consulate, Galatasaray
Tel: (0212) 251 5616.
The Anglican chaplaincy in Istanbul. Eucharist 12.30pm; on first Wednesday of the month (except Jul–Aug).
Dutch Union Church of Istanbul
Postacılar Sok. Beyoğlu
Tel: (0212) 244 5212.
Friendly New Zealand pastor and his wife welcome all comers. Sunday service at 11am.

Roman Catholic
St. Anthony of Padua
İstiklal Cad., Galatasaray-Beyoğlu
Tel: (0212) 244 09 35
One of the city's best known

Visting a Hamam

Cağaloğlu Hamam
Prof. Kazım Gürkan Cad. 34, Cağaloğlu; tel: (0212) 522 2424
Priced for tourists (up to US$50/£30 for the works) but superb attention to detail in this 400 year old bath house. Fabulous bar around the old courtyard, full of antiquities and Moorish in feel. Group bookings taken. Men: 7am–9.30pm; women: 8am–8pm.
Çemberlitaş Hamam
Vezirhan Cad. 8, Çemberlitaş; tel: (0212) 522 7974/511 2535; email: contact@cemberlitashamami.com.tr web: www.cemberlitashamami.com.tr
Another bath of great antiquity, built by the great Ottoman architect Sinan. Traditional style bathing with separate sections for the sexes. Costs around US$15–18 (£9–11) for the works.

Open 6am–midnight.
Tarişi Galatasaray Hamamı
Liva Sok, next to Greek Consulate, off İstikilal Cad, Beyoğlu
This historic bath is one of the city's best, architecturally, with great décor and comforts. However, the staff are appararently quite persistent for tips, so better to go with a Turkish friend.
Tarihi Aga Hamami
Ağa Sokak 66, Cihangir (near Taksim)
Less expensive and polished than the previous ones – a real local's hamam. For women, open 9am–6pm. Men 6pm–9am. Cost around US$10 (£6) for everything.

Many people are put off the idea of trying a Turkish bath because they simply don't know what to expect – or what to do. Don't worry. The locals will happily

steer you straight. The sexes are always segregated, either in different parts of the bath house or by allocating different times or days. You don't need to take anything with you but you can of course choose to take your own wrap, swim-suit, towels, flannel and toiletries.

The rules are simple, based on the old Roman baths or the Scandinavian sauna. Full nudity is not usual: wear a swimming costume or ask for a sarong (peştamal). You will also be given a towel and wooden clogs (takunya). Women are never attended to or massaged by men. Most five star hotels offer luxurious, modern hamams geared to western standards, but some more traditional bath houses are well worth a visit. (See feature, page 157).

functioning Roman Catholic churches.
St. Esprit Cathedral
Cumhuriyet Cad. 205/B, Harbiye.
Built by the same Italian architect who designed and built the gates of Dolmabahçe Palace.
St. Louis des Français
Postacılar Sok. 11, Beyoğlu
Tel: (0212) 244 1075

Orthodox
Aya Triada
Mehelik Sok. 11/1, Taksim
Tel: (0212) 244 13 58
St. Mary Pammakaristos
(Fethiye Cami) Fener
Tel: (0212) 522 1750 (*See page 189*).
SS Sergius and Bacchus
(Kucuk Aya Sofya), Sultanahmet
(*See page 146*).
Armenian Patriarchate
Harapnel Sok. 20, Kumkapı
Tel: (0212) 517 0970
Üç Horon
Balık Pazar (fish market), Beyoğlu
Tel: (0212) 244 1382

JEWISH

Most of the Jewish population in Turkey is Sephardic, tracing their origins to the Jews who were expelled from Spain by the Inquisition in 1492. However, over the years the community has dwindled and services are irregular. They are subject to intense security, thus it might be a good idea to phone and let them know you're coming.
Ashkenazy Synagogue
Yüksek Kaldırım 37, Karaköy
Tel: (0212) 244 2975
Neve Shalom Synagogue
Büyük Hendek Cad. 67, Beyoğlu
Tel: (0212) 244 1576
Chief Rabbinate
Yemenici Sok. 23, Tünel/Beyoğlu
Tel: (0212) 244 8794

Where to Stay

Istanbul offers all conceivable varieties of accommodation, from campsites to the most luxurious of hotels. Istanbul's five star accommodation is in line with New York or any major European city in both price and quality. *Pansiyon* accommodation, however, can be very reasonable. Visitors come to Istanbul the whole year round, but during the busiest months (July–Sept), advance booking is advisable.

Types of Lodgings

The Ministry of Tourism classifies all hotels from one to five stars. The largest number have between one and three stars – offering at the lowest level a basic en-suite room, but one which is modern and reasonably comfortable. Three-star hotels will usually have a restaurant and a bar, minibar and TV in each room.
   The five-star hotels at the top end of the market include the luxury flagships of the major international hotel chains: Intercontinental, Hilton, Hyatt, Swissotel. At this level, though the rooms are expensive, the competition is intense, and at quiet times these hotels can to offer extremely attractive packages.
   Be a little cautious when booking an unknown hotel. Ratings are awarded solely on facilities and there is no mention of ambience or even state of repair. Some 3 and 4 star hotels are way below European standards, with peeling walls and cold water; others are wonderful.

Apart-hotels
These offer some of the independence of being in your own

flat with the services associated with a comfortable hotel. In Istanbul they have been developed as a way of renovating and adapting attractive older apartment buildings without substantially changing their character. One or two conventional five-star hotels also offer apartments.

Pensions
A Turkish *pansiyon* is somewhere between a simple hotel and a bed-and-breakfast place. They can be lovely places to stay, especially if family-run. The more expensive will have en-suite facilities in every room. In some, hot water is heated by solar panels on the roof, and may run out (or simply not warm up at all in winter).

Camping
There is only one place for camping 16 km (10 miles) from the city centre, with a bar, pool, disco and tennis courts:
Ataköy Tatil Köyü
Rauf Orbay Cad., Ataköy
Tel: (0212) 559 6000/1.

Youth Hostels
Accommodation is so reasonably priced that there are very few youth hostels as such.

Hotel Listings
THE OLD CITY

Four Seasons
Tevkifhane Sok. 1, Sultanahmet
Tel: (0212) 638 8200
Fax: (0212) 638 8210
A restored neoclassical Ottoman prison is now the city's most luxurious and prestigious hotel. It has wonderful views of Aya Sofya and Blue Mosque, top-notch service, splendid décor with Ottoman antiques, and all modern conveniences. Small, and very popular. The Gazebo restaurant offers top quality Turkish and Continental cuisine. **$$$$$**
Merit Antique
Laleli
Tel: (0212) 513 9300
Fax: (0212) 512 6390/513 9340

Prices

Because of the enormous fluctuations of the lira, these price brackets are based on a US$ average and are an indication only; prices may change considerably. Bargaining is usually possible, especially out of high season. Hotels will be cheaper if part of a pre-booked package. Many cheap hotels will not accept credit cards, so check on booking.

For a double room in high season:
$ = below $50
$$ = $50 to $80
$$$ =$80 to $150
$$$$ = $150 to $250
$$$$$ = above $250

This lovingly restored early 20th-century apartment complex in the heart of the old city is now a charming hotel with 275 rooms. Superb Chinese, Turkish and Kosher restaurants. Also a patisserie, wine bar and health club. **$$$$$**
Pierre Loti
Piyerloti Cad. 5, Çemberlitaş
Tel: (0212) 518 5700
Fax: (0212) 516 1886
Attractive and intimate 36-room hotel close to Aya Sofya and other prime attractions. Airconditioning, phone, TV. **$$$**
Essel Hotel
Binbirdirek Meydanı Sok. 1–3,

Special Licence Hotels

Special Licences are granted by the municipality to hotels housed in historic buildings such as old Ottoman houses or caravanserais. Many are therefore in the oldest and most interesting parts of town, and offer the amenities (and prices) of three, four or five-star hotels, but with limitations (such as no lift), due to the historic nature of the buildings. Many are very atmospheric, decorated in old Turkish style.
The concept was first

introduced by the pioneering director of the Turkish Touring and Automobile Club, Çelik Gülersoy, a tireless conservationist and campaigner for Turkey's historical and cultural heritage. Special Licence hotels are intended to be inspirational examples for others to follow. Under his guidance and with his energy the first of these hotels were created almost 20 years ago. Prices range from luxurious (US $200) to moderate (under US $100).

Sultanahmet
Tel: (0212) 638 4428
Fax: (0212) 638 4441
Comfortable, friendly modern hotel used mainly by tour groups, 5 mins walk from Aya Sofya Square. The rooms are small, but the shortcomings are more than made up for by the superb view of Aya Sofya and the Blue Mosque from the roof terrace. Air conditioning, phone, TV. **$$$**

Historic Hotels and Pensions
Ayasofya Pansiyonlar
Soğukçeşme Sok.,
Sultanahmet
Tel: (0212) 513 3660
Fax: (0212) 513 3669
A charming cobbled lane full of restored wooden houses furnished with period furniture, located directly behind Aya Sofya. 57 rooms, 4 suites, 3 restaurants (one in a Byzantine cistern), café, bars, Turkish bath, and even a research library on old Istanbul. **$$$**
İbrahim Paşa
Terzihane Sok. 5,
Sultanahmet
Tel: (0212) 518 0394/518 0395
Fax: (0212) 518 4457
e-mail: pasha@ibm.net
web: www.all-hotels.com/a/tkpasha
This stylish, understated small hotel in a restored 19th-century townhouse next to the Hippodrome has a Parisian ambience and a spectacular view of the Sea of Marmara from its rooftop terrace. 18 rooms, one suite, all with private

bathroom and high-tech facilities including satellite TV. Café, bar, restaurant. French and English spoken. **$$$**
Yeşil Ev
Kabasakal Cad. 5,
Sultanahmet
Tel: (0212) 517 6785
Fax: (0212) 517 6780
A restored wooden mansion, previously the home of an Ottoman paşa, located between Aya Sofya and the Blue Mosque. 20 rooms with period décor, intimate walled rear garden with conservatory and good restaurant. Book well in advance. **$$$**
Empress Zoë
Akbüyük Cad., Adliya Sok. 10,
Sultanahmet
Tel: (0212) 518 2504/518 4360
Fax: (0212) 518 5699
e-mail: emzoe@ibm.net
American owner Ann Nevins has turned this small hotel (16 rooms, 3 suites) near Topkapı Palace into something unique, complete with Byzantine wall paintings and a garden which incorporates the ruins of a 15th-century Turkish bath. She can also give good advice on planning your holiday and excursions. **$$**
Hotel Celal Sultan
Salkımsögüt Sok. 16,
Sultanahmet
Tel: (0212) 520 9323
Fax: (0212) 527 2704
e-mail: csultan@ibm.net
Classically restored, cosy townhouse (16 rooms, 1 suite) with double-glazed windows and filtered water. International cable TV and great view of Aya Sofya from the roof terrace. **$$**
Hotel Kybele
Yerebatan Cad. 35,
Sultanahmet
Tel: (0212) 511 7766/67
Fax: (0212) 513 4393
A treasurehouse of Ottoman antiques with a lobby lit by over 1000 historic lamps. 16 rooms, restaurant and delightful courtyard. English, Japanese and other languages spoken. **$$**
Hotel Fehmi Bey
Üçler Sok. 15,
Sultanahmet

Old City or New City?

Most of the remains of old Constantinople are in and around Sultanahmet and for this reason it is where most visitors stay. There are a vast number of reasonably priced pensions here, pitched to international standards, and everything is geared up for the expectations of the tourist. However, like most areas designated for foreigners, there are downsides to staying in Sultanahmet: continuous harassment by hawkers or would-be guides and gigolos; over-priced, uninspired restaurants; and little

nightlife of the type for which Istanbul has become justifiably famous. In fact it is largely dead after 10pm. It will still suit those who like to go to bed early and site-hop all day, especially those who feel most comfortable in the company of compatriots rather than natives. But the younger and more adventurous might prefer to stay in old Pera, just across the Galata Bridge, where historical monuments only date from the 14th century but there's a lot more entertainment in the evening.

Tel: (0212) 638 9083/85
Fax: (0212) 518 1264
e-mail: hotelfehmibey@turk.net
web-site: www.fehmibay.com
This 18-room restored townhouse offers friendly hosts, slick décor, a sauna and a spectacular sea view from its rooftop terrace. **$$**

Hotel Nomade
Divanyolu, Ticarethane Sok. 15, Sultanahmet
Tel: (0212) 511 1296
Fax: (0212) 513 2404
Run by two French-educated twin sisters, this homely 15-room hotel will appeal to well-travelled internationalists, intellectuals and solo females. Rooftop terrace, and its own bistro (Rumeli Café) across the street. **$**

Kervan Guest House
Yerebatan Cad., Seftali Sok. 10
Tel: (0212) 528 2949
Fax: (0212) 527 2390
Bright, cheerful little guest house above a row of shops near the Yerebatan Sarayı. The owners speak excellent English, the rooms are simply but pleasantly furnished and the location is superb. **$**

THE NEW CITY

Ceylan Inter-Continental
Taksim
Tel: (0212) 231 2121
Fax: (0212) 231 2180
This luxurious hotel commands

superb views of the Bosphorus and city skylines. 390 rooms and suites, including 4 suites for the disabled. Restaurants include Turkish, French and Californian cuisine and there are bars and deluxe banqueting and convention facilities, sports facilities, shops, etc. **$$$$$**

Conrad International
Barbaros Bulvari, Beşşiktaş
Tel: (0212) 227 3000
Fax: (0212) 259 6667
web: www.HILTON.com
The biggest hotel in Istanbul, with 625 rooms and 36 suites. Excellent Italian and Turkish restaurants, French patisserie, and live jazz in the bar every night. Health club with indoor and outdoor swimming pools, 24-hour business centre. Convenient location with wonderful views of the Bosphorus and Yıldız Imperial Gardens. **$$$$$**

Çırağan Palace Hotel Kempinski
Beşiktaş
Tel: (0212) 258 3377
Fax: (0212) 259 6686
One of Istanbul's most prestigious (and expensive) hotels has been reconstructed from a ruined Ottoman palace, although most of the rooms are located in a modern extension. First member of the Leading Hotels of the World in Turkey, recently voted amongst the world's top 100 hotels by *Institutional Investor*. Superb

setting on the shore of the Bosphorus; easy proximity to the city centre a plus. Two gourmet restaurants, one Ottoman (Tuğra), one Italian (Bellini). 295 rooms and 27 suites, 12 in the palace. Outdoor swimming pool and jazz club. **$$$$$**

Divan
Elmadağ, Taksim
Tel: (0212) 231 4100
Fax: (0212) 248 8527
A relatively small, first-rate hotel with 169 rooms and 11 suites. Completely refurbished recently. The Divan has one of the most distinguished restaurants in Istanbul, serving Ottoman and international dishes, as well as a popular café for quick meals. A few rooms have private terraces. **$$$$$**

Istanbul Hilton
Harbiye
Tel: (0212) 231 4650
Fax: (0212) 240 4165
Built in the 1950s and one of the best hotels in Istanbul: fully renovated, excellent service, away from the traffic. Outdoor pool, 498 rooms, 16 suites, executive floors, and special service for business travellers. **$$$$**

Swissotel The Bosphorus
Maçka
Tel: (0212) 259 0101
Fax: (0212) 259 0105
A member of Leading Hotels of the World with 600 rooms, 17 suites, 50 executive rooms and 74 full-service apartments for longer term stays. Excellent sports and health facilities, including outdoor and indoor pools, jacuzzi, sauna, tennis, etc. Six restaurants and banqueting facilities. Superb views from hilltop location. **$$$$$**

The Marmara
Taksim
Tel: (0212) 251 4696
Fax: (0212) 244 0509
Istanbul's best known, business and conference hotel is right in the hub of the action of Taksim Square, and hosts many international events. 410 rooms, superb city view from Panorama restaurant, popular Cafe Marmara on ground floor, pool and health facilities. **$$$$$**

Mercure
Tepebaşı
Tel: (0212) 251 4646
Fax: (0212) 249 8033
Perfectly situated high-rise tourist
hotel with cracking views from many
of its 195 rooms. Close to
consulates and entertainment
facilties. Outdoor pool, rooftop club
with live music, shops, and
hairdresser. $$$$
Richmond
İstiklal Cad. 445
Tel: (0212) 252 5460
Fax: (0212) 252 5460
Great location in the heart of
Beyoğlu, perfect for entertainment
and shopping. $$$$

Historic Hotels and Pensions
Pera Palas
Tepebaşı
Tel: (0212) 251 4560
Fax: (0212) 251 4089
The historic Orient Express hotel
retains its 100-year-old aura of spy
intrigue as well as its original décor
and has hosted the likes of Agatha
Christie and Mata Hari. 139 rooms,
6 suites. $$$$$
Vardar Palace Hotel
Sıraselviler Cad. 54-56,
Taksim
Tel: (0212) 252 2896
Fax: (0212) 252 1527
For those in town for conferences or
festival-hopping this hotel offers a
great central location. The only
Special Licence hotel in the area.
Built 100 years ago in the
Levantine-Selçuk style, and
thoroughly restored with 40 en-suite
rooms, TV, minibar, etc. $
Büyük Londres
Mehrutiyet Cad. 117,
Tepebaşı
Tel: (0212) 245 0670
Fax: (0212) 245 0671
Super cheap rates for lovers of
faded grandeur, this old hotel has a
few sea-view rooms and a charming
lobby full of Italian chandeliers and
other antiques, as well as an
extremely cheap bar. Rock bottom
monthly rates in winter make sure
it's a hangout for writers and other
eccentrics. Book early and bargain
– can be as little as $25 a night
with substantial breakfast. $

Apart-Hotels
Galata Residence Hotel
Bankalar Cad., Hacı Ali Sok.,
Galata/Karaköy
Tel: (0212) 252 6062
Fax: (0212) 292 4841
e-mail: galata@escortnet.com
web-site: www.galataresidence.com
This huge 19th-century Jewish
mansion is uniquely located near
Galata Tower and has been
elegantly restored with NGO and
business conference delegates in
mind. With 14 five-person suites
and 3 doubles, all with fully
equipped kitchens and bathrooms,
prices are reasonable for group and
family travellers. Air conditioning,
television. Rooftop restaurant has
spectacular Bosphorus view,
atmospheric bar in the basement
vaults. $

OUTLYING DISTRICTS

Polat Renaissance
Sahil Cad., Yeşilyurt
Tel: (0212) 663 17 00
Fax: (0212) 663 17 55
On the shores of the Sea of
Marmara, 4 km (2.5 miles) from the
airport and the World Trade Centre.
383 deluxe rooms, one fully
equipped for handicapped, 29
suites, 2 non-smoking floors, many
bars and restaurants and Istanbul's
largest in-house conference
facilities. $$$$
Cinar Hotel
Sevketiye Mah
Fener Mevkii
Yesilkoy
Tel: (0212) 663 2900
Fax: (0212) 663 2921
Located 20 km (12 miles) from the
heart of the city, close to the
airport. 213 rooms, 8 suites, 3
restaurants, indoor and outdoor
pools, fitness centre. $$$$
Dedeman
Esentepe
Tel: (0212) 274 8800
Fax: (0212) 275 1100
Located in the business and
residential district, a modern
comfortable hotel popular with
business travellers. 335 rooms and
suites, fitness and beauty centre,

swimming pools, conference and
banqueting facilities. $$$$

Historic Hotels and Pensions
Bosphorus Paşa
Yalıboyu Cad. 64, Beylerbeyi
(Asian side of Bosphorus)
Tel: (0216) 422 0003
Fax: (0216) 422 0012
For the discerning traveller seeking
privacy, this 14-room mansion is
considered the most exclusive of
the city's Special Licence Hotels
and attracts a number of
celebrities. 4-metre (12-ft) ceilings,
spectacular views from most
rooms. No expense spared for
lavish detail and modern
convenience. The old boathouse is
now a branch of Cecconi's in
London. $$$$
Saydam Planet
İskele Meydanı
Büyükada (Princes' Islands)
Tel: (0216) 382 2670
Fax: (0216) 382 3848
There are no cars on this
spectacular island, though you can
hire a horse and trap. With 8 rooms
and 4 suites, it also falls into the
category of "exclusive" and
maintains a European ambience
and a French style restaurant on
the ground floor. Spectacular sea
view outside Istanbul's urban crush.
All amenities and big bathtubs.
$$$$
Hotel Kariye
Edirnekapı (beside the Church of
Chora or Kariye Museum)
Tel: (0212) 534 8414
Fax: (0212) 521 6631
Unique, peaceful location for lovers
of Byzantium. This elegant hotel in
a restored Ottoman mansion is right
next to one of Istanbul's most
exceptionally preserved churches.
Superb restaurant specialising in
historic Ottoman dishes and
traditional court music, 24 rooms,
3 suites, garden pavilion. $$$
Büyükada Princess
Büyükada (Princes' Island)
Tel: (0216) 382 1628
Fax: (0216) 382 1949
Housed in a 19th-century building
on the largest island, the Princess
is one of the few good hotels on
this beautiful island in the Sea of

Marmara. 24 rooms, swimming pool, restaurant, bar, patisserie, games room. **$$$**
Halki Palas
Refah Sehitleri Cad. 88, Heybeliada, Princes' Islands
Tel: (0216) 351 0025
Fax: (0216) 351 8483
Located on the second largest of the islands, a historic hotel from the mid-19th century. Great views; ideal location for a weekend break. **$$**

Şile
Şile Resort, Uzunkum, Şile
Tel: (0216) 711 4003
Comfortable modern, family-oriented beachfront hotel 5 km (3 miles) from town centre. 52 rooms with air-con, TV, balconies and sea views; outdoor pool with children's section and playroom. **$$**

THRACE AND MARMARA

Bursa
Çelik Palas Oteli
Çekirge Cad. 79
Tel: (0224) 233 38 00
Fax: (0224) 236 19 10
Bursa's finest hotel is open all year round. It is air-conditioned, has its own mineral water bath, hammam, and sauna, an excellent restaurant and beautifully decorated public rooms. Service and atmosphere excellent. **$$$$**
Kervansaray Termal Oteli
Çekirge Mah., Eski Kaplica Sokak Merkez-Bursa
Tel: (0224) 233 93 00
Fax: (0224) 233 9324
211-room luxury hotel, updated Art Deco design. The Eski Kaplicalari mineral baths adjoin the hotel, on the eastern edge of Çekirge. **$$$$**
Diamond Otel
İnönü Cad., Toyota Plaza Yan. 104
Tel: (0224) 271 4401
Fax: (0224) 271 4400
Clean, quiet, if somewhat spartan. There is rather a steep uphill walk from the hotel to the city centre. Friendly atmosphere. **$**
Safran Hotel
Ortapazar Cad.
Arka Sok. 4, Tophane
Tel: (0224) 224 7216

Fax: (0224) 224 7219
Lovingly restored wooden house in the old town. Rooms have modern amenities, such as TV and minibar. **$$**
　　Those preferring to stay out of town could try one of the many ski lodges at nearby **Uludağ**. Options include:
Grand Hotel Yazıcı
Tel: (0224) 285 2050
Fax: (0224) 285 2048, **$$$$**; and
Kar Hotel
Tel: (0224) 283 2121
Fax: (0224) 2123, **$$**.

Price Guide

For a double room in high season:
$ = below $50
$$ = $50 to $80
$$$ =$80 to $150
$$$$ = $150 to $250
$$$$$ = above $250

Çanakkale
Akol Hotel
Kordonböyü Caddesi
Tel: (0286) 217 9456
Fax: (0286) 217 2897
This seafront hotel has its own swimming pool, good restaurants, discos and satellite TV in the bedrooms. It is open throughout the year. The service is good and the atmosphere friendly. **$$$**
Anzac House
Cumhuriyet Meydanı 61, Çanakkale
Tel: (0286) 217 0156
Fax: (0286) 217 2096
Central, cheap and cheerful Australian-run backpackers' hangout, providing basic facilities. Hostel-style dormitory rooms with shared bathrooms. Book here for local tours. There are films about Gallipolli every evening. Open all year. **$**
Anzac Hotel
Saat Kulesi Meydanı 8
Tel: (0286) 217 7777
Fax: (0286) 217 2018
Conveniently central hotel, facing the clock-tower. 20 rooms with showers. Good value and comfortable. **$**

Tusan Hotel
Güzelyalı, Intepe
Tel: (0286) 232 8210
Fax: (0286) 232 8226
Popular, simple country hotel on the beach, surrounded by pine forests, 14 km (8.5 miles) south of Çanakkale on the road to Troy. Indoor and outdoor restaurants and watersports. Book well ahead. **$$**

Edirne
Rüstem Pasa Caravansaray
İki Kapılı Han Cad. 57, Sabuni Mah.
Tel: (0284) 212 6119
Fax: (0284) 212 0462
This beautifully-restored 16th-century inn, designed by Sinan, is now back in service as a pleasant, if sometimes basic hotel, with airy rooms, plain furniture and a flowery central courtyard. **$$**
Sultan Oteli
Londra Asfalti, 42
Tel: (0284) 225 1372
Fax: (0284) 225 5763
Located in the city centre, this is probably the best of Edirne's rather indifferent bunch of hotels. Rooms have shower and TV, but those at the front may be noisy. Open all the year. Service rather surly. **$$**
Edirne Park Oteli
Maarif Cad. 7
Tel: (0284) 213 5276
Fax: (0284) 225 4635
Unimaginative hotel with noisy rooms overlooking the street and indifferent service. Amongst the best of a bad lot. Open all year. **$**

Gelibolu (Gallipolli)
Abide
Alçıtepe village, Eceabat, Gelibolu
Tel: (0286) 844 6158
A charming family-run hotel. Open July–Sept only. **$**

Truva (Troy)
Hisarlık
Tevfikiye Köyü
Tel: (0286) 283 1026
Fax: (0286) 283 1087
A small hotel (11 double rooms, each named after a Trojan hero), serving individual clients only (that is, no group bookings). Good Turkish meals. **$$**

Where to Eat

Choosing a Restaurant

It is difficult to go hungry in Istanbul. From the sesame sprinkled bread rings *(simit)* sold in every street to the most elaborate Ottoman palace cuisine, there is something to cater for all appetites. There are also plenty of foreign restaurants. Urban Turks have unfortunately taken to the ubiquitous international fast food chains, but affluent Turks have travelled and love more sophisticated eating out, so you can also find fashionable restaurants offering anything from sushi to spaghetti. The best hotels often have excellent restaurants of different nationalities, plus lavish buffets available in their coffee shops, especially for Sunday brunch. However it doesn't follow that fancy décor and well-dressed waiters necessarily mean a good meal; often, the simpler restaurants give better service and more delicious food.

TYPES OF RESTAURANT

Turkish restaurants fall into clearly defined specialist categories.

Restoran
This word is applied to almost anywhere where food is served.

Lokanta
The basic neighbourhood restaurant, especially busy at lunch-times. These are reliable places to eat, and it is easy to choose as you can see what you are getting, with the food displayed cafeteria-style in hot cabinets and bubbling cauldrons. A waiter will bring your choice to your table.

Et lokantası
Restaurants specialising in meat dishes.

Balık lokantası
Fish restaurants. Serving Hot and cold *meze*, freshly caught fish and shellfish. You will be welcome to look at the fish available in order to choose. Fish is an expensive treat meal in Turkey, and is normally priced by weight.

Ocakbası
Grill restaurants, where you can sit at a table set around a charcoal fire and cook your own choice of meat (though of course if you prefer, the restaurant will do it for you). Breads, rice and salads will also be on offer.

Muhallebici
Turkish pudding shop: for milk puddings and baklava; also chicken dishes.

Meyhane
Inadequately translated as "tavern", some of these places are smoky drinking dives, dedicated to wine (and sometimes song) over food, but the best are in fact also famous for their delicious cooking. Their *meze* are often especially good.

Kebapçı (kebab house)
Various kinds of kebabs.

Ordering Food

In many Turkish restaurants there will be no printed menu, or if there is one, it may not relate to what is available. In fish restaurants and *meyhanes* large trays with assorted plates of *meze* (starters) will be brought round, and you just point to the ones which take your fancy. It is also often possible to inspect the vats in the kitchen. Later you will be asked for your choice of hot *meze* (*sıcak mezeler*), later still for your choice of main course. You can order as you go, and it is quite all right to stop after the *meze* if you feel you have had enough. Bread and bottled drinking water will be brought automatically but usually attract a modest cover charge. For a menu reader, *see Language*.

Mantı/Gözleme Evi
Turkish ravioli, filled pancakes.

Pideci/Lahmacun
Turkish pizza equivalent.

Köfteci
Meatball specialist.

Pastane
The word "pasta" means pastry or gateau in Turkish and this is where you can buy flaky borek (baked layers of pastry with assorted fillings, eg meat, spinach, cheese), as well as gâteaux and desserts. You can often sit and eat here, but some will not serve coffee and tea.

Restaurant Listings

THE OLD CITY

Many of the restaurants in this area cater solely to the tourist trade, with touts to entice in passers-by, predictable Turkish dishes, average quality of food and moderate prices. Many are spread along Divanyolu Cad. However there are a few special treats tucked amongst them.

Konyalı
Topkapı Palace, Seraglio Point
Tel: (0212) 513 9696
Set in one of the pavilions within the palace complex, this wonderful restaurant has been serving gourmet standard classical Ottoman cuisine since 1897. Superb Bosphorus views. Open 9.30am–5pm, closed Tues and evenings. All major cards. **$$$**

Rami
Utangaç Sok. 6, Sultanahmet
Tel: (0212) 517 6593
Restored wooden house with enchanting candle-lit dining on a balcony overlooking the Blue Mosque. Both food and ambience are delightful. Open daily 11am–midnight. Mastercard and Visa accepted. **$$$**

Balikci Sabahattin
Cankurtaran, Sultanahmet
Tel: (0212) 458 18 24
A local favourite operating since 1927, with wonderful selection of fresh fish and shellfish. Set menus with *mezes*, salads, desserts and wines. Very atmospheric. **$$**

Türkistan Aşevi
Tavukhane Sok. 36, Sultanahmet

Kumkapı

The former fishermen's quarter, located off the coast road behind Sultanahmet, and rather wild as a result, Kumkapı has some 50 restaurants along a few narrow streets. At times there is an an almost street carnival atmosphere. Expect voluminous alcohol consumption, strolling musicians and a few ladies of the night. Ensure you know the prices and check your bill. A few of the better restaurants to try are **Kör Agop, Olimpiyat, Cemal'in Yeri, Çamur Sevket,** and **Evren. $$**

Tel: (0212) 638 6525
A restored mansion, lavishly decorated in the Ottoman-fantasy school, with carpets, textiles, low copper tables and sofas for lounging (shoeless) over Central Asian specialities. Open daily 1am–11pm. All major cards. **$$**

The Pudding Shop
Divanyolu Cad. 18, Sultanahmet
Tel: (0212) 522 2970/511 0539
A long way from the traditional *pastahane* that was a crucial stop on the hippy trail in the 1970s, the famous Pudding Shop has remade itself as a fast food joint, more like Wimpeys. But if you are craving an omelette and chips, with fascinating reading on the walls, this is the place to come. **$**

Cennet
Divanyolu Cad. 90, Çemberlitaş
Tel: (0212) 513 1416/513 5098
Very touristy but entertaining pancake and *börek* house, with low tables, carpets and cushions, and befezzed musicians, all under startlingly bright neon lights, in a shop window. **$**

Hamdi
Tahmis Cad., Kalcin Sok., Eminönü
Tel: (0212) 528 0390/512 5424.
A well-known restaurant serving meat-based cuisine from south-eastern Turkey. Hearty, filling and tasty dishes with many types of kebabs, salads and *meze*, accompanied by wines and raki. Popular with locals. Convenient for

Spice Bazaar and ferry piers. Major credit cards. **$**

Pandeli
Mısır Çarşısı 1, Eminönü
Tel: (0212) 527 3909
Pretty İznik-tiled restaurant reached through the Spice Bazaar, serving classic Turkish food. Open Mon–Sat 11.30am–4pm. All major cards. Booking advised. **$$$**

Havuzlu
Gani Çelebi Sok. 3, Grand Bazaar, Beyazıt
Tel: (0212) 527 3346
The best of several *lokantası* in the heart of the Grand Bazaar, serving good simple kebabs and grills. Open Mon–Sat, 12 noon–6pm. All major credit cards. **$**

Darüzziyafe
Şifahane Cad. 6, Beyazıt
Tel: (0212) 511 8414
Fabulous courtyard restaurant in the elegant 16th-century kitchens of the Süleymaniye mosque complex, serving classical Ottoman cuisine. No alcohol. Open daily 12 noon–3pm, 6–11pm. All major cards. **$$**

Zeyrekhane
Sinanağa Mah., İbadethane Arkası Sok. 10, Zeyrek, Fatih
Tel: (0212) 532 2778
Recently restored Ottoman mansion next to the Byzantine Molla Zeyrek Cami, part of the grand plan to revive a run-down area of the city. Charming décor, an interesting Turkish menu, a open terrace in summer and fabulous views across the Golden Horn. **$$$**

THE NEW CITY

Brasserie
Marmara Istanbul Hotel, Taksim
Tel: (0212) 251 4696
An elegant and relaxed atmosphere, suitable for a meal, snack or cup of coffee. Enjoy Turkish and international cuisine whilst watching the world go by in Takism Square. Breakfast from 6.30–10.30am; lunch from 12 noon–3pm; dinner from 7–11pm. All major cards. **$$$**

Çatı
İstiklal Cad., Orhan Apaydın Sok. 20/7, Taksim

Prices

These are an indication only, based on a two course meal for one (eg *meze*, kebab, salad and bread, with non-alcoholic drinks). Outside the top hotels, the big differences depend more on where you go than what you eat (although fish is significantly more expensive than meat). Most larger restaurants accept credit cards. The price categories are as follows:

$ = $5 to $10
$$ = $10 to $20
$$$ = above $20

Tel: (0212) 251 0000
Top floor restaurant with city views, and entertaining decorations, its walls covered with photos, cartoons and paintings. Popular with theatre and cinema goers and the local intelligentsia. Often has live Turkish contemporary folk music. Open Mon–Sat 12 noon–1am. Mastercard and Visa. **$$**

Evim
Büyük Parmakkapı Sok 32/2, Beyoğlu
Tel: (0212) 293 4025
Superb Black Sea home cooking (including cornbread) as well as some imaginative international food. Cheap, cosy, and popular with students. No cards. **$**

Four Seasons
İstiklal Cad. 509, Tünel
Tel: (0212) 293 3941
Classy English/Turkish-owned restaurant serving outstanding international cuisine for more than 20 years. Superb service on Ottoman-style copper trays and a scrumptious dessert trolly. A bit pricey at night, but lunch set menus are excellent value at around US$10 (£6). Open 12 noon–3pm, 6pm–midnight. All major credit cards, booking advised. **$$**

Galata
İstiklal Cad., Orhan Apaydın Sok. 11, Beyoğlu
Tel: (0212) 293 1139
A glamorous, candle-lit example of the Turkish *meyhane*, offering

Cafés and Bars

Some Turkish men seem to spend their lives in their local tea or coffee house (*çayhane/ kahvehane*), smoking and playing backgammon, but it is unusual for foreigners and women to enter them. Plenty of elegant European-style cafés are springing up, offering a cosmopolitan atmosphere and food such as French-style baguette sandwiches, Italian cappuccinos, American cheesecake and English Earl Grey tea and chocolate cake. These are smart places to be seen, frequented by designer and fur-clad "ladies who lunch".

classic Istanbul Greek cuisine. Live classical Turkish (*fasıl*) music 9pm–midnight. Open Mon–Sat, 6pm–2am. No cards. $$
Hacı Abdullah
Sakız Ağa Cad. 17, Beyoğlu
Tel: (0212) 293 8561
A famous and very old Turkish restaurant serving real homestyle Ottoman cuisine. Menu changes daily. Try the *hünkar begendi kebab* (beef stew served on a bed of eggplant purée or the *kuzu tandır* (roast lamb). No alcohol. Open 11.30am–10pm. Cards: Amex, Mastercard, Visa. $$
Hacı Baba
İstiklal Cad. 49, Mehelik Sok., Taksim
Tel: (0212) 244 1886
This classic Turkish restaurant

Çiçek Pasajı

Easily recognisable for the swank, high-domed opera-set interior built at the turn of the century, the **Çiçek Pasajı** (Flower Seller's Alley) is now a raucous, touristy-covered lane full of basic *meyhanes* and gypsy music. It runs parallel to the **Balık Pazar** (Fish Market) and both open onto the main pedestrian thoroughfare of İstiklal Caddesi. The Fish Market also has good restaurants these days (some, such as **Degustasyon**, slightly

offers a superb selection of *şiş kebab* and a varied menu generally. In summers, dine on the balcony overlooking the garden of a Greek church. Booking advised. Open daily 12 noon–midnight. Amex and Visa accepted. $$
Hala
Buyukparmakkapi, Cukurlu Çeşme Sok. 26, Beyoğlu
Tel: (0212) 293 75 31
Very tasty, filling, cheap, home-made stuffed pancakes and *manti*, with friendly service. This small street contains many similar small restaurants, perfect for a quick lunch or snack. $
Hemsiye
Heybender Sok. 18, Asmalımescit, Tünel
Tel: (0212) 292 2046
A health/vegetarian interpretation of traditional Turkish home cooking and an upmarket, whole-grain décor. Open 8.30am–10.30pm. $
Kallavi 20
İstiklal Cad. Kallavi Sok. 20, Beyoğlu
Tel: (0212) 251 1010
Small, lively upmarket Turkish *meyhane* offering an all-in very reasonable price for the night including excellent food and drinks. Extremely popular with local yuppies and office party booze-ups, so often booked solid. Reservations essential. Live Turkish classical music. Not for a quiet dinner. Closed Sun. No cards. $$$
Liman
Rihtim Cad. 3rd floor (above passenger waiting room), Karaköy
Tel: (0212) 292 39 92/93

more upmarket, alongside the classical, such as the studenty **Cumhuriyet**). If you're looking for real street theatre, **Nevizade Sok.**, a right turn near the bottom of the market, is a real circus, especially in summers when the street is jammed with tables. Try **Boncuk** for Armenian specialities, **Asır** for Greek. Remember that the less decorated restaurants tend to have the best food.

Classic Istanbul favourite with great view, serving delicious Turkish food. Busy venue for businessmen at lunchtime. Open 11am–12 midnight. All major cards. $$$
Ming Garden
Hotel Lamartin, Lamartin Cad. 25, Taksim
Tel: (0212) 254 6270
Peking Duck and pork dishes both on the menu, while the plum brandy is a literal knock-out. Friendly atmosphere, authentic cuisine and reasonable prices compared to Istanbul's more chic Chinese restaurants. Open 12 noon–3pm, 6–11pm Mon–Sat. Cards: Visa, Amex, Mastercard. $$–$$$
Nuh'un Ambari
Yenicarsi Cad. 54, Beyoğlu
Tel: (0212) 292 9272
The only true vegetarian restaurant in town. Everything fresh and healthy, washed down with herbal teas and fruit juices. Also sells variety of ingredients and giftware using only natural products. $
Pars
Meşrutiyet Cad. 187, Tepebaşı
Tel: (0212) 292 1846
The only Persian restaurant in town, right across from the Pera Palace Hotel. Serves traditional Persian food, starting with breakfast at 7am, lunch 12 noon–3pm, and dinner 7pm–1am. $$
Refik's
Sofyalı Sok. 10-12, Tünel
Tel: (0212) 243 2834
A popular spot with Turkish and foreign intellectuals, embassy sorts and the occasional celeb. Part of this *meyhane's* charm is the secluded off-street location and a complete lack of concern with décor. Specialises in Black Sea dishes, especially fish. No cards. Can get crowded and service slow – if it's booked up try **Yakup 2** around the corner (Asmalımescit Sok. 35/37), owned by a relative of the avuncular Refik and quite similar but open later and takes Amex, Mastercard, Visa. Both closed Sunday. $$
Rejans
Emir Nevruz Sok. 17, Galatasaray-Beyoğlu
Tel: (0212) 244 1610

Untouched faded grandeur in this nostalgic favourite, founded in the 1920s by White Russian refugee aristocrats. Major write-ups in French guide books, however, should tell you something about the quality of the food – try the piroshki, borscht, beef stroganoff or stewed duck. Reservations are recommended for dinner. Open 12 noon–3pm, 7–11pm. Closed Sunday. Cards: Visa, Mastercard, Eurocard. **$$**

BOSPHORUS

Bellini
Çırağan Palace Hotel Kempinski
Beşiktaş
Tel: (0212) 258 3377
Exquisite Italian cuisine with superb views and live Mediterranean music, with open terrace in summer. Open 12 noon–3pm, 7–11pm. All major cards. **$$$**
Tuğra
Çırağan Palace Hotel Kempinski,
Beşiktaş
Tel: (0212) 258 3377
Ottoman-style cuisine à la carte, in a stunning setting with excellent service. Live traditional music and open-air terrace in summer. Open daily, 7.30–11.30pm. All major cards. **$$$**
Cafe Suisse
Swissotel The Bosphorus, Maçka
Tel: (0212) 259 0101
Great views, buffet and à la carte. Famous for Sunday brunch menu. Open everyday for breakfast, lunch and dinner. All major cards. **$$$**
Wine 'n Roses,
Spor Cad. 183, Beşiktaş
Tel: (0212) 236 2092
Upmarket Californian-style restaurant, serving international food and even offering imported cigars. Good selection of California wines include Sutter Home, Canyon Road and Geyser Peak. The dramatic bar is popular with jet-setters and stock brokers. Open 12 noon–midnight (bar), 12 noon–3pm (café), 7–11.30pm (dinner). All major cards. **$$$**
Bekriya
Birinci Cad. 90, 2nd floor, Arnavutköy
Tel: (0212) 257 0469

A rather eccentric, bohemian *meyhane* in an old wooden house, complete with original fixtures and pictures on the wall, and view of the Bosphorus. Menu includes Balkan specialities. Open 11am–7pm, 8pm–1am. No cards. **$$**
Kıyı
Kefeliköy Cad. 126, Tarabya
Tel: (0212) 262 0002
Swish fish restaurant featuring original Turkish art and photography by contemporary masters. Open 12 noon–midnight. Amex, Diners Club, Visa, Mastercard. **$$$**
Körfez
Körfez Cad. 78, Kanlıca
Tel: (0216) 413 4314/413 4098
A chic fish restaurant on the Asian side with romantic seaside setting. The sea bass is recommended. Private boat across the Bosphorus from Rumeli Hisarı by appointment. Open 12 noon–3pm, 7pm–midnight. Closed Monday. All major cards. **$$$**
Sirene
Mezarburnu Cad. 2, Sarıyer
Tel: (0212) 242 2621/271 6737
Gourmet Mediterranean seafood restaurant with superb Bosphorus view. Try the baked fish dish, *balık kavurma*, hard to find elsewhere. Cards: Visa, Mastercard. **$$$**
Hayal Kahvesi Çabuklu
Burunbahçe, Beykoz
Tel: (0216) 413 6880
Upmarket cousin to the Beyoğlu rock café of the same name, this is an elegant, isolated summer spot for the well-heeled, right on the water's edge (Asian shore). In summers a private boat runs every half-hour from İstinye on the European side. Restaurant and café facilities 12 noon–midnight; bar until 2am; live music after 11pm and a large dance floor. Sunday brunch 10.30am–3.30pm. All major cards accepted. **$$$**
Ali Baba
Kirecburnu Cad. 20, Kirecburnu
Tel: (0212) 262 0889
An established, respected place on the Bosphorus, serving fish, grills, stews and *meze*. Pleasant spot for lunch and dinner, outdoor seating in summer. Open 12 noon–midnight. Cards: Mastercard, Visa. **$$**

Fast Food

Rather than plump for the rather predictable international brands of burger bars and pizza parlours, do the Istanbul equivalent and head for a kebab stall, which will sell freshly cooked meat with basic salads and sandwich, and soft drinks. There is a well-known bunch, difficult to miss, at the top end of Istiklal Cad. From Taksim Square. Elsewhere in the city, it's hard to avoid them.

The Grill
Kefeliköy Cad. 128, Tarabya
Tel: (0212) 299 2666
Grilled meat dishes from around the world, including game, plus a good selection of local and international wines. Open everyday 11am–2am. Live music most nights; reservations essential at weekends. All major cards. **$$$**

OUTLYING DISTRICTS

Lütfi Convention and Exhibition Centre
Harbiye
Tel: (0212) 232 4201
Situated in the heart of commercial Istanbul, many Turkish dishes on offer and fish specialities. Popular yet relaxed atmosphere, good service. Open 12 noon–midnight. All major cards. **$$$**

Prices

The price categories used are as follows:
$ = $5 to $10
$$ = $10 to $20
$$$ = above $20

Chinese Unlimited
Ahmet Fetgari Sok. 164/1, Teşvikiye
Tel: (0212) 240 3166
Excellent selection of dishes, using authentic ingredients, served at affordable prices. Contemporary Asian décor. Cards: Visa, Mastercard. **$$**

Café du Levant
Rahmi M. Koç Museum,
Hasköy Cad. 27,
Sütlüce,
Golden Horn
Tel: (0212) 250 8938/256 7153
French-style bistro set in the
grounds of this unique urban
industrial museum, with excellent
food prepared by French chefs.
Lunch 12 noon–2.30pm; afternoon
tea 2–7.30pm; dinner
9.30–10.30pm. Closed Mon. All
major credit cards accepted. **$$$**
Le Select
Manolya Sok. 21,
Levent
Tel: (0212) 268 2120/281 7100
One of Istanbul's most exclusive,
European-style gourmet restaurants
set in a prosperous area of the city.
Reservations a must. Open daily 12
noon–3pm, 8pm–1am. All major
cards. **$$$**
Sai Thai
Aytar Cad. Levent Ishanı 3/6,
1. Levent
Tel: (0212) 283 5346

Best Thai cuisine in town in a
traditional setting complete with
kneeling tables. Open everyday 12
noon–3pm, 6.30–11pm; lunch
weekdays only. All major cards. **$$$**
Sunset Grill Bar
Ahmet Adnan Saygun Cad.,
Kireçhane Sok.,
Uluş Park
Tel: (0212) 287 0357
A Californian-style restaurant,
serving mainly grill dishes set on a
hill with an exquisite view of the
Bosphorus. Very trendy. Enjoy the
bar after sunset, 7pm–midnight. All
major credit cards. **$$$**
Süreyya
İstinye Cad. 26,
İstinye
Tel: (0212) 277 5886
One of the city's oldest established
international gourmet restaurants,
founded by a Russian emigré. Open
12 noon–3pm, 8pm–midnight.
Closed Sun; booking essential. All
major cards. **$$$**
Turquoise
Kuruçeşme Cad. 22-24

Tel: (0212) 265 8849/79
Classy French and Belgian cuisine
in a beautifully restored Ottoman
building. Has its own art gallery and
an art-deco bar. Very chic. Open
10am–2am. All major cards. **$$$**
Yirmidokuz (29)
Adnan Saygun Cad.,
inside Uluş Park
Tel: (0212) 265 6181/265 6198
Stunning Bosphorus view and
gourmet French cuisine prepared by
French chef; as well as (pricey!)
imported wines and champagne.
Open 12 noon–4pm, 8pm–1am.
Sunday brunch also served. Lunch
not served weekends. All major
cards accepted. **$$$**

THRACE AND MARMARA

On the whole, restaurants in these
areas are average provincial
establishments, with no frills, quite
unlike the luxury restaurants found
in Istanbul. Telephone reservation
is unusual and rarely necessary.

Internet Cafés

You don't have to look far to find
an internet café. There are new
ones springing up all the time and
a heavy concentration in Taksim,
Beyoğlu and Sultanahmet.
Backpacker's Internet Café
Yeni Yeni Akbiyik Cad. 22,
Sultanahmet (across from Orient
Youth hostel)
Tel: (0212) 638 6343
E-mail: backpackers@turk.net
Fast Pentium computers combined
with warm traditional Turkish décor.
Caffinet
Kurabiye Sok., Beyoğlu (behind
Fitah Cinema)
Pricey upmarket place that plays
jazz and doubles as pasta and
seafood restaurant at night.
Sanal Internet Café
14/1 Imam Adnan Sok.,
Beyoğlu
Tel: (0212) 245 6345
e-mail: sanalc@aidata.com.tr
Reasonable rates and kindly
helpers. Coffees, teas and simple
meals.

Sinera Internet Café
Mis Sok., Taksim
Cheap rates 9am–1pm, and
comfortable atmosphere while you
download. Also sells computer
components if something you've
got is on the blink.
Yagmur
Heybender Sok. 18,
Asmalımescit,
Tünel, Beyoğlu
Tel: (0212) 292 3020
E-mail: cafe@citlembik.com.tr
One of the most popular cyber-
cafés in town, thanks to the
American owner and multilingual
Scandinavian staff. Offers internet
access, e-mail addresses,
assorted computing facilities and
carrot cake. English reading
selection also available. A popular
meeting-place for foreigners living
or travelling through the city. Good
restaurant and English-language
book exchange on ground floor.
Open 11am–11pm.

Bursa
In addition to the restaurants in the
Kültürpark, which serve traditional
Turkish food, there are several fish
restaurants tucked away behind a
fishmonger's in **Alt parmak** in the
city centre. These restaurants, have
something of the lively atmosphere
of Istanbul's *meyhanler* (taverns).
Kebabçı İskender
Unlü Cad. 7,
Heykel
Tel: (0224) 221 4615
Popular with the people of Bursa.
The owners claim to be descended
from the inventor of the famed
İskender kebab. Open all year. No
credit cards. **$**
İnegol Köfteci
Atatürk Cad. 48
For a change from kebabs, try the
inegol köfte, grilled meatballs
served with raw onion rings. Open
all year. **$**
Cumurcul
Çekirge Cad.
Tel: (0224) 235 3707
Attractively converted old house in
Çekirge, with the usual range of

Tea Gardens (Çaybahçe)

Tea and coffee houses might be the domain of the local men, but tea gardens are also favoured by women and families, especially as they usually don't serve alcohol. They make the perfect place to kill time on a hot summer afternoon. Some of the best ones are:

Ikram Teahouse
Sifahane Cad.,
Beyazıt
A delightful sunken courtyard garden, set in the 16th-century soup kitchen and banqueting hall of the Süleymaniye Mosque complex, this is somewhere to take a breath of calm reflection in the midst of hectic sightseeing.

Dervis
Mimar Mehmet Aga Cad.,
Sultanahmet.
Many tea-gardens so close to the famous sights are a rip-off, but this one is reasonably priced and always busy with locals and

tourists. A great location, bang opposite the Blue Mosque, to rest weary feet and cool down with tea or a soft drink.

Cadir Köşk and Malta Köşk
Yıldız Park,
near Beşiktaş
Two old houses refurbished and now opened as cafés, both set on a huge terrace with superb views of the Bosphorus. The ideal place for an afternoon off from tiring sightseeing. Both serve tea and light refreshments, and Malta Köşk serves a buffet meal every Sunday.

Rumeli Hisari
Up the Bosphorus, (accessible by bus from Taksim or Eminönü) the old fortress has a fantastic terrace with tea, soft drinks and snacks. Tea is served in a samovar at your table. A must for a warm summer evening, with great Bosphorus views.

meze, kebabs and grills. Reservations at weekends. $$

Çanakkale
Akol Hotel Restaurant
Kordonböyü Caddesi
A varied menu of Turkish and International dishes, and fine views of shipping passing through the straits. Open all year. Major credit cards accepted. $$
Other good hotel restaurants include the **Otel Anafartalar ($)**, conveniently close to the ferry, which has a wide range of meze, kebabs and fish and the **Anzac Hotel ($)**, a popular meeting and eating place for backpackers, a few minutes walk from the ferry, which serves good snacks and light meals.
Bizim Entellektüel
On the quayside
Meze, meat or fish and salad. Popular with Turkish diners. Open all year. $
Aussie & Kiwi
Yalı Cad. 32
Antipodean haven serving homesick backpackers with such staples as Milo and Vegemite. $

Edirne
Çatı Lokantası
Hürriyet Meydanı
Tel: (0284) 225 1307
Shabby but good restaurant in the city centre, across the street from the Sultan Oteli; with a standard range of Turkish dishes. The Sultan Oteli restaurant also has a good menu. Both serve alcohol with meals. Open all year. $
Lalezar Restaurant
South of the city on the road to Karaağaç
Excellent meze and kebabs; fine views of the Meriç river and an Ottoman bridge. Open throughout the year. A nearby alternative is the Villa Restaurant. $

Gelibolu (Gallipoli)
Gelibolu Restaurant
Near the harbour
Well-known for its fish dishes, particularly Gelibolu's speciality, sardalya (sardines). Open all year.
$–$$
İpek Urfa Kebab Salonu
Towards the town centre
Tasty, spicy kebabs at low prices. $

Cafes and Patisseries

THE OLD CITY

Cafeist
Takkeciler Sok. 41–45
Grand Bazaar
Tel: (0212) 527 9853
The only café in the Grand Bazaar which, with its arty décor, doesn't look like a men's teahouse, serving typical bistro fare, and beverages – well worth the search.

Cafe Magnaura
Akbiyik Cad. 27, Sultanahmet
Tel: (0212) 518 76 22
A lively café/bar also serving meals and snacks of international cuisine. A mixed crowd, with young locals and older couples. Comfortable for women alone.

THE NEW CITY

Andon Pera
Sıraselviler Cad. 89, Taksim
Tel: (0212) 251 0222
Different floors offer different specialities, from drinks to snacks to disco. A favourite with film buffs, the bar upstairs serves deli pastries and coffees.

Burç
İstiklal Cad. 463-465, Beyoğlu
Tel: (0212) 244 2890
Understated but superb small European-style pastry shop serving perfect espresso and employing friendly staff. Try the chocolate-filled croissants.

Cadde-i-Kebir
İstiklal Caddesi
Imam Adnan Sok. 7, Beyoğlu
Tel: (0212) 251 7113
This café/bar is owned by one of Turkey's more controversial film directors, Reis Çelik. Offers imported German beer and light meals.

Prices

The price categories used are as follows:
$ = $5 to $10
$$ = $10 to $20
$$$ = above $20

Dulcinea
İstiklal Cad.,
Mehelik Sok. 20
Beyoğlu
Tel: (0212) 245 1071
e-mail: dulcinea@ihlas.net.tr
Creative modern décor and very trendy. Offers a wide selection of imported drinks and light meals from a special daily menu. Live jazz at weekends. Art gallery in the basement. A bit pricey.

Gayfe
Büyük Parmakkapı Sok. 14 A/B
Beyoğlu
Tel: (0212) 252 0694
An upmarket New York-style café/bar with good selection of music. Open everyday 11am–midnight.

Prices

The price categories used are as follows:
$ = $5 to $10
$$ = $10 to $20
$$$ = above $20

Gezi Café & Patisserie
Taksim İnönü Cad. 5/1,
Taksim (across from Marmara Hotel, next to the Atatürk Cultural Centre)
Tel: (0212) 251 7430
Great city centre meeting point, offering European pastries and coffee, or wine and cognac, all to classical music. Open 7.30am–9pm. All major credit cards accepted.

Gramafon
Istkilal Caddesi 3
Tünel (right next to tram station)
Tel: (0212) 293 0786
Pricey but exclusive café/bar specialising in live jazz most nights of the week and Sunday afternoons. It's small and definitely needs booking at weekends; attracts older monied crowd. Open everyday 9am–2am, until 8pm Sundays. Watch out for the cover charge when there's music.

Kafika
Bolahenk Sok. 8
Cihangir
Tel: (0212) 244 5167
A café in a small, cozy cinema showing classic and art-house

films. To see a film of your choice you need a group of at least four people. Reserve your film in advance. The cost is just a couple of dollars. Open 11.30am–1am

Kaktüs
Imam Adnan Sok (off İstiklal Cad.)
Tiny Parisian-style bistro with espresso, pasta, a bar, newspapers hanging on the wall and a leftist/artsy clientele.

Ora Cafe & Bar
İstiklal Cad.,
Imam Adnan Sok. 4
floors 1-3
Tel: (0212) 293 2688
A lively and usually crowded place with cramped tables but friendly atmosphere. Often customers play traditional instruments whilst having a drink. Perfect for a drink, snack or meal any time. Service a little erratic but good-natured.

Pia
Bekar Sok. (off İstkilal Cad.)
Tel: (0212) 252 7100
Similar to Kaktüs, but a younger crowd and second-floor seating.

Urban
İstiklal Cad.,
Kartal Sok. 6A
Beyoğlu
Tel: (0212) 252 1325
Hidden down a back alley, this relaxed café/bar, in a beautifully restored historical building, originally opened in the 1920s as a Jewish patisserie, constructed on earlier Ottoman foundations. Quieter than most Beyoğlu bars, with a good selection of imported drinks, coffees and light meals.

Refika
Müeyyet Sok. 11
Tünel
Beyoğlu (off İstiklal Cad., across from Swedish Consulate)
Having recently returned from four years in the States, owner Defne combines a true New York décor with American soul food such as chicken pot pie. The Sunday brunch includes pancakes, eggs benedict (real ham – a rarity for Turkey!) and bottomless cups of coffee. A little pricey, but one of the most stylish hangouts of Istanbul's intellectuals, artists and film makers. Open 10am–7pm only, closed Mon.

BOSPHORUS

Swissotel The Bosphorus
Maçka
Tel: (0212) 259 01 01
A graceful afternoon tea in the lobby with finger sandwiches and pastries, served to light piano and violin music. Open 8am–10pm.

Antre Café
Café Ağa Mah.,
Miralay Nazim Sok. 10
Kadıköy
Great fresh food and good service, run by three women who obviously love the place. Open Mon–Sat, 10am–10pm, Sunday 11am–10pm.

Café Creme
Mecidiye Koprüsü Sok. 12
Ortaköy
Tel: (0212) 227 7294
Cozy café in Ortaköy market, serving crepes, salads, cakes and coffee. Live jazz on weekend afternoons. Open 11am–11pm, weekends 9am–11pm.

Café Pi
Mualim Naci Cad. 63
Ortaköy
Tel: (0212) 236 6853
Another Ortaköy favourite, above the Gallery Pi, serving coffees and cakes. Open Tues–Sat, 11am–8pm, Sunday 11am–6pm.

OUTLYING DISTRICTS

Pierre Loti Café
Gümüşsuyu Balmumcu Sok. 1
Eyüp
Former home of 19th-century romantic writer, Pierre Loti, perched high above Eyüp and the Golden Horn. Cheerful surroundings, red-checked tablecloths and superb views make this a popular weekend outing. Open 8am–midnight.
For more bars and clubs, see
Nightlife, page 295.

Culture

The Turkish people's interest in Western arts culture began in 19th century Istanbul, but also became an important part of Atatürk's raft of reforms.

Classical Music and Dance

Western art forms such as ballet, classical music and opera are now well established among the educated, secular classes. Istanbul has large cultural centres with their own symphony orchestras, ballet and opera companies, which make forays and tours elsewhere. The standard is variable, especially for opera and ballet. It is not easy to find out programmes much in advance and tickets can be difficult to get hold of. Sometimes seats are sold out, or given to sponsors before the public can buy them.

Turkish Music and Dance

Music has an exceptionally rich tradition in Turkey. Academics and folklore groups sponsor interest in *halk müzigi* (folk music) which is still played spontaneously and genuinely at village weddings and festivals, but which visitors are most likely to encounter at a concert or dance display organised for tourists. A music and dance performance will often include a belly dancer – popular even with the most sophisticated. Some of the shows put on for tourists are shoddy, but several good hotel restaurants have excellent folk music and dance displays.

Sanat (art) and *fasıl* music (traditional Turkish styles) are best heard live, and are played in numerous bars and *meyhanes*. "Arabesque", melancholic and sentimental oriental pop ballads, will probably be the first thing you hear in Turkey, and will haunt you from every taxi and minibus. Classical Ottoman and religious

Information

Programmes are not published very far in advance, even for the state opera and ballet. The *Turkish Daily News* carries the cinema listings for Istanbul, Izmir and Ankara. Ordinary Turkish newspapers carry arts listings, obviously in Turkish, but it is fairly easy to work out what is being listed.

music is played by distinguished groups such as that of the Istanbul Municipal Conservatory, and can be heard in concert halls, and on radio and television, sometimes broadcast live. At some Dervish *tekkes* (or lodges), visitors are permitted to watch the remarkable meditative whirling dance.

Turkish pop music is increasingly popular with the younger generation, a combination of eastern and western styles, this usually takes the form of a male or female solo artist singing ballads. Also popular are modern cover versions of traditional folk songs. There are several music channels which play only Turkish music videos.

Venues for Performing Arts

Atatürk Cultural Centre (AKM)
Taksim Square
Tel: (0212) 251 5600/1023
State-owned opera house shared by the State Opera and Ballet Companies, the State Symphony Orchestra, and the State Theatre Company.
Cemal Rehit Rey Concert Hall
Harbiye
Tel: (0212) 240 5012/248 0863
Large concert hall offering varied programmes.
Lütfi Kırdar Convention & Exhibition Centre
Next to the Hilton Hotel and CRR Concert Hall, Harbiye;
Tel: (0212) 256 3055/212 7880.
One large hall (capacity 2,000), 4 smaller halls (capacity 500 each), plus 21 meeting rooms. Also a restaurant with a seating capacity

of 300, and a terrace seating 1,000.
Bursa Karagöz Sanat Evi (Theatre and Museum) Çekirge Caddesi 3
Tel: (0224) 232 1871; or speak to **Sinasi Çilekkol** at the Karagöz Antique store,
Eski Aynalı Çarşı,
Bursa Bazaar
Tel: (0224) 221 8727 or 222 6151
Karagöz puppet theatre.
Zafer Sokağı 17,
Nişantaşı, Istanbul
Tel: (0212) 240 2383
Fax: (0212) 230 0125.
The organisers have ties with UNIMA, the international marionette organisation based in Paris. Turkey's first Karagöz school in Istanbul was opened recently as part of the Children's Foundation, directed by Mustafa Ruhi Şirin.

Jazz, Rock and Pop

Istanbul is beginning to creep onto the international rock band circuit: the Rolling Stones rounded off their two-year *Bridges to Babylon* tour here. Metallica, James Brown, Madonna, Michael Jackson and many more well-known music stars have all visited. Home-grown bands thrive and you can hear live jazz in various bars, night clubs, and, more formally, concert halls.
Ada Müzik
Istiklal Caddesi, and Kumbaracı Yokuşu, Kumbaracı Iç Hanı 115/4, Beyoğlu
Tel/fax: (0212) 252 9924
Web: www.escortnet.com/adamusic
A new Turkish label and record shop featuring interesting "world" mixes.
HIP Productions
Web: www.hipproductions.com.tr
Head of the league for rave, techno and contemporary music events.

Pozitif Promotions
Havyar Sok. 54, 80060, Cihangir
Tel: (212)-249 7075/5167
Fax (0212) 249 4176
E-mail: pozitif@superonline.com.tr
Web: www.Babylon_ist.com.tr;
Pozitif_ist.com.tr
The brains (and taste) behind much of Istanbul's avant garde jazz and world music scene, Doublemoon Records and Babylon also organise an international contemporary "Music Festivity" seminar (autumn/winter), which brings together Turkish and foreign musicians with the Istanbul recording industry.

Libraries and Cultural Centres

Many foreign Cultural Centres maintain lending libraries, offer language classes and sponsor concerts, cultural activities and films.

Aksanat Cultural Centre
İstiklal Cad. Akbank Building,
Beyoglu
Tel: (0212) 252 3500
Interesting programmes of recorded jazz and classical music via a large laser-disc screen. Also painting and sculpture exhibitions and drama.

The American Library and Computer Centre
Mehrutiyet Cad. 108,
Tepebaşı
Tel: (0212) 251 2675.
CD Rom, internet, books. Open Mon–Fri 10am–3.30pm. USIS (US Information Service);
tel: (0212) 251 3602.

Atıf Efendi Library
Vefa Caddesi 44,
Beyazıt
Tel: (0212) 527 3807.
Open Tues–Fri 8.30am–5pm.
Contains more than 25,000 Ottoman manuscripts.

British Council
İstiklal Cad., Örs Turistik İş Merkezi,
Beyoğlu
Tel: (0212) 249 0574/252 7478/252 7474
Lending library open Tues–Fri 10am–5.30pm, Sat 9.30am–2.30pm. Also has a teachers' centre and gives courses.

Istanbul Festival

The annual cultural highlight in Turkey is the Istanbul Festival (April–July), which actually incorporates four linked festivals of music, theatre, cinema and jazz, organised by the Istanbul Foundation for Culture and Arts, who also organise the International Istanbul Biennial art exhibition (see feature, page 89). Banks and institutions sponsor other jazz, blues and classical music festivals which attract top level performers. At these festivals you will get the opportunity to hear major international soloists, orchestras and conductors, plus the cream of home-grown talent.

The Economics and History Foundation
Vali Konağı Cad., Samsun Apt. 57,
Nihantaşı;
E-mail: tarihvakfi@tarihvakfi.org.tr
Web: www.tarihvakfi.org.tr
This leftish intellectual think-tank puts on some of the most eye-opening exhibitions in the city (most in the Imperial Mint, next to Aya Irini in the Topkapı complex) as well as publishing a number of books and magazines, with an emphasis on social history far removed from the Turkish mainstream and Islamic nationalism.

French Cultural Centre
French Consulate, Taksim
Tel: (0212) 249 0776/252 0262
Short film festivals and other cultural events – in French.

German Cultural Centre
Odakule (İstiklal) 286/3, Beyoğlu
Tel: (0212) 249 2009/249 4582
Good reference library. You can get information here for the Goethe Institute events in Tünel.

IRCICA (Research Centre for Islamic History, Art and Culture)
Yıldız Köşk, Yıldız Palace, Barbaros Bulvarı, Beşiktaş
Tel: (0212) 260 5988
Open Mon–Fri 9am–6pm; closed July and August. Contains more than 400,000 printed books, manuscripts, atlases, maps etc.

Festival ticket booking is centralised, which makes things easier. However the festival organisers try out new systems and locations every year in an attempt to improve both service and sales, so things can change from season to season.

Istanbul Foundation for Culture and Arts
(for information about the Istanbul Festivals and Biennial)
Istiklal Cad. 146, Luvr Apt.,
Beyoglu
Tel: 212-293 3313
Fax: 212-292 0927
E-mail: ist.biennial@istfest-tr.org
Web-site: www.istfest.org.

Istanbul Contemporary Art Project
Müeyyet Sok. 11, 2nd floor, Tünel, Beyoglu (off İstiklal Cad., across from Swedish Consulate)
Tel: (0212) 245 5652
E-mail: kortun@netone.com.tr
Web: konteyner.home.mL.org
Contemporary art library and research centre which currently contains 1,200 books and catalogues in all languages, 600 periodicals, 500 titles on theory, philosophy and history, 50 contemporary art videos with visual and bibliographical records of 30 of Turkey's best artists. Set to become the hub of Istanbul's most progressive art scene, it will be rapidly expanding in 2000 to create residencies for artists, critics and curators, publish research and ultimately open an exhibition space. Open 11am–7pm.

Osmanlı Bank Gallery and Historical Archives
İstiklal Cad. 276, Beyoğlu
Tel: (0212) 245 5095
Fascinating collection of Tanzimat era social, economic, political and cultural records in this former Franco-British commercial institution, mostly in French.

Ottoman State Archives
Ticarethane Sok. 12, Sultanahmet
Tel: 212-513 8870
Open Mon–Fri 8.30am–5pm. A

"treasury of papers" – more than 500 years of bureaucracy – open to scholars.

Süleymaniye Library
Ayşekadın Hamamı Sok. 30–35, Süleymaniye complex
Tel: (0212) 520 6450
Claims to house largest collection of Islamic manuscripts in the world. A thorough reference collection on Ottoman culture and history. Photocopy, microfilm and computer research facilities available. Open 8.30am–5pm, Mon–Sat.

Topkapı Palace Library
Sultanahmet (Palace grounds)
Tel: (0212) 512 0484.
A valuable collection of miniatures, calligraphy and 15,000 Ottoman, Turkish, Persian and Arabic manuscripts. Microfilm and photocopying service available, but permission for researchers must be obtained in advance. Open 9am–5pm, Mon–Fri.

The Women's Library
across Fener jetty on Golden Horn
Tel: (0212) 534 9550
Diverse collection of works for and about women and regular cultural

Films in Istanbul

Screens are dominated by the latest Hollywood blockbusters (as well as the occasional serious art film) and usually shown in the original language with Turkish subtitles *alt yazılı*, though the title will be translated into Turkish. If the film has been dubbed, *Turkçe* (Turkish) or *ilk gösterim* (dubbed) will appear on the programme listings or poster outside the cinema – this will usually be the case with cartoons and films suitable for children. Tickets cost between US$3–7 (£2–4). At any one time there will be a choice of a dozen or so foreign films on show. If you want to see the latest Turkish movies with English subtitles, you'll have to visit during one of the major international film festivals such as the **Istanbul Film Festival** (spring).

activities. Open Mon–Sat, 9am–5.30pm.

Cinema Listings

There are over 30 cinemas in Istanbul, many of which are multiplexes attached to the major shopping areas around town. İstiklal Caddesi in Beyoğlu has the largest cluster, and certainly the most "alternative" selection of films. Check the *Turkish Daily News* (not always reliable) or *Sinema* for programme details, or just wander down and check the signs outside the cinemas.

EUROPEAN SIDE

Alkazar Cinema Centre
İstiklal Caddesi 179, Beyoğlu
Tel: (0212) 293 2466
Renovated art-nouveau cinema with 3 screens and a café/bar.
Beyoğlu
İstiklal Caddesi,
Halep Pasajı 140,
Beyoğlu
Tel: (0212) 251 3240
Two screens. The cinema runs a mini-festival from July–Sept showing the most popular art-house releases of the year.
Atlas
İstiklal Caddesi 209,
Beyoğlu
Tel: (0212) 252 8576
One of the city's best-known cinemas. Two screens.
Akmerkez Shopping Centre
Etiler
Tel: (0212) 282 0505
Four screens.

ASIAN SIDE

Atlantis
Kadıköy
Tel: (0216)-418 5491
Capitol Shopping Centre
Altunizade
Tel: (0216)-310 0616
Eight screens.
Süreyya
Bahariye Caddesi 29,
Kadıköy

Travellers' Club

A **Travellers, Club** has been organised in the Sultanahmet area by people who want to write about their journey and share their observations. The group is currently forming connections with similar clubs around the world, providing information to travellers, and organising discussions, slide and video shows. The club will also be organising tours abroad and within Turkey. Tel: (0212) 518 5409/02.

Tel: (0216)-336 0682
Late 19th century theatre.

Art Galleries

The huge Biennial exhibition brings together a heady mix of international contemporary artists; with the emphasis on showcasing Turkish artists. Turkish painting and sculpture in the modern sense have a short history, but Turkish artists are also experimenting with conceptual art and video. In architecture and design, some contemporary or recent buildings and interiors are of interest.
Borusan Culture and Art Centre
İstiklal Cad. 421,
Beyoğlu
Tel: (0212) 292 0655
Fax: (0212) 252 4591
Web: www.borusansanat.com
This corporate cultural centre includes one of the bravest art galleries in Istanbul showing work by renowned Turkish and international contemporary artists. Also a conference and concert hall, music library and publishing house.
Yapı Kredi Cultural Activities, Arts and Publishing, inc.
İstiklal Caddesi 285,
Beyoğlu
Tel: (0212) 252 4700/1/2, 280 6555
Fax: (0212) 293 3080
The Yapı Kredi bank's contemporary art and architecture galleries, publishing house and bookstores. Some texts in English.

COMMERCIAL ART AND ANTIQUE GALLERIES

Antik Palas, Spor Cad, Talimyeri Sok., Maçka
Tel: (0212) 236 2464
E-mail: antik@doruk.net
Web: www.antikpalace.com.tr
Superb collection of Ottoman and European paintings and antiques; monthly auctions and occasional exhibitions of European masters. This is the fourth largest auction house in Europe and attracts international collectors. It also has a library, organises seminars, and conferences and publishes a glossy magazine, *Antik Decor.*
Ayşe and Ercümend Kalmık Foundation
Sarayarkası Sok. 35-37, Gümüşsüyü (Taksim – behind German Consulate)
Tel: (0212) 245 0270
Unusual independent gallery in stupendously restored Ottoman house; worth the search.
Contemporary Art Marketing (C.A.M.)
Abdi Ipekçi Cad. 48/5, Nihantaşı
Tel: (0212) 234 3902
Fax: (0212) 248 3692
Trendy gallery with corporate flair.
Dulcinea
Meşelik Sok. 20, Beyoğlu

Sponsorship is Trendy

Every financial institution seems recently to have decided to sponsor modern art, including decorative arts and art jewellery, so you will find many small art galleries tucked into the ground or reception floor of office headquarters. Here, the art exhibited may or may not be for sale. There are many other small commercial galleries, some of which double up as bars or cafés and are good places to meet people. Current exhibits will be featured in city guide magazines such as *City Plus Istanbul* and *The Guide.* Istanbul is especially richly endowed with galleries large and small.

Tel: (0212) 245 1071
E-mail: art@dulcinea.org
Web: www.dulcinea.org
One of Istanbul's newest and most stylish galleries, below the popular restaurant of the same name.
Emlak Sanat Galerisi, Balyoz Sok., Yenihan 4, İstiklal Caddesi, Tünel
Tel: (0212) 252 6100
Contemporary and classical art.
Galatea
Sofyalı Sok. 16, Asmalımescit, Tünel (bottom of İstiklal Cad.)
Tel: (0212) 292 5430
E-mail: konak@turk.net.com.tr
New gallery showcasing contemporary Turkish artists. Also good restaurant and bar.
Izzet and Ipek Günay
Abide-i Hürriyet Caddesi, Tayyareci M. Ali Bey Sok. 12, Şişli
Tel: (0212) 233 0717
Ottoman antiques, calligraphy, furniture and paintings.
Galeri Baraz
Kurtuluş Caddesi 191, Kurtuluş
Tel: (0212) 240 4783
Fax: (0212) 231 6258
A wide variety of contemporary art including many of Turkey's most influential artists.
Küsav
Hasfırın Caddesi, Sinanpaşa İş Merkezi, 3rd floor, Beşiktaş
Tel: (0212) 227 3485, 260 7700
Auction house: (0212) 299 3921/23
Ottoman artworks and textiles, calligraphy and specialist collectables. Culture Ministry affiliated charitable foundation which aims to conserve and promote Turkish heritage, with regular antique auctions, valuations, and the annual **Istanbul Antiques & Decorative Arts Fair** each autumn.
Milli Reasürans Gallery
Teşvikiye Cad. 43/57, Teşvikiye
Tel: (0212) 230 1976
Fax: (0212) 231 4730
One of Istanbul's more up-market galleries featuring popular Turkish masters. Excellent contemporary Turkish and foreign works
Pamukbank Gallery of Photography
Teşvikiye Cad. 105/3, Teşvikiye
Tel: (0212) 236 6790
Fax: (0212) 236 6791

E-mail: ays.bil@pamukbank.com.tr
Historic and contemporary shows by Turkish and foreign photographers, plus a photo album library.
Sofa
Nuruosmaniye Caddesi 42 and 106/B
Tel: (0212) 527 4142, 522 1474
Fax: (0212) 527 9134
Web: www.kashifsofa.com.tr
Maps, miniatures, calligraphy, and textiles.
Sufi Gallery
Tünel Meydanı 6, Beyoğlu
Tel: (0212) 251 1966
Calligraphy, *ebru* (marbled paper), maps, engravings.
Tem
Orhan Ersek Sok. 44/2, Nimet Apt. Nişantaşı
Tel: (0212) 247 0899
Fax: (0212) 247 9756
One of Istanbul's best galleries houses an excellent collection of Turkish contemporary art and holds international exhibitions. Owner Besi Cecan speaks English.

Other Istanbul Galleries
Aksanat
İstiklal Caddesi 16-18, Beyoğlu
Tel: (0212) 252 3500
Cemal Rehit Rey Exhibition Centre
Harbiye
Tel: (0212) 240 5012
İş Sanat
Meşelik Sokak, Yürekli Han Kat. 2, Taksim
Tel: (0212) 244 2021
Galeri Nev
Maçka Caddesi 33, Maçka
Tel: (0212) 231 6782
Galeri Oda
Teşvikiye
Tel: (0212) 259 2208
Urart
Abdi Ipekçi Caddesi 21, Nişantaşı
Tel: (0212) 241 2183
Silver and gold jewellery as well as paintings and sculptures
Vakko
İstiklal Caddesi 123, Beyoğlu
Tel: (0212) 251 4092
Yapı Kredi
İstiklal Caddesi 285, Beyoğlu
Tel: (0212) 245 2041

Nightlife

Nightlife traditionally revolves around *meyhane* (taverns), bars, restaurants and *gazinos* (places where *meze* are served with accompanying Turkish cabaret or dancing). Discos and nightclubs are popular with the young and more affluent; with clubs as vulnerable to the vagaries of fashion as any in New York or London.

The best **dance clubs and discos** have up-to-date sound and lights. Entry charges vary, from about US$3–15 (£2–9).

Cabaret

Expensive, but often worth it. This form of entertainment, which can include excellently performed traditional music and belly dancing, should not be dismissed out of hand as it is not always designed just to liberate the hapless tourist's wallet. It is a genuine, popular Turkish form of entertainment, often laid on as part of lavish family

Gay Venues

There are gay bars and discos in Istanbul but as Turkish attitudes to homosexuality are both contradictory and inconsistent, and sometimes overtly hostile, you should be extremely cautious. Most gay bars and clubs are in Taksim. Try **Bar Bahçe** and **Bilsak**, off Siracevizler Cad. and **Hans Bar** at Tarlebasi Cad. 248. **Kubana Night Club 99,** Mesrutiyet Cad. 81, is a reasonably priced basement club catering for a mixed aged gay clientele. Some of the clubs in the main listings attract a mixed straight/gay crowd.

celebrations, and can be very good. Dinner and show together will come to between US$50–90 (£30–50) a head, more if you find yourself lavishly tipping the belly dancer (who will probably stuff the notes into her bra, or invite you to).

The best shows are at:
Kervansarai
Cumhuriyet Cad., Elmadağ, near the Hilton Hotel
Tel: (0212) 247 1630
Orient House
President Hotel, Tiyatro Cad. 27, Beyazıt, near the Grand Bazaar
Tel: (0212) 517 6163.
Galata Tower
Büyükhendek Cad., Galatasaray
Tel: (0212) 245 1160
Touristy, but safe and entertaining.

Bars and Clubs

Andon Pera
Siraselviler Cad. 89/2, Beyoğlu
Tel: (0212) 251 0222
Popular bar expanded to include Cafe Nisvan (10.30am–11pm), Andon Sport on 2nd floor, (6pm–2am) and Andon Dancing (9.30pm–2am).
Asterix
Kucukparmakkapi Ipek Sok. 25, Beyoğlu.
Cheap drinks, no cover charge. Open till 4am. on a good street for cheap bars.
Babylon
Şeyhbender Sok., Asmalımescit, Beyoğlu
Tel: (0212) 292 7368
Web: www.babylon-ist.com
World/jazz music. Modelled on New York's famous Knitting Factory.
Bilsak
Sıraselviler Cad., Soğancı Sok. 7, Cihangir (Taksim), 5th floor
Tel: (0212) 293 3774
Trendy, upmarket bar and restaurant with a mixed gay and straight clientele and frequented by artists, writers and journalists. Magnificent view of the city, good food and middle-range prices. Open 10am–2pm. Closed Sunday. Cards: Visa, Mastercard.
Café Mesale
Hippodrome, Sultanahmet.
One of the few places in the old city

to round off the evening. Outdoor brass tables, carpeted benches, live music, *nargile* (water pipes) and flaming torches. Even a few Turks come here.
Çubuklu 29
Paşabahçe Yolu 24, Çubuklu
Tel: (0212) 231 0356
Described as "glitterati, music, love and money." Expensive, ostentatious and entertaining.
Calinti
Ipek Sok. 27
Cheap and cheerful bar on this little street full of action. No cover charge.
Cinaralti
Balo Sok. 14
Reasonable prices, young crowd, lively. No cover charge.
English Pub
Tiyatro Cad. 25, Beyazıt
Tel: (0212) 516 6980
The oldest English Pub in Istanbul, happy hour from Mon–Fri 3pm–6pm. All major cards accepted. Open daily 11am–2pm.
Gizlibahçe
Nevizade Sok, 2/F, next to Akdeniz Restaurant.
On a narrow, lively street with plenty of bars and restaurants, this is popular with the 20s–30s age group. Good music.
Hayal Kahvesi
Büyükparmakkapı Sok. 19, Beyoğlu;
Tel: (0212) 243 6823
By day a cozy café, by night a live music venue with a young clientele featuring jazz and rock. Open daily 11am–2am. No credit cards.
High-End
Nispetiye Cad. No. 4, Etiler
Tel: (0212) 287 7380
As the name suggests, this élite and pricey disco for well-heeled youths offers the latest music and lighting, proper ventilation and a stonking cover charge (over US$25/£15). Open Wed–Sat nights.
Tarişi Pano Şaraphanesi
Balık Pazar, junction of Meşrutiyet Cad., Hamalbaşı and Kalyoncu Kulluşu Cad.
Tel: (0212) 292 6664
This old Greek wine house dates from 1898 and was recently reopened with sensitivity to its original layout, complete with the old wooden vats and rough but

Bars

Istanbul has a range of **bars** to suit any budget and taste, from the simple to the exotic and elegant. Many smart cafés turn into bars at night, and some are as fashionable as they would be in London or New York. Some have live music, but these may have a hefty cover-charge. Expensive hotels have glamorous bars – sometimes offering a spectacular view, for which you pay in the inflated price of the drinks. Some offer a "theme" – Mexican, Irish or British Pub – to bring in custom. In most you can find snacks; in some a full meal will be available.

drinkable wine on tap at low prices. Old Istanbul atmosphere.

James Joyce – The Irish Pub
Tarlabaşı Boulevard, Dernek Sok., Taksim. Tel: (0212) 238 8892
The best-known Irish Pub in Istanbul offers ceilidh dancing, and live Irish music as well as blues and African most nights. Cover charge at weekends. Rooftop barbecue on Sundays in summer. Imported Guiness and classic Irish pub grub. Very popular with foreigners.

Kafe Barinak
Ipek Sok. 21.
Narrow café/bar, mixed crowd, lively at weekends. Open late and popular for coffee. Eclectic music.

Khalkedon
Munir Nurettin Selcuk Sok., Kalamis. Tel: (0216) 349 5872
Huge night-time outdoor venue on Asian side, with same atmosphere as famous Halikarnas nightclub in Bodrum. Bar and restaurant, live Turkish music and dancing.

Madrid
Ipek Sok. 20
Regular bar, small, reasonable prices and good music.

Magma
Akarsu Sok. 5, Galatasaray (left of St Antoine's Church down the alley)
Tel: (0212) 292 1119
Very chic underground club aimed at over 25s. Speciality DJs play hip-hop, drum 'n' bass, electronica,

trip-hop, new-wave and ska; live music early on weekends. Check HIP Production website for more info. Opens at 8pm, closes 4am on weekdays; open until 6am on weekends. US$20 (£12) average cover charge.

Millennium
Nizamiye Cad. 14, Taksim
Tel: (0212) 256 4437
One of Istanbul's most frequented, celebrity packed clubs, and also one of the priciest – minimum US$25 (£15) entrance fee and expensive drinks. Two spacious rooms offer house, garage, techno and the scent of the city's wealthiest youth. Open Wed, Fri, and Sat midnight–6am. All major credit cards accepted.

Mojo
Büyükparmakkapı Sok. 26, Beyoğlu
Tel: (0212) 243 2927
A popular street for nightlife. Live bands here every night, popular with blues lovers and bohemians. 9pm–4am. Cover charge.

Peyote
Imam Adnan Sok.
Small, unique showcase venue for Istanbul's emerging alternative bands

Paşa
Muallim Naci Cad. 142, Kuruçeşme. Tel: (0212) 227 1252
"Supposedly the Hottest outdoor night-club on the Bosphorus". A place for Istanbul's glitterati, with loud music. Small restaurants inside. Cover charge, hard to get in.

Pupa's
1. Cadde 17, Arnavutköy
Tel: (0212) 265 6533
Sadly only nominally African in theme today, it is still one of the few places in town for reggae. African food on Tuesday nights, reggae disco Fri–Sat. Credit cards not accepted.

Q Bar
Çırağan Palace Hotel, Beşiktaş
Tel: (0212) 236 2121
One of Istanbul's top classical jazz venues is imaginatively run, featuring debut shows by young up-and-coming Turkish painters on "Blue Monday" nights in winter. Music outdoors on the Bosphorus in summers. Expensive, but far more interesting

than the usual hotel lounge and attractive to Istanbul's older élite.

Rock House
Dereboyu Cad. 36/38, Ortaköy
Tel: (0212) 259 8911
Another star in the crown of former Hard Rock Café supremo Richard Jacobs. "American" menu, imported beers, live rock and pool room.

Roxy
Arslan Sok. Sıraselviler Cad., Taksim
Tel: (0212) 249 4839/234 3236
Trendy, expensive youth venue with great live international bands the clientele doesn't deserve. Open 6pm–3.30am. No credit cards.

Societe Bar
İstiklal Cad., Ayhan Isik Sok. 9, Beyoğlu
Tel: (0212) 293 3323
The place to experience *fasil* (traditional Turkish song). Only open Wed–Thurs nights from 9pm.

19-20
Tepebaşı, Taksim
Tel: (0212) 235 6197
Mixed gay and straight late night haunt of the young and wild. One room for rock, another for techno.

VSOP
The Marmara Istanbul, Taksim
Tel: (0212) 251 4696
On the lobby floor of the hotel, the bar is designed to resemble a typical English library. Open 12 noon–midnight, perfect for executive drinking.

XS
Balo Sok. 37
Bar/club, popular with local bikers. Good music, cheap drinks, open until 2am.

THRACE AND MARMARA

Apart from a few local discos there is little or no nightlife – as westerners understand the term – in Thrace or Marmara. Notices of occasional concerts and plays appear on posters or in shop windows.

In **Bursa** the desperate might try:
The Club S
Kültür Park (İpekiş entrance)
Weekends only.
Bongo Bar
Clup Altınceylan, Kültür Park.

Sport

FOOTBALL

Soccer is the national obsession (*see feature, page 139*). Check fixtures from a newspaper. Matches are usually on Friday, Saturday and Sunday evenings. Try to get tickets in advance, and if your tickets are unreserved, get to the ground early as the stands fill quickly. Ticket prices are absurdly cheap for the unreserved or uncovered section, more expensive for the numbered stands. Although few women go, it's perfectly safe. Security is tight, and police confiscate water-bottles, cigarette lighters, pens and coins from being brought into the ground. Istanbul has three main teams, as detailed below.

Beşiktaş: The most picturesque ground in Turkey, with a striking view of the Bosphorus as you stand and cheer on the Black Eagles. The Stadium is situated between Gümüşsuyu Caddesi, the waterfront and Dolmabahçe Palace, an easy walk downhill from Taksim Square.

Galatasaray: Ali Sami Yen stadium is in the transport hub of Mecidiyekoy bus-station, so easily accessible, although not particularly attractive. The Galatasaray fans are probably the most noisy and fanatical, the team has been an exceptional form over the past few years.

Fenerbahce: The blues and yellows of Fenerbahce hold their games on the Asian side. The ground is quite difficult to access, and especially difficult to get back from if you're staying on the European side.

BASKETBALL

Basketball is the second most popular spectator sport in Turkey, and the country has one of the most expensive leagues in Europe, with players also from America and Yugoslavia. Watching games on TV is a very popular past-time. The season runs in the winter months. The best teams in Istanbul are Efes Pilsen, Ulker, and Fenerbahçe.

VOLLEYBALL

Volleyball is increasingly popular and both the men and women's teams have performed well in European tournaments. One Turkish woman was been picked for NBA in 1999.

OIL WRESTLING

Popular throughout Turkey, this ritualised form of wrestling, *yağlı güreh*, has been going on for six centuries. The year's highlight is the annual Kırkpınar Festival near Edirne, which takes place in late June or early July. For tickets, try the Edirne tourist office, tel: (0284) 225 1518. There are many other, smaller festivals throughout the year. See also box, *page 245*.

CAMEL WRESTLING

An annual camel-wrestling festival takes place at Selçuk in January, where two adult male camels are pitted against each other. Smaller festivals take place in Çanakkale (Dec–Mar). These events make a highly entertaining day out, with many camel-fights, folk music, barbecues and plenty of alcohol.

CIRIT (JIRIT)

A wild and ruthless game vaguely akin to polo, played on horseback with javelins. *Cirit* ponies are trained to gallop from a standing start and turn on the spot – an exciting sport showing great horsemanship. The game is played mainly in the east of Turkey, especially around Erzurum, although there is one tournament in Istanbul each July.

GOLF

In a bid to draw more wealthy, money-spending foreign tourists to Turkey, the country is rapidly developing golf as a sporting and recreational activity. Istanbul has three top quality courses. Most accept day visitors and many top hotels have arrangements for their guests. Only a few hundred Turks actually play the game.

The oldest, the **Istanbul Golf Club**, is a nine-hole course established in the late 19th century by British businessmen living in the city. For more than 100 years it remained Turkey's only golf course.

The new 18-hole **Country Club** in Istanbul has been the setting for senior European Professional Golf Association (PGA) tournaments.

Istanbul Golf Club
4 Levent
Tel: (0212) 264 0742
Kemer Golf and Country Club,
Göktürk Köyü, Kemerbürgaz
Tel: (0212) 239 7913
Fax: (0212) 239 7376
Klassis Golf Club
Seymen Köyü
Tel: (0212) 748 4600
Fax: (0212) 748 4640

TENNIS

Tennis is popular with the upper class, and remains an élitist game played in private clubs which are quite expensive. Visitors can sometimes book courts by the hour.
Enka Sports Centre
İstinye Yolu
Tel: (0212) 276 5084
Indoor tennis, swimming, basketball and volleyball

TED

İstinye. Tel: (0212) 262 0168

RIDING

Riding facilities can vary enormously, but it can be a wonderful way to explore the landscape. There are riding stables in the vicinity of Istanbul but on the whole these are open to club members only. In all cases you should be upfront about your experience or lack of it, and you will have to use your judgment as to the safety of the horses and the establishment. There are almost no ponies as we understand them in Turkey, and a lot of Arab blood in the horses which makes them pretty but skittish.

Istanbul Riding Club
Binicilik Sitesi Üçyol-Maslak
Tel: (0212) 276 1404
Open Tues–Sun 9am–7pm for hire of horses and lessons.

SKATING

Galleria Shopping Mall
Ataköy
Tel: (0212) 560 8550
Cheerful shopping centre ice-rink for fun rather than serious sport.
Open daily 9am–10pm.

SWIMMING

Many of the large hotels have pools, and it may be sensible to

use them. In winter indoor hotel pools can be a fun, though expensive treat, complete with luxurious towels and poolside service.

Public pools
Kuruçeşme Divan
Tel: (0212) 257 7150
One of the largest pools in Istanbul; open 9am–6pm. On the Bosphorus; food is available from the Teras Café.

Zekeriyakoy Divan
Tel: (0212) 202 6114
A complex consisting of a large pool, tennis and squash courts, fitness centre, sauna, massage rooms and pub.

Club 29 Çubuklu
Tel: (0212) 322 2829
On the Asian side. Not only good swimming but a great view of the Bosphorus and a delicious open buffet. Can be reached by private boat from İstinye.

Park Orman
Tel: (0212) 223 0736
Perfect also for children, situated in the Fatih Children's Forest (Fatih Orman Park) the huge pool gets crowded at weekends.

Darulsafaka
Tel: (0212) 276 8861
A sporting complex with year-round swimming facilities in an Olympic-sized pool. Also basketball courts, football, jacuzzi, sauna and fitness centre.

Beaches

There are two beaches accessible by day-trip from Istanbul. **Kilyos**, on the Black Sea coast, can be reached by bus from Sarıyer. The area also has plenty of pensions and hotels open in season. It is very popular with Russian holiday-makers, and gets even more crowded at weekends. The best beach area has a small entrance charge. The sea is cold and has a dangerous undercurrent, so better stick to areas where others are

swimming, and where there is a lifeguard. As there may be sea urchins, a pair of thongs or espadrilles for wading would be handy.

Şile is a small Black Sea resort town, 70 km (42 miles) from Üsküdar, with sandy beaches, a handy selection of cafés, bars and restaurants and a few hotels and pensions. It also gets very busy at weekends.

Shopping

Where to Shop

Shopping in Turkey is always fascinating and sometimes even educational. Istanbul offers many different shopping experiences, from the glitzy to the gritty. Vast, user-friendly shopping centres contain car parks, supermarkets, cinemas, food courts and shops selling international designer labels. But a better and older version of the same idea is the amazing Grand Bazaar, a veritable labyrinth of shops and workshops, selling every imaginable product (*see pages 101 and 176*). There are also plenty of excellent local weekly street markets, (good for wonderful fresh produce if you are self-catering), and flea markets *(bit pazarı)* if you want to go hunting for bargains. If you prefer more sophisticated, individual and independent shops, you will find them too, offering high quality fashion, interior design and gifts.

What to Buy

Textiles, clothing, carpets, pottery, metalwork, semiprecious and precious stones and jewellery, leather, glass all can vary greatly in quality and price. You can easily go home with a bag full of shoddily made but amusing souvenirs with a Turkish flavour. It is harder to find good Turkish things which are not antiques, for which you need a special export licence.

ANTIQUES AND CRAFTS

Rummaging in junk shops and flea markets is very entertaining, and although you are not supposed to take antiques out of Turkey, there is

Sales Tax

VAT (KDV) at rates between 8 and 15 percent is included in the price of most goods but you may see it itemised separately on a bill or receipt (look for the words KDV dahildir). Many carpet dealers routinely try and avoid taxes and claim that a proper receipt will bump the price up by 15 percent to cover the legalities.

You will only be able obtain a tax refund on goods bought from the relatively few shops authorised for tax free sales (mainly large department stores) to all non-residents of Turkey. The purchase must be made in TL (minimum TL5 million). Ask the shop to sign the receipt, keep it and claim back the money from the tax-office at the airport. Additional information: **Ministry of Finance and Tax Dept**, General Directorate, Ankara: (0321) 310 38 80.

no clear definition of what constitutes an antique. Old Turkish things used to be dirt cheap because newly wealthy Turks wanted everything modern, Western and glitzy. However, stylish Turks have recently become keen on old Ottoman pieces for their interior décor, so prices are rising. For items of European origin, it is possible to get export permission, and good shopkeepers will know the procedure and be able to tell you if you may legally export any particular item. Antiquities and antique Turkish things are another matter, and there are severe penalties for anyone caught trying to take these out of the country.
Artrium I. Tünel Pasajı 5 &7
Artrium II
Sofyalı Sok. 9, Tünel
Tel: (0212) 251 4302
Fax: (0212) 249 8983
Old Turkish ceramics, miniatures, calligraphy, prints, maps, paintings, frames, textiles, jewellery and gift items. Open Mon-Sat 9am–7pm.
Atlas Pasajı
İstiklal Cad. 209, Beyoğlu

Enter this unique arcade through a historic cinema complex, to find an Aladdin's cave filled with everything from antiques to costumes to Central Asian jewellery and alternative music stores.
Beyazıt Şahaflar Çarşısı
Antiquarian books and much more in this old Istanbul market on the Beyazıt side of the Grand Bazaar.
Çukurcuma
A T-shaped intersection of streets in central Beyoğlu containing at least 50 shops from those selling basic secondhand furniture and junk to top-price antiques. Follow Turnacıbaşı Sok. (sign marked Galatasaray Hamam) around to the left, where you can either continue straight for the cheaper, bohemian alleys, or turn left, down the hill at Faik Paşa Yokuşu for the more upmarket shops.

A few worth a mention are:
Alfa Ltd.
Faikpaşa Yokuşu Fazilet Apt. 47/2
Tel: (0212) 251 1672
Ottoman era books, maps and prints as well as an Ottoman miniature lead soldier collection.
Antikarnas
Faik Paşa Yokuşu 15
Tel: (0212) 251 5928/251 4135
Ottoman and European antiques, religious and decorative objects.
Hikmet & Pınar
Faikpaşa Yokuşu 36
Tel: (0212) 243 2400/293 0575
Old weapons, woodwork, and so on.
Döşem
Topkapı Palace
The state-owned gift shop has some great bargains and unquestionably the best collection of reproduction Ottoman and Byzantine jewellery, textiles, ceramics, silks and glassware going. Make time for it.
Eren
Sofyalı Sok. 34, Tünel
Tel: (0212) 251 2858
Old and new art and history books, maps and miniatures.
Horhor Bit Pazarı
Kırık Tulumba Sok. 13/22, Aksaray
A five-story, antique market with a marvellous selection.
Istanbul Handicrafts Centre
Sultanahmet, beside Yeşil Ev Hotel
Tel: (0212) 517 6782

A series of crafts workshops in a restored religious school (medrese). Visitors can watch the artisans at work and purchase their wares.
Kapalı Çarşı (Grand Bazaar)
Over 4000 tiny shops offering everything from tourist trash to gold, icons, textiles and antiques. Competition keeps prices keen. Open Mon–Sat 9am–7pm.
Küsav, Hasfırın Cad., Sinan Paşa İş Merkezi, 3rd floor, Beşiktaş
Tel: (0212) 260 7700, 227 3485
Ottoman and European antique and textile exhibits; antique auctions (see page 294).
Levant Koleksiyon
Tünel Square 8
Tel: (0212) 293 6333
Old postcards, books, and prints from the 19th century.
Librairie de Pera
Galip Dede Sok. 22, Tünel
Tel: (0212) 251 1966
One of the oldest and best antiquarian bookshops in Istanbul. A large collection of Turkish, Greek, Armenian, Arabic, and European books, maps of the Ottoman Empire, old Istanbul etchings and prints, photographs, and original water colours.
Ottomania
Sofyalı Sok. 30/32, Tünel

Bargaining

There is a subtle etiquette to haggling, which many Westerners find awkward and embarrassing at first, but then, if they get good at it, learn to love. Tradesmen in tourist areas do start their prices high, especially for tourist goods, so you can begin with at least half the initial price. It may well turn out that after a bout of intensive haggling, and several glasses of tea, the shopkeeper will respect you the more when you reach an agreed price. You can haggle a little even if you have no intention of buying, but once you have agreed a price it is very bad form to walk away. Look out too for signs spelling out that prices are fixed. They usually mean what they say.

Opening Times

Opening times are variable. Shops are open generally from Mon–Sat 9am–6/8pm (later in summer, especially in resorts). The Grand Bazaar and Spice Bazaar are open from 9am–7pm (closed Sunday). Large shops open later, and the US-style shopping malls are open seven days a week from 10am–10pm. Street markets start up around 8am, and may start packing up in the mid-afternoon. Shops do not close for lunch, but small shops may close briefly for prayers, especially for the midday prayers on Fridays. A selection of local shops in any busy neighbourhood will remain open late into the evening.

Tel: (0212) 243 2157/243 2158.
Old engravings, calligraphy, maps and some rare books.
Rölyef Art Enterprises
Emir Nevruz Sok. 16,
Galatasaray
Tel: (0212) 244 0494/293 9397
Ottoman ornaments, engravings, Islamic miniatures, calligraphy, gilding and marbling.
Urart
Abdi Ipekçi Cad. 18/1, Nişantaşı
Tel: (0212) 246 7194
Distinctive silver and gold jewellery, metal work, painting and sculpture, often based on designs of great antiquity but with a modern flair.

BOOKS

The best, large Turkish-published books on Turkey – with good photographs and English or bilingual text – are usually very expensive – often over US$100 (£60). Çelik Gülersöy, the doyen of Turkish conservation, has written many titles on the various palaces and historic areas of Istanbul, plus other areas in Turkey, and his books are reasonably priced and available in museum bookshops, though not terribly well produced. You will find cheap and not particularly good illustrated guidebooks in several languages at tourist sites. New imported foreign books are very expensive, at least a third more than at home.

There's a thriving second-hand and antiquarian book trade (see listings above): and some very good dealers with shops or stalls at flea markets in Istanbul and elsewhere.

However the appetite for foreign-language books is great and prices are not low. You'll also find maps and prints, but anything with a Turkish subject has become fashionable and expensive.
ABC
İstiklal Cad. 461, Beyoğlu
Tel: (0212) 276 2403
Books and magazines, dictionaries and language materials in English, German and French.
Aslihan Şahaflar Çarşısı
Galatasaray Fish Market, Beyoğlu
Antiquarian book market.
Dünya Bookstores
İstiklal Cad. 469, Beyoğlu
Tel: (0212) 249 1006
Books, magazines and newspapers in major European languages.
Firnas
Meşrutiyet Cad., Avrupa Pasajı 5, Beyoğlu
Tel: (0212) 244 5446
Fax: (0212) 244 5697
Small shop which orders English language books from Britain on Turkish historical and cultural subjects and translations of Turkey's best authors, selling them at their exact sterling price – no mark-ups. Some credit cards.
Homer
Yeni Çarşı Cad. 28-A,
Galatasaray
Tel: (0212) 249 5902
Great stock of books (many academic titles) in English.
Mephisto
İstiklal Cad. 173, Beyoğlu
Tel: (0212) 293 1909
Books, tapes and posters.
No Name Book Exchange
Akbiyik Cad. Bayram Firin Sok. 14, Sultanahmet

Tel: (0212) 516 9414
1200 English language books, including guidebooks, to choose from, to bring, buy or swap.
Pandora
Büyükparmakkapı Sok. 3 Beyoğlu
Tel: (0212) 245 1667
E-mail: pandorainfo-ist.comlink
Web: www.pandora.com.tr
Large selection of foreign books including many academic and regional titles.
Remzi Kitabevi
Akmerkez Shopping Mall, 121, Rumeli Cad. 44, Nişantaşı
Large and good selection of books and magazines in many languages.
Robinson Crusoe
Istiklal Cad. 389, Tünel, Beyoğlu
Tel: (0212) 293 6968/293 6977
Great selection of English language books, many of local interest. Also French- and German-language publications available.

CARPETS AND KILIMS

You do not have to be an expert to buy a good carpet, but it helps. Let yourself be guided by what you like, and most important, get your eye in first before making a commitment, and you can go home with something you really love. It is also worth remembering that London and New York are world-class carpet markets in their own right, and that department stores and chains all over the world buy new and antique Turkish carpets and flat woven kilims and offer them at competititive prices. Within Istanbul, there are certain carpet trading centres such as the Grand Bazaar and Sultanahmet. Buying a carpet can rarely be done in a hurry, and can take half a day of tea-drinking and discussion, enjoyed by both customer and dealer. If you are serious, it's worth doing a little background reading beforehand. (*See also* page 108.)
Bazaar 54
54 Nuruosmaniye Cad., Cağaloğlu
Tel: (0212) 511 2150
One of a chain of superstores claiming to be the world's largest

supplier of Turkish carpets and kilims; also a wide selection of jewellery and souvenirs. Shopping here may not be as much fun, but the quality is guaranteed.

METALWORK

You will find many wonderful things made of hand-beaten copper or brass: samovars, lunch boxes, pots and pans, cauldrons. Craftsmanship is excellent, and many items are convincingly and attractively "antiqued". Everyday household and functional metalware items can also be extremely attractive and sometimes very cheap. Stainless steel and aluminium saucepans are well-made and much cheaper than in Europe. In street markets you will also find pretty enamel tin trays, metal pots for making tea and coffee Turkish-style.

CHINA AND GLASS

Turkey has a thriving industry churning out household glass and china at extremely good prices: if your luggage allowance can take it. At a more rarefied level, some factories are making beautiful replicas of traditional and museum pieces. The Yıldız factory, beside the Yıldız Palace, makes delicately pretty porcelain in Ottoman imperial style. The state-run Döşem souvenir shops have wonderful reproduction Byzantine glass, fragile as a bubble. Paşabahçe glass factory makes the household stuff but also pretty blue and white swirled çeşmibülbül glass vases and ornaments. Elsewhere you will also see vast quantities of decorated plates and tiles in "Kütahya" or "İznik" style. Some are mass produced, some hand done; the difference is reflected in the price.

JEWELLERY, GOLD AND SILVER

Some of the most skilled craftsmen in the world work in the jewellery

and fine metal workshops of the Grand Bazaar. The choice can be overwhelming and it is also possible to order something to be made specially. Gold and silver are sold by weight, with something added on for the work involved but you can still haggle. Amber and turquoise are common. Precious and semiprecious stones are available and said to be well-priced, although you do need to know what you are doing.

MUSIC AND MUSICAL INSTRUMENTS

CDs and cassettes, either made under licence, remaindered from mainstream producers, or bootleg, can be very cheap. Up-to-date releases, though plentiful, are as expensive as at home. Traditional Turkish instruments – wind, percussion and strings – can be a good buy, and are available in specialist shops. **Galip Dede Sokak**, the neighbourhood around Tünel, at the bottom of İstiklal Cad., is Istanbul's **music** district, with an excellent selection of Turkish CDs, traditional instruments and rock and roll gear. **Zühal** is an international distributor with four different branches in this neighbourhood alone.

Shopping Centres

Should you wish for a little more of the conventional type of shopping, Istanbul has shopping malls ranging from the ordinary to the luxurious.
Akmerkez Shopping Mall, Etiler
Award-winning, giant and very luxurious, this offers exclusive international brands, food outlets, a supermarket and cinemas. Open 10am–10pm.
Capitol, Tophanelioğlu Cad., Altunizade, Üsküdar
Shopping and entertainment complex with many of Turkey's best known high-street names.
Carrefour, E-5 highway to Ankara, Icerenköy junction (Asian side).

LEATHER

There will be leather-goods shops almost anywhere you may find yourself. There can be some good buys, but look hard at the styling and finish and not just the price tag. Shoes tend to be poor quality, and anything likely to catch your eye may well be imported. Wealthy Turks are charmed by international labels, so you will see these in expensive shops at astronomical prices. However markets may well have convincing copies of this season's Prada or Gucci style.

FASHION

Turkey has its own established and sought after fashion labels. Limon Company, Yargıcı, Mudo are among the young(ish) and trendy. Vakko and Beymen equate to Harvey Nichols or Saks, with "diffusion" ranges, such as Vakkorama and Beymen Club, offering more youthful, cheaper styles. They do tend to be overwhelmed with one idea each season which can make for a cloned effect both inside the shop and out in the fashionable streets. Prices are more reasonable than in London, but it is harder to find pure natural fabrics. Turkey is

Large department store of French origin, with every category from pastries to household appliances.
Carousel, Bakırköy.
Ultra-modern, non-smoking, good for children.
Galleria, Ataköy
Outlets of most major chains.
Mayadrom Shopping Center, Yıldım Goker Cad., Akatlar.
Small centre with high quality fashion boutiques, eateries and bookshops.
Stadium Florya, Catal Sok. 2, Florya
4-storey complex devoted to sportswear and sporting goods.

also a manufacturing base for many foreign companies, so you can find very cheap jeans, teeshirts, sweatshirts and other casual gear.

The centres for designer and high fashion stores are Nişantaşı (in particular Rumeli Cad. and Abdi Ipekci Cad.), Teşvikiye, Osmanbey, Şişli, Beyoğlu, and, on the Asian side, Bağdat Cad. and Bahariye Cad. These areas contain the shops of international and Turkish designers, often competing for prices especially during the July and January sales (*indirim*).

TEXTILES

Bursa is famous both for producing silk and for its excellent cotton towels and bathrobes, but you can also find reasonably priced pure cotton sheets and pillowcases. Women's scarves, naturally, are available everywhere, from lavishly decorated silk to simple rustic cotton. Soft cotton cheesecloth, reminiscent of the 70s, is made at Şile on the Black Sea and in other places you'll find tablecloths, lace-edged scarves and embroidered cotton shirts and blouses. Everyday items which might be useful include cotton *peştemel* (sarong-style wraps worn in the *hamam*), which are good for the beach, and attractive cotton fabrics which can be bought by the metre. Specialist dealers in the Grand Bazaar and elsewhere may be able to offer you ravishing old textiles – costumes from some

Turkish Delight

Turkish Delight is said to have been created in the 18th century by one Ali Muhiddin, who came to Istanbul from the Black Sea region. His jellyish sugar-coated confection can be flavoured with anything from oranges to pistachio, lemon or almond, but the classic flavour is rose water. His shop, **Ali Muhiddin Hacı Bekir**, still owned by his descendants, is on Hamidiye Cad. (tel: (0212) 522 0666).

forgotten harem, brocade coats and waistcoats, delicately edged handkerchiefs – but these things are getting rarer.

SOUVENIRS AND GIFTS

Fun things to go home with include bowls, vases and ornaments carved from green or gold onyx, mined in Cappadocia. In the bazaars you can find embroidered or brocade leather-soled slippers, fezes, embroidered and beaded hats, and for the fancy dress cupboard any number of gaudy costumes including belly dancing outfits for all ages and sizes. A functioning *nargile* (hubble bubble pipe) together with the appropriate tobacco, might be a good souvenir or present. Meerschaum, a soft white stone, traditionally intricately carved to make pipes. Look carefully at the quality of the stone and the carving, and shop around to make sure you pay the right price. Backgammon sets (*tavla*) are plentiful and not too heavy. The *mavi boncuk*, blue glass beads used to warn off the evil eye (*nazar*), come attached to key rings, dog collars, as large ornaments, bracelets and tiny earring pendants. Karagöz shadow puppets, made of painted leather, originally come from Bursa but can be found elsewhere.

FOOD

Istanbul's markets are a treasure trove of enticing consumables, many of which make excellent presents. Some, such as the luscious tomatoes, are sadly not transportable, but large bags of pistachios, almonds or other nuts are – and they are a fraction of the European price. Also tempting are the heaped spices, including vanilla pods, peppercorns or cinnamon. Be aware that Turkish saffron is not the real thing (look for Persian saffron). Dried fruit, numerous types of tea, or even a jar of delicious Turkish honeycomb are possibilities; a box of Turkish delight (*lokum*) is essential.

Language

In 1928, Atatürk reformed the Turkish language, replacing Arabic script by the Roman alphabet, and Persian and Arabic vocabulary by words of Turkic origin. The intention was to build a sense of nationhood, westernise society, simplify the language and boost literacy.

A legacy of the flowery elaborations of late Ottoman speech lies in the way Turkish people exchange formal greetings: these pleasantries and politenesses follow a set routine in which both sides of the exchange follow formulaic patterns of questions with set answers.

Turkish is undoubtedly a difficult language for speakers of European languages to learn. Although the grammar is consistent and logical with few irregularities, and pronunciation follows phonetic spelling, both the vocabulary and structure are very different from any language that English-speakers may have tackled before. The vocabulary in particular is very foreign, and difficult to remember and use, especially over a short visit. There are a very few words, mainly of French or English origin, which you will be able to recognise once you have deciphered the Turkish spelling.

In Istanbul, English is spoken quite widely but it is useful to try to master basic pronunciation, so as to be able to say addresses and place-names correctly, and to read and use some set phrases.

Pronunciation

Pronunciation is the easiest part of Turkish, as spelling is phonetic, once you have mastered the few different

Turkish vowel and consonant sounds. Every letter is pronounced, and it is always pronounced in the same way. Only a few letters cause difficulties "c", is always pronounced "j" as in "jump", so the Turkish word "cami" (mosque) is pronounced "jah-mi", and "caddesi" (road, street) is pronounced "jah-des-i". The soft "ğ" disappears in speech, and is never voiced, but lengthens the preceding vowel. Also look out for the dotless "ı" which makes an "er" sound, quite different from the dotted "i". Compare "ızgara" (grill, pronounced uh-zgara) with "incir" (fig, pronounced in-jeer). Double consonants are both pronounced. Each syllable in a word carries equal stress, as do all the words in a phrase. The main sounds in Turkish are:

c "dj" as in jump
ç "ch" as in chill
s "s" as in sleep
ş "sh" as in sharp
g "g" as in good
ğ is silent. It lengthens the previous vowel and never begins a word
a "ah" as in father
e "e" as in let
i with a dot, "i" as in sit
ı without a dot is an "er" or "uh" sound, like the second e in ever
o "o" as in hot
ö is similar to "ur" as in spurt, or the German "oe" as in Goethe
u "oo" as in room
ü "ew" in pew, or the u-sound in French 'tu' (purse your lips).

Useful Words and Phrases

GREETINGS

Hello *Merhaba*
Good *morning* (early) *Günaydın*
Good day *İyi günler*
Good night *İyi geceler*
Good evening *İyi akşamlar*
Welcome! *Hoş geldiniz!*
Reply: **Happy to be here!** *Hoş bulduk!*
Please, with pleasure, allow me, please go first (multi-purpose, polite expression) *Buyrun*
Don't mention it *Rica ederim*

Common Signs

Giriş/Çıkış Entrance/Exit
Tehlike çıkışı Emergency exit
Giriş ücretsiz/ücretli Free/paid admission
Açık Open
Kapalı Closed
Varış Arrivals
Kalkış Departures
Askeri bölge Military zone
Sigara içilmez No smoking
Girmek yasaktır No entry
Giriş No photographs
Lütfen ayakkabılarınızı çıkartınız Please take off your shoes
Bay Men
Bayan Women
Tuvalet/WC/Umumi WC
Bozuk Out of order
İçilebilir su Drinking water

Pleased to meet you *Çok memnun oldum*
How are you? *Nasılsınız?*
Thankyou, I am/we are/fine *Teşekkürler, iyiyim/iyiyiz*
My name is ... *Adım ...*
I am English/Scottish/American/Australian *Ben İngilizim/İskoçyalım/Amerikalım/Avustralyalım*
We are sightseeing *Geziyoruz*
We'll see each other again, ("see you") *Görüşürüz*
God willing *İnşallah*
Goodbye *Hoşça kalın*
Good bye *Allaha ısmarladık*
Reply: "go happily" *Güle güle* (only said by the person staying behind)
Leave me alone *Beni rahat bırak*
Get lost *Çekil git*

ESSENTIALS

Yes *Evet*
No *Hayır/yok*
OK *Tamam*
Please *Lütfen*
Thank you *Teşekkür ederim/sağolun/mersi*
You're welcome *Bir şey değil*
Excuse me/I beg your pardon (in a crowd) *Affedersiniz*
Excuse me I don't speak Turkish *Türkçe bilmiyorum*
Do you speak English? *İngilizce biliyor musunuz?*

I don't understand/I haven't understood *Anlamıyorum/Anlamadım*
I don't know *Bilmiyorum*
Please write it down *Onu benim için heceleyebilir misiniz?*
Wait a moment! *Bir dakika!*
Slowly *Yavas*
Enough *Yeter*
Where is it? *Nerede?*
Where is the...? *... nerede?*
Where is the toilet? *Tuvalet nerede?*
What time is it? *Saatiniz var mı?*
At what time? *Saat kaçta?*
Today *Bugün*
Tomorrow *Yarın*
Yesterday *Dün*
The day after tomorrow *Öbür gün*
Now *Şimdi*
Later *Sonra*
When? *Ne zaman*
Morning/in the morning *Sabah*
Afternoon/in the afternoon *Öğleden sonra*
Evening/in the evening *Akşam*
This evening *Bu akşam*
Here *Burada*
There *Şurada*
Over there *Orada*
Is there a newspaper? *Gazete var mı?*
Is there a taxi? *Taksi var mı?*
Is there a telephone? *Telefon var mı?*
Yes, there is *Evet, var*
No, there isn't *Hayır, yok*
There is no ticket *Bilet yok*
There is no time *Zaman yok*

Road Signs

Dikkat Beware/Caution
Tehlike Danger
Yavaş Slow
Yol ver Give way
Dur Stop
Araç giremez No entry
Tek yön One way
Çıkmaz sokak No through road
Bozuk yol Poor road surface
Tamirat Roadworks
Yol kapalı Road closed
Yaya geçidi Pedestrian crossing
Şehir merkezi/Centrum City centre
Otopark/Park edilir Parking
Park edilmez No parking

Travelling

DIRECTIONS

North *Kuzey*
South *Güney*
East *Dogu*
West *Bat_*
Near *Yakın*
Far *Uzak*
Left *Sol*
On the left/to the left *Solda/sola*
Right *Sağ*
On the right/to the right *Sağda/sağa*
Straight on *Doğru*
How do I get to ...? *...'a nasıl giderim?*
How far is it to...? *...'a/'e ne kadar uzakta?*
What time does it open/close? *Kaçta açılıcak/kapanacak?*
City *Şehir*
Village *Köy*
Forest *Orman*
Sea *Deniz*
Lake *Göl*
Farm *Çiftlik*
Church *Kilise*
Mosque *Cami*
Post Office *Postane*

TRANSPORT

Car *Araba*
Petrol/gas station *Benzin istasyonu*
Petrol/gas *Benzin (super/normal)*
Fill it up, please *Doldurun, lütfen*
Flat tyre/puncture *Patlak lastik*
My car has broken down *Arabam arzalandı*
Bus station *Otogar*
Bus stop *Emanet*
Bus *Otobüs*
Train station *Gar/İstasyon*
Train *Tren*
Taxi *Taksi*
Airport *Havalimanı/Havaalanı*

Money

Bank *Banka*
Exchange office *Kamiyo büroso*
Post office *Postane*
Travellers' cheque *Seyahat çeki*
Credit card *Kredi kartı*
Exchange rate *Dövis kuru*

Aeroplane *Uçak*
Port/harbour *Liman*
Boat *Gemi*
Ferry *Feribot/Vapur*
Quay *İskele*
Ticket *Bilet*
Ticket office *Gişe*
Return ticket *Gidiş-dönüş*
Can I reserve a seat? *Reservasyon yapabilir miyim?*
What time does it leave? *Kaçta kalkıyor?*
Where does it leave from? *Nereden kalkıyor?*
How long does it take? *Ne kadar sürüyor*
Which bus? *Hangi otobüs?*

Health

Remember that in an emergency it can be quicker to get to hospital by taxi.
Hospital *Hastane*
Clinic *Klinik*
Emergency service, emergency room *Acil servis*
First aid *İlk yardım*
Doctor *Doktor*
Dentist *Dişçi*
Pharmacy *Eczane*
Pharmacist *Eczacı*
I am ill *Hastayım*
I have a fever *Ateşim var*
I have diarrhoea *İshallım*
I am diabetic *Şeker hastasıyım*
I'm allergic to... *Karşı alerjim var...*
I have asthma *Astim hastasıyım*
I have a heart condition *Kalp hastasıyım*
I am pregnant *Gebeyim*
It hurts here *Burası acıyor*
I have lost a filling *Dolgu düştü*
I need a prescription for... *... için bir reçete istiyorum*

Accommodation

Hotel *Otel*
Pension/guesthouse *Pansiyon*
Full board *Tam pansiyon*
Half board *Yarım pansiyon*
With a shower *Duşlu*
With a bathroom *Banyolu*
With a balcony *Balkonlu*
With a sea view *Deniz manzaralı*
Lift *Asansör*
Room service *Oda servisi*
Air conditioning *Havalandırma*

Emergencies

Help! *İmdat!*
Fire! *Yangın!*
Please call the police *Polis çağırın*
Please call an ambulance *Ambulans çağırın*
Please call the fire brigade *Itfaiye çağırın*
This is an emergency! *Bu acıldır!*
There has been an accident *Kaza vardı*
I'd like an interpreter *Tercüman istiyorum*
I want to speak to someone from the British Consulate *İngiltere konsoloslugundan biri ile görüşmek istiyorum*

Central heating *Kalorifer*
Key *Anahtar*
Bed *Yatak*
Blanket *Battaniye*
Pillow *Yastık*
Shower *Duş*
Soap *Sabun*
Plug *Tıkaç*
Towel *Havlu*
Basin *Lavabo*
Toilet *Tuvalet*
Toilet paper *Tuvalet kağıdı*
Hot water *Sıcak su*
Cold water *Soğuk su*
Dining-room *Yemek salonu*
I have a reservation *Reservasyonım var*
Do you have a room? *Odnız var mı?*
I'd like a room for one/three nights *Bir/üç gece için bir oda istiyorum*
Single/Double/Triple *Tek/çift/üç kişilik*
I'm sorry, we are full *Maalesef doluyuz*
I need/... is necessary *... lazım/ ...gerek*

Days of the Week

Monday *Pazartesi*
Tuesday *Salı*
Wednesday *Çarşamba*
Thursday *Perşembe*
Friday *Cuma*
Saturday *Cumartesi*
Sunday *Pazar*

Numbers

1	*bir*	60	*altmış*
2	*iki*	70	*yetmiş*
3	*üç*	80	*seksen*
4	*dört*	90	*doksan*
5	*bes*	100	*yüz*
6	*altı*	200	*iki yüz*
7	*yedi*	1,000	*bin*
8	*sekiz*	2,000	*iki bin*
9	*dokuz*	1,000,000	*bir milyon*
10	*on*	1,000,000,000	*bir milyar*
11	*on bir*		
12	*on iki*		
20	*yirmi*		
21	*yirmi bir*		
22	*yirmi iki*		
30	*otuz*		
40	*kırk*		
50	*elli*		

To make a complex number, add the components one by one eg: 5,650,000 = *bes milyon altı yüz elli bin* (in Turkish these would normally be run together). Managing huge numbers has become routine for Turks in dealing with their currency.

Shopping

I would like... *...isterim*
I don't want *Istemem*
There isn't any *Yok*
How much is it? *Ne kadar?*
Price *Fiyat*
Cheap *Ucuz*
Expensive *Pahalı*
No bargaining (sign) *Pazarlık edilmez*
Old *Eski*
New *Yeni*
Big *Büyük*
Bigger *Daha büyük*
Small *Küçük*
Smaller *Daha küçük*
Very nice/beautiful *Çok güzel*
How many? *Kaç tane?*
This *Bu*
These *Bunlar*

Months

January *Ocak*
February *Hubat*
March *Mart*
April *Nisan*
May *May_s*
June *Haziran*
July *Temmuz*
August *Agustos*
September *Eylül*
October *Ekim*
November *Kas_m*
December *Aral_k*

That *Şu*
Do you take credit cards? *Kredi karti alır mısınız?*
Receipt (for expensive item) *fatur*
(for cheap item) *fiş*

Restaurants

A table for two/four please *İki/dört kihilik bir masa, lütfen*
Can we eat outside? *Dışarıda da yiyebilir miyiz?*
Waiter! *Garson!*
Excuse me (to get service or attention) *Bakar mısınız?*
Menu *Menü*
I didn't order this *Ben bunu ısmarlamadım*
Some more water/bread/wine, please *Biraz daha su/ekmek/şarap, rica ediyoruz*
I can eat... *...yiyorum*
I cannot eat... *... yiyemiyorum*
The bill, please *Hesap, lütfen*
Service included/excluded *Servis dahil/hariç*

BASICS

Table *Masa*
Cup *Fincan*
Glass *Bardak*
Wineglass *Kadeh*
Bottle *Şişe*
Plate *Tabak*

Fork *Çatal*
Knife *Bıçak*
Spoon *Kaşık*
Napkin *Peçete*
Salt *Tuz*
Black pepper *Kara biber*
Starters *Meze*
Soup *Çorba*
Fish *Balık*
Meat dishes *Etli yemekler*
Grills *Izgara*
Eggs *Yumurta*
Vegetarian dishes *Etsiz yemekler*
Salads *Salatalar*
Fruit *Meyva*
Bread *Ekmek*
Peppery hot *Acı (a-je)*
Non-spicy *Acısız (a-je-suz)*
Water *Su*
Mineral water *Maden suyu*
Fizzy water *Soda*
Beer *Bira*
Red/white wine *Kırmızı/beyaz şarap*
Fresh orange juice *Portakal suyu*
Coffee *Kahve*
Tea *Çay*

Menu Reader

Kahvaltı Breakfast
Beyaz peynir White cheese
Kaşar peyniri Yellow cheese
Domates Tomatoes
Zeytin Olives
Salatalık Cucumber
Reçel Jam
Bal Honey
Tereyağ Butter

Extra dishes which you may order for a more substantial breakfast:
Haşlanmış yumurta Boiled egg (hard)
Rafadan yumurta Soft-boiled eggs
Menemen Scrambled egg omelette with tomatoes, peppers, onion and cheese
Sahanda yumurta Fried eggs
Pastırmalı yumurta Eggs fried with pastırma (Turkish cured beef, like pastrami)
Sade/peynirli/mantarlı omlet Plain/cheese/mushroom omelette

Çorbalar/Soups
Haşlama Mutton broth
Tavuk çorbası/tavuk suyu Chicken soup

For Vegetarians

I only eat fruit and vegetables
Yalnız meyve ve sebze yiyorum
I cannot eat any meat at all *Hiç et yiyemiyorum*
I can eat fish *Balık yiyorum*

Düğün çorbası Wedding soup (thickened with eggs and lemon)
Ezogelin çorbası Lentil soup with rice
Mercimek çorbası Red lentil soup
Domates çorbası Tomato soup
İşkembe çorbası Tripe soup
Paça çorbası Lamb's feet soup
Şehriye çorbası Fine noodle soup
Yayla çorbası Yoghurt soup
Tarhana çorbası Soup made from a dried yoghurt base

Soğuk meze/Cold starters
These are usually offered from a large tray of assorted dishes, or you can choose from a cold cabinet – there are dozens of variations.

Beyaz peynir White cheese
Kavun Honeydew melon
Zeytin Olives
Patlıcan ezmesi Aubergine purée
Piyaz/pilaki White bean salad with olive oil and lemon
Acı Spicy hot red paste or salad of chopped peppers and tomato
Tarama Purée of fish roe
Çerkez tavuğu Shredded chicken in walnut sauce
Haydari Dip of chopped dill and garlic in thick yoghurt
Fava Purée of beans
Dolma Vegetables or other things stuffed with rice mixed with dill, pinenuts and currants
Yalancı yaprak dolması Stuffed vine leaves
Midye dolması Stuffed mussels
Biber dolması Stuffed peppers
Lakerda Sliced smoked tuna
Hamsi Fresh anchovies preserved in oil
Zeytinyağlı Vegetables cooked with olive oil, served cold
Zeytinyağlı kereviz Celeriac in olive oil
İmam bayıldı Aubergine stuffed with tomato and onion, cooked with olive oil

Sıcak mezeler/Hot starters
Sigara böreği Crisp fried rolls of pastry with cheese or meat filling (can also be triangular: *muska*)
Arnavut ciğeri Albanian-style fried diced lamb's liver
Kalamar tava Deep-fried squid rings
Midye tava Deep-fried mussels
Tarator Nut and garlic sauce served with above, or with fried vegetables
Patates köfte Potato croquettes

Salata/Salad
Karışık Mixed
Çoban salatası "Shepherd's salad": chopped mixed tomato, cucumber, pepper, onion and parsley
Yeşil salata Green salad
Mevsim salatası Seasonal salad
Roka Rocket/arugula
Salatalık Cucumber
Domates Tomatoes
Marul Cos/romaine lettuce
Semizotu Lamb's lettuce/purslane
Söğüş Sliced salad vegetables with no dressing

Et yemekleri/Meat dishes
Kebap Kebab
Döner Sliced, layered lamb grilled on revolving spit
Tavuk döner As above, made with chicken
Şiş kebap Cubed meat grilled on skewer eg *kuzu şiş* (lamb), *tavuk şiş* (chicken)
Adana kebap Minced lamb grilled on skewer, spicy
Urfa kebap As above, not spicy
Bursa/İskender/yoğurtlu kebap Dish of döner slices laid on pieces of bread, with tomato sauce, melted butter and yoghurt with garlic
Pirzola Cutlets
Izgara Grill/grilled – usually over charcoal
Köfte Meatballs
Köfte ızgara Grilled meatballs
Bıldırcın ızgara Grilled quail
Kuzu tandır/fırın Lamb baked on the bone
Hünkár begendili köfte Meatballs with aubergine purée
Kadınbudu köfte "Ladies' thighs": meat and rice croquettes in gravy

Karnıyarık Aubergines split in half and filled with minced lamb mixed with pinenuts and currants
Kavurma Meat stir-fried or braised, cooked in its own fat and juices
Çoban kavurma Lamb fried with peppers, tomatoes and onions
Saç kavurma Wok-fried meat with vegetables and spices
Etli dolması Dolma stuffed with meat and rice (eaten hot)
Etli kabak dolması Courgettes stuffed with meat
Etli nohut Chickpea and lamb stew
Etli kuru fasuliye Haricot beans and lamb stew
Kağıt kebabı Lamb and vegetables cooked in paper
Kıymalı with minced meat
Güveç Casserole

Balık yemekleri/Fish dishes
Most fish is eaten plainly grilled or fried, and priced by weight. It will be less expensive if it is local and in season. Always ask the price, "*ne kadar?*" before ordering.

Balık ızgara Grilled fish
Balık kızartması Fried fish
Balık şiş Cubed fish grilled on skewers
Alabalık Trout
Levrek Seabass
Lüfer Bluefish
Hamsi Anchovies
Sardalye Sardines
Karagöz Black bream
Uskumru Mackerel
Palamut Tunny
Kalkan Turbot
Gümüş Silverfish (like whitebait)
Barbunya Red mullet
Kefal Grey mullet
Kılıç balığı Swordfish
Dil balığı Sole
Karides Shrimp, prawns
Karides güveç Prawn casserole with peppers, tomato and melted cheese
Hamsi pilav Rice baked with anchovies
Levrek pilakisi Sea bass stew with onion, potato, tomato and garlic
Kiremitte balık Fish baked on a tile
Kağıtta barbunya Mullet (or other fish) baked in a paper case

Snacks and side orders

Makarna Macaroni, noodles
Patates puresi Mashed/puréed potatoes
Patates kızartması/tava Chips (french fries), sometimes eaten with *meze*
Pilav Cooked rice. Can be a rice dish with meat, chicken, pulses or noodles
Tost Toasted cheese sandwich
Turşu Pickles – Turkish pickles are sour and salty, sometimes spicy but never sweet – eaten with *meze*.

Tatlı/Sweets and desserts

Baklava Layers of wafer-thin pastry with nuts and syrup
Ekmek kadayıf Bread pudding soaked in syrup
Güllaç Dessert made with layers of rice wafer, sugar and milk
Tavuk gögsü Milk pudding made with pounded chicken breast
Kazandibi Glazed, with a browned, caramelised top
Dondurma Ice cream
Muhallebi Rice flour, milk and rosewater blancmange
Sütlaç Rice pudding
Aşure "Noah's pudding" made with dried fruits, nuts, seeds, and pulses
Kabak tatlısı Candied pumpkin
Ayva tatlısı Candied quince
Kaymaklı with clotted cream
Komposto Poached fruit
Krem caramel Caramel custard, French crême caramel
Pasta Gâteau-style cake, patisserie

Drinks

Cold drinks

Su Water
Memba suyu Mineral water
Maden suyu gazoz/soda Sparkling water
Ayran Yoghurt whisked with cold water and salt
Meyva suyu Fruit juice
Vişne suyu Sourcherry juice
Kayısı suyu Apricot juice
Taze portakal suyu Freshly squeezed orange juice
Şerbet Sweetened, iced fruit juice drink
Limonata Lemon drink
Buz Ice

Hot drinks

Çay Tea
Açık Weak
Demli Brewed
Bir bardak çay Glass of tea
Bir fincan kahve Cup of coffee
Ada çayı "Island tea" made with dried wild sage
Elma çayı Apple tea
Kahve Coffee
Neskafe any instant coffee
Sutlu with milk
Şeker Sugar
Türk kahvesi Turkish coffee
Az şekerli with little sugar
Orta Medium sweet
Şekerli Sweet
Sade without sugar
Süzme kahve Filter coffee
Sahlep Hot, thick sweet winter drink made of *sahlep* root, milk and cinnamon

Alcohol

Bira Beer
Siyah Dark (beer)
Beyaz Light (beer)
Cintonik Gin and tonic
Votka Vodka
Yerli Local, Turkish
Şarap Wine
Şarap listesi Wine list
Kırmızı şarap Red wine
Beyaz şarap White wine
Roze şarap Rosé
Sek Dry
Antik Aged
Özel Special
Tatlı Sweet
Şişe Bottle
Yarım şişe Half bottle
Rakı Turkish national alcoholic drink, strongly aniseed-flavoured. Yeni Rakı Chief brand of rakı

Turkish wine labels: *Doluca, Villa Doluca, Doluca Antik, Kavaklıdere Yakut* (red), *Kavaklıdere Çankaya* (white), *Kavaklıdere Lal* (rosé), *Turasan* (Cappadocian)
Turkish beers: *Efes Pilsen, Efes Light* (low alcohol), *Venus, Marmara, Tuborg, Troy*
Spirits are made in Turkey by Tekel, the state tobacco and liquor concern, and a variety of private companies.

Further Reading

There are plenty of books about all aspects of Turkey in English. Such a complex country with so many layers of history and culture couldn't fail to generate a wealth of histories, memoirs, poetry, fiction, biographies and travel writing. Not much Turkish writing has been translated into English. Some good books in English have been written and issued by Turkish publishers, but are difficult to obtain outside Turkey.

History

Constantinople, City of the World's Desire, 1453–1924, by Philip Mansel. Penguin 1997. Outstandingly researched portrait of the imperial city, scholarly, gripping – a mass of information, anecdote and analysis.
Istanbul, The Imperial City, by John Freely. Viking 1996. Illustrated introductory biography of the city and its social life through twenty-seven centuries. The most recent publication by this long-time resident and knowledgeable lover of Turkey.
Turkey Unveiled, Atatürk and After, by Nicole and Hugh Pope. John Murray 1997. Excellent, readable account of the intricacies of Turkish political affairs in the recent past, written by journalists who have been living in and covering the country for the last ten years.
Orientalism, Western Conceptions of the Orient, by Edward W. Said. Penguin 1995. Highly acclaimed overview of Western attitudes towards the East, analysing literature, arts and culture.
Byzantium, three volumes: *The Early Centuries, The Apogee, The Decline and Fall*, by John Julius Norwich. Penguin 1993–1996. Thorough, accessible, readable and

entertaining account of the history of the empire up to the Ottoman conquest of 1453.

The Ottomans, Dissolving Images, by Andrew Wheatcroft. Penguin 1995.
Colourful, readable account of the development of Ottoman power and empire, with good detail about social life.

On Secret Service East of Constantinople, by Peter Hopkirk. Oxford Paperbacks 1995.
Brilliant account of Turkish and German conspiracies against Britain and Russia after 1914, by the author of *The Great Game*. The true story behind *Greenmantle* (see below).

Black Sea, The Birthplace of Civilisation and Barbarism, by Neal Ascherson. Vintage 1996.
Compelling, brilliantly written book about the cultures surrounding this great inland sea; from Herodotus to the fall of Communism.

The Greeks in Ionia and the East, by John Cook. Thames and Hudson 1962.

Troy and the Trojans, by Carl Blegen. Thames and Hudson 1963.

The Armenians, by Sirapie der Nersessian. Thames and Hudson 1979.

A History of the Crusades, by Steven Runciman. Cambridge University Press 1952–4.
Still the definitive history of the Crusades by one of Britain's greatest medieval historians.

The Fall of Constantinople, 1453, by Steven Runciman. Cambridge University Press 1965.

Byzantine Civilisation, by Steven Runciman. Cambridge University Press 1933.
Also wrote The Last Byzantine Renaissance (1971).

Alexander of Macedon, by Peter Green. Penguin Books 1970.

The Ottoman Empire: The Classical Age, 1300-1600, by Halil Inalcik. Weidenfeld and Nicolson 1973.

Atatürk: The Rebirth of a Nation, by Lord Kinross. Weidenfeld and Nicolson 1964.

The Ottoman Centuries, by Lord Kinross. Morrow Quill 1977.

The Emergence of Modern Turkey, by Bernard Lewis. Oxford University Press 1968.

History of the Byzantine State, by Georg Ostrogorsky. Blackwell 1968.

History of the Ottoman Empire and Modern Turkey, by Stanford J. Shaw and Ezel Kural Shaw. Cambridge University Press 1976.

The Harvest of Hellenism, by F.E Peters. Simon and Schuster 1970.

Lives and Letters

The Turkish Embassy Letters, by Lady Mary Wortley Montagu. Virago 1995.
Newly edited edition of these lively and intelligent letters, written in 1716 when the writer's husband had just been appointed ambassador. One of the most fascinating of early travel writers.

The Imperial Harem of the Sultans, the memoirs of Leyla Hanımefendi. Peva Publications, Istanbul, 1995 (available in Istanbul).
The only contemporary account of daily life at the Çirağan Palace during the 19th century, originally published in French in 1925, which gives a vivid portrait of this hidden world.

Portrait of a Turkish Family, by Irfan Orga. Eland Books, 1993.
Vividly and movingly describes the author's family life and his growing up, first as a child in Ottoman Turkey before the First World War, then through the war and the years of Atatürk's reforms.

Everyday Life in Ottoman Turkey, by Raphaela Lewis. Batsford 1971.

Art and architecture

A History of Ottoman Architecture by Godfrey Goodwin. Thames and Hudson 1987.
Comprehensive and definitive, covering every kind of building all over Turkey. Goodwin's other great book is a monograph on Sinan, the greatest of the Ottoman architects (Saqi Books).

Ancient Civilizations and Ruins of Turkey, by Ekrem Akurgal. 3rd edition. Haset Kitabevi, 1973.

Turkish Art and Architecture, by Oktay Aslanapa. Faber and Faber 1971.

The Palace of Topkapı, by Fanny Davis. Scribners 1970.

Early Christian and Byzantine Architecture, by Richard Krautheimer. Penguin Books 1965.

Sinan, the Grand Old Man of Ottoman Architecture, by Aptullah Kuran. Washington DC 1986.

Carpets

Halı Magazine, Halı Publications.
Six issues a year dedicated to rug commerce and scholarship, with frequent articles on Turkish textiles and carpets. They also publish **Istanbul, the Halı Rug Guide,** and **Orient Stars,** by E. Heinrich Kirchheim, a lavishly illustrated book with 250 colour plates of classical Turkish carpets.

Oriental Carpets: A Buyer's Guide, by Essie Sakhai. Parkway 1995.
Detailed information on history, design and buying tips.

Travel Writing

The Total Discourse of the Rare Adventures and Painful Peregrinations of Long Nineteene Yeares Travayles from Scotland to the Most Famous Kingdoms in Europe, Asia and Africa, 1645, by William Lithgow.
The title says it all. Entertaining 17th century account of the city.

The City of the Sultan and the Domestic Manners of the Turks, by Julia Pardoe, 1839.
English lady traveller; also wrote The Beauties of the Bosphorus.

A Fez of the Heart by Jeremy Seal. Picador 1996.
Travels around Turkey in search of a real fez, the red felt hat banned in 1925. A perceptive, alternative view of modern Turkey.

The Crossing Place, A Journey among the Armenians, by Philip Marsden. Flamingo 1994.
Travels in search of this remarkable people – one of Turkey's most important minorities – the remaining traces of their culture and their diaspora.

From the Holy Mountain, A Journey in the Shadow of Byzantium, by William Dalrymple. Flamingo 1998. Starting from Mount Athos, the Holy Mountain in Greece, the author follows the trail of Eastern Christianity, travelling into Eastern Turkey and beyond. Dalrymple has been hailed as a successor to Patrick Leigh Fermor; he is certainly adventurous and his writing is lively and erudite.

Anthologies

Istanbul, Tales of the City, selected by John Miller. Chronicle Books. San Francisco 1995. Pocket-sized eclectic collection of prose and poetry including pieces by Simone de Beauvoir, Disraeli and Gore Vidal.
Istanbul, a Traveller's Companion, selected and introduced by Laurence Kelly. Constable. A wonderful collection of extracts from fourteen centuries of writing, arranged around landmark buildings to act as a background guide, and which brings to life sites which visitors can still see.
Across the Hellespont: Travellers in Turkey from Herodotus to Freya Stark, by Richard Stoneham. Harmondsworth 1984.
Turkish Verse, by Nermin Menemencioglu. Penguin Books 1978.

Fiction

Greenmantle, by John Buchan. Penguin.
First published in 1916, the immortal Richard Hannay adventures across the Balkans into Anatolia.
The Bride of Suleiman, by Aileen Crawley.
Fascinating fictionalised account of the life of Roxelana, wife of Süleyman the Magnificent.
Julian, by Gore Vidal. New York: Signet, 1962.
The White Castle (1991), **The Black Book** (1996), **The New Life** (1997). Novels by Orhan Pamuk, translated by Güneli Gün. Faber. Introspective, perceptive,

sometimes over-complex but much lauded contemporary Turkish writer. *The New Life* was the fastest selling book in Turkish history.
Mehmet My Hawk, by Yahar Kemal. Harvill 1993.
The best-known Turkish novelist in translation. This is just one, the most famous, of many novels, some set in and around Istanbul, some epics set in rural Anatolia.
The Rage of the Vulture, by Barry Unsworth. Granada.
Historical novel by the best-selling author, set in the twilight years of the Ottoman Empire and focusing on the sultan, Abdülhamid.

Food and Cooking

Classic Turkish Cookery by Ghillie and Jonathan Başan, introduced by Josceline Dimbleby. Tauris Parke Books 1997.
A beautiful large hardback illustrated book which places Turkish cooking in its geographical and cultural context; the recipes are a practical, authentic introduction to the best of Turkish dishes, gleaned from sources all over Turkey.
Timeless Tastes, Turkish Culinary Culture, project director Semahat Arsel. Vehbi Koç Vakfı and Divan Istanbul 1996.
Published to celebrate the 40th anniversary of the Divan Hotel, long renowned for its kitchen and its patisserie. The book has several authors: experts on culinary art and history, and professional chefs who give their recipes. This history of Turkish cooking at the most elevated level is illustrated with Ottoman miniatures and engravings.
The Art of Turkish Cooking, by Nehet Eren. Hippocrene Books 1996.
Written in 1969, the excellence of this book lies in its simple instructions, and the use of simple ingredients which are readily available (a characteristic of Turkish cooking anyway). The style is a little dated, but the recipes are authentic. A less lavish choice than the above two books.
Eat Smart in Turkey, by Joan and David Peterson. Gingo Press.

Excellent guide to Turkish food from the market to the table, complete with entertaining historical notes.

Guides

Strolling through Istanbul, A Guide to the City, by Hilary Sumner-Boyd and John Freely. Redhouse Press, Istanbul 1996. Also Harvill.
First written and published in the early 70s and one of the first proper guides to the city, this book is still valuable, though it has outlived one of its authors. The other, John Freely, still lives and works in Istanbul, and few are more knowledgeable than he. His other useful book is **The Companion Guide to Turkey,** Harper Collins, 1996. This was first published in 1979 but revised in 1992. Freely's knowledge of and affection for the country is palpable in its pages.
Istanbul, an Archeological Guide, by Christa Beck and Christiane Forsting. Ellipsis 1997.
Neatly designed, tiny pocket size book with black and white photographs, the only guide to include some of Istanbul's most interesting recently-built, renovated or redesigned buildings and structures. Compiled by two architects currently practising in Berlin.
Blue Guide Turkey, by Bernard McDonagh. A&C Black 1999. Latest edition of the classic fount of all wisdom on history and archaeology.

Other Insight Guides

Other Insight Guides which highlight destinations in this region include the comprehensive **Insight Guide: Turkey** with background essays, detailed countrywide Places chapters and practical information sections and lavish photography. There are also **Insight Compact Guide: Istanbul,** a handy fact-packed reference guide to the city, and **Insight Pocket Guide: Istanbul,** written by a local host and offering tailor-made itineraries plus a useful pull-out map.

ART & PHOTO CREDITS

Picture Spreads

INSIGHT GUIDE
ISTANBUL

Cartographic Editor **Zoë Goodwin**
Production **Stuart A Everitt**
Design Consultants
Carlotta Junger, Graham Mitchener
Picture Research **Hilary Genin, Britta Jaschinski**

Index

Numbers in italics refer to photographs

Top 5 Suggestions

1) HAgia Sophia p.146 (need head covering)
2) Blue mosque p.154 (need head cover)
3) GRAND Bazaar p.176
4) spice market p.182
5) Bosphorus cruise p.217
6) Turkish Bath p.156

INSIGHT GUIDES

The world's largest collection of visual travel guides

A range of guides and maps to meet every travel need

Insight Guides

This classic series gives you the complete picture of a destination through expert, well written and informative text and stunning photography. Each book is an ideal background information and travel planner, serves as an on-the-spot companion – and is a superb visual souvenir of a trip. Nearly 200 titles.

Insight Pocket Guides

focus on the best choices for places to see and things to do, picked by our local correspondents. They are ideal for visitors new to a destination. To help readers follow the routes easily, the books contain full-size pull-out maps. 120 titles.

Insight Maps

are designed to complement the guides. They provide full mapping of major cities, regions and countries, and their laminated finish makes them easy to fold and gives them durability. 60 titles.

Insight Compact Guides

are convenient, comprehensive reference books, modestly priced. The text, photographs and maps are all carefully cross-referenced, making the books ideal for on-the-spot use when in a destination. 120 titles.

Different travellers have different needs. Since 1970, Insight Guides has been meeting these needs with a range of practical and stimulating guidebooks and maps

66 I was first drawn to the Insight Guides by the excellent "Nepal" volume. I can think of no book which so effectively captures the essence of a country. Out of these pages leaped the Nepal I know – the captivating charm of a people and their culture. I've since discovered and enjoyed the entire Insight Guide series. Each volume deals with a country in the same sensitive depth, which is nowhere more evident than in the superb photography. 99

Sir Edmund Hillary

☀ INSIGHT GUIDES

The world's largest collection of visual travel guides

Insight Guides – the Classic Series that puts you in the picture

Alaska	China	Hong Kong	Morocco	Singapore
Alsace	Cologne	Hungary	Moscow	South Africa
Amazon Wildlife	Continental Europe		Munich	South America
American Southwest	Corsica	Iceland		South Tyrol
Amsterdam	Costa Rica	India	Namibia	Southeast Asia
Argentina	Crete	India's Western	Native America	Wildlife
Asia, East	Crossing America	Himalayas	Nepal	Spain
Asia, South	Cuba	India, South	Netherlands	Spain, Northern
Asia, Southeast	Cyprus	Indian Wildlife	New England	Spain, Southern
Athens	Czech & Slovak	Indonesia	New Orleans	Sri Lanka
Atlanta	Republic	Ireland	New York City	Sweden
Australia		Israel	New York State	Switzerland
Austria	Delhi, Jaipur & Agra	Istanbul	New Zealand	Sydney
	Denmark	Italy	Nile	Syria & Lebanon
Bahamas	Dominican Republic	Italy, Northern	Normandy	
Bali	Dresden		Norway	Taiwan
Baltic States	Dublin	Jamaica		Tenerife
Bangkok	Düsseldorf	Japan	Old South	Texas
Barbados		Java	Oman & The UAE	Thailand
Barcelona	East African Wildlife	Jerusalem	Oxford	Tokyo
Bay of Naples	Eastern Europe	Jordan		Trinidad & Tobago
Beijing	Ecuador		Pacific Northwest	Tunisia
Belgium	Edinburgh	Kathmandu	Pakistan	Turkey
Belize	Egypt	Kenya	Paris	Turkish Coast
Berlin	England	Korea	Peru	Tuscany
Bermuda			Philadelphia	
Boston	Finland	Laos & Cambodia	Philippines	Umbria
Brazil	Florence	Lisbon	Poland	USA: Eastern States
Brittany	Florida	Loire Valley	Portugal	USA: Western States
Brussels	France	London	Prague	US National Parks:
Budapest	Frankfurt	Los Angeles	Provence	East
Buenos Aires	French Riviera		Puerto Rico	US National Parks:
Burgundy		Madeira		West
Burma (Myanmar)	Gambia & Senegal	Madrid	Rajasthan	
	Germany	Malaysia	Rhine	Vancouver
Cairo	Glasgow	Mallorca & Ibiza	Rio de Janeiro	Venezuela
Calcutta	Gran Canaria	Malta	Rockies	Venice
California	Great Barrier Reef	Marine Life ot the	Rome	Vienna
California, Northern	Great Britain	South China Sea	Russia	Vietnam
California, Southern	Greece	Mauritius &		
Canada	Greek Islands	Seychelles	St. Petersburg	Wales
Caribbean	Guatemala, Belize &	Melbourne	San Francisco	Washington DC
Catalonia	Yucatán	Mexico City	Sardinia	Waterways of Europe
Channel Islands		Mexico	Scotland	Wild West
Chicago	Hamburg	Miami	Seattle	
Chile	Hawaii	Montreal	Sicily	Yemen

Complementing the above titles are 120 easy-to-carry Insight Compact Guides, 120 Insight Pocket Guides with full-size pull-out maps and more than 60 laminated easy-fold Insight Maps

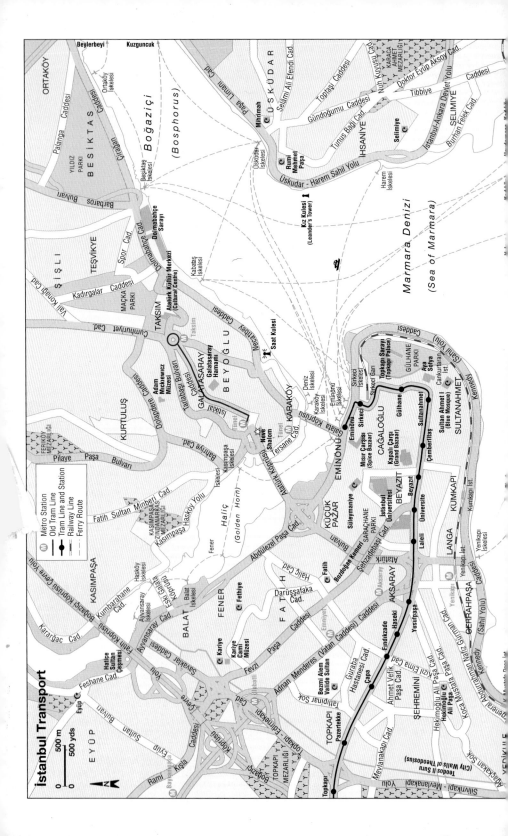